THE AQUARIAN
BOOK OF
FORTUNE ~ TELLING

Telling your future with Tarot, numbers, playing cards and runes

THE AQUARIAN BOOK OF FORTUNE~TELLING

INTRODUCTION BY
SASHA FENTON

THE AQUARIAN PRESS
Wellingborough, Northamptonshire

This edition first published in 1987

British Library Cataloguing in Publication Data

The Aquarian book of fortune telling.
1. Fortune telling
133.3'24   BF1861

ISBN 0-85030-587-X

The Aquarian Press is part of the
Thorsons Publishing Group

Printed and bound in Great Britain

CONTENTS

INTRODUCTION

by Sasha Fenton

It has been said that the oldest professions in the world are medicine and prostitution, but I maintain that divination would be a strong contender for the title. Human nature doesn't change, people have always wanted help in coping with their lives and have always been keen to know what lies just around the corner, even if the corner hides nothing but horror and destruction.

Who visits the diviner? The answer has been the same throughout the ages. For instance, a young girl may ask, 'Who will I marry?' – an important question when marriage was for life. Today's Asian client wants to know what kind of a man her father will choose for her. 'Will my father only think of a possible business alliance or will he consider *my* needs? Will my husband be kind and gentle or will he beat me? Will he learn to like me, or just to put up with me?' This client of today's world has much in common with a girl from a time in the past, slipping out cloaked and hooded in the dead of a moonless night, with only her maid for company, to consult the old lady who lives outside the village. ('Who will my father choose for me?')

Divination combines a number of factors; the first being the diagnosis of illness, the second the reading of character and the third the divination of the future, or 'fortune-telling'. Taking the diagnosis of illness first, astrology was once a useful diagnostic tool; even now a good astrologer would be able to point out to his client areas of potential weakness or suggest the probable course of an illness which is giving trouble to the client at the time of the reading. Herbalists and healers have always understood the nature of man and the connection between mind, body and spirit. The healer/doctors of olden days may have lacked modern knowledge and the panoply of drugs which are now available but they have been replaced by the busy General Practitioner who is short of time and may appear rather remote to a poorly educated person. Today's surgeon makes his assessments from a sheaf of clinical test results; perhaps we have lost something while we were gaining knowledge.

While on a visit to friends in Zambia, my daughter Helen came across a stall in the market place in Lusaka belonging to 'Doctor Zulu' who advertises himself as 'The healer with a difference' and goes on to say that he is 'here to solve your problems – VD, evil spirits, TB, asthma plus *at home, marriage, jobless* problems.' Who's to say that asthma is not exacerbated by 'at home, marriage and jobless problems'. I for one am quite prepared to believe that a full-blown migraine attack is, at least in part, caused by evil spirits – it certainly feels like it! The point of this touch of levity is that Doctor Zulu is certainly *not* a healer with a difference; versions of him exist among the Eskino, Red Indian, and African tribes. In Europe witches did the same kind of work and Doctor Zulu's modern equivalent can be seen at psychic festivals around the world.

On a less personal scale, the population of a city in ancient times would have been interested in the chances of a good harvest plus the likelihood of war, famine, pestilence and plague. Cassandra warned the citizens of Pompeii (woe, woe and thrice woe), but to little avail. Perhaps life in Pompeii had been too good for too long. The predictions of Nostradamus have been read down the centuries and many of the predictions have been attributed to our century, especially to the time of dictatorships in Europe. According to Nostradamus, the world as we know it will end when the Soviet Union and America join up against China and all three happily lob parcel loads of nuclear bombs at each other over the polar ice cap. Unthinkable? Russia and America ganging up against China? Well, how did those historic enemies Russia and Germany manage to sell their populations the idea of a non-aggression pact at the beginning of the Second World War? Put that way it is quite a chilling thought.

In eastern countries it has always been usual for kings and princes to have horoscopes charted for them either at the time of their birth or at their accession. Even now Indian astrologers make up marvellous illuminated life-charts for their Rajahs. The earliest known records of royal charts come from Chaldea in what is now Mesopotamia. The first record of astrology being used for divination is in the year 2872 BC when Sargon of Agarde used astrologer priests for purposes of prediction.

Primitive man was far more tuned in to the forces of nature than is civilized man. Nomadic tribes certainly used the Moon, planets and stars for a calender; they also found omens, probably based on patterns which they observed in the natural world around them. Divination by means of the behaviour of animals and the appearance of trees and so forth would have been treated with respect. Even now we are aware that a good crop of berries in the autumn will herald a long hard winter.

The remnants of stone age people still survive on the face of the earth in the form of Australian Aborigines and also in the Eskimo tribes. Both of these peoples are well known to be religious and superstitious and to use rituals of magic and divination, even to the point of *making* things happen for them, such as pointing the bone. The most primitive people may be the hunter-gatherers of the Kalahari Desert who have a rich tradition of divination by all forms of natural phenomena which is passed on verbally to the younger members of the tribe.

People don't change. Wherever you look on the face of the Earth, from Silicon Valley to the most primitive Amazon tribesman (and woman), we all want to know what our chances are for health, wealth and happiness and above all love, love, love.

The Three Uses of Divination

I have already mentioned divination for the purposes of diagnosis. This fell out of general use with the advances of science, technology and medicine but in some small measure divination is beginning to creep back, not only in the sphere of alternative medicine but in the 'legitimate' world of hospitals. For instance, the alternative practitioner may make use of something like Kirlian photography for diagnosis but in some hospitals which specialize in research into the disease of cancer, spectrum photography of patients' hands is being used. In other words, the patient's *aura* is being captured on film and interpreted! Some years ago, my friend's daughter underwent treatment for lymphatic leukaemia, and we were amazed to find that one of the doctors at Great Ormond Street Hospital for Sick Children had taken inked prints of her feet for the purposes of research! Incidentally, the child survived the illness and is now living a normal adult life.

Character Reading

There are a number of practical uses for character reading; one such instance would be career guidance. Many people consult a divinator when they are not sure what to do with their working lives and they frequently gain much insight into their potential, talents and abilities as a result. For example, a skilled palmist would be able to tell a client if her leanings were practical or creative by the course of her head line, towards working for others or being self employed (fate line), towards manual desterity, an active or a sedentary type of job (hand shape etc.). A really experienced palmist would be able to pick out specific career possibilities. I have used palmistry as an example, but a skilled graphologist (handwriting analyst) could probably do even better. There are other learned skills such as numerology and astrology which would have much the same results. The partly or wholly psychic skills of divination by tea leaves, cards, clairvoyance, sand etc. could also be used.

An important part of one's character is the ability to relate to others, and in particular to find someone to live with and to love. A skilled consultant would be able to tell his client where she keeps going wrong in relationships and why. He would be able to delve into her childhood and see the patterns which were formed there; obviously a psychiatrist can do the same thing, and counselling is counselling whoever is doing it. There is one mammoth difference between a divinator and a psychological counsellor, between a divinator and a good doctor, between a divinator and a good careers guidance officer, however, and that is the *sheer absolute magic of being able to see into the future.*

Character reading, therefore, is useful as a tool for helping the client understand herself and the nature of the people around her but it has a couple of other surprising benefits. It helps the *divinator* in two important ways. First,it is useful for him to understand which type of personality he is dealing with as this tells him how he must treat her. Second, it gives confidence to a client during the beginning stages of a reading to hear something to which she can immediately relate, as this helps her to relax and accept the rest of the reading. One could say that it establishes the *credibility* of the divinator.

Divination for the Purposes of Fortune-telling

I saw a television programme about the continent of Africa recently which covered many aspect of the countries of Africa from the point of view of history, economics, geography etc., but one piece which dwelt on some of the beliefs and superstitions held my attention. This particular episode showed a divinator preparing an area of ground by making a smooth sandy pathway, then sticking twigs into it at strategic intervals and finally making a pattern of squares over the pathway with pieces of meat. During the following night foxes walked over the pathway and took the bait, and the divinator used the pattern of the footprints which the foxes left behind in order to work out the fate of the village during the next few months. Fascinating, but does it work? The answer must be a resounding *yes*.

All these methods however ridiculous they may appear at first glance do work very well. In most situations there is a certain amount of preparation which is part and parcel of building up the correct atmosphere and of concentrating the divinator's mind on the job in hand.

Categories of Divination

I have decided to divide the methods of fortune-telling into three categories, with a possible addition of a fourth. The first one would be the *scientific skills*, the second the *interpretative skills* and the third the *psychic skills*. The fourth would be the *spiritual link* which may or may not to be used to foretell future events. Obviously there is a lot of cross fertilization between these categories as the same consultant may work in two, three or even all of the categories in order to obtain a good reading. He may use different skills for different clients or he may use several in the course of one reading. Even those who are committed to one way of working will have interests in other methods. One classic example is my friend Renee Hindle who works purely on a psychic wavelength but is also learning how to read the Runes for her own pleasure and enlightenment.

The Scientific Skills

I classify the scientific skills as those which don't rely on psychic or even intuitive gifts. Character reading without fortune telling can be done by means of graphology, which is the study of hand-writing, and by phrenology which is the study of bumps on the skull, much beloved of Victorian divinators. A skill which is very definitely divinatory, but not actually *learned*, is the I Ching. This has to be looked up in a book; no-one could possibly be expected to remember all the 'changes' which are possible. A similar idea to the I Ching is the Oracle de Napoleon, invented by Napoleon Bonaparte. This looks a bit like dominoes as it can be made up of pieces which have dots on them. Pieces of paper with the dot patterns already made can be used, or they can be picked out from a printed list with a pin (in the same way that I choose my Derby winners!). The reading is given by looking up the meanings of the dotted shapes which have been chosen.

Astrology, which is divination by the movements of the planets and stars, and numerology, divination by numbers, are very definitely learned skills which don't rely on anything but themselves. They are particularly useful when the consultant and his client are at a distance from one another because they can be done through the post. Palmistry can, theoretically, be done by post as it is possible to get a reasonable hand print using a photocopier, but it is far better for the palmist to see the hand close up so as to assess colour, texture, back of the hands etc. Some consultants are quite happy to give readings through the post, but most prefer to deal with their clients face to face. There are a number of good reasons for this. First, an important part of any consultation is the counselling and advice which comes out of the reading. This is often a two-way business with the client talking about her problems and asking questions which the consultant may not have thought of. The second reason is that consultants are human and they like to feel that they are helping their clients rather than just sending their work off into a vacuum. Consultants also need feedback in order to measure their own performance. As the old saying goes 'man does not live by bread alone', he needs his ego fed as well.

It is often better for the consultant and his client to be together for the simple reason that most consultants *are* intuitive and often actually *psychic* and they need their client near them, preferably in a quiet room where they can build up a trusting and relaxed atmosphere and can 'tune in' to their clients, thereby gaining that extra push that intuition gives. This intuition can be a mixture of understanding people and their problems due to experience and of the ability to 'read' people by body language etc. Often it is nothing less than psychic ability which must be brought into play to bring what might have otherwise been a rather mechanical reading into life.

The Interpretative Skills
This is by far the largest category and makes up three of the four books which are included in this compendium. This category can be further broken down into two sections, the first being the *learned/ interpretative skills* of readings by such items as dice, Tarot, playing cards, dominoes, Rune stones etc. It is perfectly possible to give a reading from the 'book meanings' of cards, Runes, dice etc. but it can be rather sterile without that extra intuitive 'push'.

I am in a good position to give some excellent examples of this problem due to the feedback which I have been receiving from people who have bought my book *Fortune-telling by Tarot Cards*. They find the meanings of each card easy enough to grasp but they have difficulty in stringing them together in order to make a reading. They find that some of the cards which they draw contradict other cards. They don't yet have the knack of applying the cards to specific areas of their 'client's' lives and they haven't yet learned to allow their own inner feelings to tell them what they are seeing. The art, of course, is to *think* less and to *feel* more, but it takes time to come. Often the answer is to go and have a couple of readings from other consultants and then to ask them if they would be prepared to give a couple of lessons at a reasonable price. A few examples from an expert can be worth a year of struggling along on one's own.

Books which give examples of actual readings are most helpful in showing the student how to relate what he is seeing to reality. All the books in this compendium show actual examples for the student to work through. Incidentally, all professional consultants themselves seek readings from other consultants. They do this for a variety of reasons, partly because they, like all of us, find life confusing at times and partly to see how their work compares in price, length of reading and content to that of their competitors!

My second sub-division would be the *intuitive/interpretative skills*. These are many and varied, but all of them work basically in the same way as they require imagination to make them come alive. As my friend Douglas Ashby points out to his students, the heart of the word 'imagination' is the word 'image' and *that* is what it's all about. To some extent, Tarot can cross over into this category as the images on some of the cards will spark the divinator's imagination into action. Even dice could be used partly in this way if, in addition to the numbers on the dice, the way they lay were taken into account; e.g., do the dice fall into a shape reminiscent of a ship at sea or look like the tiers on a wedding cake? Considerable imagination might be needed to work with such hard-edged objects, therefore how much easier with something soft and malleable such as sand. David Bingham introduced me to sand reading a couple of years ago. This is a very old art which came originally from Egypt and is rather like tea leaf reading in its effect. The art of sand reading has to be learned to some extent; for instance, the back of the tray being the past, one side being nearby circumstances and the other being distant ones and so on. However, the major part of this kind of reading is imagination and an artistic eye.

Tea leaf reading, which is similar in nature to sand reading, has rather gone out of fashion, possibly killed off by the invention of tea bags! Mainly killed off, like so much, by the invention of television. Before the days of TV people messed around with all kinds of things out of boredom half the time and therefore many home skills were developed. People played cards and games together and learned to tell each other's fortune for fun and enlightenment, often by the nearest means to hand. We are probably the first generation not to spend hours staring into a fire watching shapes in the coals and in the flames. Maybe we are the first generation not to lie out under the sky on country walks and see shapes in the clouds as they pass by. This kind of imaginative divination is closely allied to the whole business of omens and superstitions.

Those who had a religious turn of mind used the bible to find answers, not just by reading the wisdom in its pages but by opening the book, shutting their eyes and picking words at random. The idea behind this is that divine guidance would be obtained due to the holiness of the book. The less holy used the same method with poetry books.

Omens can be seen anywhere one chooses to look, but a good starting point is dreams. Most people are shaken if they have a disturbing dream and it is hard for *anyone* to dismiss this kind of thing. Dreams may be nothing more than a mixture of too much mental stimulation absorbed from radio, television and the day's papers, but they frequently show our state of mind. I occasionally dream of losing luggage or forgetting where I parked the car. Dreams can, of course, be prophetic, either directly by coming true exactly as per the dream or symbolically. My mother taught me an old saying which referred to dreams.

'Friday night dreamt, Saturday told
Sure to come true, though ever so old.'

The idea behind this superstition is that any dream which you have on a Friday night will be sure to come true if you tell someone about it on Saturday.

Omens can be seen in everyday events or can be 'read into' almost anything. Some people react strangely to colours, feeling that wearing such and such a colour will affect their day. Others are affected by things people say, by the placement of an object on a table or some other unusual event. I know that certain times of the year bring events into my life, the months of May and October being particularly important for both good and ill. I have learned to be watchful of anything which happens at those times of the year.

Superstitions are close to this kind of thinking. Many superstitions seem to involve avoiding trouble; some of these have a basis in truth; for example, it may or may not be unlucky to open an umbrella indoors, but it *can* be downright *dangerous*. Similarly walking under a ladder, passing on stairs and so on. I grew up in a *very* superstitious household where the family had a mixture of Jewish superstitions plus Polish, Russian, Portugese, German, Austrian, Dutch and French ones in addition to the many and varied superstitions attached to the tailoring trade which most of the family were involved in. I learned that putting keys on the table 'locked the table', which meant possible starvation for the family, this being a constant reality of life in the ghettos of Poland and Russia.

I also learned that buying one's own tape measure meant that one bought seven years of working in the sweated sewing trades and therefore was to be avoided. Later on I became a dancer and spent some years on the stage, the theatre being a hot-bed of superstitions which if accidentally transgressed caused backstage hysterics brought about by wrought nerves. (The net result of all this is that I cannot stand *any* superstition and frequently pass people on stairs, walk under ladders, cross knives and break mirrors!)

The other aspect of omens and superstitions is the idea of 'propitiating the gods'. In many cultures certain sayings, behaviours and actions are supposed to please or to infuriate the local deities. Practices vary from making offerings of flowers and food or lighting candles before prayer. In some Central American cultures in previous centuries, the sacrifices were of human life. Talismans and amulets come into this category as protection and bringers of luck as does white heather, the corn dolly or the strange rabbit's foot. I have always considered this to be particularly *unlucky* for the rabbit. However, this is taking us rather a long way from the subject of divination. The following are a few amusing ideas which you could try out for yourself.

1. When you see a number of magpies, remember the old saying, 'One for sorrow, two for joy, three for a girl and four for a boy.'

2. Heat a little sealing wax in a spoon, pour this into a glass of cold water and interpret the shapes which are formed.

3. Fill a wide bowl with water and ask a question, then drop a small stone into the water and count the ripples. If there is an even number the answer is no.

4. Place your pet cat out in the hall, and mentally ask a question. If the cat places his right paw round the door first, the answer will be yes.

5.   An itchy right eye means that you will meet an old friend while an itchy left shoulder brings sorrow; an itchy right palm means that money is on the way.

6.   A mole on a woman's left breast indicates an ardent temperament, sometimes leading to foolish attachments!

Obviously the whole business of divination has its daft side but it has a deadly serious side too and this is well known to every professional consultant. Some people go and have their fortune told for fun, but many consult the divinator because they are in great distress. A quiet atmosphere with a sense of respect for the client is essential. Some consultants perform a little ritual before working, either says a prayer, lighting a candle or burning a little incense while playing some gential meditative music on a tape recorder. This is not merely mumbo-jumbo, it creates an atmosphere which helps to tune in and calm down the minds of both the client and the consultant. As it happens *I* do none of these things, but I do use my own room which is part office and part consulting room. This room seems to have a calming and healing atmosphere of its own. I do say a little prayer from time to time to give me the strength and wisdom to help those who come to see me.

Pure Psychic Skills
Psychics can work in many ways but they all require a certain kind of sensitivity. This sensitivity *can* be trained and developed but it cannot be put into a person if it is not there in the first place. Psychic ability comes in many forms, the most well known being clairvoyance or the ability to 'see clearly'. (Clairaudience is the ability to 'hear clearly', clairsentience the ability to 'feel clearly' etc.) Eve Bingham once told me that pure psychic work should be done on foot, moving around the room rather than sitting in one spot and concentrating, because the whole body needs to be free to come into contact with whatever feelings are around. Many psychics work on a level of mental impression. This is a very common phenomenon but it is hard to explain; these psychics just get feelings and impressions which they can use and interpret. Many ordinary people have these feelings which they tend to ignore and then they wonder why they 'knew' that something important was about to happen.

There are many psychics who see, hear, feel, smell things as if they were re-playing a television or radio programme in their heads. Others see things in symbolic form. If a client asked a psychic whether her marriage was likely to break up, the psychic would mentally *ask* to be shown an image. A typical image in this case would be a vision of a broken wedding ring. If there was another wedding ring being shown in the background the psychic would pass this information on to the client, telling her that she would (according to the images shown) be ending this marriage, but would eventually have another marriage to look forward to.

Aided Psychic Skills

Psychics can use any amount of aids to help them get the answers that they want and these cross over into the interpretative field, but still require that special something before they can be used successfully. Card reading is a good example of this; a psychic may start by interpreting the cards but soon 'rise over' the cards and read from mental impressions, clairvoyance and so forth. There are many psychic hand readers who work in this way too. Another common method of psychic divination is to use a crystal ball. This is really a focus for the clairvoyant psychic to 'throw' his images. I personally cannot use a crystal, but do very well with a glass of liquid.

Dowsing is another form of psychic work which can be used for divination. Pendulums have been used throughout the ages to answer yes/no questions. A well-known old tradition is to hold a wedding ring tied to a hair taken from a pregnant woman's head, over her stomach to see whether it swings around and around or up and down signifying a girl or a boy. Dowsing is a useful tool for finding drains and water courses underground and could be used to find oil-fields. One does not need actually to stand at the oil-field to accomplish this, dowsing with wires or a pendulum over a map will do. A good dowser can find lost objects and even lost people in the same manner, either by using a map of the relevant country or city or by drawing a plan of the house where the lost object is hiding itself and then dowsing over the plan of the house. Some psychics just use their hands for this as they are able to pick up a 'hot spot' on the plan or map.

There are many ways that a psychic can augment his skills, but the idea is always to make a contact between himself and his client. Psychometry is a popular method; this means that the psychic asks his client for a watch or piece of jewellery which he then holds in his hand while he 'tunes in'. The psychic then tells the client what he can see, or interprets any symbols which he is 'shown'.

There are probably many forms of psychism which I have left out, but there is one strange one which I must mention although it is not really a form of divination. It is the strange ability of some people to transmit and or receive by means of telepathy. My daughter is such a strong telepath that she can even get through to my non-psychic husband, while she absolutely deafens me!

The Spiritual Link

This last section does not really come into the realms of divination at all as it is rarely the intention of those who contact 'spirit' to predict the future. The purpose of Spiritualism is to prove that another world exists beyond the confines of this one. Those who 'pass over' are in some cases able to pass messages which would only be understood by those who are still here on earth. The messages are often extremely mundane, such as 'I gave the vase with blue flowers on it to your Aunty Pat'. The sole purpose of this is to prove beyond doubt that the dead relative is living in another world, therefore the other world *has to exist*! The fact that these messages bring comfort to the bereaved is almost a spin off, a side effect which, while being a worthwhile thing to do, is not the main purpose of Spiritualism at all. Occasionally there are messages of warning or advice from the spirit world which are passed on to those down here. These are predictive, of course, and very useful if they are heeded, but this too is a spin off and not really relevant to the original intention.

Many psychics do use mediumistic abilities in order to give predictive messages and this is by means of their ability to link in with their spirit guides. The whole concept of spiritual guides is difficult to explain but I shall do my best. Every person on the face of the earth has the ability to contact his or her spiritual guides. Very few people ever know that they have such guides and therefore go through life using only their own intuition and only very occasionally wonder why they were led into certain paths of behaviour. Those who do become aware of guides are probably being pushed by those guides into that very awareness for some purpose that the guide himself (or herself) has in mind. This may be to take up something like healing, spiritualism, predictive work or psychology. These people, born sensitive in the first place, seem to be drawn to seek the inward path and to find their spiritual guidance; they may even find that they are being forced into it in some way. Some people have strange experiences which seem to force their chakra centres open and to create a bond with the spirit world. If this happens it feels almost like spiritual rape and as such, is quite unstoppable. In such a case, the only thing to do is to take the confusion line and 'relax and enjoy it'.

People who are able to link with their guides for the purposes of prediction are often the very best predictive divinators. Whether these people also use learned and interpretative skills to augment the ideas which come into their minds doesn't matter. If they are receptive to their guides and able to make that connection clearly and to articulate what they see, feel and hear, they are the tops, the very tops and there aren't many of those around. These divinators may also be healers and/or good psychologists, but they have a golden gift which in reality boils down to nothing more than the ability to turn themselves into a kind of telephone line between this world and worlds past and future, but it really is something wonderful to observe in action.

What Makes a Diviner
The answer to this is the same as 'what makes a winning golfer', or 'what makes a concert pianist?' It is a mixture of talent, motivation and an irresistible urge. There may also be some kind of irresistible push from the divinator's own spirit guides, to do this kind of work.

Why Aren't Diviners All Rich?
Why can't we all win on the pools? Pick out the winner of the 2.30 at Epsom? Find the best kind of job and keep it? Why? Why? Why? – Why not?

The answer seems to be that this gift is *not* to be used for the purposes of making money the easy way or even getting through life the easy way. Good diviners actually seem to do *more* than their fair share of suffering and, therefore, are able to understand the sufferings of their clients very well. There is some force in action which keeps just enough money rolling in for most diviners to keep them afloat but rarely riches, or success. Some do, of course, have a great deal of success but this very success itself seems to be aimed at keeping the diviner's nose fixed firmly to the grindstone.

PART ONE

FORTUNE-TELLING BY TAROT CARDS

SASHA FENTON

INTRODUCTION

The Origins of the Tarot
Nobody knows for certain where Tarot cards originally came from
but they seem to share the same roots as playing cards and the game
of chess. There are claims put forward that China, India or Egypt is
the birthplace of the Tarot; I feel sure that influences from all these
places, and a good many more, have been drawn on by the early card
designers. It is probable that the packs which finally emerged, more
or less in their present form, in the fourteenth century were
developed from those which were carried by travelling people and
gypsies during their periodic westerly migrations.

An early card game which was called 'Tarocco' in Italy and 'Tarot'
in France used the now familiar format of four suits of cards
numbered from Ace to 10 with figures of King, Queen, Cavalier
and Page. The suits were in the familiar form of Cups, Staves (Rods
or Wands), Swords and Coins (or Pentacles) – although the names
changed slightly from one country to another, or even from one area
to another. This game actually used the 22 Major Arcana cards which
were used as trump cards; the only one which still remains in playing
card packs is the Fool which is now called the Joker.

There is an account of cards being used for fortune-telling in the
fourteenth century French court, when a gypsy was brought in to
entertain the King. She was able to describe intimate details of the
people around him and tell him of future events with such accuracy
that fortune-telling by cards became tremendously popular. So
much so that the King became thoroughly fed-up with it and banned
the cards from the court altogether.

Since then, Tarot cards have gone through a number of phases of
popularity and banishment over the years, and are at the moment
once more extremely popular. The image that they have of being
slightly dangerous in some unspecified way, only serves to increase
their attraction. In actual fact, Tarot cards are not in the least
dangerous as they rely upon the intuition, and possible psychic

powers of the reader and in no way release dangerous or frightening forces. If the reader treats them with respect but does not worry too much about any one particular reading then they can be entertaining, informative and a useful guide to future actions.

1
RITUAL AND PROCEDURE

Looking After the Cards
Tarot cards which are meant to be used for divination should not be used for card games. They should be kept either in their box or in a drawstring bag. Many professional readers like to wrap their cards in a silk scarf to insulate the cards from outside influences. I have never done this, I just keep them in their box. The cards should be used only by you, the Reader, except when being shuffled by the Questioner prior to a reading. Other people should not be allowed to mess about with them or they will pick up too many cross-vibrations.

New Cards
It is a good idea to 'work up' a new pack by laying each card on top of the same cards from an old deck. If you have no old deck of your own, then be careful whose deck you use for this. If this idea does not appeal to you, then just keep on shuffling the cards and doing some test readings for yourself and your family until they lose their newness.

Guidelines for Readers
Always be careful not to frighten a Questioner when you are giving a reading. Most people tend to take what is said to them very seriously, even if they are outwardly sceptical or even derisory. It would be unforgivable to frighten or upset someone needlessly. Even a very experienced professional Reader has to take care when giving bad news, but in the case of an absolute beginner, if your Questioner should happen to pick out a set of really black cards, I would actually advise you to tone your interpretation right down, even to the point of risking your credibility. If you maintain your interest in the Tarot, you will soon learn to judge people and develop an instinct for giving bad news tactfully but confidently.

People are funny; the majority of us are quite happy to be gently

For a reading using upright and reversed cards
The Questioner cuts the cards into three decks
and then chooses one of them.

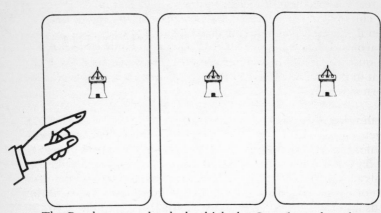

The Reader turns the deck which the Questioner has chosen.

The end which was nearest to the Questioner must be placed
nearest to the Reader.

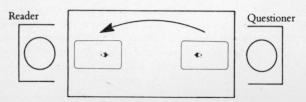

criticized by a Reader, we also enjoy being told that we have had a lot to put up with in the past (who hasn't?). We don't even mind being told that we will have to face a few more problems in the future, but we really hate to hear of specific health problems, troubles affecting out children, or that a loved one is being unfaithful. So as a Reader, even if you are absolutely convinced that the Questioner sitting in front of you has a youngster who will soon be in trouble with the law, a spouse who is putting it about and a really majestic cancer growing right in the middle of his middle – do yourself a favour, tone it all down a little!

Dealing the Cards

When you are ready to try a reading, sit somewhere quiet and comfortable. Use a table which is large enough to spread the cards out on; the dining table is often a popular place for this. Shuffle the cards a little if you wish, then pass them on to the Questioner and let him or her give them a good shuffle. Ask the Questioner to cut the cards into three decks, using the left hand (nearest to the heart). If you wish to give an upright and reversed reading, you can also ask the Questioner to choose one of the three decks which you can then turn round. The Questioner should then put all the cards back together again in any order he or she prefers. Then you should pick up the cards so that the end that pointed towards the Questioner now points towards you. Now you are ready to begin.

2

INTRODUCTION TO THE MINOR ARCANA AND THE COURT CARDS

THE MINOR ARCANA

The Minor Arcana of the Tarot is composed of four suits of cards, these are Cups, Staves (Rods or Wands), Swords and Coins (or Pentacles). Each of these suits have numbered cards from Ace to 10, plus four court cards which are the Page, Knight, Queen and King.

In some European countries, the Minor Arcana cards are still actually used as playing cards. Some of the packs which are meant for card games have heads at both ends in the same way that our playing cards do.

It is just about feasible for someone to give a reading by means of the Minor Arcana only – after all there are many skilled playing card readers around, but it is unusual for both the Major and the Minor Arcana cards to be used together. A good many readers like to give a reading using just the Major Arcana first, then another reading using the complete pack.

THE COURT CARDS

The court cards cause quite a lot of confusion for those wishing to learn the Tarot as they *may* represent actual people who are already in the Questioner's environment or who may yet come into his life. The court cards may also represent situations and events rather than actual persons in the Questioner's life, or they may be people to meet and deal with who will leave no great or lasting impression on the Questioner but who may spark off events and turning points as they pass by. There is also the fraught question of how to identify specific people in the subject's life from the court cards – even the simple act of choosing a Significator* to represent the Questioner is filled with

*The Significator is a card which has been chosen by the Reader to represent the Questioner.

problems. So let us try to analyse and deal with these questions in a fairly logical manner.

CHOOSING A SIGNIFICATOR

The Gipsy Method
In earlier times, before the advent of television and radio, people were forced to find ways to entertain themselves in order to combat boredom. We have all heard about the singsongs around the piano that people supposedly enjoyed in the old days, haven't we? Well, along other things, fortune-telling was a much more popular pastime than it is today, and one could almost guarantee that in every family there would be an old auntie somewhere who had a 'way' with tea leaves or playing cards. The usual method of telling fortunes by means of playing cards was to allocate certain categories of age and general appearance to each of the court cards, and this is still used by many readers today, both by means of Tarot cards and ordinary playing cards. The following analysis will demonstrate the method.

Kings   – These are mature men of at least 35 years of age, possibly older.

Queens – These are mature adult women.

Knights – These are young adult men.

Pages   – These are children and young people of both sexes.

Cups   – Blonde haired, light skinned people.

Staves – Brown haired, light skinned people.

Swords – Dark complexioned, dark haired people.

Coins   – Very dark complexioned, dark haired people.

If the reader wants to use ordinary playing cards they can be treated as follows:

Combine the Knight and Page cards to make the Jack; i.e. young or immature persons of either sex.

Cups are like Hearts
Staves are like Clubs
Swords are like Spades
Coins are like Diamonds

In fact our familiar playing cards developed from the same source as the Minor Arcana of the Tarot. One can see an immediate correlation between Staves and Clubs. The Diamond probably got its name from its shape – remember the Coins are often called Pentacles because of the five pointed star on each coin in some packs. The Hearts are harder to find an explanation for, but it might again stem from the shape of the Cups or the designs on them on some of the ancient packs. The name 'Spade' is a corruption of 'Espada' which is Spanish for Sword!

The Astrological Method
This method is based on astrology with the theory being that the four suits relate to the four astrological elements, and therefore to the signs of the zodiac.

Cups   – Water signs, i.e. Cancer, Scorpio and Pisces.

Staves – Air signs, i.e. Gemini, Libra and Aquarius.
            Or Fire signs, i.e. Aries, Leo and Sagittarius.

Swords – Air signs, i.e. Gemini, Libra and Aquarius.
            Or Fire signs, i.e. Aries, Leo and Sagittarius.

Coins   – Earth signs, i.e. Taurus, Virgo and Capricorn.

As you can see, Tarot readers cannot agree about the Air and Fire signs and this is in my opinion a particularly awkward method of interpretation.
   The way a Court Card might be used goes something like this. Say, for instance, the King of Swords was prominent in the layout, the Reader might say to the Questioner 'you are going to have a significant meeting with someone born under the sign of Gemini, Libra or Aquarius (*or* Aries, Leo or Sagittarius)'. I personally have never really felt at home with this method, but that is not in any way to disparage those who get good results by using it. In many ways this dilemma isolates the chief problem with regard to the Tarot (or any other form of interpretative work), that every Reader or potential Reader must find out what works for him or her and must not necessarily follow a rigid patterns. Any book on the Tarot can only give guidelines and the Reader must find his own way to success by trial, error and practice. *This is a most important point.*

Other Popular Ideas
Some Readers associate particular professions with particular cards such as a doctor or lawyer for the King of Swords or a business

woman for the Queen of Staves. The booklets which come with the packs of cards when one buys them often mention such things as 'A man, kindly disposed to the Questioner, who lives in the country'. All this is fair enough but is not really sufficiently flexible.

Sasha's Method
This really is a mixture of all the other methods. First of all, if I happen to be using a Significator to represent the Questioner, I will choose one to fit his appearance and what little I may know of his nature. Therefore, I may choose the Queen of Staves for a chatty working woman with medium colouring, and the King of Coins for a steady, quiet, down-to-earth (if not an actual earth sign), darkish haired man.

Kings and Queens, on the whole, are actual people who are now, or shortly will be, a part of the Questioner's life. The Reader should always use his or her own intuition with regard to the type of person any court card represents. If my description does not *feel* right, then by all means change it. My interpretations are tried and tested, but nevertheless time and practice will show the Reader the type of person each court card represents to him or her.

Knights, of course, can represent people, and in general the colouring and the behaviour of these people is rather like that of the King's, but possibly in a watered down form. Another curious thing about the Knights is that they may actually represent a mature person – the type who would normally be represented by the King, but this person may be diminishing in importance to the Questioner in the future. For instance, a person who has had a central and significant effect on the Questioner in recent years will either shortly move away, or for some other reason, just become less important (either for good or ill) to the Questioner. I call this the 'law of diminishing persons' and it is quite strange how it seems to work. The former star performer in our Questioner's life may reduce from a King, to a Knight and then to a Page before disappearing completely out of his or her sphere of interest. This 'diminishing' situation may be temporary or permanent, a glance at other cards in the spread may help the Reader here. It is also worth noting that this kind of situation requires fairly frequent readings and a Questioner who already knows which card signifies whom in his life.

Pages are often children or very youthful people. Generally speaking, the Page of Cups and Coins will be fairly steady and peaceful children while the Pages of Staves and Swords signify the more active type of child. The colouring of the child is blonde for Cups, brown for Staves, darkish for Swords and very dark for Coins.

If more than one Page appears in a spread, then children are in the forefront of the Questioner's mind, or there may just be a lot of documentation, telephone calls, letters and general communications on the way to the Questioner. There may be scandal or gossip, mixed up communications and misunderstandings, especially if the Pages are reversed.

So to sum up the Court cards; it is generally assumed that a King represents a lover, husband, boss, authority figure, father, brother or friend. A Queen represents a lover, wife, boss, mother, sister or friend. A Knight represents a lover, friend, brother (or sister) or a colleague. A Page represents a child, friend or messenger. However, these people may not even stay for very long in the Questioner's life and the cards will show the *impact* that the character has on the Questioner at the time of the reading and this may be the impact of a situation rather than a person.

3
THE SUIT OF CUPS

The suit of Cups is associated with romance, marriage and material goods and possessions. Cups also indicate warmth and friendship, partnerships and even the kind of affection a person may have for their pet! Educational matters and the visual arts are also associated with Cup cards.

ACE OF CUPS

Meaning

The beginning of an affectionate loving or friendly association for the questioner. At best this may be the romance of a lifetime, or a marriage made in heaven, at the very least it indicates new friendships, good social life and good companionship. It also may indicate that a gift is coming to the questioner, often a ring – even a wedding ring! A birth is also possible.

Reversed Meaning

This gives a watered down version of the upright Ace. Therefore, affection rather than outright *love* could be on the way to the Questioner, or more sadly someone who did not love the Questioner could be losing interest at the time of reading.

TWO OF CUPS

Meaning

A partnership. This may be romantic or to do with business.

Therefore if the Questioner has just met somebody interesting, this card would indicate that romance will blossom. Even if this is a business partnership, there will be a liking and friendship for the people involved – whatever sex they may be. It can also mean two people making up after an argument or getting engaged, or making a commitment to each other.

Reversed Meaning
This reverses the above reading. There will be a parting which might be temporary and due to unforseen circumstances or there may be a complete split in the relationship. Other cards in the reading will help to clarify matters. It is possible that the desired relationship will not get off the ground in the first place.

THREE OF CUPS

Meaning
This is a fun card which shows up when pleasant celebrations are due to occur. There might be a wedding for the Questioner soon, or he may officiate at somebody else's wedding. There may be the birth of a child, a house-warming or any reason for a celebration.

Reversed Meaning
A confusing card, it may indicate fun, frivolity and sex, however, it can show that an expected or hoped for marriage will not take place. There may even be a divorce, or it could indicate that an affair which is taking place will not turn into marriage later on.

FOUR OF CUPS

Meaning
This is a peculiar card as it shows dissatisfaction. It shows that the

Questioner has advantages under his nose which he cannot see, but wants something which he does not have, or even does not really know what it is that he wants. Perhaps the grass is greener on the other side of the hill.

Reversed Meaning
The meaning of the upright card is reversed here. The Questioner makes up his mind as to what it is that he wants, or decides to make the best of what he already has. Also new friends and experiences are on the way.

FIVE OF CUPS

Meaning
This is a miserable card which shows loss and sadness. However, this is not total loss, there is definitely something left to look forward to, whatever has been lost, there is still something left from which to begin to build for the future. There is a sense of looking back with regret, possibly even some kind of mourning.

Reversed Meaning
A sense of loss and a period of unhappiness is passing away and there
will be good times again in the future, possibly meeting up with old
friends again.

SIX OF CUPS

Meaning
This card shows a need to reach back into the past in order to build
for the future. Therefore, the Questioner should go back to his roots
in some way, either by using some old skill or experience or by
getting in touch with old friends and family contacts. It often comes
up just before a happy family gathering.

Reversed Meaning
This reverses the meaning of the upright card. It can indicate that a
planned family get-together will be a disaster, or that the answer to
the Questioner's problems does not lie in the past but will require a
new outlook on life. The family are not likely to help and perhaps it is
time to admit to personal mistakes and *grow up*.

SEVEN OF CUPS

Meaning
This card show confusion. There are too many roads to choose from
and some of them will be dead ends. Perhaps it is best for the
Questioner to coast along for a while rather than trying to make far
reaching decisions at this time. If the money is a stumbling block in a
romance, this should soon be sorted out.

Reversed Meaning
Muddles and indecision will soon sort themselves out.

EIGHT OF CUPS

Meaning
There is a miserable situation involving the Questioner just now, but
there *is* light at the end of the tunnel. The message is to be
courageous and patient, things will work out eventually. It is possible
that a blonde woman will change the Questioner's life in some way
soon.

Reversed Meaning
A definite end to a rotten situation is now in view. There should be
some joy and fun ahead.

NINE OF CUPS

Meaning
This card shows that the Questioner is (or soon will be) very pleased

with himself. This is fine as long as he remembers not to appear too smug to less fortunate people. Marriage to a mature type of person may be on the way.

Reversed Meaning
Not a bad card as it shows some satisfaction to come, but there may still be a slight touch of irritation. If, for instance, the Questioner failed in an exam, he would not have failed by a great margin and would be advised to try again. Any problems should be sorted out soon.

TEN OF CUPS

Meaning
This is sometimes called the 'wish' card, if this shows up in a reading, the Questioner can expect to get all that he desires.

Reversed Meaning
This may be a watered down version of the upright card, i.e. partial success in obtaining one's desires, but it may be that someone else

will be getting a fair bit of the Questioner's share of the spoils. There may be arguments in a relationship or within the family. A complete split up is possible. A look at other cards nearby will give some more clues about this one.

PAGE OF CUPS

Meaning
A loving gentle youngster, possibly blonde with fair colouring.

Often the Pages are not people but situations. The Page of Cups indicates a time to think and study and possibly the passing of exams. If often shows up before the Questioner embarks on a course of study. Also there may be business matters but they will proceed slowly and will need thinking about rather than rushing in boldly.

Reversed Meaning
This may indicate trouble to come for the Page of Cups (see upright description). There may be some studying which has to be done or an exam which must be passed. This is more of a chore than a pleasure.

KNIGHT OF CUPS

Meaning
A kindly, good natured youngish man, possibly fair haired. A Man who has feelings of love and affection for the Questioner is coming to or going away from the Questioner. The Questioner's lover or husband could have a journey ahead of him. Changes with regard to romance and relationships *may* soon be on the way.

Reversed Meaning
Love could be fading; a lover could be unfaithful, unloving or just not in a position at present to do what the Questioner wants.

QUEEN OF CUPS

Meaning
This woman will bring love and comfort to the Questioner. She is a good friend to the Questioner of either sex and will do her best to help in any situation. However, she may be somewhat possessive and materialistic. She should be maternal and home-loving and especially fond of animals. Either way up, she may be a bit spoiled and selfish.

Reversed Meaning
This lady may be disappointed in love in the near future, or intrinsically unable to give her affections freely. Possibly she is not sincere, she may be greedy, materialistic and jealous, it may be that she has been hurt before and is holding back rather than be hurt again.

KING OF CUPS

Meaning
Probably, but not necessarily, fair or reddish in hair and skin colouring.

Lover or husband, kindly warmhearted man who cares for the Questioner. Could be a bit possessive but would be successful and happy in love relationships himself and would make other people around him happy too. This man could be rather self indulgent and not always too reliable, although he is affectionate by nature.

Reversed Meaning
Probably quite caring and well meaning but not really that reliable. This could indicate to the Questioner that he is losing interest in this relationship or is not in a position to do much to help the Questioner. There could be jealousy or possessiveness here and the King could himself be a loser in the game of love.

4
THE SUIT OF STAVES

The suit of Staves (or Wands) is associated with negotiations of one kind or another. This may be to do with business, legal matters, clubs and societies, neighbourhood events or family business matters. Overseas travel is associated with some of the Stave cards, otherwise plenty of local trips and journeys are indicated. Creativity in the form of words is represented by these cards too. Often property dealings, home decorations and renovations are indicated by the appearance of Stave cards.

ACE OF STAVES

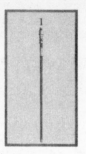

Meaning
This is the birth of an idea, even in some cases the birth of a child. There could be a significant letter or phone call to do with business – or businesslike matters. This should bring good news, and should be the beginning of a successful enterprise.

Reversed Meaning
Indicates a new beginning but there will be problems attached. It is still worth doing, but possibly the time is not quite right just now.

TWO OF STAVES

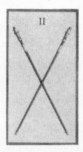

Meaning
This could be a partnership or some sort of joint arrangement which will come into being but, in my experience, this has something to do with property or premises and may indicate a good property deal to come. Watch out for the competition though! There may also be a proud man who is, or shortly will be, important in the Questioner's life.

Reversed Meaning
Delays in the sale or purchase of property. Possibly a badly starred business partnership. Wait and try again another time. There may be unexpected news. A proud man may cause trouble.

THREE OF STAVES

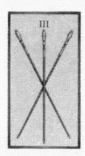

Meaning
A new deal, new job or new beginning. There could be travel in connection with work, or just an important letter or phone call with good news on the way. Marriages and partnerships will go well in the future.

Reversed Meaning
Wait, try again later. There will be nothing good about going ahead with business matters just now.

FOUR OF STAVES

Meaning
This is a card of security and of putting down roots. It may indicate the purchase of a house or premises, or it may just indicate a good holiday in the near future. There could be a house-warming soon.

Reversed Meaning
Similar to above but may be delayed or surrounded by problems.

FIVE OF STAVES

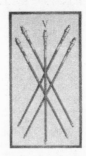

Meaning
Something of a struggle in matters of negotiation, however, despite the aggravation there should be a good outcome in the end. Courage and endurance may be needed before the Questioner arrives where he wants to be. Travel plans may have to be put back.

Reversed Meaning
Leave it, try again another time. There may be legal problems ahead.

SIX OF STAVES

Meaning
Victory! Great news! Legal battles will be won, negotiations will succeed, agreement will be reached and problems will be overcome.

Reversed Meaning
If there is a forthcoming battle, the other side will win. Leave it for the time being if you can, try again later. Other people may not do *their* jobs properly and that may affect your life in some way.

SEVEN OF STAVES

Meaning
Problems which can be overcome, but they may have to be isolated and sorted out one at a time. A constant battle, but with courage and determination this will be won. This may be a health problem or just the opposition of other people around the Questioner.

Reversed Meaning
There are just too many obstacles at the moment, try to sort out the worst of your problems now and leave chancy new decisions for another time. There could be some sort of puzzling or potentially embarrassing situation developing in the future.

EIGHT OF STAVES

Meaning
There will soon be an expansion of the Questioner's horizons, taking the form of mind broadening experiences and new people. Travel is very likely and among the new faces and places there may well be friendship and love to be found.

Reversed Meaning
Cancelled plans. Do not move away from familiar ground just now.
There could be jealousy and spite around the Questioner (or he may
feel jealous himself soon). The Questioner may even be affected by
strike action!

NINE OF STAVES

Meaning
The message to the Questioner from this card is to hang on to what
he or she has got. There will not be too much opportunity to expand
one's life and horizons just at the moment as one may be
surrounded by people who are making demands. The best bet is to
stay put, be prudent and keep the present lifestyle intact. This card
shows the Questioner to be in a *temporarily* secure position.

Reversed Meaning
There is a danger of loss of status or loss of position with this card.
There may be illness on the way now.

TEN OF STAVES

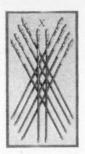

Meaning
There will be added burdens or more responsibilty to come –
whichever way the Questioner likes to look at it. He or she could
receive a promotion to a more responsible position at work or could
find themselves lumbered in some way, though not necessarily at
work.

Reversed Meaning
Burdens can and will be put down shortly – but that promotion and
extra responsibility will not be forthcoming just yet.

PAGE OF STAVES

Meaning
An intelligent rather restless youngster who has charm and plenty to
say. This card shows up when the Questioner is going on a journey.
This will be fine if the Page is upright, but may involve a problem if
the card is reversed. There may also be visitors (most probably

young ones) from a long way off. There may also be surprising news on the way. Also letter and news about work and from old friends. Minor property or premises matters may go ahead now.

Reversed Meaning
There could be a problem for this youngster. There may be a delay or some sort of problem with regard to contracts or travel. Negotiations may be temporarily held up.

KNIGHT OF STAVES

Meaning
Business or news to do with travel, also a visitor to or from afar. A move of house may be in the offing, changes are coming and they will require phone calls, letters and journeys. There may be romantic or business dealings with a chatty, pleasant young man.

Reversed Meaning
Something to do with travel or travellers may be disappointing. A promise may be broken. There may be a set-back with regard to property matters. A brown-haired young man may let the Questioner down or may prove to be insincere.

QUEEN OF STAVES

Meaning
A charming and clever woman, a good companion and a good talker. This lady is great fun, reliable in her affections and very loving but possibly a bit hard to pin down and possess as she has a definite mind of her own. She is a good business woman, adept in dealing with people and a reliable worker but not necessarily all that

successful, she needs a good, helpful man behind her to boost her confidence in herself before she can really succeed.

Reversed Meaning
Either this lady is well meaning but unable to be reliable as a friend or successful in business because of circumstances, or she really is an unreliable and unfaithful type of person.

KING OF STAVES

Meaning
Probably light to medium colouring, fair skinned with lightish hair, slimly built. An amusing, chatty, friendly man who is fond of the Questioner but not necessarily going to become heavily involved emotionally. This man is good company, will cheer the Questioner up and may be very helpful in the working environment. Good at selling, communicating or marketing.

Reversed Meaning
At worst this may be a sly liar, at best this man is unreliable and

untrustworthy. He may be great fun but do not take him too seriously or get heavily involved with him in ways that matter. He may be full of promises but not willing (or able) to deliver the goods just now.

5
THE SUIT OF SWORDS

The Sword cards indicate trouble and strife, swift action to be taken, and health matters. Sometimes they represent travel over, or to, watery places. These cards can also indicate courage and authority figures as well as sadness and betrayal. The Swords get right to the heart of any matter, and for that reason they represent areas of life and experience which have to be taken very seriously.

ACE OF SWORDS

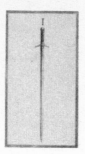

Meaning
This may indicate an operation, as the presence of this card can
mean a cut to the body, or at least an injection. Like all Aces, this card
may indicate the beginning of a new cycle but in this case it will be
something all absorbing such as a very difficult but rewarding job, or
a really passionate love affair. Whatever is coming to the Questioner,
it will do so with quite a bang. There may also be power and justice
coming to (or for) the Questioner.

Reversed Meaning
Similar to above, but the events which are on the way are likely to be
milder and not so all absorbing. This could be a warning card that a
business deal will turn out to be an absolute disaster. This can also
show that the Questioner may take too much action in some way and
may 'go over the top' so to speak, or react too strongly to a situation.

TWO OF SWORDS

Meaning
There is a strange situation going on when this card appears. The
Questioner cannot make a move and cannot see his way forward. It is
a card of suspension, no change, possibly of delay. If the Questioner
has fears about a relationship breaking up, or the loss of a job, then
the appearance of this card would give reassurance that things would
remain as they are. However, on the other hand no improvement in
life can be expected either at this time. There may be an agreement,
settlement or some sort of peace treaty.

Reversed Meaning
The end of stalemate, things are about to start moving. There may be relief and release from a difficult situation now, or the Questioner, or someone close, may travel away soon.

THREE OF SWORDS

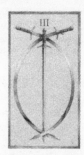

Meaning
There may be loss or heartache to be faced. This could be the end of a relationship or some other sad event. Some say that this card indicates blood, therefore there could be illness or an operation coming soon.

Reversed Meaning
The end of a period of heartbreak, the beginning of learning to cope with a loss or rejection. There may be a minor surgical procedure soon. The Questioner may attend a funeral in the near future.

FOUR OF SWORDS

Meaning
This is a card of recovery from illness. (It is amazing how often this card will come up near someone who is in hospital and it is always good news for the sick person.) The other indication is that the Questioner needs to take a break from present stressful situations.

Reversed Meaning
This is not too optimistic for a sick person as it indicates that the illness is still there and more treatment is needed. In other circumstances there may be recovery from financial losses.

FIVE OF SWORDS

Meaning
This card shows quarrels, possibly even violence. There may be ruined plans and a rather bad time all around. Someone the Questioner loves may suddenly go away – possibly even overseas. There might be people who are jealous and spiteful to the Questioner.

Reversed Meaning
Similar to upright but the problem is probably passing from the
Questioner's life shortly. The Questioner may attend a funeral
shortly.

SIX OF SWORDS

Meaning
Travel over water, there could be an element of gradual release from
poverty or unhappiness now and a move or journey may be the
turning point. There may be a visitor from overseas coming into the
Questioner's life – check other cards nearby for this.

Reversed Meaning
Journeys – even holidays will be delayed. There may be financial
losses due to carelessness.

SEVEN OF SWORDS

Meaning
This card is hard to interpret. It may indicate a robbery or rip-off to

come or it may mean that the Questioner is due to gather up his resources, cut his losses and sort out some difficult situation once and for all. There is often legal or business advice here – but there is also the desire to escape from overwhelming problems.

Reversed Meaning
There will be advice (possibly legal) forthcoming soon. However, beware of thieves.

EIGHT OF SWORDS

Meaning
The Questioner is temporarily tied down and cannot do much to change the circumstances. This could be due to all sorts of reasons and the only thing to do is to wait and see how things go for a while before attempting to make major changes. There should be light at the end of the tunnel here.

Reversed Meaning
Restrictions will soon lift but depressions and hard times must be coped with first. There may be accidents, disappointments or even deaths in the Questioner's environment.

NINE OF SWORDS

Meaning
There could be illness, even a miscarriage or some nagging worry. I find that this card often shows up shortly before the Questioner's mother gets into difficulties or causes problems for others.

Reversed Meanings
The worry and sleepless nights will shortly come to an end. There may be unpleasant rumours being put around about the Questioner.

TEN OF SWORDS

Meaning
There will be treachery – a stab in the back. This is an unfortunate card as it can indicate divorce, work problems and general unhappiness. There could be a forced change coming, not of the Questioner's choosing.

Reversed Meaning
Minor disappointment, a person may try to slander the Questioner or may let him or her down. However, hard times will come to an end soon and in the case of ill health, there will soon be recovery.

PAGE OF SWORDS

Meaning
This is an active, possibly sporty child, who is dark haired. There may be good news about business but the Questioner is being told to keep his eyes open because either opportunity, or possibly scandal, are on the way. A contract may shortly need to be signed.

Reversed Meaning
The young person described in the upright section may have problems to face. Indicates arguments and problems but these could be settled soon. There could be disappointments regarding work and business matters, especially those concerning contracts. There may be someone unpleasant who is spying on the Questioner and hoping to land the Questioner in trouble.

KNIGHT OF SWORDS

Meaning
A tough, brave and very intelligent young man may help the

Questioner soon. There will be a young and energetic environment. Possibly swift changes and decisions to be made soon. An assertive dark young man may come along soon. The Questioner may make hasty decisions or sudden changes in the near future.

Reversed Meaning
This could indicate an agressive, destructive, argumentative young man, or just an active and amibitious man who has temporary difficulties. Arguments coming soon and swift action to be taken shortly. There could be some medical or surgical treatment soon.

QUEEN OF SWORDS

QUEEN OF SWORDS

Meaning
A sharp, clever woman, either a teacher, doctor or lawyer. She should be good to the Questioner but although helpful with the kind of problem which requires professional help, she might be a bit too cool and prickly to make a good loving companion. It depends really on the Questioner's priorities at the time of the reading. This lady commands respect.

Reversed Meaning
This lady is sharp and unpleasant. She may be professionally in opposition to the Questioner, or just a strong and difficult influence in the Questioner's life. She may be cold-hearted and possibly spiteful.

KING OF SWORDS

Meaning
Possibly dark haired and rather sharp featured, this could well be a

KING OF SWORDS

doctor, lawyer or professional man who is about to have some important influence on the Questioner's life. Of course, he may be the Questioner's boss – however, any of the Kings would fit into that category. This man could bring problems which have to be dealt with, literally speaking, there could be trouble ahead which he may (or may not) help the Questioner to deal with. He appears to lack a sense of humour and to be a tough, uncompromising professional man; however, there could be a good reason to need a man like this on one's side in the near future. Put it this way; if I was faced with some sort of financial or medical problem, I would be quite glad to see this card turn up in a spread as it would show me that I would soon find the right man for the job in hand.

Reversed Meaning
This is an aggressive man who is bent on stirring up trouble – he may be the lawyer who is representing the opposition in an impending law suit. He may be a particularly unhelpful medical or professional man whom the Questioner will shortly be up against, or he may be closely involved in the Questioner's private or business life. He may not actually be all that evil, just angry because he cannot help much at present. If this is so, then the Questioner may expect aggression, tantrums, possibly even violence from this man.

6
THE SUIT OF COINS

The Suit of Coins is associated with money, goods and services, the organization of work and of business; also matters relating to the Questioner's status and his or her larger possessions such as property.

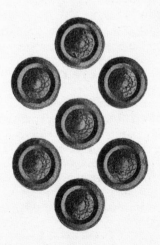

ACE OF COINS

Meaning
Money coming to the Questioner, this may be a win, bonus or a raise or it may be associated with a better job – a step up in the Questioner's financial position. It could be a letter about money but the news will be good.

Reversed Meaning
Same as upright but the significance (and amounts of cash) will be less.

TWO OF COINS

Meaning
Separation, possibly the breakup of a partnership or of a home. Property may be divided either by agreement or by law. Alternatively, this card may indicate a lack of ability either through the Questioner's nature, or circumstances, to cope with all the different demands that are being made on him or her. The Questioner will be

borrowing from Peter to pay Paul.

Reversed Meaning
In my experience this card is much the same either way up, except
that the problem may be coming to an end if the card is reversed,

THREE OF COINS

Meaning
Buying a home, or extending or improving of property or premises.
Also success in business due to cashing in on some talent or learned
skill.

Reversed Meaning
Same as above but beset by problems, probably indicating that the
Questioner has bitten off more than he can chew.

FOUR OF COINS

Meaning
Financial security is on the way, but there may be too much emphasis on money in the Questioner's outlook on life at this time. This card also shows that the *long term* financial outlook is going to be good.

Reversed Meaning
Money may be short, security will be hard to come by in the short term. Exam failures and delays in payments are possible.

FIVE OF COINS

Meaning
A sense of loss and loneliness prevails, however there is warmth and love to be found but probably not from the place where the Questioner most wishes it to come. Oddly enough, affairs and romances flourish when this card shows up but they are not going to be deeply satisfying emotionally. Financial loss is the most likely outcome from this card.

Reversed Meaning
A period of loss and loneliness will end soon.

SIX OF COINS

Meaning
This indicates that money will have to be shared out soon. Other cards nearby will help to indicate why, but it may be the result of a divorce, redundancy or an inheritance. The Questioner's finances will have to be sorted out, there may be too many people around who are trying to drain the Questioner of money or of energy. There

is another meaning to this card and that is of benevolence, i.e. that the Questioner will be in such a good position that he will be able and willing to help out other people. Personally, I have found that the former is more likely to be the case.

Reversed Meaning
Similar to upright but the problem may be passing away by now.

SEVEN OF COINS

Meaning
This card indicates slow growth, achievement or advancement by dint of long term efforts. Therefore, hard work will bring just rewards – keep at it. Even if things are bad now, don't give up, keep trying.

Reversed Meaning
A period of hard work will come to an end soon, frankly it is just not worth battling on just now. Wait and try again later.

EIGHT OF COINS

Meaning
A new job or promotion, there may be a raise or just praise. The Questioner will soon learn a new skill which will be relevant to a future career.

Reversed Meaning
Problem at work, could just be that the Questioner's present job will come to an end soon or will need to take a new direction. The Questioner may be put into a position where he has to learn new methods whether he wants to or not.

NINE OF COINS

Meaning
Money and success are on the way. This will be a good time to buy goods for the home. Domestic matters will go well.

Reversed Meaning
There will be no success and not much money coming from this project. The Questioner may be selling some of his belongings soon.

TEN OF COINS

Meaning
This card brings money and success but also great pleasure from personal achievement. Can bring travel in connection with business and it can also indicate a good future marriage and family life. Commercial matters will be an integral part of any marriage when this card is involved.

Reversed Meaning
Some success is on the way. There may be a gift coming or some sort of charitable benefit such as winning a raffle prize. There may even be a state (or private) pension on the way.

PAGE OF COINS

Meaning
A steady business-like youngster probably with very dark hair.

This card brings news about money matters and possibly travel; however, in this case it would be on business rather than for pleasure. There may be news of a promotion at work too. A youngster could have some good news soon, or may do something to make people proud of him.

Reversed Meaning
The young person described above could have some problems to come. There could be some slight temporary shortage of money, also business and money news will be poor for a while.

KNIGHT OF COINS

Meaning
This should be a youngish man with a cautious nature. A young man coming with news about business, money, etc. Even travel and business are possible now due to the restless nature of the Knight card.

Reversed Meaning
Problems with regard to work, money or people who have great ideas that cost the Questioner money. Could be a warning not to travel on business just now.

QUEEN OF COINS

Meaning
This lady is money-minded. She may be comfortably off, or just determined to be so. She commands respect because of her status

and possessions – or would like to do so. She is a skilled negotiator and an honest and reliable business woman. She would be a comfortable and warm-hearted love companion, but only to the man who will give her a decent standard of living.

Reversed Meaning
This lady will win if involved in a fight against the Questioner, especially if money is involved. She is tough and materialistic. However, she may be perfectly kind and reasonable, but temporarily down on her own luck.

KING OF COINS

Meaning
Dark haired and complexioned, possibly a rather thick-set build. A sound solid citizen, conservative and reliable if rather boring. He should have good business sense but will be cautious rather than a gambler or experimenter. He should be very close to his family. He is basically kind but may be somewhat mean, over-careful, or nervous of spending unnecessarily. He is a tough but honest bargainer and negotiator.

Reversed Meaning

A hard headed business man who is not on the Questioner's side. Alternatively , he may look steady but actually turn out to be a loser. He could be mean, untrustworthy, unfair or possessive. He may even be quite a good person who is temporarily down on his luck.

7
THE MAJOR ARCANA

The Major Arcana is so powerful in its imagery that it can be used on its own, without the Minor Arcana, even though there are only twenty-two cards. Many readers will give a Major Arcana reading followed by another reading using the whole pack. This gives them the outline of the Questioner's problems and lifestyle before going on to give the complete reading. In a mixture of Major and Minor cards, it is interesting to note how many of the Major cards appear and where.

Even though packs vary somewhat, the overall symbolism of the Major cards remains the same (i.e. the Emperor may be dressed or seated differently in different packs, but he is still the Emperor!).

There is a certain amount of controversy these days about whether to give reverse readings for cards and I believe that the majority of professional readers *do not* reverse their cards at all. The idea is that all the cards have their good and bad (weak or strong might be a better description) aspects, and this is especially true of the Major Arcana cards. I have broken the explanations down into 'positive' and 'negative' to make them a bit easier for the novice reader to understand and the 'negative' can be given as a reversed reading if so desired. Frankly, I feel that each card encompasses both sides within its nature, but I leave it to you to experiment with these cards for yourself.

O
THE FOOL

Positive
This can be shown as the first or last card in the Major Arcana. I tend to think of it as the first card as it represents a fresh start or the discovery of talents and abilities that the Questioner did not know were there. It represents a person stepping out into a new future which could take them anywhere. It is a chance to start again and it

can be applied to any aspect of life, such as a new relationship, a new area to live in, a new job, a change of direction generally. Its message is that a new door is opening and there will be challenges ahead which can be taken advantage of. The Fool can also tell of fun ahead and light hearted enjoyable people and events to come. However, even as a 'positive' card, there is a warning not to be rash, or to rush in to a new situation in a blind and undisciplined manner. Positive or negative, the Fool tells the Questioner that he is going to have to use his willpower and to exercise restraint in some future situation.

Negative
There is a clear warning here to give thought and consideration to any new situation. The Questioner will be tempted to act in an immature, possibly even irrational manner, and may become obsessed by some craze which leads them to extravagance and loss. There may be an overwhelming passion for somebody tremendously exciting, but there will be problems attached to this affair which *must* be taken into consideration before plunging in. If the warnings are ignored then at best, the outcome will make the Questioner look and feel like a prize idiot, and at worst this could be tragic.

I
THE MAGICIAN

Positive
This card depicts new opportunities, it may be the start of an enterprise or even of an important relationship, though in general, I feel that is has more to do with business matters and worldly affairs than with love and romance. There may be several courses of action to be looked at in the near future, and thought must be paid to new decisions and actions. There will soon be a chance to use skills and

education in a practical manner, but there should be some kind of politics or salesmanship involved in this somewhere.

A friend once described the Magician as indicating a 'bold step' and this is probably right as there is a somewhat chancy element attached to this card. It tells the Questioner to go ahead and blind them all with science, use the new found confidence and have a go. All in all, an important new cycle in the Questioner's life, especially that part of it which is carried on outside the home. There is definitely a feeling of the Questioner being urged to put ideas into practice because there will be great rewards for use of one's imagination, original ideas, flair, art, craft or subtlety that he or she possesses. This card could show up just as the Questioner is going to start a business using the skills and talents they possess. This is a good example because it pre-supposes self-reliance, flexibility and the ability to choose one's own action. It also shows determination to see the task through to the end.

Negative

The warning here is not to miss an opportunity that is coming up. Also to look carefully at any new enterprise which is presented to the Questioner by *other people*. They may not be all that honest. There is always an air of trickery around the Magician, either the good trickery of the successful salesman or the heartlessness of the 'cowboy' or 'con artist'. If this card depicts a person around the Questioner, he may be about to take on just the right one for the job; alternatively, the Questioner may go headlong into a business where he may find himself being controlled by a team of crooks or fools! The warning as with all the cards is that everything in life can go either way. Although consideration is essential before action when this card shows up, especially if it is upright and in a prominent part of a spread, then for goodness sake have a go!

II
THE HIGH PRIESTESS

Positive

If students of the occult finds this card upright and in a prominent place in the reading, then they are being told to go ahead with their studies; they *have* the ability and will make positive and helpful use of it. The Priestess has both intuition and common-sense, there is a feeling of ancient knowledge about her, about the hidden and mysterious things in life. I feel that if this card shows up when decisions are to be made, then one should follow one's feelings and let one's natural intuition be the guide, also to make allowances for somebody else's intuition particularly if they are close and trusted friends.

The Priestess also indicates scholarship in its widest sense. The card can foretell a period of study to come and of a good teacher who will be very helpful to the Questioner. It may point to a particular person about to help the Questioner, this would be a woman who is clever, rather remote but informative, if not very motherly in manner, a professionally qualified person most likely. The Questioner may take on some of the mantle of the High Priestess and find himself in a position to apple common sense and understanding. The card is also associated with integrity and honesty, so although the tongue may be sharp, the sentiments and the heart are in the right place. Of course, the Priestess, like all the cards, is somewhat androgynous, which means that 'she' may actually be a 'he'!

There is one other rather tantalizing point about the Priestess which is that it points out to the Questioner that they are not yet in possession of all the facts. The Reader must note the area of the spread in which this card falls and tell the Questioner that something pertaining to this subject has yet to be revealed.

Negative

The negative side is the opposite of cool commonsensical control, i.e. uncontrolled emotional outbursts and stupid careless remarks. Selfishness and impatience make for rows, and the Questioner is reminded to make sure that they really know what they are talking about before getting into an argument. There is a feeling of high sexual tension here as the image of the High Priestess is of an untouchable and apparently cool natured woman which makes us wonder what passions may be boiling away under her habit! However, even if uncontrolled passion is about to enter one's life, there could be something to learn, even if it is only to improve one's sexual technique!

Another aspect of this card sometimes shows up when a female Questioner is being so mindful of her family's needs that she neglects her own. She is being told not to sacrifice so much time and money on them, especially on their education, as they would learn some good practical lessons from life if she left them alone and attended to *her own* requirements a bit more.

III
THE EMPRESS

Positive

This card represents feminity in abundance, like the goddess Venus, with all her sexual charms on the one hand, and a plump loving mother caring for her children on the other. On a more down-to-earth note, there could be a child on the way when this card shows up. If the Questioner is too old to have children, this can indicate the birth of a grandchild, nephew or neice. In a man's reading, the Empress represents a warm and loving woman who makes him feel that all's right with the world. If the Questioner is thinking of getting married, then the Empress will show that the marriage will take place and be satisfying and happy. If there is nothing dramatic going on in the Questioner's love life, then this card shows that there is material satisfaction and comfort around the corner.

As a situation rather than an actual woman, the theme of fertility and abundance still counts. Like the planet Venus in astrology, the Empress is concerned with fruits of the earth, personal values and possessions, especially large and important ones. Therefore, this could show up when the Questioner is just about to move from town to country, or to buy a house with a garden. If this is the case, then the move would be beneficial. There could be more money after a pretty lean period, or just a feeling of satisfaction with oneself and one's life. A generous warm and satisfying card which is especially concerned with ownership of goods, that is of material things rather than spiritual or mental activity. The 'proprietary' feelings attached to the Empress extend to people in the sense that one says 'This is *my* child', of 'Let me introduce you to *my* wife'!

Negative
There is not much that is negative about this card but it can suggest that one is overdoing the self-indulgence bit and will regret this later. It also tends to indicate possessiveness and jealousy born of fear of rejection and loss. There is also a strong possibility of either infertility (probably temporary) or on the other hand an unwanted pregnancy. I often find that sterilization, vasectomy and abortion, or operations involving the reproductive organs, show up when this card is reversed in an important position in a spread. This does not indicate whether these situations are chosen by or forced upon the Questioner, just as the fact that they are there. There can be emotional disappointments, disenchantment with a new property, especially if it has no garden – the Empress *likes* growing things. There could be financial loss, therefore no abundance and short shrift for a time.

IIII
THE EMPEROR

Positive
The Emperor is definitely the boss! If this card represents a person who is a part of or is about to enter the Questioner's sphere of

interest, then the Questioner will definitely not be able to ignore him. This man might be a skilled business man, an elder statesman in government, or a powerful, firm but benevolent husband or father figure. If a woman is enquiring about a man she has just met and the Emperor card shows up, she can be sure that he *is* all he appears to be and will stand by her and support her. He is strong and steady by nature, with both the will and the ability to take charge in any situation. He is a good manager and reliable partner. He may not be too much fun at times, and will probably not be very talkative and entertaining, but he will stand fast and cope with any situation. Think of Jack Hawkins as the captain in 'The Cruel Sea' and you will be on the right track!

As a situation rather than a person, the Emperor represents the ability to influence people and events. The Questioner may take on some of the Emperor's personality and find him or herself moving steadily up into a position of power and influence. This indicates a firm base, a sound financial position and perhaps a secure and respected position in the community. The Questioner will be able to reach his goals and will use intelligence and reason, rather than make emotional or even intuitive judgements.

Negative
There is not much that *is* negative about this card. However, if the Questioner wants to know whether a particular person is as reliable and responsible as he seems to be, and the card comes out reversed, then I would suggest that he is not, at least for the moment, all that he is cracked up to be. This may be because he is not as strong a character as he wants others to think he is, not as reliable as the Questioner would like him to be; or is just temporarily out of stock of stiff upper lips. The reverse of the Emperor is immaturity and a lack of concentration, the inability to finish what has been started, too

much dependence upon others instead of self reliance and faith in one's own abilities. This man's apparent weakness may be due to poor health which could, of course, be a temporary situation or a sad warning that a strong and good man is not going to be able to continue with a full and active life.

V
THE HIEROPHANT

Positive

The ideas behind this card are rather difficult to put across, as the general feeling is of kindness, conformity and spiritual guidance. The Hierophant *may* turn up as a person in the Questioner's life, but this would be unusual, somehow he seems to represent situations rather than people. However, if he does, then he may literally be a teacher (especially in the sense that a Rabbi is a teacher) or even a personnel officer. He will advise the Questioner to take a good look at his motives and even to pray for guidance. When the guidance does come, it will emphasize right from wrong and will be along the lines of conventional, possibly religious thought.

As a situation, the Hierophant represents conventional behaviour. Therefore if a Questioner wants to know whether the person he or she fancies wants a conventional marriage, or prefers to live together and still go out with others, then the Hierophant, upright and in a relevant part of the spread, will definitely show that the conventional is wanted. If there is some doubt in the Questioner's mind about how to go about achieving his aims in life, the Hierophant will show that the traditional ways will lead to success. In fact tradition, spirituality and following the dictates of God, one's conscience and the tried and tested methods of working and living are going to be the most successful in this case. There will be kindness and help from people around the Questioner. The older, more staid people will be the ones to offer useful advice and help. If this card shows up when the Questioner's affairs are being held up, it signifies that the delay will not be for much longer.

Negative

There really is not much that is negative about this card except to say that the Questioner may be his own worst enemy by being too timid and too aware of other people's requirements while neglecting his own. It is strange that the two cards who represent people who train and teach us (the Hierophant and the High Priestess) should also warn against being *too* kind-hearted. They are telling us that making excuses for other people's weaknesses is not going to do anyone any good and a dose of firmness may be of more benefit in the long run to all concerned. It is better to stand up for yourself when you know you are right. The other problems are of hypocrisy and self doubt. Be honest, at least with yourself, *that* is the message here.

When the Hierophant is reversed, then non-conformity will be the order of the day. For instance, if the Questioner wants to know whether the person they are interested in desires marriage, then the answer will be negative. There is also the feeling that a more relaxed attitude to matters of business may be more productive, therefore, the Questioner would be better not to put things on a firm traditional footing, but just let things slide along for a while and see what turns up. In others words, do not try to coerce someone into marraige, or into strict modes of operating which will not suit. The Questioner should be prepared to accept novel ways of thinking and not be captive to their own ideas or too full of their own opinions.

VI
THE LOVERS

Positive

There are two distinct and very different messages from this card. On the one hand it can mean exactly what it looks like, i.e. that love, romance and passion are coming to the Questioner. In this context it means that a relationship is just around the corner or one which is worrying the Questioner will bloom into love and marriage. On a milder note this card means friendship and harmony. Therefore, if it shows up in an area relating to work, it would mean that relationships

with colleagues at work or with business partners will be happy and productive. As well as meaning attraction, this card is often interpreted as beauty. When one finds someone attractive, they become beautiful even if they are, strictly speaking, not good looking. If there has been a parting, for whatever reason, the Lovers card indicates that the partners will soon be reunited.

The other meaning attached to the Lovers is of *choice*. This means that the Questioner is soon going to have to choose between two people, two courses of action, two jobs or two of anything, and that the matter of choosing is going to be very important in its outcome. The obvious impression is of choosing between sacred and profane love, and this may well be the case; but the general idea is that the choice has some sort of right or wrong influence, selfish or unselfish, easy or tough. A common matter of choice for women these days is whether to have a career, or opt for an old fashioned family life.

Negative

When the Lover appears reversed, it can mean a temporary or permanent parting, the end of a relationship rather than the beginning, but this will be made clearer by reference to the rest of the reading. It also warns of making a mistake, tying oneself up with the wrong person or for the wrong reasons. The Questioner will remain frustrated in their desires (carnal or otherwise) if they do not make an effort or make their feelings a bit more obvious to the other person. Another problem is infatuation, wanting someone who is clearly wrong for all concerned.

VII
THE CHARIOT

Positive

The Chariot is associated with a time of hard work and major effort, and it is often retro-active, which means that it is just as likely to show the phase which has recently passed by as to indicate something which has yet to come. Either way, it is associated with a struggle, and a time when one does not know whether one is on one's head or one's heels. There could be a great ordeal here, a time of strain and overwork but the feeling is that the outcome makes all the effort worthwhile. This may be a course of action which is deliberately chosen by the Questioner like going into business or moving house, thereby incurring a lot of work in getting the project off the ground. The troubles may, of course, be something not of the Questioner's choosing, which would mean dealing with a knotty problem which is definitely going to need hard work, patience and endurance to solve. The feeling is that a victory is achieved here despite setbacks. In a way it is quite a simple card to interpret, because it means that things have been, still are, or about to be, very hard to handle for a while – but that the outcome is good. The general feeling of the Chariot is of purposeful activity.

On a more practical note, this card often shows up when the Questioner is about to buy a new vehicle, or to have one MoT'd or set to rights, in this case it is a good omen. The Chariot may also indicate that the Questioner will be travelling soon, possibly in connection with work. I have noticed that vehicles – planes, boats, even bicycles – enter the life of the Questioner after this card turns up in a spread.

Negative

The meaning here is much the same as above, but the Questioner has less chance of winning outright, or the struggle is going against them at the moment. This does not mean that it will always be that way, things may change. The one sure thing about the Chariot is that it shows a time of tension and hard work which cannot and will not go on forever. If this card *is* reversed, then the problems are more likely to have been presented *to*, rather than chosen *by*, the Questioner. This card sometimes predicts problems with regard to vehicles.

VIII
JUSTICE

Positive

The meaning of this card is actually quite obvious – it represents justice, fairness, balance, etc. This card often comes up when there are legal matters to be dealt with, and on the whole it can be taken to mean that the outcome will be good. If the card shows up *reversed* in the ninth position in an Astrological spread (see page 147), it would not be good news legally.

The Justice card does not restrict itself strictly to legal matters, it encompasses all matters relating to fairness and justice in the wider sense. For instance, this would be a terrific card to have if a partnership or joint venture is about to be entered. Although it is stretching things somewhat, even a forthcoming marriage could show up with this card, as it would show that the union would bring harmony and a feeling of completeness and balance to the couple involved. If the Questioner is involved in any kind of argument, or has been in any way accused of doing something wrong, he will soon be proved right. There could be agreements through discussion, or a situation where the Questioner acts in an honest manner when others around them do not and this honesty, loyalty and idealism are shown to be right.

Negative
This is one of those cards which does need some extra consideration if it comes out reversed, as it does appear to reverse the meaning of the upright version. That is to say, legal problems will continue or will not be resolved to the Questioner's satisfaction. If there are no legal matters concerning the Questioner, then he or she is being warned of some sort of unfair treatment or unfair accusation to come. There could be a lack of promotion, or some other setback due to somebody who is engaging in underhand politics. The Questioner may have to apologise to someone or make a special effort to keep the peace.

VIIII
THE HERMIT

Positive
This is not an easy card to interpret as its meaning is subtle, it also tends to give advice to the Questioner rather than show a forthcoming event. It indicates that the Questioner will need to take some time out to think things over.

There could be an important decision to make, or just one of those times when there will be a need for reflection and consideration of long term aims and ambitions. This may show that the Questioner would benefit from the advice of an expert, or just a sensible and sympathetic friend. He or she could do well to withdraw from active life for a while in order to meditate, pray and give some thought to the larger issues of life and death. There is another meaning to this card and that means that the Questioner will need to be cautious and prudent in some forthcoming situation. This card contains an element of self denial, and it all fits in with the idea of living quietly for a while, possibly doing without something or someone. It can mean a time of loneliness ahead, which may be self-imposed. There could even be a time of convalescence. The retreat from life and company may be self-imposed or imposed from outside, but it will be beneficial if the Questioner makes the most of the peaceful and reflective period.

Negative
In my experience there are two or three meanings to this. Firstly, there may be a petulant refusal of help in a difficult situation. The Questioner could turn away from family or friends, and cut his nose to spite his face.

Secondly, there could be a failure to grow up and see things as they really are. Both of these are the kind of state of mind which results from a person being hurt or rejected in some way, jealousy or fear are likely to be at the back of this behaviour.

The third ideas is that the Questioner might be left alone, bereaved or let down by a lover or partner and may feel very lonely, rejected and down-hearted for a while. Sometimes the questioner, 'Is he coming back?' is answered by a reversed Hermit (plus other pointers) as being 'no'.

X
WHEEL OF FORTUNE

Positive
Whenever the Wheel of Fortune appears in a spread it signifies

change. The Questioner is being told that nothing stays the same forever, and in this particular case changes are definitely on the way. It would be nice to suggest that the changes are for the better, but this is not necessarily so. Just think of a ferris wheel in a fairground, the little seats with their cargo of laughing passengers are travelling *up* on one side of the wheel, at the same time others are travelling *down* on the other side. Therefore let us be optimists and suggest that the Wheel indicates a turn for the better, a chance coming from out of the blue, a stroke of luck, great opportunity or even a godsend. Certainly this card shows that events related to the sphere of life it represents in the spread are going to be changing.

Most Readers like to see this as an optimistic card, but it may not be so – the best that one can say is that any sudden setbacks can be viewed as a challenge which give the Questioner a chance to grow in whatever area of life is affected by the changes to come. The *placement* of this card in a spread is actually more important than the card itself as it is meant to show *where* the greatest changes will come.

Negative
There really isn't a reverse meaning for this card except that if the upright Wheel can be taken to represent an upturn in fortunes, then the reversed Wheel may bring unexpected setbacks. This may herald the end of a rather easy phase and the beginning of a stressful time to come. There are challenges here and the Questioner will be given the chance to rise to the occasion or let himself become downhearted.

XI
STRENGTH

Positive

On a very simple and straightforward level this card shows that somebody who has been ill is going to recover soon. If the person indicated in the spread has been feeling tired, down-hearted or has just not been coping with things too well lately, then things are bound to improve.

On another level, this card shows that the Questioner will be able to overcome future obstacles, have the courage and resolution to cope. There will be calm perseverence and determination, especially when under pressure. Plans may be put into action soon, achievements and success lie ahead. This is a good card to have when interviews and exams are due.

Above all, the mood of the Strength card is of quiet courage of the unspectacular kind in the face of long term challenges. Conscience will be the guide and the forces of truth and light will triumph over spiteful and jealous behaviour. Ignorance and oppression will be overcome, goodwill will win over evil intentions.

Negative

This shows that the Questioner, or the relevant person in their environment, is not yet well. It is a warning of continued health problems, or that someone is drained of energy and hope.

There is also the possibility that a struggle will be just too much and that an enemy will gain ascendency over the Questioner. There may have to be a postponement or abandonment of plans soon. There is a lack of courage and resolution and the Questioner is warned that underhanded behaviour will land them in trouble.

XII
THE HANGED MAN

Positive

This card represents a suspension in affairs which will be followed by a turning point in the Questioner's life. However, the changes are more likely to be in *mental attitude* rather than in actual events – although events could conspire to cause this. The general impression is that the Questioner will soon abandon outmoded methods of thought in favour of a more philosophical outlook on life. The effect of this card is often descirbed as taking someone away from materialism towards a more spiritual outlook on life. This concept involves sacrifice in some form or other. A good illustration of this idea carried out to the ultimate, would be that of St Francis of Assisi who gave up a comfortable life for something which seemed to make more sense to him.

This card may show up when a destructive relationship is coming to an end, and it shows the Questioner that, although they may be lonely (i.e. suspended) for a while, it really will be for the best in the long run. If there are financial or other losses, then the Questioner is being told that they will 'grow' in character as a result of dealing with these problems, and that perhaps this is needed in order to make somebody more appreciative of the non-material aspects of life such as love, friendship or self respect. One simple instance of this kind of gradual change in circumstances is when loving parents find that their brood is leaving the nest.

On a practical level this card says that there may be something very good which results from difficult circumstances, such as the Questioner being given the sack from his job, a situation which will require the Questioner to assess his or her abilities and could, when seen in the long run, be very beneficial. There will definitely be some form of hiatus between the former situation and what is yet to come, there must be some sacrifices made, this should be used constructively so as to create a satisfactory future outlook on life.

Negative

There is not much that *is* negative about this card except that it advises the Questioner to take a philosophical view of any sacrifices that he or she may have to make. It also shows that the Questioner may be longing for change and not able to accept the rather stagnant situation that is going to prevail over the next few months. This card shows the need to grow up and accept that situations are not always of one's own choosing but occasionally have to be endured for a while.

There is a warning against making *useless* sacrifices, or putting up with a poor situation because it is easier and less frightening than taking the risk of making changes. The Questioner should stop banging his or her head against the same old brick wall. Clear and objective thought is required now, seek guidance, then take the road which feels right inside.

XIII
DEATH

Positive

This card usually puts the wind up people when it appears in a spread, but I have *never* known it to mean that the Questioner is about to die! To be honest, in certain circumstances I *have* seen this card foretell the death of somebody in the life of the Questioner, but this is usually no great surprise as the dying person is generally old and very sick by the time of the reading.

The more usual meaning of this card is *change*. This means that the Questioner can expect some situation to come to a complete end which clears the way for a fresh start. An apparent misfortune may be a blessing in disguise. There may be death of the old self, inner or outer changes that will lead shortly to a new way of life. On the whole, I would suggest that the events which cause changes are not going to be pleasant to begin with, there may be the loss of a friendship or relationship of long standing. Somebody may leave, there may be financial losses or, in extreme circumstances, the loss of a home or a change in one's health (look at other cards for some sort of indication). However, the meaning here is that there is always a chance to make good. Changes which may be hard to cope with will clear away a certain amount of unnecessary rubbish from the past and leave the Questioner free to make a new start.

Negative
There is really no different from the 'positive' reading except that on
the one hand the effects should not be quite so drastic or so out of the
blue. There is a warning that this situation should be dealt with in a
fairly positive and active manner or a terrible feeling of lethargy and
depression might set in. This card also indicates that the Questioner
may be stagnating, afraid of losing what he now has.

XIIII
TEMPERANCE

Positive
This is a very pleasant card, it foretells a time of peace and harmony
to come. If the Questioner has been going through a rather fraught
period, he will soon be feeling calmer and coping better. In fact, the
central impression of the Temperance card is of coping well and
relaxing. There is harmony here, this may be applied to future
relationships, family situations, work, money, health, in fact any
aspect of life. The position of this card in a spread will give the
Reader an idea of how to interpret this.

The other theme of this card is that of *moderation*. Therefore, if the
Questioner has been overdoing anything, be it work or play, good
sense and a balanced attitude will apply in the future. There may be a
time of frugality when this card appears, this should not be too much
of a struggle as it will give the Questioner a chance to make good use
of what he already has. There may be some slight material hardships,
but spirituality will bring comfort. To my mind this card says, 'Put
your feet up, you've done enough'.

Negative

The only negative ideas that this card suggests are that the Questioner will be too busy in the future to be able to see where he is really going. There may be continued pressures and anxieties and the Questioner may find it difficult to cope with all the separate demands that there are on his or her time. Frankly, the answer here is to make an assessment of what can be left for another time and to concentrate on what absolutely must be done.

Intemperance is also a possibility, so if the Questioner is overdoing the good things of life, the advice is to cut back a bit.

XV
THE DEVIL

Positive

This is the card which upsets people who are religious or are afraid of Tarot cards in general because we all know that the Devil is evil. Well, so he is, but the evil can be of our making in that we allow ourselves to behave stupidly. There is a strong warning here not to be talked into evil (or even black magic) by dangerous people. There is also an element of bondage; enslavement to outmoded ideas possibly, or to a job or house which needs to be left for good. The most obvious form of slavery comes from being tied to people who are no good for you. Perhaps it is time to take a realistic look at current relationships and to stop blaming others without also looking inwardly. The Devil urges the Questioner to be very practical, even with essentially non-practical matters.

The Questioner needs to become more independent and to stop accepting unpleasant situations just for the sake of peace. The message here is that one will continue to be oppressed unless the chains are broken. If this card shows up in an area concerned with money, then it might show that for the time being, the Questioner will be tied to a particular job because he or she cannot afford to do otherwise. Perhaps there is a way out, it is possible to gain qualifications and become trained for something better, even though it might take a long time. It is worth thinking positively and practically about future improvements and changes. Above all, the Devil is a practical lad, not spiritual at all!

This card is also concerned with sexual matters. There are many reasons why sex could present problems, but the message of this card is that sex may well become an important factor in any future decisions. Also that the Questioner may soon be involved in an extremely hot and passionate love affair.

Negative

Frankly, this card is fairly negative whichever way up it is, but the reverse meaning can show that the influence is passing, and that the chains which have held the Questioner are shortly going to be broken. The Questioner is beginning to wake up about the situation and may shortly be able to do something really positive to break out.

This card still warns of becoming involved with evil people and of dirty deeds to come. Follow your conscience, take good advice and when in doubt, keep to the straight and narrow.

XVI
THE TOWER

Positive

This is a most unpleasant card to find in a reading. To be honest, I advise people not to get *too* worried unless it comes up in repeated readings, but whatever way one cares to look at it the Tower brings bad news. There is definitely going to be some sort of loss, even a calamity of some kind. Security, as the Questioner has known it in the past, is going to be destroyed and the troubles are likely to come amazingly quickly when they start. Illusions are going to be shattered and the truth about people and situations will be revealed in startling clarity. There will be a questioning of previously accepted beliefs, trust will be destroyed. There could even be some sort of disgrace.

I am by nature an optimist, but even I cannot find much that is good about this card. At one time I kept getting the Tower in my own readings, and sure enough, our family suffered an appalling financial loss, but we fought our way back to solvency and feel quite proud of ourselves having done so.

Negative
Negative and positive are not really apt terms for this card; however, to see this card reversed in a spread does seem to show that the problems are here and now rather than in the future. The reversed Tower indicates something in the nature of a long term misery, rather than a sudden catastrophe, although current and future difficulties may be stemming from a sudden disaster in the recent past. Also, the Questioner can now either make strides to overcome difficult circumstances or remain in the midst of them. There is likely to be continued oppression, the problems are not solved yet.

XVII
THE STAR

Positive

This card is truly the 'Star of Hope'. amd it brings hope, faith and optimism to any part of the spread that it touches. In general, it is a clear indication that things will go well in the future. If the Questioner has been going through a particularly rough patch, then life will soon become smooth again. If there has been a health problem, then this is a wonderful card to see in a reading.

On a more practical note, it is worth taking account of the position of the Star in a spread as its message may apply to a particular area of life. For instance, if applied to career matters, it could show that a problem will soon be solved, past efforts will be appreciated and rewarded. New enterprises or new jobs will go well, promotion could be on the way and any new venture will flourish. Obviously, this hopeful message can be applied to relationships, exam prospects – even the driving test. If it seems to show up in a relatively unimportant area of the spread, such as a holiday, then it would be telling the Reader that this particular holiday is going to be a good deal more for the Questioner than they imagine.

There is something of an educational slant to this card as it can mean that educational and artistic matters are soon going to be important and that the Questioner would soon be able to make good use of his or her talents. Travel could be on the way, because the general idea of this card is expansion of the horizons and very positive new experiences. It sometimes indicates an increasing and purely beneficial interest in the occult.

Negative

This card does not really have a negative side to it except that it can show some doubts about a new venture, there is a touch of pessimism when the Star is reversed, and perhaps a warning not to expand one's horizons too much just at the moment. It just shows some doubt about the future.

XVIII
THE MOON

Positive

The central theme of this card is one of illusion. This is rather a difficult concept to understand as mystery and illusion can be both good and bad depending on the nature of the Questioner and the area of life that this card affects. Experience has taught me that if this

card pops up early on in a Tarot session, then I am dealing with highly charged emotions. If the Questioner has just fallen in love and is not sure how things are going, if a relationship seems to be going nowhere, or working its way to a close, then the Moon will often be one of the first cards to appear. This card clearly shows that everybody concerned in the relationship is muddled, not sure about what they want or where they are going. There could be a good deal of insincerity on both sides. There is no sensible advice that a Reader can hope to give as these kinds of problems defy logic. The Questioner's best hope is to avoid making too many concrete plans and let things float along for a while.

If the Moon card points to other areas of life, such as finances or work, then deception and trickery are definitely in the air. On a very mundane level, even simple plans can be screwed up when the Moon arrives on the scene, letters will go awry, travel plans will be completely fouled up. Messes, muddles, deception, lies and frustration are on the way for sure, and if there is a woman around who can give the Questioner trouble, she will not hesitate to do so.

On a more positive side, the Moon gives the Questioner a chance to use his or her imagination, and this can be positively channelled into artistic pursuits. There could soon be a development of occult powers. The Questioner would do well to rely on 'gut feelings' in relation to any doubtful situations, as they are going to be far more accurate than reason.

Negative
This card is much the same either way up, but lies and insincerity will definitely be around the Questioner, the muddles and failures may be of a fairly minor matter, but they will be irritating just the same. Either way up, this annoying card can tease the poor Questioner by showing that the future is yet to be revealed and that the cards are not

in the mood to be particularly informative just now.

XVIIII
THE SUN

Positive

This is a lovely card, as it means joy and happiness are on the way. The sun is about to shine on the Questioner and will soon make him feel very good. There is not much to say about this card except that whatever area of the Questioner's life is touched by it will bring happiness and success. If there has been poor health, then there could be no better card to turn up. All efforts will be rewarded, trials overcome, there will be good friends, comfort and happiness. Marriage will be happy and successful, there will be unselfish love and a great deal of fun and frolic ahead. All proposed enterprises will go well.

I have often seen this card show up shortly before the birth of a child, and if the Questioner is doubtful about the ability to have children, then there could be no better card to find than the Sun. There may be grandchildren soon, or just neighbourhood children, the Questioner may even be working among children, but whatever the connection, there will be joy and fun of a youthful and exuberant nature.

Negative

This shows that there is *potential* for happiness ahead but that it is rather clouded at the moment. There will be success and achievement, but it may take a bit of time to come along. There will be great improvements but complete satisfaction will take a little longer to achieve.

This card can sometimes be a little sad when associated with children. It may show that a child is shortly to become sick, or that there may be difficulties related to pregnancy or birth. It is even possible, when looked at with other cards in the spread, that a child could prove to be a nuisance in the eyes of the Questioner, or the cause of disagreements. The reversed Sun sometimes shows up when the Questioner decides against having a child and can indicate a forthcoming sterilization, vasectomy or even an abortion (especially if the reversed Empress is also in the spread).

This card also indicates that the Questioner's marriage is not a great success and that he or she is not appreciated.

XX
JUDGEMENT

Positive
This card indicates that a phase is definitely coming to an end. The Questioner will soon be able to look back over what they have been doing and make a clear evaluation of past events. In practical terms, the Judgement card could mean rewards, promotions or even a retirement party with gifts and good wishes for the future. Although this card represents an ending, it is more of a logical conclusion than a wrench, and in any circumstances the Questioner will feel that he has done his duty and now has a clear conscience.

All endings are also beginnings, the end of a project also means the chance to start a new one, and at least the Questioner will start out with the confidence of having accomplished the previous project satisfactorily. There is a feeling of rejuvenation attached to this card, therefore if one has been tied down looking after a sick or demanding relative who is possibly soon to be released from suffering, then the

Questioner will feel satisfied that they have done all that could be done and at the same time will also relish the freedom of being able to make a fresh and unfettered start.

There is another far more practical level to this card, and that is of strictly *legal* judgments. If the Questioner is due to have any dealings with the law, then the outcome will be favourable. I suppose it is not surprising but I often find this card turning up when the Questioner is on the point of a divorce as, on the one hand, it shows the end of the marriage and on the other, the legal settlements which are to come.

Negative
The reversed Judgment card still refers to endings but the feeling is that the Questioner will not be too satisfied with the circumstances surrounding the events. This could mean that the Questioner would know in his heart of hearts that he could have done much better. That could apply to educational matters, work or relationships. The Questioner knows that they could have been a better friend, or just done more for others. There has been a shortsighted and selfish attitude somewhere along the line.

On another level, legal matters are not well starred when this card turns up reversed – especially in any position in a spread which refers specifically to the law.

XXI
THE WORLD

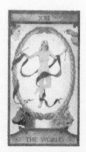

Positive
If the Questioner is nearing the end of a project, then he will soon be able to survey the work done with a sense of pride and accomplishment.

This card, like so many of the Major Arcana, is about turning points but in this case a gradual and satisfactory ending with the implicit feeling that new projects soon to be embarked upon will go well too. There is success on the way, there will be praise and reward for satisfactory completion. The Questioner will elicit the admiration of others and will have reason to feel proud. There will be good fortune and above all spiritual enlightenment. The World card shows clearly that the Questioner is about to gain some insight and a sense of inner peace.

On a more mundane level, this card often indicates travel and can even go as far as to suggest emigration because it carries the notion of a new life in a new place. This may just be a move of house, particularly if it is in connection with a change in the Questioner's circumstances, for example, children being born or becoming independent. But in my experience there is more than a hint of foreign places and of new adventures to come.

Negative
The Questioner might display an ability to accept change and an unreasonable desire to stick in a rut, but on the other hand, this could be a good thing as it shows stability and permanence rather than uncertainty and restlessness.

The worst aspect of the negative World is that the Questioner may find himself envious of other people and unsatisfied with his own progress. However, all is not lost even now, there can be fulfilled ambitions and a fair amount of success, but only after a bit of trime has passed. Be patient, keep trying, that is the message here.

8
SPREADS

Before Spreading the Cards
Shuffle the cards a little, then ask the Questioner to shuffle them well. If the Questioner finds it too hard to shuffle them, then you might suggest that the cards are put face downwards on the table and stirred around, touching as many of them as possible. When the Questioner has finished shuffling (or stirring), ask them to cut the pack into three decks, using the left hand – because it is closest to the heart.

If you wish to give an upright and reversed reading, you may ask the Questioner to point to one of the decks, which you can then turn around. The Questioner should then put all the cards back into one pack, there is no special order for this; and finally the Questioner should put them down on the table. You then take the cards *with the end which was nearest to the Questioner now nearest to you* and you can start to take the cards from the top of the deck for your reading. In the case of a reading which uses only a few cards, you may ask the Questioner to spread them out on the table and to pick out the relevant number of cards for the subsequent reading.

How to Spread the Cards
The first and most vital point to grasp is to get into the habit of turning the cards over from side to side, not from top to bottom. This is so that you do not reverse cards which are upright or put reversed cards up the right way.

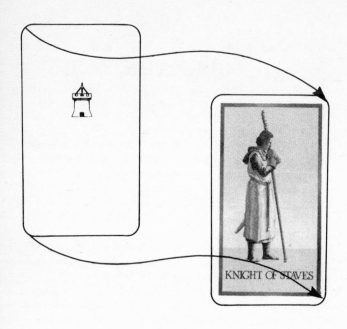

Remember – Turn the cards from side to side.

THE SIX CARD CHOOSE-IT-YOURSELF SPREAD

The easiest way for a complete beginner to start to read the cards is to make a list on a piece of paper of six areas of life which are of special interest to the Questioner at that particular time. Of course, the Reader may also *be* the Questioner. Then pick out six cards, either from the top of the deck or at random and make up a story based on the cards' meanings. (See page 103ff.)

Once you have grasped this method, go over the six again, either right off the top of the deck or with selected cards and see how the 'story' progresses. Alternatively, choose one or two categories out of the six and put another card or two on top of them to 'zoom in' onto a particularly important area of interest.

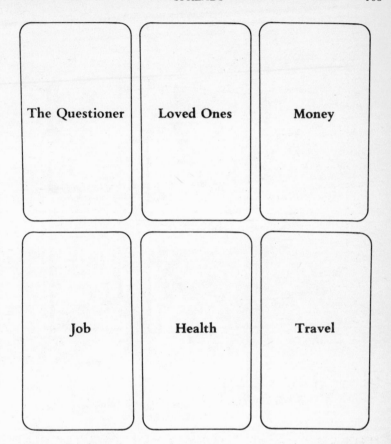

| The Questioner | Loved Ones | Money |

| Job | Health | Travel |

The Questioner

Two of Staves (reversed)
In the case of this reading, there appears to be a break up of a partnership concerned with business matters. It is possible that pride on one or both sides was a contributory factor here, also bad luck or bad timing in business matters.

Loved Ones

Page of Staves
On one level this card tells us that the Questioner has children and

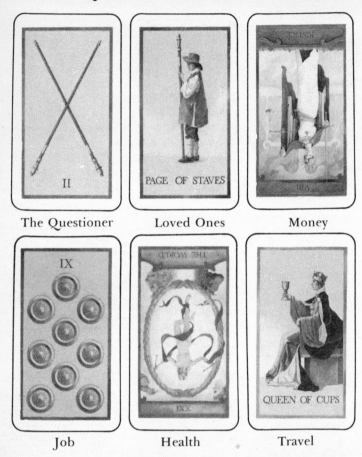

The Questioner	Loved Ones	Money

Job	Health	Travel

may be worried about one of them. On another level, there is a lot of correspondence, writing, telephoning, travel and business to be done by and for the family.

Money

Justice (reversed)

This is a Major Arcana card and it is reversed, therefore it points to a major problem in the life of the Questioner at the time of the reading. The Justice card is all about balance and fair play, and with regard to this reading, I would suspect a good deal of worry in this area in the near future. There is even an indication that a legal matter will rear its head and soon cause the Questioner some trouble.

Job

Nine of Coins
This is clearly a good omen, but it shows that work carried out in or near the home is more likely to lead to success (and money) than that which is done away from the home. There is an element of things yet to be revealed, and a feeling that something, probably involving work in or near the home, is likely to turn out well.

Health

The World (reversed)
This card appears to be presenting a major problem for the Questioner. It seems as if health matters are changing the Questioner's life. This may be the Questioner's own health or that of acquaintances. The message here is that the health problems will not go away, and that the changes, although not liked, have to be lived with. One thing is certain, the World that the Questioner has occupied until recently will never be the same again. A deeper reading will show how this will ultimately affect the Questioner.

Travel

Queen of Cups
I chose this category because it is less 'weighty' than the preceding ones. This card clearly indicates that travel will be a pleasurable experience for the Questioner. He or she can expect to meet a fair woman, possibly a foreigner, who will be kind and helpful. There could be fun, good food, laughter and romance connected with travel in the future.

THE 'CONSEQUENCES' SPREAD

This spread is used by some professional Readers when the Questioner wants to focus on a particular problem. The Reader ought to choose a Significator for this spread (see page 29).

The spread should be interpreted as follows:

1. The Significator.

2. The Questioner, or some clue as to the circumstances surrounding him or her.

3. The background to, or the cause of the problem.

4. The past.

5. The future.

6. Suggestions as to future actions.

7. Environment or persons close to the Questioner.

8. Outcome or consequence of actions.

Sample Reading for the 'Consequences' Spread

1. *King of Coins (Significator)*

2. *Four of Staves*
The Questioner is worried about an established business that they own, possibly the cost of the upkeep of the premises is worrying them.

3. *Nine of Coins (reversed)*
Confirms the reading from card number 2. Money and the recession are worrying the Questioner.

4. *The Lovers (reversed)*
Partnership problems, decisions have been made by both partners. This does not seem to have been easy for them.

5. *The Moon*
Some deception to come, problems ahead which cannot be foreseen. Decisions will be made on an emotional basis.

6. *Six of Swords*
Travel will be required in order to secure more business. This may even be overseas travel. There will be a slow improvement, calmer financial waters are on the way.

7. *Nine of Swords*
Other people in the business environment will cause worries and problems, there may be a few sleepless nights for the *partner* of this business.

8. *Eight of Staves (reversed)*
There will be some jealousy or spite coming to the Questioner. The business must not expand too quickly. There could be confusions and problems relating to the *partner's* emotional state and woolly state of mind over the next few months. The overall message is to keep to a steady course and be prepared to become independent of the partner (Six of Swords) if necessary.

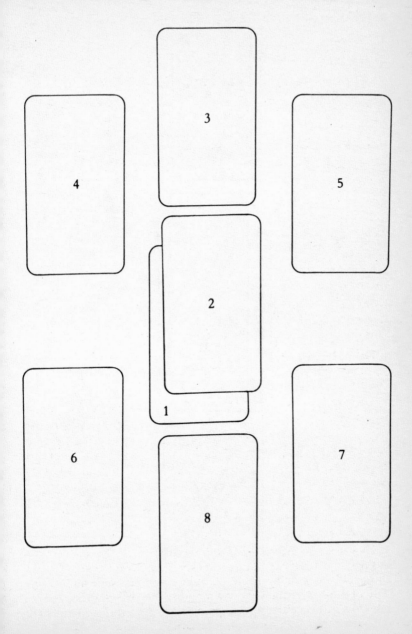

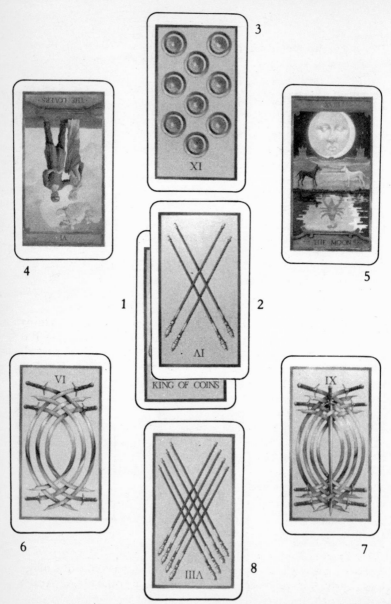

THE ANNUAL SPREAD

This is a useful spread for those who wish to know when a proposed event is going to take place. It is also good for a general twelve month reading.

The method is simple. Just lay out the cards in the form of a clock and read them month by month, starting with the current month unless the reading is done very near the end of a month, when it would make sense to start from the next month. This can be done with just one card for each month, but two or three cards per month give a fuller, more complex reading.

It is a good idea to take note of the position of any Major Arcana cards, and in particular, any month where two or three Major Arcana cards fall together. This will show the most important times in the year ahead.

This method can be used for the timing of more immediate events, as the twelve card circle can be adapted to show twelve *weeks* ahead, or even twelve *days* ahead. However, it is more usual to use this spread for the coming year.

Sample Reading for the Annual Spread

I have deliberately made the interpretation of this sample reading rather brief in order to simplify what can be a very long reading. It is a good idea to put one extra card right in the middle of the spread, which may give a powerful clue as to the main event of the forthcoming year. I have used all the cards in an the upright position for this reading.

'One for Luck'

Three of Staves
New projects this year, probably involving travel and negotiations.

1. *The Emperor + Ace of Swords*
Something begins now, this should be very satisfying and possibly profitable. Passion and sexual satisfaction *might* enter the life of the Questioner now.

2. *The Tower + The Hanged Man*
A shock involving some sacrifice. A truth of some kind will emerge very clearly. A very significant month as these are both Major Arcana cards.

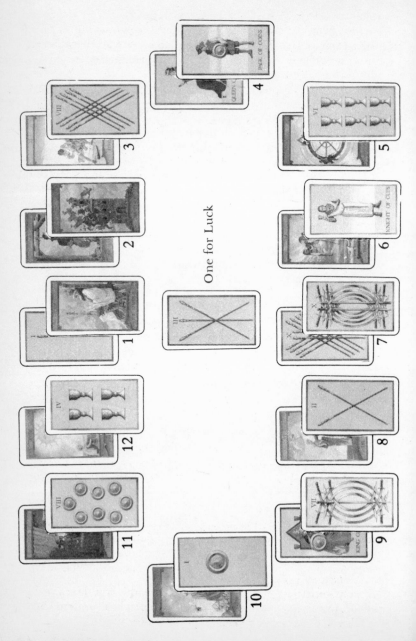

One for Luck

3. *Strength + Eight of Staves*
Recovery from the previous month's events, bouncing back to health and control of situations. Travel, new horizons, and negotiations are indicated here.

4. *Queen of Swords + Page of Coins*
There could be a problem regarding a youngster and/or a dark haired woman. If not, then this could be a business matter between the Questioner and a woman.

5. *Six of Cups + Wheel of Fortune*
This has got to be a turning point, but somehow the past is wrapped up in all this. Past skills and past friends may be helpful (or harmful) now. Past emotional ties may be reformed or completely broken now.

6. *Knight of Cups + The Hermit*
A fairish man may give the Questioner very good advice. This man may be a rather lonely, introspective person, but he will be friendly or even loving towards the Questioner.

7. *Ten of Staves + Ten of Swords*
A very trying month when there is just too much to do and the Questioner will be carrying the can for other people's failings. Hard work and difficult people mark this month.

8. *The Lovers + Two of Staves*
A temporary or permanent partnership. This looks like business rather than pleasure but could be a bit of both. Decisions will have to be jointly taken now. Alternatively, a love relationship may now begin to include work related matters.

9. *King of Coins + Seven of Swords*
There could be some sort of split up with the Questioner taking part of something that is shared, and leaving some to a man of business. There may be legal forms to sign. The business man could give good advice to the Questioner.

10. *The Star + Ace of Coins*
There are great opportunities to make money now. The future looks very bright and hopeful with regard to business and money matters now. There could even be a win.

11. *The Magician + Eight of Coins*
Definitely something good to do with money, this could be a really good job, promotion or a business matter. Success in all undertakings which involve money and skills, especially new skills.

12. *The Sun + Four of Cups*
Things are going to be very good, but emotionally there will be just a hint of sadness. It looks like a year of success in financial and business matters for the Questioner, but a little sad and lacking in the area of love and romance.

THE CELTIC CROSS

This spread is depicted in every book I have ever seen on the Tarot. I personally think it is a confusing spread for a beginner to deal with, but I will show a couple of sample readings for those who would like to be able to use it. It can be done with either the Major Arcana alone or with a mixture of both Arcanas. It is usual to select a Significator from the court cards to represent the Questioner. (See page 29.)

The spread works as follows:

1. The Significator.

2. The Questioner's present situation.

3. Whatever is causing or influencing the situation.

4. The goal, aim or ideal. Alternatively, the best that the Questioner can hope for under the present circumstances.

5. The distant past.

6. The recent past.

7. People or events which will figure in the life of the Questioner in the near future.

8. More information about the Questioner and how he or she affects the surrounding environment.

9. Other people or situations around the Questioner and how *they* affect the Questioner.

10. Inner feelings, hopes and fears.

11. Outcome.

Timing Events, using the Celtic Cross
A friend of mine, Jean Goode, who works under the name of Aquarius, has been a professional Reader for many years. Jean has passed on this unique method of timing events to me for inclusion in this book.

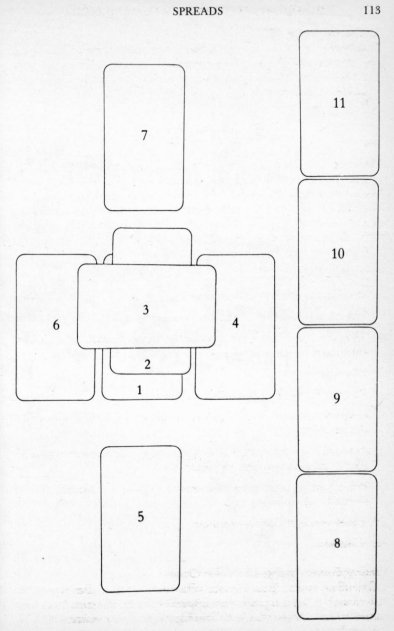

7

QUEEN OF COINS

6

PAGE OF COINS

1, 2 and 3

KING OF SWORDS

4

KING OF CUPS

5

VII

11

10

9

I

8

Firstly, lay out the Celtic Cross spread using both Arcanas of the Tarot. Then go *backwards* through the spread until you reach a number card (that is a card of the Minor Arcana which has a number from 1 to 10). Then work out your timing like this:

Years are indicated by a Coin card.

Months are indicated by a Sword card.

Weeks are indicated by a Stave card.

Days are indicated by a Cup card *but only if it is next to a Coin card!*

Jean tells me that she usually encounters her first numbered card among the four cards which are alongside the Cross itself. In the case of this not being so, she says that the Reader should just keep on going backwards until a numbered card is found.

A Sample Reading Using the Celtic Cross
I have used a mixture of the Major and Minor Arcanas for this, and I have kept all the cards in the upright position. The Questioner is a young woman who feels the need to progress in her career.

1. *Page of Coins (Significator)*

2. *The Hierophant*
This is a young person who has had a rather traditional upbringing and who is conservative by nature. She is very good-natured, especially towards her family and close friends.

3. *Nine of Cups*
She is looking for emotional and financial stability and satisfaction. She has a good deal of this already.

4. *King of Swords*
This card sometimes indicates medical people and in this case, there has been a history of illness and operations in the past.

5. *King of Cups*
She has a lot of love and affection around her from her family and friends. She trusts men because her father and brother love and protect her.

6. *Wheel of Fortune*
Change is coming now. The Questioner admits that she would like to improve her job situation and hopes that this card indicates a change for the better.

7. *Queen of Coins*
The Questioner is aiming high in her career, she wants to be a

business woman in her own right – the cards so far, indicate that this will happen.

8. *Ace of Swords*
The Questioner wants change and is prepared to cope with any problems that will bring change. She knows that she will have to leave her rather cozy situation and take a chance on life.

9. *The Hanged Man*
Her environment is static. There will be no change unless *she* seeks it herself – she must make the future happen, she must turn her own Wheel of Fortune, no one will do this for her. She will cause other people to make sacrifices for her and she may have to make some herself for the benefit of others.

10. *The Star*
This card is the wish card of the Major Arcana (the Ten of Cups is the wish card in the Minor Arcana) and this area of the Celtic Cross refers to hopes and wishes. It appears that the Questioner can expect to get what she is wishing for.

11. *Seven of Swords (Timing card)*
The Questioner will have to move on in some way, either from her home or her job. She will have to be a little more adventurous. She will leave something of herself behind and will never forget the good things of the past, but she must gather up her resources and make a move within the next year. She will receive good advice (possibly from the King cards in the spread) and she will act upon this.

In fact, I continued with this reading, took another card from the top of the deck and put over the top of the final card. It turned out to be the Death card which signifies tremendous change coming soon. I also put another card over the Queen of Coins, this turned out to be the Ace of Staves – the Questioner says that she ultimately wants to have her own business. It seems clear from this reading that she will get her desire. This young woman is at the point of changing from being the girlish Page of Coins, to the womanly Queen of Coins. She has very dark hair and is a natural business woman. She likes comfort and stability and a good home and family life.

Jean Goode's Timing Device in Action
This reading was done in December 1983. In August 1984 the Questioner handed in her notice in order to take up a managerial job with much better pay and prospects. This job came her way in July. *This is exactly seven months after the reading was done!*

PART TWO

FORTUNE-TELLING WITH NUMBERS

RODNEY DAVIES

INTRODUCTION

This book shows you how to understand your character and your talents through numbers, and how number can reveal the general pattern of your life, so enabling you to know your destiny. It also tells you how to find your lucky days and dates, and how to use numbers to improve your fortune.

The use of numbers in this way constitutes numerology, which is an ancient divinatory art dating back at least as far as the sixth century BC, when the Greek mathematician and philosopher Pythagoras taught at his school at Croton, in Italy, that everything is number.

In a very real sense Pythagoras was right, because number is an integral part of the natural world. Each of us, for example, is formed from a genetically predetermined number of bodily parts – one heart, two eyes, ten fingers, and so on – which makes us the beings we are, and every scientist knows that counting is as important to the classifier as the examination of shape, colour and size. Indeed, the chemical elements that are the building blocks of life differ from one another only because their atoms are made up of different numbers of protons, neutrons and electrons.

Number imposes order on nature and in doing so creates its beauty – think for a moment of the hexagonal ice crystals of snowflakes and the trefoil leaves of clover – because line, form and symmetry are the products of number. And it is because numbers comprise the essence of ourselves that they can be used as keys to our personality and our abilities and to our path through life.

The numbers that we are going to be concerned with are the nine single numbers running from 1 to 9. These, together with zero, constitute the bricks and mortar of numeration because every number, from 10 up, is expressed as combinations of them. Where appropriate we shall reduce all numbers larger than 9 to a single number. This is done by adding the constituent numbers together. Take the number 301, for example, which is made of 3, 0 and 1.

When these are added together they total 4:

$$3 + 0 + 1 = 4$$

For numbers whose constituents when first added give a double number, the addition must be continued until a single number is obtained. Consider 989, for example:

$$9 + 8 + 9 = 26$$

The product is 26. To get a single number the 2 and the 6 must be added together:

$$2 + 6 = 8$$

Of course, for larger numbers further additions may be necessary.

In numerology both the individual digits of a number (the 3, 0 and 1 of 301, and the 9, 8 and 9 of 989) and its single product are important, although zero, not being a number, has qualities only of space and not of character.

Your most important numbers are those of your birthdate. Taken individually, these represent the day, the month and the year of your birth.

The day number always falls somewhere between 1 and 31.

The month number depends on the placement of the month in the year, January is the first month. February the second month, and so on, right through to December, which is the twelfth month. Each month is numbered accordingly.

The year of birth may be in the late 1800s for someone who is very old, but for most people the birth year will be 1900 and something.

For example, consider the birthdate 7 April 1963. Because April is the fourth month of the year this date is expressed numerically as 7-4-1963.

The *day number* is always placed first, the *month number* second and the *year* last. This is because the day number is most personal to you, while the year is least personal. Many millions of people were born throughout the world in 1963, for instance. About a twelfth of them were born in the month of April, and of these about a thirtieth were born on the 7th.

In Britain it is usual to write the above date as 7-4-1963, but in America it is the practice to put the month number first, followed by the day number and then the year. Thus in America 7 April 1963 is written 4-7-1963. This would be as confusing to a Briton, who would think it meant 4 July 1963, as the Briton's 7-4-1963 would be to an American, who would read it as the same date, 4 July 1963.

Your birthdate will give a similar sequence of numbers, which together represent your character and your talents, just as the planets and their placement in the zodiac do on your day of birth. In fact, as we shall shortly discover, the link between numerology and astrology is close.

When the numbers of your birthdate are added together and the product reduced to a single number, the result is the *birth* or *destiny number*. This number symbolizes the course and general tenor of your life, or your destiny.

This is how your example birthdate adds up:

$$7 + 4 + 1 + 9 + 6 + 3 = 30$$
$$3 + 0 = 3$$

The birth or destiny number of someone born on 7 April 1963 is therefore 3. You can calculate your birth number in the same way. This is also your *lucky number* because it rules those periods of your life which are luckiest for you. These periods are dealt with later.

The other numbers which are personally important to you are the ones that can be obtained from your name. There are three of these: the *vowel number*, the *consonant number* and the *name number* itself. They are calculated using the table below, which gives the number equivalents of the letters of the alphabet:

1	2	3	4	5	6	7	8	9
A	B	C	D	E	F	G	H	I
J	K	L	M	N	O	P	Q	R
S	T	U	V	W	X	Y	Z	

The five vowels are *a, e, i, o,* and *u,* and these have the values 1, 5, 9, 6 and 3 respectively. The vowel number of a name is determined by adding together the values of its vowels. Let us take the name John Smith by way of example, which has two vowels, *o* and *i.*

JOHN SMITH
6   +   9   = 15 = 6

The vowel number of John Smith's name is therefore 6.

The consonant number is obtained in an identical way, by adding together the number values of the name's consonants:

J O H N   S M I T H
1   8 5   1 4   2 8 = 29 = 11 = 2

The consonant number of John Smith's name is 2. (Note that here we have had to go one stage further in our additions, since 11 is a two-digit number.)

Likewise, the name number is obtained by adding together all the letter values and by reducing the product to a single number:

$$
\begin{array}{ll}
\text{J O H N} & \text{S M I T H} \\
1\ 6\ 8\ 5 & 1\ 4\ 9\ 2\ 8 = 44 = 8
\end{array}
$$

More simply, the name number can be determined by adding together the vowel number and the consonant number:

$$6 + 2 = 8$$

The three numbers which can be obtained from the name John Smith are therefore 6, 2 and 8.

But what if John Smith has a middle name, such as Arthur? Should all three names be used to determine the vowel number, the consonant number and the name number? The answer if No – unless Mr Smith thinks of himself as and calls himself John Arthur Smith. Numerologists are agreed that, in general, the only names that should be considered numerologically are the family name or surname and the commonly used Christian or first name, or its contraction, or the pet name.

So while Mr Smith's full name is John Arthur Smith, he is for numerological purposes John Smith – or Arthur Smith if he uses the name Arthur in preference to John. Of course, if he has taken to using the name Arthur but has contracted it to Art, he must be considered as Art Smith.

In a similar way, pet names must be evaluated if they are used by the people concerrned, just as Mo must be for Maureen, Bill for William, Jack for John and Sandy for Sandra if Mo, Bill, Jack and Sandy call themselves by these names.

Because our name reflects our sense of self, it is hardly surprising that we may change it as we grow and mature. Thus someone named Elizabeth might prefer to be known as Betty when she's a schoolgirl, as Liz when she's a young woman and as Elizabeth only when she's married and settled down.

In contrast to the birthdate numbers, which represent our basic or inherited character, the name numbers represent our character as it is moulded by our environment.

The vowel number symbolizes our exposed or conscious self. In Freudian terms it represents our *ego*.

The consonant number symbolizes our hidden or unconscious self. In Freudian terms it therefore represents our *id*.

Together, the vowel number and the consonant number combine to give the name number, which in turn represents our total personality. Thus the name is the measure of the man.

As the vowel number can be matched with any one of the nine possible consonant numbers, this means that although there are only nine ego personalities and nine id personalities, there are eighty-one total personalities (9 x 9 = 81).

A balanced personality has an ego and an id which interact harmoniously with each other, while an unbalanced personality does not. Such harmony or disharmony is revealed by the degree of compatability or incompatability between the vowel and the consonant numbers. Incompatible numbers point to personality problems of one sort or another.

There are five *odd* single numbers – 1, 3, 5, 7 and 9 – and four *even* single numbers – 2, 4, 6 and 8. In general, odd and even numbers are incompatible, thus their presence together usually indicates inner tensions and difficulties.

The odd numbers represent the qualities of hardness, action, extroversion, leadership, aggression, motivation, domination and ambition – in other words, those qualities traditionally linked with the male – while the even numbers symbolize female softness, stillness, passiveness, introversion, submission and unambition. More widely, odd numbers stand for active qualities – heat, light, strength, weight, speed, etc. – and even numbers for inactive qualities – cold, darkness, weakness, lightness, slowness, and so on.

Equally, the odds are linked with the good forces of the world, with honesty, openness, truth, etc., and thus ultimately with God Himself, while the evens are the numbers of the Left-Hand Path, of dishonesty, concealment, untruth, etc., and hence of the Devil. Yet it would be wrong to pursue this too far and to equate the male and the active only with good and the female and inactive only with evil, for this is simply not true. The universe is built of opposites and these have equal importance in its construction, thus they are in themselves neither good nor bad. In this respect we should remember that philosophers and mystics have long said that in terms of achieving the best from life, one should always seek out a Middle Way, the Golden Mean.

1
NUMBERS AND YOU

There exists, as the last chapter mentioned, a close connection between numerology and astrology. This is hardly surprising in view of the fact that everything in the universe has a numerical base. Indeed, we can even go so far as to say that if the planets circling the Sun control our destiny, then their power derives from number. And this means that because the secret of life and of those forces acting on living things lies with numbers, we can, through a study of numbers, understand mysteries that have long seemed impenetrable.

Each planet has a certain influence over an individual's person and life. When one planet's influence is strong the individual shows signs of it, both in looks and character and in life pattern. This is in accordance with the central dictum of astrology – as above, so below. Of course, it is impossible for anyone to be wholly under the influence of one planet. We are all planetary mixtures, and have variable life patterns to match.

The ancient astrologers knew of only five planets – Mercury, Venus, Mars, Jupiter and Saturn – and the Sun and the Moon. But because the latter were also called planets, the ancients spoke of 'the seven planets' and gave due reverence to the number 7. But more importantly, as far as we are concerned, they identified each of the nine single numbers with one of the seven planets, thus linking each number with distinct planetary characteristics and powers. The list below gives these traditional number/planet matchings:

1 and 4 :	THE SUN
2 and 7 :	THE MOON
3 :	JUPITER
5 :	MERCURY
6 :	VENUS
8 :	SATURN
9 :	MARS

Two numbers, 1 and 4, are associated with the Sun, and two, 2 and 7, with the Moon. This 'doubling up' with respect to two of the planets is necessary because there are nine single numbers but only seven planets. However, since the discovery of the 'new' planets Uranus, Neptune and Pluto, some numerologists have ascribed 4 to Uranus and 7 to Neptune, while Pluto has been linked with both 8 and 9. But because these associations are both uncomfortable and disputed they will, for the purpose of this book, be ignored.

Just as the nine single numbers represent natural order, so zero – 0 – stands for space and emptiness, the original Chaos from which matter arose. Such formlessness was the starting point of creation in most mythologies. In the Greek Pelagian creation myth, for example, the goddess Eurynome ('wide wandering') rises naked from Chaos, and, finding nothing on which to rest her feet, separates the sea from the sky and dances upon the waves.

The nothingness which preceded the creation was called Nirgun Brahman, or Brahma's Night, by the Hindus. Creation or the start of Brahma's Day was brought about by the explosive creative principle named Savitar, the Sun god, who manifested in a manner resembling the Big Bang of modern astronomy, suddenly flooding the universe with light and heat.

In Genesis, Chapter 1, God says on the fourth day of creation, 'Let there be lights in the firmament to divide the day from the night.' He then made 'the greater light' – that is, the Sun – 'to rule the day, and the lesser light' – the Moon – 'to rule the night.' This Biblical story partly explains why the Sun, the first celestial body to be created on the fourth day, is linked with numbers 1 and 4, and why the Moon, the second celestial body to be created, is linked with 2. The Moon is also associated with 7 because each stage of its cycle takes seven days.

The five remaining numbers, viz. 3, 5, 6, 8 and 9, each became associated with one of the five visible planets. How this came about and the effect that it had on the meanings of the numbers themselves is dealt with in detail on the following pages.

THE NUMBER 1

1 is an enigmatic number, despite its apparent simplicity. One of anything may represent the least you can have, yet it is also the first step in gaining more of the same. Indeed, the notion of the first – 'the first step', 'first place', 'first in line' – is as much one of making the initial move as it is of being the winner. But while 'first away, first home' seems a persuasive argument, one should never forget Aesop's fable of the tortoise and the hare.

Because 1 is the first number, rising from zero just as Eurynome rose from Chaos, it stands for both new beginnings and for all that may follow. After all, every succeeding number is only an ever growing group of 1's: 2 is two 1's, 3 is three 1's, and so on *ad infinitum*.

As one of the two numbers linked specifically with the Sun, 1 is the number of the rising Sun (called Khepri by the Egyptians) which brings the new day. Yet because 1 comprises every other number, they, too, can be identified with different stages of the Sun's cycle. The sequence 1 to 9 is a solar sequence, endlessly repeated as 10 to 18, 19 to 27, 28 to 36, 37 to 45, 46 to 54, 55 to 63, 64 to 72, 73 to 81, 82 to 90, 91 to 99, etc.

2 represents the Sun at mid-morning, when it is still rising and when its heat is not too intense. 3 is the Sun at noon, the all-seeing Re of the Egyptians, at the height of its power and splendour. 4 is the Sun of mid-afternoon, sinking towards the western horizon, and 5 is the number of the setting Sun, Atum.

6, 7 and 8 are the numbers of the Sun in the underworld. 6 symbolizes the Sun's descent into the nether regions, 7 the Sun at its nadir, its deepest and most mysterious point, and 8 represents the Sun beginning its journey back to the world of men.

9 stands for the final stage of the Sun's journey, which is both an end and a beginning, for a 'new' and rejuvenated solar disc is about to appear in the sky. Indeed, if 1 is envisaged as symbolizing the half of the Sun above the horizon, 9 represents the half still below it.

The diagram at the top of the next page makes these number equivalents clear.

1 is the number of birth and of new life generally, of new starts and of confident moves forward, of climbing above difficulties, of aiming high, of breaking with the past, and of energy and enthusiasm. It is the number of youth, daring, single-mindedness, sexual awakening and adventure. It is also the number of the risen God, the deity who dies, but who overcomes death to be born again, as did Tammuz, the vegetation god of the Babylonians, the Egyptian Osiris, who rose from the dead as Horus, and Jesus Christ who 'rose from the dead and who ascended into heaven'.

1 is plentifully endowed with the qualities of the first: activity, motivation, leadership, pluck, ambition, direction and purpose, that is, with those qualities that are masculine and aggressive. But in keeping with the Sun's placement on the horizon, where it is just starting its climb into the sky, 1 is also the number of the child and of childish traits: naïvety, awkwardness, self-consciousness, selfishness,

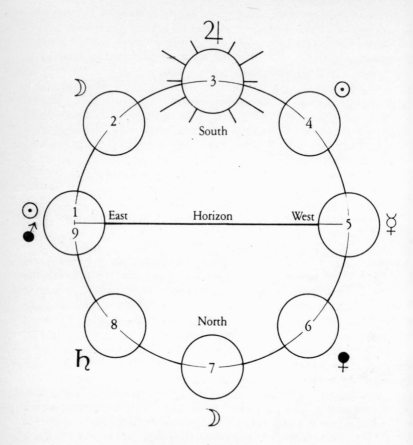

The Solar Cycle

cruelty and gullibility. 1 thus symbolizes strength, vigour and immaturity.

If you were born on the 1st of any month, 1 is an important influence in your life, as it is if you were born on the 10th or the 11th. Indeed, the 11th born are doubly influenced by 1. 1 traits are also found in those birthdays on the 12th, 13th, 14th, 15th, 16th, 17th, 18th, 21st and 31st, although these are admixed with those represented by the other number. 1 is also important in the lives of those born in January, the first month, as well as those born in

October (the tenth month), November (the eleventh month) and, although to a lesser extent, December (the twelfth month). Famous people with birthdays on the 1st include Louis Bleriot (1-7-1872), Jimmy Carter (1-10-1924), Olivia de Havilland (1-7-1916), Marilyn Monroe (1-6-1926), Joe Orton (1-1-1933), Lytton Strachey (1-3-1880) and Edgar Wallace (1-4-1895).

If 1 is strongly represented in your birthdate you are of average height or above and have a lean athletic body. You carry yourself well, keeping your head up and your shoulders back. You have large, striking eyes, a lot of hair and a very good skin. Indeed, your whole appearance and demeanour suggest vibrancy and confidence, which is why heads turn when you enter the room. Because you love being the centre of attention you may behave childishly if you're ignored. If this doesn't bring results, you quickly return to those who know your worth. Your immaturity is often expressed by an over-eagerness for new and different things, by a readiness to support crank causes and by your tendency to sulk when you cannot get your own way. Yet your positive and enthusiastic nature is stimulating and attractive, gaining you many friends and admirers. Because you are by nature a leader, and not a follower, you find it hard to take orders or even to work with others on an equal footing, for you like being the boss and directing operations. However, you are basically rather conservative, thus you never intentionally kick against the pricks. You also have a strong sense of loyalty and a love of fair play.

1 is the number of gold and of similar light, bright colours. In physical terms it represents health and fitness, fleetness of foot, blonde hair, skin that tans easily and attractive features. The direction of 1 is east, and travel to the east or residence in that part of the country is fortunate for those with 1 prominent in their birthdate. The luckiest period of the year for 1s is between 20 March and 20 April, when the Sun passes through Aries, where it is exalted, while the worst is between 24 September and 23 October, when the Sun is debilitated in Libra.

Should you possess a 1 vowel number, which is symbolic of your ego personality, you are blessed with an open, friendly and confident manner. Yet your nature is paradoxical because your confidence stems from a childish belief in your own superiority. Indeed, you are basically selfish, to the extent that you only give your friendship to those who accept your elevated ideas about yourself. You are, however, a good leader and organizer, and you are not afraid of making decisions or of taking responsibility. You hate work that is boring or repetitive, or that requires you to dirty your hands, which is why manual jobs are not for you. In fact, your love of being in the public eye means that work as an actor, entertainer or politician represents your employment ideal. If you are a woman you don't much like housework or looking after children. Money is important to you and you have quite expensive tastes: you like to dress well, live in elegant surroundings, and entertain in some style. You are probably not a smoker or a drinker. You dislike rudeness, and those that behave badly in your house never get invited back. You hate being on your own; thus you can only feel complete in the company of others. Your generosity and warmth make you popular and win you friends, although your friendship, as noted above, is not readily given. You are proud of your family and interested in its history.

An ego symbolized by 1, the number of the rising Sun, is ideally complemented by an id represented by 5, the number of the setting Sun. A 7 id is also a satisfactory match because it gives you an emotional depth that might otherwise be lacking. You are similarly well served by a 3 id, which not only realistically increases your self-confidence but matures and stabilizes you. But a 1 id or a 9 id cannot make your ego a good partner because their characters are too close to its own, especially inasmuch as they are selfish and immature. An id symbolized by an even number – 2, 4, 6 or 8 – is not generally favourable, with perhaps the exception of a 4 id, which can, 4 being the second solar number, provide sufficient strength and stability to balance you. Of the rest, a 6 id is better than a 2 id or an 8 id.

If 1 is your consonant number, representing your id or unconscious, you have a strong innate sense of your own self-worth and of the general rightness of your ideas. How this inner certainty manifests depends on your ego type, but you will always feel driven to put the world to rights; thus you have a tendency to tell others how they should behave. You have very high standards and you are contemptuous of the morally weak. Indeed, your 1 id is something of a taskmaster because it demands much from you: it won't let you settle for second-best in either your working life or your relationships and it constantly pressurizes you to improve yourself. In this respect, Excelsior is your watchword. Yet because 1 ids are the sunniest of all, you seldom get depressed and when you do, your black mood does not last for long. This helps you to recover quickly from set-backs and disappointments and prevents you from being self-pitying. Such an id also gives you stable and sustained emotions, thus when you give your heart you give it completely. Promiscuity is not your style, which means that if your ego decides to have a fling you will feel both guilty and ashamed. You enjoy being at home with your family and if you have to travel you will try to take your loved ones with you.

If your name number is 1 you adore sunny days, the open air and visits to forests and mountains. You are fascinated by old forts, castles and battle sites. You enjoy giving advice, helping others, bitter tastes, gold jewellery, thick clothes, your father's company, being with members of the armed forces, dogs and horses, and anything to do with royalty. Your lucky day of the week is Sunday; your lucky gemstones are the diamond, the amber, the sardonyx and the topaz; your lucky flowers are the cowslip, the heliotrope, the marigold and the sunflower; and your lucky colours are gold, orange, yellow and yellow-green.

THE NUMBER 2

2 is one of the two numbers linked with the Moon and it is called the number of the Positive Moon. In the solar cycle 2 represents the Sun at mid-morning, when it is well above the horizon but not yet too hot.

The Moon is identified with two numbers because it follows a continuously changing cycle, one consisting of a waxing or growth phase and the other of a waning or shrinkage phase. These two phases also naturally link the Moon with 2, as do the Moon's two horns which it displays when New. And because each stage of the Moon's cycle, from New Moon to First Quarter Moon, from First Quarter Moon to Full Moon, from Full Moon to Second Quarter Moon, and from Second Quarter Moon to Old Moon takes seven days, the number 7 is similarly associated with the Moon. Indeed, 7 is known as the number of the Negative Moon. Taken together, 2 represents the waxing Moon, its positive phase, and 7 the waning Moon, its negative phase.

The Moon is, without doubt, the most interesting of the heavenly bodies. It is large, easily observable and ever-changing. It greatly impressed early man, who revered it above the Sun. And while we think of the Moon as having female characteristics, many ancient socities regarded the Moon as a male god. The Sumerians believed that the Moon, whom they called Nanna, was the father of both the Sun (or Utu) and Venus (or Inanna). And as late as the Middle Ages the Scandinavians thought that the Moon was a boy and the Sun a girl, who rode across the sky in chariots fleeing from pursuing wolves. The world would end, they said, when the wolves caught the Sun and ate her.

But since mankind's discovery that the Moon is a cold, dark body that shines only with the reflected light of the Sun, it has been demoted to second place in the heavens, which is, of course, another reason why it is associated with 2. In our society, being 'number two' means that although one has tried, one is not 'first among men' but 'second rate'. It is no coincidence that those who come second in sports events are awarded a silver medal, for silver is the metal of the Moon. Nor is it surprising that the winner gets the gold.

To us the Moon is female, its twenty-eight-day cycle matching that of the female menstrual period and its grace, coolness and aura of mystery the feminine character. So also is 2, which follows 1 and is created from it, just as Eve was fashioned from Adam, the first man. 2 is thus connected with all those traits, foibles, attractions and weaknesses that are characteristically feminine. 1 is bright and hot, 2 is shadowy and cold; 1 is simple and rational, 2 is complex and intuitive; 1 is upright and erect, 2 is curved and smooth. And because all living things, in the ancient view, were created by the divine pairing of earth and sky, 2 is also the number of pregnancy and birth.

Less favourably, 2 represents that which opposes: the contrary, the antagonistic and the enemy. For if 1 symbolizes God, 2 is Satan, the Devil, whose two horns and cloven feet show his numerical standing. And by association 2 is the number of the Left-Hand Path, of night and darkness, of secret things and hidden things, and of witches, warlocks and the undead. 2 is duplicity, untruth, 'speaking with a forked tongue'. It is also the number of passivity, submissiveness, pliability, restraint, and of all that is uncertain and obscure.

Many myths and legends involve that most enigmatic of twosomes, twins. Typically, mythical twins, while born of the same mother, different fathers, one a god, the other mortal, this difference lying at the root of their subsequent conflict. For twins, again typically, fight each other, with the result that one usually kills the other. Indeed, the quarrel between the Greek twins Proteus and Acrisius began while they were still in the womb.

The myths in which a semi-divine human twin fights his mortal brother are symbolic of the struggles between the worshippers of the celestial twins, the Sun and the Moon, which took place at the dawn of history. To early man the Sun and the Moon were the most obvious and potent celestial objects, whose circular shape and apparent identical size suggests a brotherly relationship, but whose differences of brightness, heat production and times of appearance pointed to an underlying dissimilarity. And while the sun's dominance of the day and the Moon's of the night suggested that the two brothers had successfully divided the sky between them, each seemed jealous of the other and schemed to snatch his portion of the sky for himself. The Sun's power grew during the spring and summer, when the days lengthened, and Moon's in the autumn and winter, when the night became longer. Such cosmic contention reached a climax when a solar eclipse occurred, the darkness it brought threatening the end of the world.

The most famous twins in Greek myth are Castor and Polydeuces (or Pollux), the Dioscuri, whose symbol, the *docana*, representing two upright pillars, is still used for Gemini, the sign of the Twins. Polydeuces, being the son of Zeus, is the immortal solar twin, and Castor, the son of an ordinary mortal, is the lunar twin. Castor's name, which means 'beaver', links him with water and wood, both of which are lunar substances. In numerological terms Polydeuces is 1 and Castor 2. The Dioscuri are unusual in that instead of quarrelling with each other, they do so with another pair of twins, Idas and Lynceus, which eventually leads to the two lunar brothers, Castor and Lynceus, being killed by their respective solar opposites.

The Greeks said that the Moon's chariot was drawn by two white horses, as was Eos' (or Dawn's). Both the Moon and 2 are associated with mares, cows and with female animals in general, and with dogs. Orthrus, the two-headed hound of Geryon, was the legendary progenitor of the Sphinx and the Nemean Lion (lions once being sacred to the Moon).

If you were born on the 2nd, the 20th or the 22nd, the influence of 2 is strong in your life and you are, like Castor, a lunar child. The influence of 2 is similarly strong if you were born on the 12th, 21st, 23rd, 24th, 25th, 26th, 27th, 28th or 29th, although the conjoined numbers represent moderating characteristics. Lunar influences are likewise potent in the lives of those born in February, the second month of the year. The Romans associated February with the dead and believed it to be unlucky, which is why they made it the shortest month. Famous people born on the 2nd include Marie Antoinette (2-11-1755), Arthur Bliss (2-8-1891), Edward Elgar (2-6-1857), Nell Gwynn (2-1-1650), Alec Douglas-Home (2-7-1903), Warren Harding (2-11-1865) and the Marquis de Sade (2-6-1740).

Should 2 figure strongly in your birthdate, you are an introverted and thoughtful type, possessing great sensitivity and intuition. If you are a man you probably have a slender, rather feminine physique, one not suited to rough games or physical work. You are the victim of much uncertainty about yourself, which makes you tense and anxious, this in turn preventing you from sleeping well. Your tenseness is exacerbated by the changeable nature of your life, which suggests to you that you are not in control of your destiny. Your lack of confidence makes it hard for you to stick up for yourself or to freely express your point of view. It also adversely affects your relationships.

2 is the number of white and of very pale colours, of bloodlessness, and of intuition and instinct. In the human body it represents fair skin that reacts badly to sunlight, hair that is blonde, lank and fine, weak bones and muscles, worried-looking eyes and a soft-spoken voice. The direction of 2 is south-east, whence travel or residence is favourable for the 2 born. The best times of the year for 2s occur whenever the Moon is lodged in Taurus, where it is exalted, although a waxing Moon is generally good for them. Their worst periods happen when the Moon is located in Scorpio, which is the sign of its debilitation.

A 2 vowel number indicates that you are rather laid-back and repressed, but also that you have creative talents and a strong desire to learn. Others find you hard to get to know because you are not particularly vocal or demonstrative, and they tend to think that you have something to hide. You are quite shy and you lack self-confidence. This makes you a follower, not a leader, and you prefer to suggest rather than instruct. Because you are impressionable, your surroundings have a strong effect on your mood and you are very much influenced by the opinions and actions of others. Security is important to you and this is why you must be very careful when choosing a marraige partner. With someone who gives you the right amount of love and respect you blossom into a warm and delightful human being but when these are lacking you shrivel up and die inwardly, and you may have self-destructive thoughts. You are a good listener and because you instinctively know where others are going wrong, you give excellent advice. This is why you do very well in fields like counselling, social work and psychiatry, whose aim is to help others. Indeed, your ability to put yourself in another's shoes makes you a natural champion of the poor and oppressed. But because you constantly question your own beliefs and goals, you are your own worst enemy. Thus, it is essential for you to have the support of someone who has the confidence you lack and who can focus both your mind and your energies.

The functioning of your ego personality is helped or hindered by your id nature, which is symbolized by your consonant number. Because odd numbers represent qualities that do not go well with those symbolized by the even numbers, your 2 ego is best served by an id symbolized by 4, 6 or 8, all of which are stronger and more stable than 2. In the solar cycle 2 is opposed by 6, the number of the descended Sun, which is therefore the most compatible id type for you to have.

If your consonant number is 2 you have a very rich and imaginative inner life, which sometimes seems more real than the world around you. You are strongly psychic and you are often troubled by strange dreams and presentiments. Indeed, should you wish to develop these talents you could become a gifted medium or clairvoyant. But if you have an odd ego number, particularly if this is 1, you may ignore these insights and try to repress them, preferring instead to trust to logic. You enjoy reading and artistic activities like painting and drawing, and you rather like being alone. Your 2 id indicates that you were frightened of the dark and of nameless terrors as a child, and that you are prone to nervous disorders and to superstitious fears, which may debilitate you. In your negative periods you are restless and moody, to the extent that others find you unpredictable and unreliable. You dislike responsibility and you will, if you're not careful, drift through life. You have a tendency to change both your job and your residence often. You have a need to serve others, which is why you find nursing, social work, fund-raising and allied work attractive.

If 2 is your name number you are a night person, preferring to stay out late instead of hitting the hay at a reasonable hour. The Moon affects you quite drastically, and you are restless and unsettled at Full Moon. You like salty food, silver jewellery, rainy weather, new clothes, places close to the sea or beside rivers, journeys by boat, the feel of metal and minerals, clean living, religion and positive people. Your lucky day of the week is Monday; your lucky gemstones are the emerald, the moonstone, the ruby and the turquoise; your lucky flowers are the peony, the poppy and the water lily; and your lucky colours are amber, emerald green and white.

THE NUMBER 3

3 is the most potent, mysterious and religious of the nine single numbers, for it is the number of the divine force manifesting in human life creatively and procreatively. Folk-tales are replete with threesomes – three wishes, three questions, three truths, three sisters, etc. – and triplets and triads figure extensively in the myths and legends of every age and country. As a holy number 3 appears in Christian belief as the Trinity of Father, Son and Holy Ghost. 'The way begets one' said the Chinese sage Lao Tzu; 'one begets two; two

begets three; three begets the myriad creatures. The myriad creatures carry on their backs the yin and embrace in their arms the yang and are the blending of the generative forces of the two.'

It is probable that 3 became linked with the divine at an early age because in those countries where civilization began – in the Middle East, particularly Egypt – the year had only three seasons, spring, summer and winter, which naturally seemed to represent the three aspects of the generative force, the risen, the whole and the dying god, whose yearly cycle mirrored the daily genesis and nemesis of the Sun as Khepri, Re and Atum.

In Sumerian myth the universe was said to have been created by Enhil, the child of An (heaven) and Ki (earth), forcing apart his copulating parents, while the Egyptians had Shu, who, like Enlil, is the air, separating the similarity entwined Nut (heaven) and Geb (earth), to bring the world into existence. The third entity is thus creative in an active, forceful way, while at the same time being, like the air itself, empty and invisible. Here, surely, is the root of all religion.

In Greek myth Rhea, the earth, gives birth to three sons, Hades, Poseidon and Zeus, who respectively take command of the underworld, the sea and the sky, and three daughters, Hestia, Demeter and Hera. Zeus (the Roman Jupiter), who becomes the king of the gods, is the third son and is nursed by three nymphs. Together the sons represent the three-season year: Poseidon, whose symbol is the bull, is the deity of the spring; Zeus, whose symbol is the lion, is the deity of the summer; and Hades, symbolized by the serpent, is the god of the winter. Poseidon bears a trident, as did Britannia on the old British penny to symbolize Britain's sea power, and fathers three children on the nymph Amphitrite ('the third one who encircles'), while Tartarus, Hades' realm, is guarded by the three-headed dog Cerberus, and has three regions and a trio of judges, Minos, Rhadamanthys and Aecus, who try the souls of the dead at a place where three roads meet.

Greek mythology also provides us with the three Erinnyes or Furies, who avenge the crimes of parricide and perjury, the three Fates, the three Muses, the three Hesperides, the three Harpies, the three Graeae, the three Gorgons, and Hecate, the third aspect of the Moon and the goddess of witches, who has three bodies and three heads.

In addition to being the number of the divine, 3 also symbolizes intelligence, knowledge, wisdom, creative expression, good living and sexual union for procreative purposes. Astrologically, it is linked with Jupiter, the largest planet of the solar system, and thus with the zodiac signs of Sagittarius and Pisces, which respectively represent the worldly and the spiritual aspects of both Jupiter and 3.

If you were born on the 3rd or the 30th of any month you are strongly influenced by 3, as you are, although less forcibly, if you were born on the 13th, 23rd or 31st. 3 similarly exerts an influence over those born in March, the third month, and December, the twelfth month (1 + 2 = 3). Famous people born on the 3rd include Clement Attlee (3-1-1883), Marlon Brando (3-4-1924), Rupert Brooke (3-8-1887), Felix Mendelssohn (3-2-1809), Dolly Parton (3-1-1946) and Burt Reynolds (3-11-1936). And it was the thrice-married film actress Jean Harlow (3-3-1911) who once said, 'I like to wake up in the morning and feel a new man.'

If three is prominent in your birthdate you are tall and strong-boned with a tendency to run to fat. You have a hearty appetite and a love of good food and drink. You are sociable and convivial, and you enjoy making whoopee. Because you are an extrovert you don't like being alone, which is why you would rather associate with dubious types than spend an evening without company. You are basically a cheery, open and frank person, who likes to spend money and gamble. Yet you have a spiritual side and a psychic's sensitivity. You enjoy learning and you are naturally attracted to teaching, law, journalism and the arts.

3 is the number of purple, the imperial colour, and of brown and yellow. This is why 3 people often have a blotchy complexion, which is caused by their over-indulgence in rich food and strong drink. Typically, 3s have rather plump, full faces, long noses and a lot of fine, healthy hair. The direction of 3 is to the south, and residence or travel in that direction is fortunate for 3s. Their best period takes place when Jupiter transits the zodiac sign of Cancer, where it is exalted, their worst when Jupiter passes through Capricorn, where it is debilitated. Jupiter will return to Cancer on 5 August 1989, and will remain in the sign for a little over a year, until 19 August 1990. It won't be back in Capricorn until 4 January 1996, and because it will stay in the sign until 22 January 1997, the year 1996 will be a rather difficult one for 3s.

If your ego personality is symbolized by a 3 vowel number, you are an extroverted, friendly and likeable soul. You have a lot of confidence, although you do occasionally experience periods of uncertainty, when you may drink too heavily or abuse your body in other ways. In fact, you don't take very good care of yourself, especially in the middle part of your life when you risk becoming flabby and out of shape. You are easily bored and this may prompt you to change your job quite often in an effort to find something that can stimulate and challenge you. You enjoy the outdoors and you are a keen sportsman, although typically as a spectator rather than as a participant. You are frank, honest and forthright, and you expect others to be similarly open. Indeed, you despise the hypocrite and the dissembler. Because you are quite humorous and optimistic, you are popular. You possess musical and artistic gifts, and you love to learn. You are also a natural teacher, with an enthusiasm for transmitting knowledge that is infectious. You like money and all that it can buy, yet despite your materialism you sense that there is a dimension of the spirit which not only attracts you but which helps guard you against excess. Being independent, you like to play the field in love and you certainly won't rush into marriage.

Because 3 represents the Sun at noon, when it has reached its zenith, your ego is best served by an id whose qualities are symbolized by 7, the number of both the Sun at its nadir and the waning Moon. Other odd numbered ids also serve you well, but if you have an id represented by 2, 4, 6 or 8 you will be less confident, shyer and more troubled, although your creativity and psychic ability will be greater.

If you have an id symbolized by 3 you feel different from your fellows, mainly because you recognize the presence of the divine in your life. Indeed, religion is important to you and quite probably you are a regular church-goer. You may even have thought about entering the ministry. Your id, however, is its own worst enemy because although it tries to act as your spiritual guardian, it is also the source of your strong sexual urges, thus it constantly tempts your ego with erotic images ony to condemn it – and so making you feel guilty and ashamed – when you give way to temptation. Because 3 is the most intuitive of the odd numbers, your id from time to time gives you amazing insights and prophetic dreams, although the use you make of these depends very much on your ego. While you try to behave in a mature and responsible way, both in your work and at home, you periodically have lapses, when you act foolishly and out of character. At such times you tend to take unnecessary risks, such as gambling money you can ill-afford to lose. Indeed, you rather like betting and occasionally – but not always – you are blessed with incredible luck.

Should 3 be your name number you love the open air, driving in fast cars, hiking and cycling, and attending sports events. Because you are a night person, you don't like rising early. You are fond of animals, sweet foods, expensive clothes and furnishings, children, fruit and orchards, churches, cathedrals and holy places generally, and cultivated people. Your lucky day of the week is Thursday; your lucky gemstones are the amethyst, the sapphire and the turquoise; your lucky flowers are the carnation, the pimpernel and the wallflower; and your lucky colours are blue, mauve, orange and purple.

THE NUMBER 4

4 is the number of the Negative Sun and it is the second of the Sun's two number. The Sun is given two numbers because its daily and its yearly cycles are divided into two. During the morning the Sun rises into the sky to reach its zenith at noon, from where it descends to vanish finally beneath the horizon. Likewise, during the first half of the year, through the spring and summer, the Sun gains height and grows hotter, while in the autumn and winter it steadily loses altitude and gives less heat. In fact, during both cycles the Sun waxes and wanes. 1 is therefore the number of the waxing Sun, symbolized by the lion, and 4 is the number of the waning Sun, whose animal symbol is the serpent.

In Greek myth the Sun-god Helius' chariot is pulled by four white horses, while that of Hades, the first son of Rhea, who can be identified with both the waning Sun and the Sun which has sunk beneath the horizon, is drawn by four black horses. The ancient anxieties generated by the Sun's nightly disappearance lie behind the myth of Theseus' and Peirithous' descent into Tartarus, where Hades confines them for four years. Theseus (whose name means 'he who lays down') represents the setting Sun and Peirithous ('he who turns around') the rising Sun. It is no coincidence that the two men are released from Tartarus by Heracles, the archetypal solar hero.

Because 4 is the number of the waning Sun and of the Sun at night, it is linked with inward and hidden things, with death and the afterlife, and with the earth and the treasures of the earth. 4 is also the number of divine revelation – Helius being the god of divination – and of stability and fertility. This is perhaps why Lao Tzu said, 'Within the realms there are four things that are great . . . the way is great; heaven is great; earth is great; and the king also is great.'

Greek myth records that Zeus fathered four of the Olympian deities – Hermes, Apollo, Artemis and Dionysus – out of wedlock; that Artemis practised four times with the silver bow made for her by the Cyclopes; that the Sphinx, child of the two-headed hound Orthrus, had a body made from the parts of four different creatures;

and that Peleus was given four wedding gifts, a spear, a suit of golden armour, and two horses.

Important tetrads include the four temperate seasons, the four points of the year (the two solstices and the two equinoxes), the four elements, the four humours, the four winds, the four cardinal virtues and the four letters of the Tetragrammaton, YHVH, which represent the secret name of God.

Marduk, the Babylonian god of lightning, the flood-storm and the four winds, who was all-seeing and all-hearing, possessed a double number of sense organs:

> Four were his eyes, four were his ears;
> When he moved his lips, fire blazed forth.
> Large were all four hearing organs,
> And the eyes, in like number, scanned all things.

If you were born on the 4th of any month the influence of 4 is strong in your life; it is also important if you were born on the 14th or the 24th. Indeed, the 14th is a very special birthdate because it is made up of both the Sun's numbers, 1 and 4, and those whose birthday it is have demonstable light and dark sides, which were evident in photographer Cecil Beaton's (14-1-1904) job, the morals of Frank Harris (14-2-1856), and the life of Che Guevara (14-6-1928), who said: 'In a revolution one wins or dies.' 4 is likewise important in the lives of the April born, for April is the fourth month of the year. The Romans held celebrations in honour of Magna Mater, the Great Mother, that is, the earth, on 4 April. Famous people with birthdays on the 4th include Anton Bruckner (4-9-1824), Calvin Coolidge (4-7-1872), Queen Elizabeth, the Queen Mother (4-8-1900), Charles Lindbergh (4-2-1902) and Clyde Tombaugh (4-2-1906), the discoverer of Pluto.

If 4 is well represented in your birthdate you are a reticent person with a good sense of humour and a calm, steady demeanour, both of which belie a rather rough, aggressive and volatile inner you that is only shown when you are angered or pushed too far. You are quite tall and have a strong, muscular body and regular features. You are not as confident in yourself as you would like to be, and you suffer from periods of self-doubt and anxiety, which you keep carefully hidden. You enjoy working hard and you see nothing wrong in wealth and luxury as long as they have been earned. Although others find you difficult to get to know, you are a faithful friend once your friendship has been won. You are honest and law-abiding, and you believe in fair play.

The colour of 4 is brown, the colour of the soil, but it is also linked with lighter and brighter colours, such as blue and violet. Similarly, the coluring of 4 people is either dark (the colour of the Negative Sun) or light (the colour of the Positive Sun). The physique may also be tall and slim or short and stout. One characteristic feature of 4s is the Greek nose, which lacks an indentation between the nose bridge and the forehead. The direction of 4 is to the south-west, and travel or residence in that part of the country or globe is fortunate for 4s. Like 1s, 4 individuals find life easiest when the Sun transits Aries, which it does every year between 20 March and 20 April, and most difficult when it passes through Libra, which it does annually between 24 September and 23 October.

If 4 is your vowel number you have a strong and stable ego and you are generally responsible and dependable. Yet you are not as confident or as well adjusted as you would wish, and you are plagued by periodic bouts of self-doubts and uncertainty. You are unusual in that while you need to live a structured life, you also like change and variety, which means that you are happiest working freelance or at a job that allows you a good deal of freedom and the opportunity to travel. Should your work or your home life prove too restricting you will suffer in silence for a long while before suddenly and dramatically breaking away, to pick up the pieces elsewhere. Indeed, such volcanic changes are typical of the 4 character. You can work quite well with others, although you don't much like taking orders. Because you are creative and clever with your hands, you are naturally attracted to music and art and to jobs which combine creativity with practical application, such as that of the architect, engineer and designer. You are friendly, yet your need to remain independent makes you somewhat aloof, which is why you have more aquaintances than friends. You were rather moody and difficult when young, and you can still plunge into unfathomable silences, much to everyone's puzzlement. You don't give much away about yourself, which gives you a certain mystery. Your pleasures tend to be on the unusual side, so allowing you to get out of yourself, thus you're more likely to be learning kung-fu or going scuba-diving than playing golf. Marriage doesn't appeal to you all that much and you will try to put it off for as long as you decently can.

Your 4 ego is moderated by your id, whose character and state is represented by the consonant number of your name. Because 4 is an even number, you are best served by an even-numbered id, for otherwise your ego's stability will be constantly threatened by restless urges from below. An 8 id is most compatible with a 4 ego, because such an id is balanced and comparatively quiescent. 2, 4 and 6 id types are also compatible, but less so than an 8 id. Of course, a 4 id is essentially the same as a 4 ego: it won't create problems but it won't provide stimulant pressures either. Less favourable are ids represented by the odd numbers 1, 3, 5, 7 and 9, although 1 ids, being solar by nature, have natural affinities with 4 egos that the others lack.

A 4 consonant number reveals that you have an id rich in creative ideas and intuitive awareness, which makes you something of a primary source when it comes to producing brainwaves and insights. Yet despite this you are noted for your stubborn persistence, thus you don't find it easy to alter course once you have started something. However, if you have a less persistent and rather contrary ego number, a 4 id will act as a positive counterweight, helping you keep your nose to the grindstone. You are concerned about the state of the world and about the lot of your fellow man, which is why you tend to give to charities and protest against things like seal hunting and nuclear waste disposal. Ideally, you like to live in quiet, pleasant surroundings, and you need the support and respect of your colleagues and friends. Yet, ironically, security makes you feel uneasy because you sense that it could trap you. This is why you are always planning travel trips and activities that are different and exotic.

If your name number is 4 you reach your daily peak in the afternoon and early evening. You dress oddly and somewhat unconventionally, and you are generous where big sums of money are involved but mean with small expenditures. You like dry river beds and salt flats, pottery items and watching pots being made, birds, plants, especially shrubs, and you have a penchant for the occult. Your lucky day of the week is Saturday; your lucky gemstones are the amethyst, the aquamarine and the lapis lazuli; your lucky flowers are the buttercup, the fennel and the foxglove; and your lucky colours are electric blue and green, brown, violet and off-white.

THE NUMBER 5

The number 5 is perhaps the most interesting of the nine single numbers, not least because it is the number of sexual pleasure, deception and magic. Astrologically, 5 is the number of the planet Mercury and the setting Sun. Mercury is identified with the setting Sun because, lying so near the Sun, it only becomes visible just after sunset. In Greek and Roman mythology Mercury (or Hermes) is the god who conducts the souls of the dead to the underworld and he was originally the god of the twilight. In Tartarus Mercury delivers the ghosts to Charon, the ferryman, who rows them across the black waters of the river Styx. In keeping with Mercury's numerological associations, the Styx has five tributaries: Acheron, Phlegethon, Cocytus, Aornis and Lethe.

Mercury's mother is Maia, one of the Pleiades nymphs, who were pursued by Orion for five years before being transformed into stars. Maia gave her name to May, the fifth month, during which the Pleiades rise with the Sun to mark the start of the nautical year. This is probably why Mercury became the god of mariners. In fact, Mercury's jurisdiction was wide, as befits his restless character, and he was the god of invention, soothsaying, musicianship, treaties, trade and commerce, theft, travel, artifice and mathematics. He was also the messenger of Zeus. Mercury wears winged sandals and carries a magic wand with which he can induce sleep.

Additionally, as the god of intelligence, speech and communication, Mercury was credited with the invention of the alphabet, which has five vowels, while the five fingers of the hand link both Mercury and the number 5 with manual skills. Indeed, the right hand symbolizes Mercury as an Olympian deity, this being the hand with which most of us write, throw dice, strum a musical instrument, seal bargains, etc., while the left, the awkward or sinister hand, is the hand of Mercury as conductor of the dead.

The names of the five fingers of the right hand derive from those of the five male Dactyls who sprang into life when Rhea, giving birth to Zeus, dug her fingers into the ground. Each finger of the right hand is also identified with one of the vowels of the alphabet. The thumb is the digit of the vowel A and is named Heracles; the index finger, that of O, is named Paeonis; the middle finger, that of U, is named Epimedes; the third finger, that of E, is named Iasius; and the little finger, which palmists link specifically with Mercury, is that of the vowel I and is called Acesidas. In a similar manner the thumb is identified with the winter solstice, when the Sun is reborn, the index finger with the spring equinox, the middle finger with the summer solstice, the third finger with the autumn equinox, and the little finger with the winter solstice again, when the Sun dies. In the ancient tree alphabet, A, the vowel of the thumb, was the first letter, and I, the vowel of the little finger, the last. This old alphabet is recalled in the expression 'from A to Izzard', meaning from start to finish, 'Izzard' being a variant of Z.

The names of the five female Dactyls who are personified by the fingers of the left hand have been lost, probably because their repetition was considered unlucky.

The hands can thus be considered as representing the polarities of nature, the right hand being the male and hence symbolizing light, logic, dexterity, action, openness, etc. – that is, the good, and the left the female, or darkness, intuition, clumsiness, passiveness, conceal-ment, etc. – in other words, the bad.

As Hermes Trismegistus – Hermes 'three times very, very great' – Mercury was said to have introduced astrology and its philosophical system, which is summed up by the dictum 'as above, so below', to mankind.

Astrology interprets the movements of the five planets and the two lights, the Sun and the Moon, in terms of human destiny. It is not surprising, therefore, to find that the fingers and the other parts of the hand – the hands being the bodily parts by which man imposes his will on the world – are linked with these celestial bodies. The thumb is the digit of Venus; the index finger, Jupiter; the middle finger, Saturn; the third finger, the Sun; and the little finger, Mercury.

But despite 5's close association with Mercury and his many attributes, the number never became as important in the West as it did in China, where, no doubt because of the special attention given to the five planets, 5 was the only number worthy of serious study. The Chinese recognized five zones of space, five odours, five musical notes, five human senses, five vital facial features, five metals, five duties, five elements, five colours, five directions and a plethora of other fives, each fifth part of which was ruled by one of the five planets. Mercury, for example, was the planet of the element *water*, the metal *iron*, the colour *black*, and the direction *north*. The other planets were linked with the following elements, metals, colours and directions.

	Element	*Metal*	*Colour*	*Direction*
VENUS	Metal	Silver	White	West
MARS	Fire	Copper	Red	South
JUPITER	Wood	Lead	Blue	East
SATURN	Earth	Gold	Yellow	Centre

In fact, the Chinese were so five-minded that they saw 5 wherever they looked, which is perhaps why the sage Lao Tzu warned, 'The five colours makes a man's eyes blind; the five notes makes his ears deaf; the five tastes injure his palate.'

But although 5 symbolizes intelligence, cleverness and versatility, it is also the number of instability, irresponsibility and indeterminancy, which is why it has been called the Errol Flynn of numbers. Thus, it is perhaps hardly surprising that 5 turns up with alarming frequency in the names and birthdates of those who are sexually promiscuous or sexually abnormal, or criminally predisposed or psychologically disturbed. 5 is the number of genius, but genius is next to madness.

The influence of 5 is strong in your life if you were born on the 5th, as it is, but to a lesser degree, if your birthday is the 15th or the 25th. The addition of 1 and 2 to the birthdate gives 5 a stability it lacks on its own. New projects, for instance, are often successfully launched on the 15th, such as the founding of the McDonald's hamburger chain (15-4-1955), the launch of decimalization in Britain (15-2-1971), and the publication of Sir Isaac Pitman's Stenographic Sound-hand book (15-11-1837). The 5th, by contrast, saw the arrest of Oscar Wilde for homosexuality (5-4-1895), the assassination of Robert Kennedy (5-6-1968), and the start of the unsuccessful Sino-Soviet talks (5-7-1963) which led to the rift between the two countries. Because 5 is the number of May, the fifth month, those born in May tend to be rather restless and footloose. Famous people with birthdays on the 5th include Walt Disney (5-12-1901), Henry II of England (5-3-1133), John Huston (5-8-1906), Tatum O'Neal (5-11-1963) and Sir Robert Peel (5-2-1788).

If 5 is prominent in your birthdate you are likely to be of slender build, 5 being the number of the ectomorph. Quite possibly you would like to be heavier than you are, but find it difficult to put on weight. Your gauntness stems from your high metabolic rate, which readily burns up what you eat. You also tend not to bother about eating regularly. Although you are generally outgoing and cheerful, your natural anxiety and impatience sometimes makes you irritable and short-tempered, to the detriment of your relationships. You suffer periodic bouts of moodiness and almost manic restlessness, especially during your twenties and thirties. You have a clear speaking voice and a love of words. Indeed, you are an effective communicator. You also like reading and writing. You are blessed with a good sense of humour and you enjoy playing jokes and making others laugh.

The colour of 5 is yellow, which, being close to gold, reflects Mercury's proximity to the Sun. 5 people frequently have a sallow complexion, a yellowness that also tends to appear in the white of the eyes and on the teeth. The typical 5 person has a thin, long-limbed body, straight, fine hair, thin eyebrows and lips, weak teeth, and quick, restless movements. The direction of 5 is west, whence travel or residence is fortunate for 5s. All 5 types find life easier for them when Mercury transits the zodiac sign of Virgo, where it is exalted, and at a low ebb when the little planet passes through Pisces, where it is debilitated. Because Mercury usually spends no more than about one month in each sign, it returns to Virgo every year.

If 5 is the vowel number of your name, you have a 5 ego and a personality to match. This means that you have a clever mind which enables you to learn new skills and absorb facts quickly. However, your mental sharpness makes you rather impatient with those less able than yourself. You love to talk and argue – especially the latter – and you are good at languages. Because you enjoy a challenge, you readily tackle any problem that comes your way, even though you may not be qualified to solve it. You like games such as chess and backgammon, which enable you to pit your wits against an opponent, but not rough, body contact games, such as rugby or football. You are not, however, blessed with much persistence, thus you often give up if you can't solve a problem or get your own way easily or quickly. You have a persuasive tongue, which allows you to manipulate others, and a good sense of humour. But although your knowledge is wide, you tend to know a little about a lot. Because you are quick, light and funny you find it easy to meet people and as a result you have an active and interesting social life. Yet you have few close friends because any emotional commitment scares you. You keep your own emotions under tight control, to the extent that your friends and colleagues seldom know what you are really feeling. You tend to be neurotic, and if typical, you pay too much attention to your appearance and to the tidiness of your home. Indeed, dirt and dust make you uncomfortable and angry, so do slovenly habits. You also worry too much about your health and you are something of a sucker for quack remedies. While you are both attractive to and interested in the opposite sex, you shy away from serious commitment and may flit from one relationship to the next. Also, you have a tendency to kiss and tell, which can hurt your ex-partners. Fortunately, however, sex is not all that important to you. What you like is the chase!

Because 5 represents the setting Sun, poised on the brink of the abyss, your 5 ego is perhaps the most unstable of the ego types and it takes relatively little to push you 'over the edge'. This is why you need to have a stable id, for this will provide a psychic counterweight to your natural restlessness and impatience. In this respect the numbers of the rising Sun – 1 and 9 – are ideal consonant numbers for you, for such an id will balance your ego. 3 and 7 consonant numbers likewise indicate a favourable id. However, a 5 id is not suitable for a 5 ego and should you have such an id you will find it hard to cope. Ids represented by the even numbers – 2, 4, 6 and 8 – suggest that you are at odds with your emotions and that you tend to suffer from self-doubt and depression.

If your consonant number is 5, your id is very much a thorn in your side because it constantly throws up all manner of restless, critical and exotic ideas and images, which make it difficult for you to feel at peace with yourself. It continually says, 'Come on! Get up, get out and get going!' so pressurizing you to run in all directions at once. Of course, such an id is stimulating and even positive if you have an ego that can successfully channel its demands, but if not it will prompt a lot of silly desires and irrational actions. At its best, a 5 id gives you a love of learning, travel and adventure, an interest in progress and change, and a talent for social intercourse. Because it is oddly in tune with natural forces, your id can warn you of future dangers and tell you if someone is trying to con you. If you're wise you'll trust your hunches – but not when you're near a roulette wheel or a racetrack. You do like to gamble and this can cause you a lot of problems with your finances. In a similar way, your 5 id encourages you to put up a false front behind which you hide your real self.

If 5 is your name number you like public places, gossip, going to the theatre, listening to music and finding things out. Your best time of the day is early evening, and you love watching the Sun go down. The autumn is your favourite season. You enjoy spending time in gardens, walking in the rain, watching birds, eating different foods, sitting beneath leafy trees, and the company of your maternal uncles. Your lucky day of the week is Wednesday; your lucky gemstones are the agate, Alexandrite, the opal and the onyx; your lucky flowers are the gladiolus, the orchid and the snapdragon; and your lucky colours are light green, orange and yellow.

THE NUMBER 6

The number 6 is undoubtedly the most attractive of the nine single numbers because it symbolizes love and marriage, birth and growth, and peace. Its planet is Venus, who in mythology was the goddess of love. Yet in the solar cycle 6 is the number of the descended Sun, poised mid-way between its setting and its nadir. This indicates that 6 has a dark side to it, that its presence as a birth number or as a name number does not always augur happiness. Indeed, love as often brings pain as it does pleasure, and the divorce statistics speak eloquently of the problems and difficulties of marriage.

Like 3, which symbolizes the male sex urge and procreation, 6 is the number of female sexuality, children and family life. It is also the number of simplicity, neatness, hard work, happiness and art.

The generative nature of 6 is illustrated by the biblical account of God's creation of the world and everything in it in six days, and in myth by the Greek goddess Rhea giving birth to six children, three of whom were male and three female, and by the story in the Epic of Gilgamesh of how Enkidu, the wild man, was tamed by a harlot after six days of sexual passion, which gave him wisdom and put 'the thoughts of man . . . in his heart.' Heroic acts are rarely associated with 6: Theseus' departure for Crete, where he slew the Minotaur, on 6 April, being but one of the few examples.

In very ancient times the goddess of the planet Venus had a dual character and a dual role: she was both the amorous and enticing Queen of Love and the destructive and murderous Lady of Battles. This duality derived from the planet Venus' appearance in the sky as either the morning star or the evening star, the former representing the goddess in her benign aspect, the latter the goddess in her warlike aspect. Indeed, Venus was known as the 'Star of Lamentation' when it shone at night.

Venus was called Inanna by the Sumerians. Her brother and husband was Utu, the Sun, a relationship suggested by the planet Venus' proximity to that body, and her sister was Ereshkigal, the Queen of the Underworld. One myth describes how Inanna descends into Ereshkigal's realm to liberate her love Dumuzi, the god of the harvest, who had been imprisoned there. Angered by Inanna's insolent intrusion into the land of death, Ereshkigal captures her and subjects her to the ravages of sixty illnesses. She remains in the nether world until Utu and Nanna, the Moon, get help from Enki, the god of the planet Jupiter, who secures her release.

This descent of Venus/Inanna into the underworld explains why 6 occupies the position that it does in the solar cycle, a placement that also symbolizes Venus as the feared goddess of war, who despatches the souls of slain warriors to Tartarus.

In our discussion of the number 3 we noted how God or 'the divine' is often represented by a triad of male deities. This threesome typically becomes increased to six by the gods' marriage to their sisters, a doubling which reveals why 6 symbolizes both marriage and family life. Thus, the trio of Babylonian high gods – Anu, Enlil and Ea – marry, respectively, their sisters Antu, Ninlil and Ninki.

This incestuous union must also have originally taken place between the six children of Rhea, but because the Greeks came to abhor such marriages, only Zeus' marriage to Hera was allowed to stand. Yet there is evidence that Poseidon was once the spouse of his sister Demeter, and Hades of Hestia.

However, despite the close association of 6 with Venus, its appearance in Greek myth is infrequent. It generally occurs only as numbers of children. For example, the Greeks said that Poseidon fathered six sons of the nymph Halia; that Aeolus, the guardian of the winds, had six sons and six daughters by his wife Enarete; and that Apollo killed six of Niobe's seven sons and his sister, Artemis, six of her daughters. It is, however, worth remembering that the first Olympian family consisted of six gods, Zeus, Poseidon, Apollo, Hermes, Hephaistos and Ares, and six goddesses, Hera, Demeter, Artemis, Athene, Aphrodite and Hestia. This company of double sixes was only altered when Dionysus, the god of wine, took the place of the self-effacing Hestia, the goddess of the hearth. Hades, being the god of the underworld, was never an Olympian.

If you were born on the 6th of any month the influence of 6 is strong in your life, as it is, although to a lesser degree, if your birthday falls on the 16th or the 26th. 6 is also a potent factor in the lives of those born in June, the sixth month. The name June derives from Juno, the Roman goddess of marriage, who had the power to make a marriage both happy and fertile. Famous people with birthdays on the 6th include the German composer Max Bruch (6-1-1838), Henry VI of England (6-12-1421), Robert Mitchum (6-8-1917), Ronald Reagan (6-2-1911) and baseball player 'Babe' Ruth (6-2-1895).

If 6 is well represented in your birthdate, you are probably quite tall, although the height of 6 people is very variable. You have an attractive, well-proportioned body, but because you gain weight easily, you have to work at keeping your figure. Your manner is pleasant and friendly and although you are rather introverted, you enjoy the comapny of others. You don't, however, like being with noisy or ill-mannered people. Yet despite having a lot of friends, your friendships are not very close or enduring, chiefly because you are too selfish and opportunistic where others are concerned. When alone you like reading or listening to music, and you may play a musical instrument or have some other artistic hobby. You are happiest in your home, which is the most important place in your life. If you are not yet married you will certainly be looking forward to the day when you are. You enjoy spending money on clothes and cosmetics, because you think it is important to be attractive to the opposite sex.

6 is the number of green, the colour of plant life. 6 people are blessed with regular features, clear skin and silky, light-coloured hair. Their most beautiful facial features are their large and lustrous eyes. The direction of 6 is to the north-west, and travel or residence in that direction is fortunate for the 6 born. The best period for them is when Venus transits the zodiacal sign of Pisces, where it is exalted, the worst when Venus transits Virgo, the sign of its debilitation. Because Venus generally stays in each zodiac sign for about a month, it passes through both Pisces and Virgo once every year.

Should you possess a 6 vowel number, symbolizing your ego, you have a well-balanced personality, one that stands on the mid-line between extroversion and introversion. You are naturally reserved, polite and diffident, yet when the mood takes you or the moment is right you can party with the best of them. You feel happiest in surroundings that are bright, colourful and tastefully furnished. You hate dirt and untidiness, and you will go to great lengths to stay clean and neat. Because the notion of balance is important to you, you avoid people and situations that are controversial or upsetting. Indeed, you are both fair and honest, and you believe that the rule of law is central to civilized life. Thus you support the police, order and strong government. However, you dislike injustice, particularly social injustice, and you will always protest against it. But although you have strong views, your ability to see things from the other's point of view stops you from becoming blinkered, thus you are often unsure of your ground when the time comes to cast your vote. In this respect you are a fence-sitter. You are generally careful in your handling of money, although the urge to gamble, to gain riches without effort, can sometimes get the better of you. Because you have an attractive appearance and manner you are popular with the opposite sex, hence you are seldom without a partner of some sort. But you are less successful at ending relationships than beginning them, simply because you find it hard to make a clean break.

An ego symbolized by 6, the number of the Sun mid-way between its setting and its nadir, is best served by an id symbolized by 2, the number of the mid-morning Sun. However, an id represented by any of the even numbers – 2, 4, 6 and 8 – will satisfactorily complement a 6 ego, although a 6 id won't provide the contrast and stimulation that the other id types will. Ids symbolized by the odd numbers – 1, 3, 5, 7 and 9 – will create difficulties because they will rob you of your equanimity by presenting you with all sorts of troublesome feelings and ideas.

If you have a 6 id the deeper levels of your mind are calmer than most, and in your quiet moments you have an inner sense of harmony and peace. You may practise meditation and be interested in mystical and philosophical teachings. A stable, happy home situation is very important to you and you suffer a great deal if things are wrong for you in this respect. This is why the best part of travelling for you is the returning home. Likewise, your strong urge to marry and settle down means that although you may decide to travel, achieve some educational goal or make a career for yourself, you won't feel whole until you have a mate, a home and one or two children. Your id tends to make you resistant to change, thus you are by nature very conservative. However, you will always support changes that right a wrong. You like art and you have an eye for line, form and colour. Indeed, you are creative yourself. Your worst faults are your self-absorption, your vacillation and your tendency to manipulate others.

If 6 is your name number you enjoy the outdoors, especially those places where cereals are grown or where cattle are pastured, or where there are trees. Summer is your favourite season. You also like shops and window-gazing for bargains. Somewhat oddly, you have a taste for sour foods. You like eating out, going to the theatre or cinema, and talking to clergymen. You also like singing, reading, poetry, smelling nice, wearing jewellery and colourful clothes and flowers. Your lucky day of the week is Friday, your lucky gemstones are the chrysolite, the jade and the opal; your lucky flowers are the violet and the white rose; and your lucky colours are blue, emerald green and violet.

THE NUMBER 7

There is no doubt that 7 is generally considered to be the most intriguing, mysterious and fortunate of the nine single numbers. And to us in the West the world seems full of sevens, just as it appeared replete with fives to the Chinese. Our heptads include the seven wonders of the world, the seven seas, the seven continents, the seven colours of the rainbow, the seven notes of a musical scale, the seven days of the week, the seven league boots, the seven churches, the seven champions of Christendom, the seven seals, the seven stars, the seven angels and the seven pillars of wisdom.

But this positive view of 7 is not generally met with in mythology or suggested by 7's astrological associations. 7 is the number of the Negative Moon and of the Sun at its nadir, the lowest point of its cycle, which links it with darkness and the land of the dead.

The ancient myths reveal that 7 was associated with rest, sleep, peace and death at the earliest of times. In Genesis, for example, we learn that God, having created the world in six days, 'rested on the seventh day from all his work that he had made'. A similar cessation of divine activity on the seventh day is recounted by Utnapishtim, the hero of the flood, in the Epic of Gilgamesh. Describing the deluge Utnapishtim says,

> For six days and six nights the winds blew, torrent and tempest and flood overwhelmed the world, tempest and flood raged together like warring hosts. When the seventh day dawned the storm from the south subsided, the sea grew calm, the flood was stilled; I looked at the face of the world and there was silence, all mankind was turned to clay.

And Greek myth recounts the strange story of the twins Agamedes and Trophonius, who were advised by the oracle of Apollo to 'live merrily and indulge yourselves in every pleasure for six days; on the seventh, your heart's desire shall be granted.' On that day Agamedes and Trophonius died quietly in their beds.

It is therefore perhaps hardly surprising to find that the Babylonian underworld contains almost as many heptads as the Greek Tartarus does triads. Ereshkigal's dark realm is surrounded by seven walls, and access to it is only gained by passing through seven gates, each of which is secured by seven bolts. Because every soul has to remove one article of clothing at each gate, so as to arrive naked in the underworld, seven divestments have to be made. And once there the dead are judged by the seven Annunaki.

It was earlier pointed out that both 2 and 7 are identified with the Moon, 2 being the number of the waxing Moon and thus of growth, expansion, moistness, health and life, and 7 the number of the waning Moon, that is, of reduction, shrinkage, dryness, sickness and death. Also 2, being even, is a female number, while 7 being odd, is male. These correspondences indicate that 2 and 7 stand for the opposite of existence, the Yin and the Yang.

But while we with out numerate sophistication can readily accept that because 2 precedes 7 in the number sequence it should be identified with the first, rather than the second phase of the Moon's cycle, we would be wrong in assuming that the ancients celebrated so simply. Indeed, their close association of 2 with life and 7 with death suggests that they had a much stronger argument for this than the mere fact that 2 lies before 7 in the number sequence. Their reasons must surely have been based on their observations of the natural world, which provided them with the examples of power, change and contrast that formed the framework of their religion.

In Sumer and Babylonia both the Moon and the Sun were worshipped as powerful gods. Each was regarded as an all-seeing deity, who knew the secrets of mankind. There is also evidence of early Moon worship in Egypt, where the Moon may have once been ranked as equal to the Sun, the immortal Re. Indeed, the Sun's and the Moon's equality and their all-seeing power is suggested by the fact that the Egyptians believed them to be the two eyes of Horus, the falcon god, the Sun being Horus' right eye, the Moon his left.

The idea of the Sun and Moon being eyes forms part of a very ancient creation myth, which told how the world was made from the bodily parts of a gigantic god, who had been murdered and dismembered. Echoes of this gruesome story occur in the myth of Uranus, the Greek sky-god, who was castrated by his son Cronus – and who was, incidentally, his seventh son – and from whose blood were created the three Furies and the ash nymphs, the goddess Aphrodite arising from the foam that collected around Uranus' genitals, which Cronus threw into the sea. Somewhat similarly, Egyptian myth records the dismemberment of Osiris by Seth, who then scattered his bodily parts around the land of Egypt.

Fortunately, however, a complete version of this creation myth is found in Scandinavian folklore, which tells us that the first sentient being was the giant Ymir, who is spontaneously created by the interaction of ice and fire. Not long afterwards the god Buri is generated by the divine cow Avonhumla licking salty ice blocks. Buri then gives life to Bor, who in turn fathers the three gods Odin, Vili and Ve. These three kill Ymir and cut him up to create the world – 'From his blood the seas and lakes, from his flesh the earth, and from his bones the mountains; from his teeth and jaws and such bones as were broken they formed the rocks and the pebbles.'

What is particularly interesting about this Norse myth is the fact that the three gods fashion the sky from Ymir's skull, placing it over the earth to create the vault of heaven. In this way Ymir's eyes become the Sun and the Moon.

A living human head has five visible openings: two ears, two nostrils and a mouth. A skull, however, shows two more, the orbits or eye sockets, giving a total of seven (an eighth, the *foramen magnum*, through which passes the spinal cord, can only be seen if the skull is detached from the backbone). It was this number of skull openings which surely suggested to ancient man, to whom the skull was the most potent symbol of death and mortality, that 7 and death are linked, and that the number is also associated with sleep, peace and darkness.

Likewise, 7 is also the number of wisdom and occult knowledge, of thought and learning, and of the unconscious mind.

Since the Sun traditionally represents the right eye and the Moon the left, the question naturally arises as to whether the other skull openings are linked with the five planets. This indeed is the case. Astrology gives Jupiter rulership of the right ear and Saturn of the left ear. Mars likewise governs the right nostril, Venus the left. And Mercury, as might be expected, is the lord of the mouth.

The influence of 7 is strong in your life if you were born on the 7th, as it is, although to a lesser extent, if you were born on the 17th. A birthday on the 27th introduces both lunar numbers into your life, thus making you a distinct Moon person. You are powerfully affected by the Moon, to the extent that your moods and the very pattern of your life ebb and flow in a cyclical manner. 7 is also an important influence in the lives of those born in July, the seventh month. July was named after Julius Caesar, the Roman emperor, at whose death a comet appeared and shone for seven days. Famous people with birthdays on the 7th include Gary Cooper (7-5-1901), Charles Dickens (7-2-1812), Queen Elizabeth I of England (7-9-1533), Billy Graham (7-11-1918), Billie Holiday (7-4-1915), Gustav Mahler (7-7-1860) and Ringo Starr (7-7-1940).

You probably are not very tall if 7 is well represented in your birthdate, and you are likely to be on the plump side. Indeed, your metabolism is slow, which explains why you easily gain weight, a tendency aggravated by your liking for rich foods and alcohol. You probably suffered quite badly from acne and other skin disorders during adolescence, and you may still wish that your complexion was better. You have a poor dress sense, which is not helped by your odd shape, thus you never really look or feel as smart as you would like. But if your appearance needs work, your personality could hardly be bettered, for you are a gentle, friendly and pleasant soul, who has a liking for others and an intuitive understanding of them. Although you are not very ambitious, you place a high value on education. Your main weakness is your tendency to turn to drink or drugs when faced with life's problems.

The colour of 7 is blue, the colour of tropical seas and the sky. 7 people have rather plump facial features and short necks, but are blessed with very attractive eyes. Their foreheads are full and wide and their hair is fine and dark. The direction of 7 is north, and travel or residence in that direction is fortunate for 7 people. The best period for 7s, as it is also for 2s, occurs when the Moon is lodged in the zodiac sign of Taurus, where it is exalted, and the worst is when the Moon is placed in Scorpio, where it is debilitated. Such lunar placements last for about two days every month and their dates can be found by consulting an ephemeris.

If 7 is your vowel number, symbolizing your ego or manifest personality, you are a bright, quite creative type, whose biggest fault in terms of getting ahead is your lack of direction. You also have little staying power. This means that if you are to achieve anything solid you need a lot of support and encouragement, particularly in your marriage and business partnerships. Yet you are certainly no fool, either intellectually or intuitively, and you love to learn. Indeed, academic qualifications are important to you. Because you can both understand and give a sympathetic ear to the problems of others, you are attracted to social work, counselling and psychiatry. However, your dislike of taking on too much responsibility means that you often miss out on the top jobs. You enjoy creative acitivies, such as drama, writing and music, and these take up much of your spare time. Your warm and sociable nature makes you popular, yet others find you hard to get to know because you tend to change your views and behaviour to suit the company. Thus, you are all things to men. You have difficulty in starting new projects because you are a chronic procrastinator, which is another reason why you need a strong partner to give you a push. You dislike upsets and arguments, and you worry too much. Because you are poor at handling money, you often have problems with your finances. However, your intuitive abilities can give you good guidance – if you let them.

One of the biggest faults of a 7 ego is its tendency to be depressive and self-pitying. This is why its ideal complement is an id symbolized by 3, the number of the Sun at noon and of expansive Jupiter. But an id represented by 1, 5 or 9 can also stop a 7 ego from falling into the Slough of Despond too often. Yet this won't be the case if its partner is an id symbolized by 2, 4 6 or 8, or by 7, for none of these can prevent it becoming depressed and miserable. In fact, they may worsen such tendencies.

An id symbolized by 7 however, is not a bad one to have, because 7, being the number of the Sun at its nadir, shows it to be well suited to its unconscious environment. Thus if you have a 7 id the deeper parts of your mind are not likely to contain much troublesome psychic material, so you should feel relatively at peace with yourself.

You are very intuitive and you instinctively know how things will turn out. Indeed, with the right training you could make a competent medium or psychic. You are probably very interested in the occult and in mysterious happenings, and you may even like walking in cemetries and attending funerals. Your dreams are vivid and colourful, and some of them are prophetic. You rather enjoy the ego-destabilizing effects of drink and drugs – even if the latter are only tranquillizers – and you need to use both cautiously. Your 7 id makes it easy for you to be alone, because you retreat into yourself, and you spend a lot of time day-dreaming. Your excellent understanding of human nature gives you a natural sympathy for others and the ability to give sensible advice. Yet because your conscience is poorly developed, you find it easy to fall down on your responsibilities. You rarely feel guilty!

If 7 is your name number you don't much like the outdoors, unless you are near water – by a lake, a river or the sea. You love visiting churches and cathedrals, indeed anywhere with religious connections, and places where the dead are buried. You prefer the company of women, especially after dark, your favourite time of the day. You like history and archaeology, stories about the sea, and anything strange or mysterious. In manner, you are truthful, God-fearing and reserved. Your lucky day of the week is Thursday; your lucky gemstones are the bloodstone, coral, the emerald and the sapphire; your lucky flower is the heliotrope; and your lucky colours are blue, mauve, purple and sea-green.

THE NUMBER 8

The number 8 is the last of the even single numbers, its smoothly curved shape suggesting balance and harmony. Its planet is Saturn, the faintest and the slowest-moving of the visible planets. In the solar cycle 8 represents the Sun's final placement before it rises to bring the new day. Thus it is, like 6 and 7, a number of the underworld.

But while 8 and Saturn are linked in a numerological sense, in myth Saturn is generally associated with 7, which as we have seen is one of the numbers of the Moon. To the Greeks, Cronus (or Saturn) was the seventh son of Uranus and Mother Earth, and was, as one of the Titans, the ruler of the seventh day, which is Saturday, the day of Saturn. Indeed, Saturn is the seventh planet.

We do know, however, that the ancient Greeks sacrificed to Selene, the Moon Goddess, on the eighth day of each lunation, when the Moon enters its second phase. To them the eighth day was sacred to the Moon.

More importantly, the god Saturn was originally both an agricultural deity and an aspect of the Moon, his lunar connections being made evident by his possession of an adamantine sickle, made for him by his mother, which is a symbol of the Moon. It is with the sickle that he castrates his father Uranus. The poet Hesiod describes what happened next:

> The genitals, cut off with adamant
> And thrown from land into the stormy sea,
> Were carried for a long time on the waves
> White foam surrounded the immortal flesh,
> And in it grew a girl.

The girl is Aphrodite, the 'foam-born' goddess of love, who in reality is a third aspect of the Moon. Together, Aphrodite, Selene and Cronus – or, to give them their Latin names, Venus, Luna and Saturn – represent the Moon's three phases: New, Full and Old. This adds new meaning to the numbers 6, 7 and 8, the numbers of Venus, the Moon and Saturn, whose placement at the lowest point of the solar cycle reveals them to be not only numbers of the underworld, but of darkness and the night. Indeed, Venus, Luna and Saturn form the divine lunar triad, which is why their numbers, when added together, total 21 (6 + 7 + 8 = 21), which in turn reduces to 3 (2 + 1 = 3). The myth of Saturn's seizure of heavenly power by castrating his father is symbolic of that distant period of human history when agriculture was fast supplanting hunting, and when life for many people was becoming much more stable, settled and peaceful. This golden 'age of Saturn', which was apparently initiated by women, who mastered agricultural production, brought about the eclipse of the old sky gods, symbolized by the castration of Uranus, and the worship in their place of Mother Earth and her celestial handmaiden, the Moon. The Greeks looked back longingly to this joyous and peaceful time, when people, so Hesiod tells us . . .

> . . . lived with happy hearts
> Untouched by work or sorrow . . .
> . . . ungrudgingly, the fertile land
> Gave up her fruits unasked. Happy to be
> At peace, they lived with every want supplied.

The Old Moon's reaping of his father's genitals perhaps explains why Jehovah instructed Abraham that 'he that is eight days old shall be circumsized among you.' Circumcision exposes the hidden lunar glans of the penis, from whose centre emerges yellow urine and white fertilizing semen. Liquids have long been ruled by the Moon because it brings rain, and yellow and white are both lunar colours. The eighth day is wholly suitable for circumcision because the eighth day of the lunar cycle was, as we have seen, specially sacred to the Moon.

In keeping with Saturn's identification with the Old Moon, the number 8 symbolizes old age and those qualities of life that the later years bring forth, such as wisdom, self-control and patience. 8 is also the number of intuition and psychic ability, as well as being linked with money and business skills. Less happily, 8 represents gloom, despondency, regret and disillusion, and also obstacles, losses and difficulties.

8 is a potent factor in your life if you were born on the 8th, as it is, although less directly, if you started life on the 18th or the 28th. However, if your birthday falls on the latter date, you should appreciate that 28 is closely connected with the Moon, not only because 2 and 8 are both lunar numbers, but because the lunar cycle lasts for twenty-eight days. A birthday on the 28th makes you a Moon person; your life will wax and wane in keeping with the lunar rhythms, and you will feel peculiarly out-of-sorts at Full Moon. 8 is also important in the lives of those born in August, the eighth month. August was named for the Roman emperor Augustus to mark the month of his death. Coincidentally, Augustus was born in September when the Moon was lodged in the zodiac sign of Capricorn, whose planetary ruler is Saturn. Famous people with birthdays on the 8th include Sammy Davis Junior (8-12-1925), James Dean (8-2-1931), Dame Edith Evans (8-2-1888), Elvis Presley (8-1-1935), Robert Schumann (8-6-1810) and Harry S. Truman (8-5-1884).

If 8 is prominent in your birthdate you are tall and slim, with long limbs and somewhat starkly outlined bones. You have large teeth but because you don't smile very often they are seldom seen. By nature you are retiring, introspective and unemotional. You are a loner, not simply because you enjoy your own company, but because you have difficulties in getting along with others. In fact, your personal relationships are always a bit fraught, due to your lack of sense of humour and your somewhat acid tongue. You don't much care for the opposite sex and you may not marry until quite late in life, if at all. You have strong principles and a rather set way of looking at the world. You matured early and you will always seem old for your age. You dislike youthful high spirits and unruliness, as you do obvious displays of emotion. Because you have a good intuitive understanding of life, others find your thoughts and opinions valuable. However, although you are naturally conservative and law-abiding, you are quite capable of behaving aggressively if you feel you've been treated unfairly.

The colour of 8 is black, although any dark shade belongs to the number. The facial features of 8 people are strongly etched, their skin dry and sallow, and their hair coarse, straight and dark-coloured. The knees and knuckles are prominent. The direction of 8 is north-east, which is favourable for travel and residence for the 8 born. The best period for 8s occur when Saturn passes through the zodiac sign of Libra, where it is exalted, the worst when Saturn is lodged in Aries, where it is debilitated. Because Saturn moves slowly through the sky, it stays in each sign for about two years. It ended its last transit of Libra in August, 1983 and it won't be back in the sign until early next century. Likewise, Saturn won't return to Aries until April 1996.

If your vowel number is 8, you have a stable and cautious ego personality, despite your occasional odd dreams and 'I know what's going to happen' hunches. You are conventional by instinct – some would say old-fashioned – and you dress and behave prudently and sensibly. Your chief personal fault is your relaxed attitude to cleanliness, which means that your finger nails and shirt collars are likely to be grubby. Sudden change alarms you, and indeed you can't stand people who are always changing their minds or who crave excitement. Your strategy of living is to plan ahead and work towards your goals slowly and carefully. You seldom experience immediate success. In fact, success for you is always viewed as a thing of the future, the pot of gold at the end of the rainbow which gives your life a point and a purpose. This is why many 8s feel decidedly unsettled when they reach their goals and why they immediately set new ones for themselves. You are patient and determined, traits which allow you to plod on determinedly for years. You are very careful with your money, to the extent that others regard you as being tight with it, and you're certainly not the sort who splashes money around. You like to have a sum of money salted away for emergencies, and you're very keen on investing anything extra, particularly in property or land. But what is most surprising about you in view of your carefully controlled emotions is your strong sex urge. Indeed, you don't like to waste any time in gratifying your sexual desires, thus sex is one of the few things that hurries you up.

Because 8 is the number of the Sun ascending from the underworld, your ego is ideally complemented by an id symbolized by 4, the number of the afternoon Sun. You are also well served by a

2 id, for such an id, like the one symbolized by 4, has qualities that can alleviate your depressive tendencies. Less suitable is an id symbolized by 6 or 8, for both id types are too similar to your ego to be able to give it the necessary balance and lift. Similarly, an id represented by an odd number – 1, 3, 5, 7 or 9 – is unsatisfactory because it generates disruptive desires and changeable ideas which make it hard for you to feel at peace with yourself. This is especially true of a 7 id despite the lunar connections between 7 and 8. In fact, a 7 id is likely to weaken your confidence and increase your depression.

If you possess an 8 id you constantly sense that you must be careful and hold back, because such an id acts as a brake on your conscious self. In some respects this is advantageous to you, yet it may mean that you react too slowly when the circumstances call for fast action. Indeed, caution is your watchword and the slow, steady way always appeals to you more than the mad scramble. Waste, imprudence and poor organization upset you, and you feel ill-at-ease in situations where these are evident. You have great sympathy for those who want to preserve and conserve, and quite probably you belong to a conservation group yourself. You are loyal and dutiful, and your word is your bond. You hate behaving in ways that offend your sense of decency, no matter what the circumstances. But while your id seldom makes emotional demands on you, it is the source of your strong sex urge. How this is expressed depends, of course, on your ego type, but if it is adequately controlled and directed it can be a powerful aid, giving you tremendous energy and drive. Uncontrolled, it may bring you much distress and many problems. You also have trouble in forgiving and forgetting, which means you tend to waste too much time in righting old wrongs. Others find you cool and laid-back and they sense, no matter what your ego type, that you keep things from them.

If 8 your name number you are happiest outdoors at places that are wooded or mountainous, or that are near lakes and rivers. You prefer foods that grow beneath the earth, like potatoes, or those that are dark in colour, like prunes. You also enjoy eating meat and fish and all food and drink that has been matured for a long time. In particular, you like sharp tastes. Your favourite season of the year is winter, and you are strongly attracted to old people, rubbish tips, unsavoury places like brothels and low-class nightclubs, and areas of town frequented by workers, rough-necks and vagabonds. You have a talent for languages and a love of anything to do with the soil. Your lucky day of the week is Saturdya; your lucky gemstones are the garnet, the black opal and the tourmaline; your lucky flowers are the nightshade, the rose and the thistle; and your lucky colours are black, grey and indigo.

THE NUMBER 9

The number 9 is the last single odd number as well as being the last single number. In the solar cycle it corresponds to the rising Sun, specifically to that half of the Sun which is still below the horizon. Its planet is Mars, the red planet, who in mythology was the god of war.

In ancient times 9 was also linked with the Moon. We have already seen how the Moon's three phases – New, Full and Old – were represented by a trio of deities, such as Venus, Luna and Saturn. In time each god or goddess of the Moon's three phases similarly became represented by a triad, thereby increasing the number of lunar deities to nine.

9 is the number of birth and new life because the period of human gestation is nine months. Indeed, the mystery of birth and the mechanics of addition give 9 its secret meaning: it is the number of endings but also of beginnings. Gestation takes nine months and terminates with the birth of the child, while 9 itself is followed by 10, which reduces to 1 $(1 + 0 = 1)$ to start a new sequence. Thus 9 is the final stage of a continually repeated series.

Greek mythology provides many examples of 9 representing the end of one activity and the start of another. Typically, some significant event occurs on the ninth day, in the ninth month or in the ninth year.

For instance, when Phyllis, the lover of Acamas, heard that Troy had fallen she went each night to the sea-shore to watch for his ship. When it failed to appear on her ninth visit she died of grief and was transformed into an almond tree. Again, Deucalion and Pyrrha, the Greek survivors of the flood, floated helplessly in their ark for nine days before it came to rest on Mount Parnassus, while Britomartis, the daughter, like Artemis, of Leto and thus a lunar deity, was chased by Minos for nine months before eluding capture by throwing herself into the sea.

The ninth year was especially important to the Greeks because nine years comprised the Great Year of one hundred lunations, and because childhood ended for the Greeks at age nine.

Thus the god Hephaistos, having been flung from Olympus at birth by his mother Hera, is restored by her to the sacred mountain in his ninth year. And it was at the age of nine that the twins Otus and Ephialtes, both of whom stood nine fathoms tall and measured nine cubits across, attempted to scale Mount Olympus by piling Mount Pelion on Mount Ossa. Similarly, it was every ninth year that the Athenians were obliged to send a tribute of seven youths and seven maidens to Crete as an offering for the Minotaur.

9 is therefore the number of both completion and incipient regeneration, and hence of wisdom and the expert as well as ignorance and the novice, of sense and nonsense, of caution and imprudence, of virtue and licence, and of the follower and the leader. In these respects it accords with the mythological nature of the god Mars, who while being strong, fearless and skilled in warfare, was also impetuous, impatient and rash, characteristics that led to his defeat in battle on more than one occasion.

If you were born on the 9th of any month, 9 is an important influence in your life. This is also true, albeit to a lesser extent, if you were born on the 19th or the 29th. 9 is likewise important in the lives of those born in September, the ninth month, although it was originally the seventh month of the year (*Septem* is Latin for 'seven'). The Romans held games called the *Ludi Romani* in September, which ran from the 5th to the 19th of the month. Famous people with birthdays on the 9th include Kirk Douglas (9-12-1916), Edward Heath (9-7-1916), John Lennon (9-10-1940), Richard Nixon (9-1-1913), Donny Osmond (9-12-1957) and Peter the Great of Russia (9-5-1672).

Should 9 be well represented in your birthdate you are probably of average height with a strong, muscular body. If you are a man you are likely to have a moustache or a beard, or both, and if you are a woman you may be troubled with unwanted facial or body hair. Also, you possess a mark, such as a prominent mole, birthmark or scar, on your head or face. You are an outgoing, confident type with a lot of energy, courage and panache. Unfortunately, you like your own way and you can't stand being frustrated. If you are, you quickly lose your cool. Your impatience makes you accident-prone and thus a danger to both yourself and others. Because you like change, excitement and adventure, you are always ready to accept new ideas and new challenges. Yet you all too frequently start new schemes without adequate planning or thought, with the result that they often come to grief. Similarly, you just as quickly lose interest, for you are by nature a starter rather than a finisher. This is why others are wary of asking you for help because they know you cannot be relied upon.

9 is the number of red and of all roseate shades. 9 people usually have ruddy faces and curly red, brown or black hair. Their voices are loud and rather coarse and their movements are clumsy. The

direction of 9, like that of 1, is east, which is fortunate for travel and residence for both 1s and 9s. The best period for 9 people occurs when Mars passes through Capricorn, where it is exalted, their worse when Mars transits Cancer, where it is debilitated. Mars generally stays for about five weeks in each of the signs, although this can be considerably lengthened by its retrogradation. Mars next travels through Cancer between 21 May and 6 July 1987 and through Capricorn between 23 February 1988 and 6 April 1988.

If you have a 9 vowel number, which is symbolic of your ego, you possess an excitable, hot-blooded personality, which makes you both extroverted and pushy. You like to be noticed and for this reason you tend to favour brash, eye-catching clothes. Because you see things in black-and-white terms, you're either for or against in your attitudes, there being no in-between for you. You like to deal with your problems promptly and decisively, which is why you will resort to violence if all else fails. You are touchy about how others treat you, because you want and expect their deference and admiration. For this reason you have constant arguments with your friends, simply to maintain your place in the pecking order. But while you are selfish and somewhat arrogant, you more than make up for those faults with your enthusiasm and generosity. If you like someone you'll go overboard in supporting him or her, thus you make a powerful and stimulating ally. Also, because you like facing challenges and opposing those in authority, you are always ready to help someone in trouble, especially if this means you have to take on those in government or the police. Because you are open and forthright, you don't pull any punches when it comes to saying what you think. Thus you're not a hypocrite or a dissembler. You're just as open with your heart, which you lose very easily. In fact, you love the company of the opposite sex. But unfortunately, although you are always open to new ideas and experiences – to the extent that you know more about life than most – your impatience and impulsiveness often gets in the way of your wisdom and developed caution. In this respect you are the eternal optimist.

Because 9 is the number of the rising Sun, you are best served by an id symbolized by 5, the number of the setting Sun. But an id symbolized by 3 or 7 is also suitable for you, as both types complement your conscious self. This is not the case if your id is symbolized by 1, because it will be very similar to your ego in character, or by 9 itself. Your ego type is the exception where even-numbered ids are concerrned, for such ids reduce your tendency to run out of control. However, they may make you somewhat manic-depressive.

If you have a 9 id you have a turbulent inner life, and your unconscious is likely to be the source of all manner of desires, urges and images that not only make it hard for you to relax but which may upset you. You probably feel dissatisfied with what you have achieved and are constantly trying to do better. But, of course, your dissatisfaction depends on your ego type, although if you're the sort of person who likes to think ahead and plan your moves, your 9 id will naturally encourage you to take short-cuts and to run instead of walk. Such advice isn't always wrong, however, and for this reason you are well advised to pay attention to your dreams and hunches, which can guide you as to how you should proceed. Because you are inquisitive and curious you need to work in a field that satisfies your desire to know. Your sexual urge is strong and you spend quite a lot of time thinking about sex. You fall in love quickly, but not always wisely. You are not very constant in your affections, which may provoke strong guilt feelings if your ego nature believes in loyalty and fair play. You hate to be enclosed, thus you can't stand small rooms, closed doors and windows, or lifts. Indeed, any form of restriction makes you uncomfortable.

If 9 is your name number you like being in the country during the day and in town at night. You enjoy noise, colour, activity and crowds – and you can't resist watching a military display. You are fond of sports and games, pungent tastes, gold or copper jewellery and ornaments, warm temperatures, fire and fireworks, your brothers, horses and a good laugh. Your lucky day of the week is Tuesday; your lucky gemstones are the diamond and the ruby; your lucky flowers are the geranium, the gorse, the thistle and the wild rose; and your lucky colours are bright green, pink, red and russet.

2
NUMBERS AND INNER HARMONY

The two areas of the mind, the ego and the id, together reflect the polarity of nature. The ego or conscious is the part of the mind that is self-aware, the part with which we think and reflect. The id or unconscious is the part of the mind that is hidden, wherein memories, feelings and emotions are kept essentially locked away. The ego corresponds to the positive pole – to light, openness and freedom – and the id to the negative pole, that is, to darkness, confinement and restriction.

Yet there is a constant two-way interaction between the ego and the id. During the day the active ego sends all its sense impressions and thoughts to the id, where they are stored as memory. At night, when the ego is relatively quiescent, the id communicates with it symbolically through dreams. This is why Freud called dreams the 'royal road to the unconscious'.

For a person to be happy with himself and with the world harmony must exist between his ego and id. Such harmony only occurs when the id is free of troublesome feelings or when the ego ceases to be bothered by them. Disharmony thus results from tensions between the ego and the id, to the extent that meaningful interaction between them has ceased, so that they are in essence separate poles instead of being two sides of the same coin.

As we have seen, a person's ego is represented by the vowel value of his name, and his id by the consonant value. This naturally implies that the name itself symbolizes the whole man or woman.

There is nothing far-fetched about this. After all, if I ask you who you are, you will reply, 'I am John Smith', or whatever. Your name, to all intents and purposes, is you. It stands for all that you are. Indeed, there is evidence which suggests that a name is more than just symbol, but rather a shaping force. It has been shown, for example, that those with impressive or remarkable names often become impressive or remarkable people while those with ordinary names tend to stay ordinary. But there is nothing new in the idea that names have power. Down the ages countless statesmen, politicians, artists, actors and entertainers have transformed themselves by taking pseudonyms, and without their adopted names we would probably have never heard of Caligula, N. Lenin, Joseph Stalin, Leon Trotsky, Mark Twain, George Eliot, George Sand, Samuel Goldwyn, George Orwell, Ginger Rogers, Tony Curtis, Kirk Douglas, Ringo Starr, Cliff Richard, Alvin Stardust and Engelbert Humperdinck, to name but a few.

But more importantly, we can, by using our name's vowel and consonant values, determine how well each relates to the other and thus the degree of compatibility that exists between our ego and id.

This numerological way of discovering how balanced we are psychically also works practically in the other direction. For if we find that our ego and id types are incompatible, we can, by changing our names, alter either our ego or id numbers, or both, and thereby bring about a healthy change in our psyche. Such a change can and will bring about quite amazing results, as many thousands of people have discovered, while at the same time having the added advantage of being free, which qualified psychiatric help is most certainly not.

Of course, the idea of changing your name might sound daunting to you. But then, you would be very unusual if it didn't because your name is you. Yet such a change is a small price to pay for becoming a happier and better adjusted person. And anyhow, if you want to create a new you, there's no reason why the new you shouldn't have a new name.

Fortunately, however, a name change doesn't have to be radical and quite possibly you can achieve an improved vowel/consonant relationship by tinkering with your given names. Consider, for example, the case of a man named John Peter Jones, who grew up calling himself John Jones and who wasn't at all happy. Now John Jones has a vowel number of 8 and a consonant number of 3:

$$\begin{array}{llll} \text{J O H N J O N E S} \\ \quad 6 \qquad 6 \quad 5 \qquad = 17 = 8 \end{array}$$

$$\begin{array}{llll} \text{J O H N J O N E S} \\ 1 \quad 8 \; 5 \; 1 \quad 5 \quad 1 \quad = 21 = 3 \end{array}$$

John Jones thus has an 8 ego type and a 3 id type, which as we know, are incompatible, one being even numbered and one odd numbered.

But John Peter Jones has a remedy at hand by dropping his first Christian name, John, in favour of his second, Peter. Peter Jones gives him a 3 vowel number and a 7 consonant number:

$$\begin{array}{c} \text{PETER J ONES} \\ 5 \quad 5 \quad\quad 6 \quad 5 \quad\quad = 21 = 3 \end{array}$$

$$\begin{array}{c} \text{PETER J ONES} \\ 7 \quad 2 \quad 9 \quad 1 \quad 5 \quad 1 \quad = 25 = 7 \end{array}$$

A 3 ego and a 7 id are a perfect match because not only are they both odd numbered, but their numbers are opposites. Moreover, 3 is a natural ego number because it is the number of the Sun at midday, while 7 is a natural id number because it is the number of the Sun at its nadir. Furthermore, John Jones had a 3 id. By becoming Peter Jones he is able to release his troublesome id contents into his ego, his new id thereby becoming transformed into a healthier 7 type.

The name Peter Jones has another advantage, for Peter, in common with many other first names, is often shortened – to Pete. But fortunately, the name Pete Jones gives exactly the same vowel/consonant number values as Peter Jones:

$$\begin{array}{c} \text{PETE J ONES} \\ 5 \quad 5 \quad\quad 6 \quad 5 \quad\quad = 21 = 3 \end{array}$$

$$\begin{array}{c} \text{PETE J ONES} \\ 7 \quad 2 \quad\quad 1 \quad 5 \quad 1 \quad = 16 = 7 \end{array}$$

Thus Peter Jones, in terms of producing a psychologically well-adjusted person, is a perfect name.

Should it be necessary, you may also be able to improve your psychological balance just as easily, if not by using one of your other Christian names in full, then perhaps by shortening it, in the manner that Maureen can be abbreviated to Mo, Elizabeth to Liz, Reginald to Reg, Herbert to Herb or Bert, and so on. If not, you will have to adopt an entirely new Christian name to give you the number balance that you require.

It is normal, of course, for women to take a new surname when they marry and such a change either gives them improved vowel/consonant number values or worse ones. Only rarely do their vowel and consonant numbers stay the same. These changes reflect the changes in their lives that the married state brings about, improved vowel/consonant number values usually indicating a happy marriage and worsened vowel/consonant number values the reverse. It therefore follows that if an unhappily married woman alters her name in the manner described above to give herself better vowel/consonant number values, the improvement in her mental state that this will cause will enable her to function more effectively, which many in turn make her marriage happier.

Finally, it remains to be said that the profound mental changes that can be brought about by a change of name do not happen overnight. They take time, often quite a long time. How long? Well, about as long as it took Peter Jones to feel that he really is Peter Jones, and not John Jones, that is, for as long as it takes your new name to sink totally into your mind, so that it, and not your old name is you.

3
NUMBERS AND DESTINY

Our existence, it has been said, has only two certainties: one, nothing remains the same; two, life ends in death. Everything else is a guess, a perhaps and a maybe.

But not quite. There are ways of lifting Fortuna's veils and taking a peek at what lies ahead, and some of these – like astrology, palmistry and the interpretation of omens – have been used for millennia. Yet despite their age and accuracy, such methods have one major drawback: they require expert knowledge, knowledge that most people nowadays are too busy to acquire for themselves.

Fortunately, however, numerology gives anyone the power to understand the course of his or her life, in a way that is both easy to use and mathematically precise.

The most important number in this respect is the birth or destiny number. You will remember that this is obtained by adding together the numbers of one's birthdate and reducing the result to a single number.

Again, consider the birthdate 7 April 1963. This reduces to 3, the birth number:

$$7 + 4 + 1 + 9 + 6 + 3 = 30$$
$$3 + 0 = 3$$

If you haven't already done so, now is the time to calculate your own birth number.

Using your birth number, you can determine those periods of your life which are generally favourable, those which are generally unfavourable, and those which are neutral, that is, which bring good and bad in roughly equal amounts.

The system we shall use to do this is based on the seven planets of traditional astrology and the numbers associated with them. It is a very accurate method of elucidating future trends, as the examples discussed demonstrate, and should be considered carefully.

The first important fact to appreciate is that each stage of your life – or, for that matter, anyone's life – is governed by one of the planets. The order in which they govern is determined by their apparent distance from the earth. The Moon, for example, rules us at birth because it is closest to us: then comes Mercury, Venus, the Sun, Mars, Jupiter and Saturn. This order does not entirely agree with the discoveries of modern astronomy, yet it is surprisingly close.

The length of each planetary period derives from the number linked with the governing planet, which represents the same number of years. Thus because the number linked with Mars is 9, the period governed by Mars lasts for nine years.

The Moon is associated with two numbers, 2 and 7. At birth the first of these is operative, which means that the first two years of anyone's life are ruled by the Moon.

The planet Mercury is linked with 5, hence the next five years of life are ruled by Mercury.

Similarly, the next years are ruled by Venus, whose number is 6. But because the Sun, like the Moon, is linked with two numbers, 1 and 4, and because 1 is initially operative, only the succeeding year is governed by the Sun. The following nine years are ruled by Mars (9), the next three by Jupiter (3), and the next eight by Saturn (8). this takes us up to our 34th birthday.

From this age the cycle of planets repeats itself, except that instead of the Moon ruling the following two years it governs the next seven, because 7 is the second of its two numbers. Likewise, the Sun rules four years instead of only one. This second planetary cycle takes us to our 76th birthday. From then on the first cycle operates again, with the Moon ruling the next two years, so taking us to age 110 which is the greatest age that anyone can realistically hope to live to. (The oldest authenticated age to which anyone has ever lived is 113 years, 124 days, which was achieved by the French-Canadian bootmaker Pierre Joubert.)

These three complete planetary cycles correspond to the three lengths of life referred to by Indian astrologers: *Alpayu* or short life (birth to age 32), *Madhyayu* or medium life (age 32 to age 75), and *Purnayu* or full life (age 75 to 120). The Indians believe that the full human lifespan is 120, which accords with Genesis 5:3 – 'And the Lord said, My spirit shall not always strive with man, for that he also is flesh: yet his days shall be an hundred and twenty years.'

The table below shows the planetary periods of human life and their length:

	Planet	Number	Age
First Cycle	Moon	2	0-2
	Mercury	5	2-7
	Venus	6	7-13
	Sun	1	13-14
	Mars	9	14-23
	Jupiter	3	23-26
	Saturn	8	26-34
Second Cycle	Moon	7	34-41
	Mercury	5	41-46
	Venus	6	46-52
	Sun	4	52-56
	Mars	9	56-65
	Jupiter	3	65-68
	Saturn	8	68-76
Third Cycle	Moon	2	76-78
	Mercury	5	78-83
	Venus	6	83-89
	Sun	1	89-90
	Mars	9	90-99
	Jupiter	3	99-102
	Saturn	8	102-110

This table will enable you to discover which plantary period you are currently in. Obviously, if you are 24 years old you are under the rulership of Jupiter, if 70 years old you are under the rulership of Saturn.

The first point of importance about these planetary periods is that each will treat you in a manner determined by your birth number. Some will be favourable, some unfavourable and some neutral. Thus a continuous, yet consistent cycle of change threads its way through your life, the key to which is provided by your birth number.

There are two types of favourable period: the good or single positive (+) and the very good or double positive (++). Likewise, there are two types of unfavourable period, the bad or single negative (−) and the very bad or double negative (− −). By contrast, there is only one type of neutral period (0). These periods correspond to the positive, negative and neutral points of the solar cycle, which are illustrated over the page.

To determine the nature of your own life periods, you must put your birth number at the double positive (++) sunrise position and

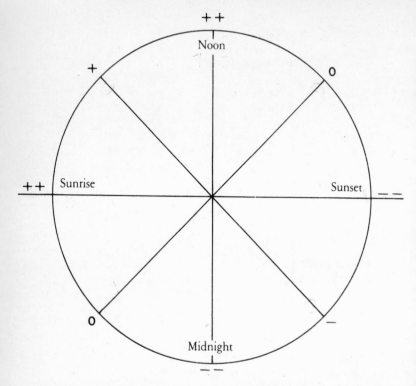

place the remaining numbers in sequence around the circle. The numbers and the periods they and their planets rule all take the positive, negative and neutral qualities of the points where they fall. The diagram at the top of the next page shows how the sequence would look if your birth number is 7.

This tells us that the most favourable or double positive periods (++) are linked with 7, 1 and 9 and the favourable or single positive periods (+) with 8, that the most unfavourable or double negative periods (− −) are linked with 3 and 5 and the unfavourable or single negative periods (−) with 4, and that the neutral periods are linked with 2 and 6. The table opposite shows how these would appear in your life.

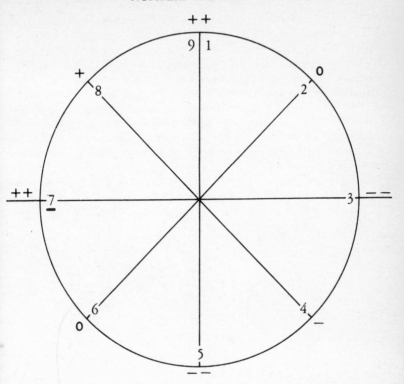

Planet	Number	Age	Nature	
Moon	2	0-2	0	
Mercury	5	2-7	− −	
Venus	6	7-13	0	
Sun	1	13-14	+ +	
Mars	9	14-23	+ +	
Jupiter	3	23-26	− −	
Saturn	8	26-34	+	
Moon	7	34-41	+ +	
Mercury	5	41-46	− −	
Venus	6	46-52	0	
Sun	4	52-56	−	
Mars	9	56-65	+ +	
Jupiter	3	65-68	− −	
Saturn	8	68-76	+	etc.

This means that up until the age of 76 your best life periods would lie between the ages of 13 and 14 (1), 14 and 23 (9), 34 and 41 (7) and 56 and 65 (9). Conversely, your most difficult periods would lie between the ages of 2 and 7 (5), 23 and 26 (3), 41 and 46 (5) and 65 and 68 (3). The other periods would all fall somewhere between these two extremes, being either single positive, single negative or neutral.

The nature of the life periods are obviously different for those with different birth numbers, withe the exception of those with a birth number of either 1 or 9, who, because their birth numbers occupy the same point in the solar cycle, share life periods having the same nature.

The following solar wheel shows the positive, negative and neutral number points of someone having a 4 birth number:

For this person the double positive periods (++) lie between the

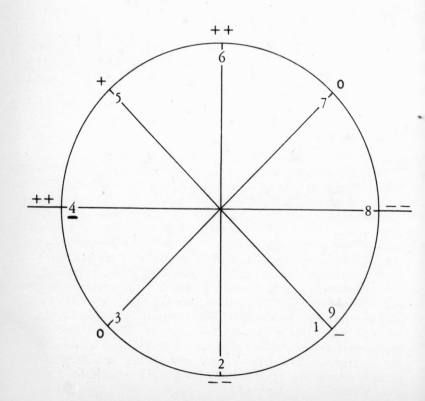

ages of 7 and 13 (6), 46 and 52 (6) and 51 and 56 (4), at least up until the age of 76. The double negative periods lie between birth and the age of 2 (2), 26 and 34 (8) and 68 and 76 (8).

The table below shows the nature of the life periods for each of the nine birth number types:

Planet	Age	Birth Number								
		1	2	3	4	5	6	7	8	9
Moon (2)	0-2	+	++	0	- -	-	- -	0	++	+
Mercury (5)	2-7	- -	0	++	+	++	0	- -	-	- -
Venus (6)	7-13	-	- -	0	++	+	++	0	- -	-
Sun (1)	13-14	++	0	- -	-	- -	0	++	+	++
Mars (9)	14-23	++	0	- -	-	- -	0	++	+	++
Jupiter (3)	23-26	++	+	++	0	- -	-	- -	0	++
Saturn (8)	26-34	0	- -	-	- -	0	++	+	++	0
Moon (7)	34-41	- -	-	- -	0	++	+	++	0	- -
Mercury (5)	41-46	- -	0	++	+	++	0	- -	-	- -
Venus (6)	46-52	-	- -	0	++	+	++	0	- -	-
Sun (4)	52-56	0	++	+	++	0	- -	-	- -	0
Mars (9)	56-65	++	0	- -	-	- -	0	++	+	++
Jupiter (3)	65-68	++	+	++	0	- -	-	- -	0	++
Saturn (8)	68-76	0	- -	-	- -	0	++	+	++	0
Moon (2)	76-78	+	++	0	- -	-	- -	0	++	+
Mercury (5)	78-83	- -	0	++	+	++	0	- -	-	- -
Venus (6)	83-89	-	- -	0	++	+	++	0	- -	-
Sun (1)	89-90	++	0	- -	-	- -	0	++	+	++

By looking down the column under your birth number you can now see which life periods (or ages) will be good for you, which bad and which neutral. The good periods are the ones which have the greatest potential for happiness and success, when things tend to fall into place for you and when life is generally easier. The bad periods – especially the ones that are double negative (– –) – are those which throw up the biggest problems and difficulties, when life tends to be less enjoyable and more fraught. In particular, these are more likely to produce illness, accidents and death, although the worst does not by any means always happen in a double negative period. For just as a double positive period has the most potential for good, so the double negative period has the most potential for bad. If you are wise you will take maximum advantage of the former – to study, to start a business, to marry – while proceeding cautiously and prudently during the latter. In this way you can accentuate the good and minimize the bad.

An examination of the lives of the famous reveals that most reached the pinnacle of their success during a double positive period, and that their major difficulties, sometimes even their deaths, happen in a double negative period. A few examples will demonstate this.

Elvis Presley, nicknamed 'the Pelvis', burst onto the music scene in the mid-1950s, to quickly become the most dynamic singing star the world has ever seen. He almost single-handedly launched rock 'n' roll, and his driving singing style, sexy movements and outrageous clothes were widely admired and imitated.

But although Elvis Presley was destined to become very rich and famous, he was born into humble circumstances on 8 January 1935, the son of Vernon and Gladys Presley, both poor, working-class whites.

Elvis's birthdate gave him a 9 birth number:

$$8+1+1+9+3+5 = 27$$
$$2 + 7 = 9$$

As can be seen from the above table, the first two years of Elvis Presley's life were single positive ones; the following eleven years, however, weren't nearly so good. His five-year Mercury period from age 2 to 7 was double negative and his six-year Venus period from the age of 7 to 13 was single negative. His family's fortunes remained at a low ebb at this time, both parents working at a succession of low-paid jobs, their joint income too low to enable them to move from the two-room wood shack where Elvis had been born. Their nadir happened during Elvis's five-year Mercury period, when father Vernon was sent to gaol for trying to cash a forged cheque.

Elvis started a double positive (++) Sun period on his 13th birthday and that year – 1948 – things started to change for the better. The Presley family moved to Memphis, a city of some size and a growing music centre, and it wasn't long before they were housed in a large and quite pleasant apartment at Lauderdale Court. Elvis was sent to Humes High School and on graduating in 1952 he found himself a job as a truck-driver, while making tentative efforts to launch a singing career.

Elvis left school and started work during his double positive Mars period, which began for him at the age of 14 and continued until his 23rd birthday (1949-58). It was during this period that he leapt to stardom. In 1954 he had gained the stage at Overton Park Shell in Memphis, making up part of a local music show. In 1955, 'That's All

Right, Mama' was released, making him a local celebrity. Then in 1956 'Heartbreak Hotel' became a national hit, and Elvis's appearance on the Ed Sullivan show sent him rocketing into orbit. From that moment on his records consistently topped the charts and teenagers everywhere went wild for him.

The Mars period ended on his birthday in 1958. It was followed, however, by another double positive period, one which lasted for three years and was ruled by the planet Jupiter (1958-61).

Apart from being the planet of growth and increase, Jupiter governs religion, education and travel. Thus it was perhaps not surprising that Elvis was inducted into the Army in March 1958 and was soon afterwards posted to Germany. But the stunned world had no reason to worry about his fortunes. He remained as popular as ever and his records continued to sell like hot cakes.

Elvis's two-year Army stint ended in March 1960, when he returned to America. He immediately made some new records, employing both a different style and a different band. Two of these records – 'It's Now or Never' and 'Are you Lonesome Tonight?' – became his biggest sellers.

il1Elvis Presley's decline as a singing star can be dated to 1961, when he started an eight-year neutral period ruled by Saturn (1961-9). It was during this period that he stopped making live appearances and instead concentrated on becoming a film-star. He was to appear in a total of thirty-three films, the majority of which were candy floss epics, characterized by poor acting, poor plots and poor songs. Never again was Elvis Presley to be the raunchy rocker of his pre-Army days.

In 1967 he married Priscilla Beaulieu, and their daughter Lisa was born on 1 February 1968 – exactly nine months to the day after their marriage. Like her father, Lisa Presley has a 9 birth number.

The eight-year neutral period, which was more than a little disappointing to Elvis's fans, ended on the singer's birthday in 1969. It was followed by two double negative periods, the first lasting seven years and ruled by the Moon (1969-76), the second lasting five years and ruled by Mercury (1976-81). These periods were to be the most difficult and tragic of Elvis's life, notwithstanding the fact that he began touring again. For he had become a drug addict, a habit begun in his neutral period but which became far more serious in 1969. After his divorce from Priscilla in 1973, a break-up that affected him deeply, he went into a steady decline, his health rapidly worsening: he suffered from a chronic weight problem, diabetes, digestive disorders, glaucoma and heart irregularities, all of which were adversely affected by his heavy drug-taking.

Elvis Presley died suddenly in his bathroom on 16 August 1977, about eighteen months after the start of his second double negative period.

Of course, Elvis Presley is a special case and his life should not be regarded as a mirror for those with a 9 birth number. Few people with this birth number will experience either the huge success or the steep decline and early death of Elvis Presley. Yet they will find that the same double positive periods off them their greatest advantages and the same double negative periods their biggest difficulties.

By way of contrast, we will next consider the life of Adolf Hitler, the German dictator and founder of Nazism.

Hitler was born in Braunau-am-Inn, Austria, on 20 April 1889. He therefore had a birth number of 5:

$$2+0+4+1+8+8+9=32$$
$$3+2=5$$

Despite the fact that the first two years of his life were single negative (1889-91), he survived them, which was more than his two brothers had done, and the close relationship he enjoyed with his mother doubtless helped make the following five years (1891-6) as positive as they were. He began a single positive period on his 7th birthday in 1896, and this lasted until his 13th birthday in 1902, when he began three consecutive double negative periods. The first, ruled by the Sun, lasted for one year (1902-3). The second, ruled by Mars, ran for nine years (1903-12), and the third, ruled by Jupiter, lasted for three years (1912-15). This long and difficult period had a decisive psychological effect on Hitler, for it was during this time that he acquired his deep hatred of Jews and of liberal values and developed his admiration for Germany.

Hitler's father Alois died in 1903, at the start of young Adolf's double negative Mars period. He left school in 1905 without the normal leaving certificate, one of his masters describing him as being 'notoriously cantankerous, wilful, arrogant and bad-tempered', and spend the next two years drifitng around Linz, where he and his sick mother Klara were then living. In 1907 he went to Vienna, where he twice unsuccessfully tried to gain a place at the Academy of Fine Arts. For the next three years he lived in a men's hostel and supported himself by doing odd jobs. He said later, 'Vienna was a hard school for me, but it taught me the most profound lessons of my life.'

In 1913, during the three-year double negative Jupiter period,

Hitler moved to Munich in German Bavaria. The following year the First World War broke out and he immediately volunteered for active service. He was in uniform throughout the war, and he was wounded twice and twice decorated with the Iron Cross. He never rose, however, above the rank of corporal.

Hitler began a neutral period on his 26th birthday in 1915 and it was after this date that he won the decorations mentioned above. Certainly the quality of his life improved. At the end of the war he stayed on in the Army, was made an education officer and was sent to Munich to counter Communist propaganda and to observe the activities of small political groups.

In September 1919 he attended a meeting of the German Workers' Party and was immediately attracted by its policies. He joined it and became, oddly enough, its fifty-fifth member, receiving a membership card numbered 555. He rose quickly through its ranks, helped swell its membership with his rousing speeches, and on 24 February 1920 announced its anti-Semitic, pro-Aryan racial policies to a crowd of 2,000 at the Hofbrauhous beer cellar in Munich. The party's name was augmented to the National Socialist German Workers' Party – or Nazi Party, for short – and the swastika and the raised arm salute were adopted as its symbols. The following year Adolf Hitler became its leader.

But things did not go entirely Hitler's way during this neutral period. He injudiciously proclaimed a revolution in 1923, but his 'march on Berlin' was broken up by the police, who shot and killed sixteen of his followers. For this debacle Hitler was sent to gaol for nine months.

Hitler's birthday in 1923 saw the end of the eight-year neutral period which had governed his life since 1915 and the start of a double positive period. In fact, two double positive periods ran consecutively for him, the first a seven-year period ruled by the Negative Moon (1923-30), the second a five-year period ruled by Mercury (1930-35). It was during this long twelve-year period that Adolf Hitler rose to supreme power in Germany, for despite the Nazis' defeat in the 1928 elections, the continuing economic downswing ensured that they more than recouped their losses in the elections of 1930, when they became the second largest political party in Germany. Chancellor Franz von Papen called another election in 1932, in the hope of factionalizing the Nazis, but their share of the Reichstag seats again increased. The following year, after von Papen had been forced to resign, Adolf Hitler was made Chancellor. In 1934 Hitler eliminated his rivals in the Nazi Party and on Hindenberg's death in the August of that year he assumed the title of President. He had become the Führer, the leader.

Hitler began a single positive period on his birthday in 1935 which lasted for six years (1935-41). During this period he successfully reduced German unemployment and began to put his plans for German reunification, which he had described in *Mein Kampf*, into action. He stripped German Jews of their citizenship and initiated the 'Final Solution'. In 1936 he invaded the Rhineland and in 1938 he annexed Austria. In September 1938 he signed the Munich Agreement with Neville Chamberlain, Daladier and Mussolini. The following year he annexed Bohemia and Morovia, thereafter signing the Pact of Steel with Italy on 22 May and, to everybody's amazement, a non-aggression treaty with Russia on 23 August. On 1 September 1939 Hitler ordered his troops into Poland, to which Britain and France responded by declaring war on Germany on 3 September. The Second World War had begun.

The success of the German forces continued, however, due largely to the unpreparedness of the Allies. Hitler's Stormtroops quickly overran Denmark and Norway, then France, Belgium, Holland and Luxenburg. Yet the planned invasion of Britain was not mounted, because the Luftwaffe were defeated by the RAF in the Battle of Britain. It was this reverse that persuaded Hitler to go ahead with his plans for the invasion of Russia. Operation Barbarossa was launched on 22 June 1941, just two months after the start of the four-year neutral period which governed Hitler's life until 1945. The invasion of Russia proceeded far more quickly and successfully than Hitler expected, and it seemed likely that the German Army would reach Moscow by Christmas 1941. But there was a sudden stiffening of Russian resolve, which had been badly shaken by the speed and force of the German attack, and the rate of the Wermacht's advance was slowed. This marked, although Hitler did not know it at the time, the beginning of the end for the Third Reich. Hitler's days were numbered.

It is unnecessary to chart the remaining course of the war – the retreat from Moscow, the entry into the conflict of the United States, the allied victories – except to remark that the noose kept tightening around Germany's neck. By April 1945 the Russians had surrounded Berlin, trapping the Führer in his underground bunker. On 20 April Hitler celebrated his 56th birthday, which also marked the start of a double negative period ruled by Mars. Nine days later he married his mistress Eva Braun. The following day – 30 April 1945 – he shot himself. Not long afterwards the war ended and Europe began picking up the pieces. The nightmare was over.

Adolf Hitler's life demonstrates, like that of Elvis Presley's, that it is the double positive periods which offer the greatest potential for advancement. The key double positive period in this respect is the one ruled by the planet associated with one's birth number. Elvis Presley (birth number 9) became internationally famous as a singer during the nine-year Mars period that governed his life between the ages of 13 and 23, and Adolf Hitler (birth number 5) became dictator of Germany during the five-year Mercury period that governed him between the ages of 41 and 46. But such a period is, however, a moment of time which has to be seized: it does not automatically confer its blessing upon those living through it. Both Elvis Presley and Adolf Hitler had set their goals and were working towards them when their moment came. They made their right time work for them.

Similarly, the most hazardous double negative period is the one linked with the number that lies opposite one's birth number in the solar cycle. For example, 5 is the number lying opposite 9 in the solar cycle and it was during the five-year Mercury period that ruled his life between ages 41 and 46 that Elvis Presley died (at age 42). Likewise, 1 and 9 are the numbers that lie opposite 5 in the solar cycle and it was during the nine-year Mars period that ruled his life between the ages of 56 and 65 that Adolf Hitler died (at age 56). Of course, death does not always happen during such a period, but one is always at risk.

Finally, let us take a brief look at the career of Margaret Thatcher, the Prime Minister of Britain.

Margaret Hilda Thatcher was born on 13 October 1925. She thus has a 4 birth number

$$1 + 3 + 1 + 0 + 1 + 9 + 2 + 5 = 22$$
$$2 + 2 = 4$$

Mrs Thatcher spent her childhood in the town of her birth – Grantham in Lincolnshire – and she has often said how happy it was and how she draws strength from the values it taught her. It is therefore not surprising to find that she enjoyed a five-year single positive period between the ages of 2 and 7 (1927-32), which was followed by a six-year double positive period between the ages of 7 and 13 (1932-38). She then began a long and less fortunate period which ran from her 13th birthday to her 41st. This consisted of (1) two consecutive single negative periods, the first lasting a year (1938-

39), the second nine years (1939-48), during the latter part of which she attended Oxford University and gained a degree in Chemistry, (2) a three-year neutral period (1948-51) when she worked as a research chemist and began to study law, (3) an eight-year double negative period (1951-9), during which she completed her law studies, being called to the Bar in 1953, and (4) another neutral period which lasted for seven years (1959-66). She married her husband Denis when she was 25, just before she began the double negative period, and she entered Parliament in 1959, shortly after the double negative period ended.

Although we know little about Mrs Thatcher's private life and inner feelings between 1938 and 1966, the fact that she changed her career three times – from research chemist to lawyer to politician – while coping with being a wife and mother, suggests that the period was neither easy nor particularly satisfying for her.

Mrs Thatcher's fortunes improved at the age of 41 when she began a five-year single positive period ruled by Mercury (1966-71). She served with distinction in Edward Heath's government (1970-74), which overlapped the start of her six-year double positive Venus period in 1971. After the Conservatives' 1974 electoral defeat she stood as party leader, which she became in 1975, at 49. The double positive period ended on her 52nd birthday in 1977, but was immediately followed by another, a four-year period ruled by the Negative Sun (1977-81) and linked with her 4 birth number. It was during this period, in 1979 at age 53, that Mrs Thatcher became Prime Minister..

Mrs Thatcher began a Mars-ruled single negative period on her 56th birthday in 1981 and this will run for nine years until her 65th birthday in 1990. In all probability this period won't be as successful for her as the two previous periods, despite the increased popularity she gained as a result of the 1982 Falklands Crisis and her resounding election victory of 1983. Indeed, she will need to guide the Ship of State with great care if she is to save both it and herself from the rocks.

4

NUMBERS AND PATHWAYS

Just as your birth number creates the good, the bad and the neutral periods of our life, so it also gives your life direction. Birth presents the individual with a bewildering range of possibilites which are narrowed down by the birth number, to give you or anyone else a reduced number of pathways to follow. Thus the individual is free, but not entirely free. He or she can make choices but the choices are restricted.

Such pathways are by no means limited to only one birth number. In fact, they often join with those originating from other numbers, forming common routes down which many can pass. But the going is not equally easy for all. Some will find the way straight and smooth, while others will have a difficult time of it. And some won't get started at all. To them the way is effectively barred.

An example will make this clear. Since the Second World War, Great Britain has had nine different prime ministers: Clement Attlee, Winston Churchill, Anthony Eden, Harold Macmillan, Alec Douglas-Home, Harold Wilson, Edward Heath, James Callaghan and Margaret Thatcher. We might expect, if the birth number is entirely unrelated to one's path in life, these nine to have a varied selection of birth numbers, not all nine perhaps, but two of one, two of another, one of this and one of that, etc. But nothing could be further from the truth. The nine prime ministers each have either a 4 birth number, a 6 birth number or a 7 birth number.

The actual birth numbers possessed by each are: Clement Attlee, 6; Winston Churchill, 7; Anthony Eden, 7; Harold Macmillan, 7; Alec Douglas-Home, 4; Harold Wilson, 4; Edward Heath, 6; James Callaghan, 7; and Margaret Thatcher, 4.

Four prime ministers had a 7 birth number, three had (or have) a 4 birth number and two had a 6 birth number. Thus, judged on this group of post-war prime ministers, it would seem that the pathway to premiership is only open to those with a 4, 6 or 7 birth number, and that the going is easiest for those with a 7 birth number, somewhat harder for those with a 4 birth number, and hardest for those with a 6 birth number.

If we examine the birth numbers of the remaining twentieth-century British prime ministers we find that while other numbers do turn up, there is still a bias in favour of 4, 6 and 7. These are the birth numbers of the other prime ministers of this century: Archibald Rosebury, 5; Arthur Balfour, 8; Henry Campbell-Bannerman, 7; Herbert Asquith, 1; David Lloyd George, 9; Andrew Bonar Law, 2; Stanley Baldwin, 6; Ramsay MacDonald, 7; and Neville Chamberlain, 9.

Out of this total of eighteen people who reached the highest political office in the land six had a 7 birth number, three a 4 birth number, three a 6 birth number, two a 9 birth number, one a 1 birth number, one a 2 birth number, one a 5 birth number and one an 8 birth number. No prime minister had a 3 birth number. This demonstrates that while the pathway to Number 10 is very difficult to negotiate for those with a 1, 2, 5 or an 8 birth number, it is impassible for those having a birth number of 3.

Despite the good intentions of those entering politics, it remains a dirty business. Those that get to the top are the toughest, sharpest and most ambitious of the lot. Luck plays its part, yet it is a particular personality that wins the olive wreath. It therefore isn't surprising that those with a 7 birth number are most likely to succeed. 7 is the number of the Negative Moon and it gives its possessor access to those negative qualities stemming from the dark side of the Moon, such as duplicity, stealth, guile and charm, as well as the power of hypnotic influence. And because 7 is the number of death, it is, like death, 'all-conquering' – or, at least, very nearly. Likewise, 4 is the number of the Negative Sun, the number of the Sun descending towards the underworld, and its qualities of strength and determination are admixed with the darker one of ruthless ambition and the need to be in charge. No one can deny the attractiveness and charm of Alec Douglas-Home, Harold Wilson and Margaret Thatcher, each of whom has a 4 birth number, or the mailed fist that each conceals in a velvet glove. The other number bringing greatest success in British politics is 6, the number of Venus, which is, like 7, a number of the underworld. For while we now think of Venus as the most delightful of the ancient goddesses, she in fact had two sides: she was a love goddess and a war goddess, just as her planet appears as the lucky morning star and as the malevolent evening star. Thus depite the beauty and artistic talents of those born with a 6 birth number, such people are the possessors of altogether darker gifts.

In the United States, where good looks and a pleasing personality are more important in political life than they are in Britain, those with a 6 birth number have the most success in getting into the White House. Indeed, of the sixteen presidents that America has had this century, four have had a 6 birth number, the last being Richard Nixon. In second place come those with a 2 birth number, of whom there have been three, the most recent being Ronald Reagan. However, the possession of a 7 birth number, which is so important for political success in Britain, gives no more advantage than a birth number of 5, 8 or 9, each of which have belonged to two presidents. Yet it is significant that the two presidents who had a 7 birth number – Harry S. Truman and John F. Kennedy – were the most memorable.

In strange contrast to the British experience, a 4 birth number worked against those hoping to become President, for nobody having this number has reached the White House this century. The American people don't care for the concealed, yet evident ruthlessness of the Negative Moon.

But as in Britain, those born with a 3 birth number don't make it to the top of the political tree either. This century has produced no presidents with such a birth number. Thus it's thumbs down on both sides of the Atlantic for the poor 3s. Indeed, Edward Kennedy (birth number 3) was perhaps wiser than we think when he withdrew from the last presidential election.

It is now time to describe the chief pathways belonging to each of the nine birth numbers. But first it must be pointed out that because the birth number represents certain character traits possessed by its owner, these will either be the same as or similar to the ego character delineated by the vowel number or quite different. If your birth number is the same as your vowel number, then the description of your character traits and job preferences given below will be exact. But if they are different you should take the information given for your birth number as your primary guide and that given for your vowel as your secondary guide. The truth will be a mix of the two.

If your birth number is 1: 1 is the number of the Positive Sun and gives you the twin advantages of self-confidence and self assurance. You are determined and resourceful and you are quick to make the most of whatever opportunities come your way. These traits, combined with your solar energy, aggression and desire to succeed, help you get to the top, which is where you believe you deserve to be. You enjoy being in charge: you like organizing, directing and giving orders.

And because you believe in yourself and your ideas, you are not shy of taking responsibility and making decisions. Yet you are by no means power-mad, and your innate sympathy and understanding usually enable you to enjoy good relations with your subordinates. Also, you are fortunate in being able to instil confidence and provide inspiration. Because you work hard and have clear goals, you always stand a good chance of getting where you want to be. Your chief fault is your extravagance, thus you should avoid handling other people's money. Other handicaps include your conservatism and your gullibility. You are attracted to and function well in all areas of business and commerce, the Church, the legal profession, local politics, political science, community work, teaching and lecturing, government service, medicine (especially the care of the heart and blood system), public relations and any occupation having to do with gold. You also enjoy involvement in trade unions, working for royalty or the aristocracy in a supervisory capacity, and participation in those artistic activities such as acting, which can bring both fame and financial reward. In a similar way you are attracted to military service. In short, you want to be respected, honoured and appreciated.

If your birth number is 2: 2 is the number of the Positive Moon and gives you both a rising spirit and the important quality of quiet persistence. You are not, however, as go-getting as those with a 1 birth number, thus you seldom desire the top job. You get on well with other people and you usually enjoy good relations with your workmates. Indeed, you prefer working with others than by yourself. Your natural concern for your fellows inclines you to work for charities, clinics or hospitals, or as a social worker, counsellor or probation officer – that is, in some role that allows you to be of service to others. In a similar way, your unique ability to understand the point of view and the problems of others, makes you a natural diplomat, advisor and mediator. Because you also have a good imagination and artistic talent, you are drawn to work in advertising, interior and architectual design, public relations, painting and decorating, and also to the legal profession, journalism, the Church, catering, domestic work, building, estate agencing, buying and selling antiques and second-hand goods, farming, bartending, waiting, teaching and anything to do with the sea and with fluids. Ideally, you want to give rather than to receive and to be valued for yourself.

If your birth number is 3: 3 is the number of Jupiter and it marks you out as a higher soul, as someone who is less concerned with selfish ends than with promoting justice, helping others and increasing knowledge. Your kindly and generous character stops you from doing work that is at all dishonest or disreputable, or that requires you to be pushy and assertive. Yet your love of travel and change makes you avoid those jobs that are dull and repetitive, or which tie you down. You are naturally optimistic and cheerful, and you rarely flinch from taking on something that others find too difficult. Because you enjoy being outdoors, you are attracted to any work that gets you outside, particularly if this involves sport, animals or defending your country. You are also interested in community work, the Church, teaching and academic research, medicine and hospital work, editing and publishing, writing, civil engineering, the civil service, insurance, archaeology, music, dowsing and mediumship, geology, travel agencing, hairstyling, the sale of drugs and herbalism. But no matter what job you do you will always strive to increase your knowledge through study, just as you will always adhere to your religious beliefs.

If your birth number is 4: 4 is the number of the Negative Sun and it gives you a friendly public face which masks a deeper, more complex hidden person. This means that despite your friendliness you are very detached, and indeed you place great importance on your independence. You hate being tied down or ordered about, thus you are only really happy in a job which allows you to be your own boss. You benefit from your solar energy, which enables you to keep plugging away at something long after others would have called it a day. This can, however, be both a strength and a weakness, for sometimes you refuse to give up despite there being no chance of success. Indeed, you are motivated chiefly by the desire for success, which goads you constantly like a spur. You are attracted to those occupations that allow you to be both independent and creative, thus freelance creative work is ideal for you, such as freelance photography, journalism, song-writing, designing, entertaining, etc. You are also drawn to the occult and to anything strange or bizarre, as well as to astronomy and science, dancing and choreography, theatre direction and singing, writing and publishing, engineering, computing, anything electrical, banking, surveying, psychiatry, the post office and railways, teaching,laboratory work, politics and office work. Because self-realization is so important to you, you care very little about what others think of you. You always try to do your own thing.

If your birth number is 5: 5 is the number of Mercury and it indicates you have a quick, active brain, a persuasive tongue and a desire to go ahead. You function best in jobs that allow you to use your wits and your powers of persuasion, thus manual work or work that is uninteresting is not for you. You also require plenty of change and variety in your work and this can lead you to change your job quite often. You will also moonlight if the opportunity arises. But you are not overly ambitious and you do not want to be encumbered with heavy responsibilities. Your anxious disposition may make you too fussy and too preoccupied with details, which can have a deleterious effect on your working relationships. Yet you generally get on well with others, for you prefer to work as part of a team rather than alone. The following jobs are examples of those that both attract you and which can give you fulfilment: salesman, journalist, writer, teacher or instructor, tour guide, advertising copy-writer, public relations consultant, lawyer, government official, political scientist, engineer, radio and television announcer, record producer, actor, courier, taxi-driver, transport manager, architect and inventor. You will inevitably face set-backs and disappointments in your career, but your high spirits and ready sense of fun will help you to cope with these.

If your birth number is 6: 6 is the number of Venus and it indicates that you have a natural distaste for any job that is dirty and unpleasant. Thus, in general, manual work does not appeal to you. Your friendly and easy manner enables you to get on well with others, to the extent that you seldom have conflicts with your colleagues. Although you like the outdoors and anything to do with farming and gardening, you are drawn to jobs that are glamorous, such as those connected with the arts, with fashion and beauty, and with health care. You have a talent for buying and selling, for arbitration and for pleasing others. You also enjoy acting as an intermediary, which is required in public relations, law and diplomacy. You don't, however, like work that is too taxing, for you are rather lazy. But you do like money and you expect to be well-paid for what you do. Generally speaking, you favour those jobs that bring you into contact with the public and which allow you to exercise certain skills, such as hairdressing, massage, social work, sports training, decorating and designing, selling perfume and cosmetics, art work and stationery, publishing, engraving, pawnbroking, bartending and retailing second-hand goods. But you should be aware of your darker side which could, in the wrong circumstances, lead you into pornography, drug-dealing and prostitution.

If your birth number is 7: 7 is the number of the Negative Moon and it reveals that you have a rather romantic attitude to life as well as strange yearnings. You have a restless disposition, which not only prompts you to change your job quite often but makes you impatient with anything that stops you going forwards as fast as you would like. Because your colleagues tend to misunderstand you, your relations with them are often fraught. You like having money, yet you are careless with it, hence you should avoid handling other people's money. You are imaginative and creative, but although you can work hard to achieve a particular goal, you dislike discipline and routine. You are attracted to glamorous jobs, such as those connected with the arts or with entertainment, and to politics, community work and academic research, to maritime activities (especially those having to do with overseas trade), and to any work that is theoretical rather than practical. Your interest in the welfare of others can lead you into medicine (you are fascinated by disorders of the nervous system), nursing, social work, veterinary science, chiropody, chiropractic and the rehabilitation of those with drink or drug problems. Also, you enjoy writing, trade union activities, selling drugs and medicines, playing a musical instrument, and restaurant work. Your sensitivity to the needs of others and your natural psychic gifts give you an almost mystical power, which can, of course, be used for either good or evil.

If your birth number is 8: 8 is the number of Saturn and it indicates that you have a sober and practical approach to life. Your logical and analytical brain enables you to plan and organize; it allows you to take responsibility. You are patient, persistent and ambitious, thus you are quite capable of working towards long-term goals. Indeed, you rarely expect overnight success. Additionally, you have a good memory, a talent for languages and an ability to keep your temper. Despite the fact that you are a loner, you get on well with others, especially if they are older than you. The sort of job that most attracts you is one that both offers security and the chance to move ahead. But you are paradoxical in that although you are conservative and conventional, your type of job can be drawn from a very wide field. You are interested in commerce and government service, building and architectural design, mining and farming, science and engineering, law and police work, musical composition and singing (you are blessed with an excellent voice), dentistry and medicine (especially disorders of the bones and skin), boxing, both as a fighter and promoter, estate agencing, funeral directing, computer programming and systems analysis. You are the archetypal strong, silent type and you set your goals when you are quite young: you then dedicate your life to achieving them.

If your birth number is 9: 9 is the number of Mars and it reveals that you have a complex character, because it marks the end of one solar cycle and the start of another. Thus while you are mature and wise, you also have a youthful naîvety and a restless desire for adventure. In a similar way you are selfish and aggressive but also introspective and uncertain. Yet your readiness to get up and get going makes you a pioneer, and your enthusiasm, for the task ahead gives inspiration to others. Less happily, you lose interest quickly and so seldom complete what you begin. Because you are very independent and like being in charge, you hate any work that puts you in a subservient role. You are attracted to the Armed Forces, although you would not wish to remain a foot soldier, and to the manufacture of weapons and machine tools. You are likewise interested in surgery and medical research (especially that relating to cancer, blood ailments and bowel and bladder disorders), science (especially biology, genetics and physics), advertising, banking, stockbroking, insurance, accountancy, acting and entertaining, butchering, sport and farming, and to hunting, animal-training and zoo-keeping. You love tinkering with machinery and you enjoy fixing things. But despite all your energy and enthusiasm you are always aware that you could be doing better.

5
NUMBER-RHYTHMS

In Chapter Three it was shown how everyone's life is made up of an alternating series of positive, negative and neutral periods, which can be determined by using the birth number and the solar cycle. The shortest of these periods lasts for one year (a 1 or Positive Sun period) and the longest for nine years (a 9 or Mars period). Quite often periods having a similar value follow one another, to give an extended positive, negative or neutral period. For example, those with a birth number of 1 or 9 enjoy three consecutive double positive periods between the ages of 13 and 26, while those with a 5 birth number experience three double negative periods running consecutively at this time, which is why their teens and years of early adulthood are so difficult.

But the terms 'positive', 'negative' and 'neutral' only apply to the period they describe as a whole, not to all of the days that make it up. Thus while a double positive period may bring the happiest moments, the best opportunities and the greatest triumphs of a person's life, some of its individual days will be difficult and some unhappy. And likewise, a double negative period has plenty of days that contrast with its overall nature and which in fact make it bearable.

Indeed, each life period is made up of good or positive days, bad or negative days and neutral days. Of course, the best days are the good days of a double positive period, the worst are the bad days of a double negative period. The wise man and woman will take maximum advantage of the former and be extra careful on the latter.

The first step in determining the nature of any day is to reduce its date to a single number. Let us take as our example 10 June 1984. Because June is the sixth month of the year this date reduces as follows:

$$1+0+6+1+9+8+4 = 29$$
$$2 + 9 = 11$$
$$1 + 1 = 2$$

10 June 1984 is thus a 2 day. How it will respond to you depends on your birth number, for days are like the life periods: they can either be single positive or double positive, single negative or double negative, or neutral. In fact any day will be all of these to people with different birth numbers. This explains why a day that is good for me may be bad for you.

To discover the nature of any day we must again refer to the solar cycle, except that this time we have to turn the 'number wheel' to bring your birth number to the westerly sunset position, whose value is double negative. Thus it is the sunrise position which determines the life periods and the sunset position the day type. Let us suppose that you have a 3 birth number. This is how the solar cycle arranges itself for you:

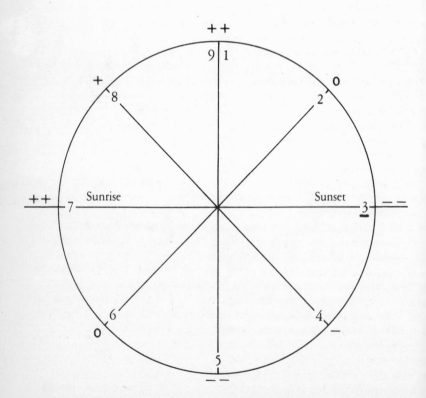

Because 2 is placed against a neutral point this indicates that any date that reduces to 2 – and hence 10 June 1984 – is a neutral day for you. Likewise, those dates that reduce to 1 and 9 are double positive, those that reduce to 3 are double negative, those that reduce to 4 are single negative, those that reduce to 5 are double negative, those that reduce to 6 are neutral, those that reduce to 7 are double positive, and those that reduce to 8 are single positive.

By turning the other numbers to the western horizon, we can in a similar manner determine the nature of any day or date for each birth number. These day values are summarized in the table below:

Birth Number

		1	2	3	4	5	6	7	8	9
	1	– –	0	+ +	+	+ +	0	– –	–	– –
	2	–	– –	0	+ +	+	+ +	0	– –	–
	3	– –	–	– –	0	+ +	+	+ +	0	– –
	4	0	– –	–	– –	0	+ +	+	+ +	0
Date	5	+ +	0	– –	–	– –	0	+ +	+	+ +
Number	6	+	+ +	0	– –	–	– –	0	+ +	+
	7	+ +	+	+ +	0	– –	–	– –	0	+ +
	8	0	+ +	+	+ +	0	– –	–	– –	0
	9	– –	0	+ +	+	+ +	0	– –	–	– –

Because every date can be reduced to one of the nine single numbers, this means that behind every date sequence lies a cycle of enneads, which in turn gives a recurring cycle of positive, negative and neutral days which is unique to each birth number, with the exception of 1 and 9, which share the same place in the solar cycle and thus the same days.

These cycles form a background rhythm to human life which are, with their constant risings and fallings, very similar to bio-rhythms. For this reason we can call them *number-rhythms*. At the top of the next page for example, is the number-rhythm cycle of someone who has a 3 birth number.

And beneath is the number-rhythm cycle of someone with a 1 or 9 birth number.

Generally speaking, we feel at our best mentally and physically on

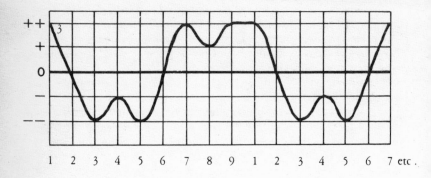

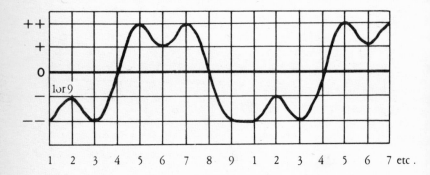

positive days and at our worst on negative days. Positive days are also potentially luckier. These are the days when things tend to go right for us, when we make a better impression on others and when, sometimes, our dreams become true. By contrast, negative days are potentially less fortunate. They are the days when we tend to make mistakes, when we have difficulties with others and when our schemes fail. And on double negative days we are more likely to have accidents, sometimes fatal ones. For example, Buddy Holly (birth number 8), the singer, died in a plane crash on what was for him a double negative day, 3 February 1959. A double negative day was also unfortunate for President Richard Nixon (birth number 6). It was on such a day – 17 June 1972 – that the Watergate conspirators were arrested, an event which led directly to his impeachment. Similarly Elvis Presley (birth number 9) died suddenly on one of his double negative days, 16 August 1977.

One is also more likely to die violently on a double negative day. President James Garfield (birth number 7) was assassinated on such a day – 19 September 1881 – as was President John Kennedy (birth number 7), who was shot by Lee Harvey Oswald on 22 November 1963.

But although the risk of accidental or violent death is higher on a double negative day, this is not to say that death always occurs on negative days, whether these be single negative or double negative. Death is not, *per se*, a negative experience. It is as much a part of life as birth, thus when it happens naturally at the end of a long life it must surely be regarded as a positive event. This is why America's oldest man John B. Salling (birth number 1), who died at 113, left this world on one of his double positive days, 16 March 1959.

Thus, no matter what your birth number, each day that you live through will be potentially either good (+) or very good (++), bad (–) or very bad (––), or neutral (0). The key word here is 'potentially'. Days are like wound springs, most of which never unwind. Yet if the right action is performed on the right day, the result can be marvellous, while if the wrong action is performed on the wrong day, a catastrophe can occur. This is why one should only take risks on positive days, never on negative days. Neutral days are usually just that, uneventful and unexciting. But surprises do sometimes happen on them, not all of them nice. Film-star James Dean (birth number 6) crashed his Porsche and killed himself on one of his neutral days, 30 September 1955, while President William McKinley (birth number 1) was shot by the anarchist Leon Czolgosz on one of his, 6 September 1901.

However, the number-rhythm cycles do not flow smoothly throughout the entire year because they are interrupted at the end of every month. For example, take 31 December 1984, which reduces to 2:

$$3 + 1 + 1 + 2 + 1 + 9 + 8 + 4 = 29$$
$$2 + 9 = 11$$
$$1 + 1 = 2$$

But the following day, 1 January 1985, reduces to 7:

$$1 + 1 + 1 + 9 + 8 + 5 = 25$$
$$2 + 5 = 7$$

This means that from Christmas Day, 25 December 1984 (which reduces to 5) to 6 January 1985 (which reduces to 3) the number sequence runs:

5 6 7 8 9 1 2 / 7 8 9 1 2 3, etc.

This particular interruption will be to the advantage of some number types, who will gain a longer positive period because of it, but to the disadvantage of others, who will be subjected to an extra-long negative period. Thus the period between Christmas Day 1984 and Twelfth Night 1985 was fortunate for those with a 3 birth number but unfortunate for those with a 7 birth number, as the graph below illustrates:

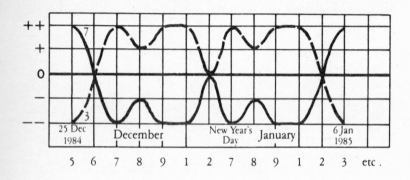

This graph also shows that the number-rhythms of those with a 3 birth number and those with a 7 birth number are mirror images of each other. Thus when the 3s have positive days the 7s have negative days, and vice versa. This 'mirror image' effect happens to those numbers that stand opposite each other in the solar cycle. It is most clearly seen in the top graph opposite, which shows the uninterrupted number rhythms of those having a 4 birth number and those having an 8 birth number.

In fact, such number-rhythms are complementary. For although the 4s are at their worst on days four, five and six, their low spirits are matched by the more buoyant mood of the 8s on these days. The reverse is true on days one, two, eight and nine, when the 4s are at their best and the 8s are at their worst. In the first instance the 8s will be able to shrug their shoulders at the cranky 4s, whereas the reverse will be true in the second. On two days, however, their moods exactly coincide, for on days three and seven they are both in neutral.

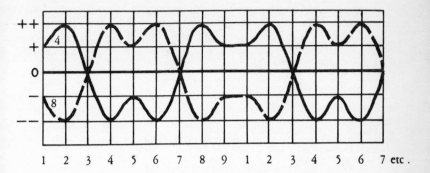

They will then be able to settle any differences that may have arisen between them.

But now compare the number-rhythms of those with a 5 birth number and those with a 6 birth number:

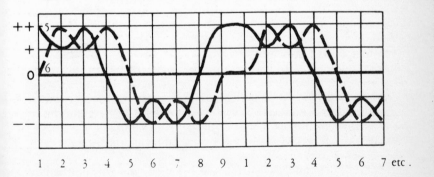

In this case the number-rhythms closely coincide, so that both have up-swings and down-swings together. On no day are their moods ever identical. Thus 5 and 6 types get on well on days two and three, when both have their moods uplifted by what is for them either a single positive day or a double positive day. The same is true, although to a lesser degree, on days one and four, when one of them enjoys a double positive day and the other has a neutral day. Their number-rhythms work against them, however, on days five, six, seven and eight, when the mood of one or the other is always depressed by a double negative day, while that of the other is never lifted above neutral. This produces a tense period when arguments and disagreements are likely to occur. Hence we can summarize the character of the relationship between those with a 5 birth number and those with a 6 birth number as unstable. For while 4s and 8s are true opposites, whose balanced opposition can lead to mutual respect and friendship, the 5s and the 6s are never in 'synch'. Indeed, their low periods can engender sufficient hostility to neutralize the effect of their positive periods. They tend therefore to become polarized and to avoid one another. They have no common ground in an emotional sense on which they can build friendship.

But what of those with a 1 or a 9 birth number, who have identical number-rhythms, or those who have the same birth number? How do they get on together?

The answer, quite simple, is well. For because their moods exactly coincide, they experience the same peaks and slumps. Thus they feel kindred spirits, which is of course, what they are. They will get on famously on those days which are single positive or double positive for them, while on single negative days or double negative days they will either keep themselves to themselves to avoid conflict or they will commiserate with each other because they know how the other feels.

From this we can conclude that we get on best with those who have the same birth number as ourselves or whose birth number lies opposite ours in the solar cycle, 1 and 9 being the opposites of 5, 2 the opposite of 6, 3 of 7, and 4 of 8. Likewise, we also enjoy quite good relations with those whose birth number stands at right angles to our own in the solar cycle. Consider, for example, the number-rhythms of those possessing a 2 birth number and those possessing an 8 birth number, which are shown opposite.

Here we see an exact correlation of mood on day two, which is double negative for both, and on day six, which is double positive for them, while on days four and eight their moods are polarized. As we saw earlier, such mood matchings promote good relations, thus we can expect the two types either to get on well or to sensibly shun each other on these days. They will also enjoy tolerably good relations on days five and seven, when the mood of one is single positive and that of the other is neutral. The only danger days are one, three and nine,

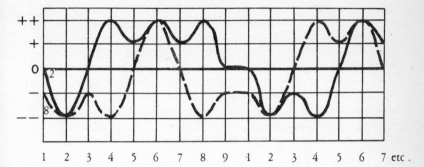

when the irritated single negative mood of the one could provoke anger in the neutral, and therefore unstable mood of the other.

But the situation is complicated by the fact that the number rhythms work against a background provided by the life periods, whose own nature can either be positive, negative or neutral. This means that if we take the days of a neutral period as representing the norm, then those of a positive period are potentially better and those of a negative period are potentially worse. Hence the days with the greatest potential are the double positive days of a double positive life period, whilst those with the worst potential are the double negative days of a double negative period.

Yet quite often the nature of a day can override that of the period in which it falls, which is why good things can happen in negative periods and bad things in positive periods. For example, Russian cosmonaut Yuri Gargarin (birth number 2) was launched into space on one of his double positive days, 12 April 1961, and became the first man to orbit the earth despite the double negative life period he was then undergoing. And French aviator Louis Bleriot (birth number 8) successfully flew the English Channel on what was for him a double positive day, 25 July 1909, even though he made the attempt in a neutral period.

Similarly, the nature of the period can outweigh that of its days. President Abraham Lincoln (birth number 5) was assassinated during a double negative period, yet on a day that was for him single positive, 14 April 1965. Martin Luther King (birth number 1) was even more unfortunate. He was shot to death during a double negative period, yet on a day that was for him double positive, 4 April 1968. Contrariwise, Roger Bannister (birth number 2) became the first man to run a mile in under four minutes on 6 May 1954. This was a single negative day for him but fortunately the attempt was made during a single positive period. And Charles Lindbergh (birth number 9) took off to fly the Atlantic on one of his neutral days – 20 May 1927 – and successfully landed in France on the following day, which was for him a double negative one. However, he was lucky enough to have made the attempt in a double positive life period.

Because the life periods can last a maximum of nine years and because their nature is representative of the period as a whole rather than parts of it, individual days often express themselves more forcibly than might be expected. This accounts for the success that some people enjoy when in competition with others who are undergoing a more positive life period. Such people win because the day is right for them.

In this respect it is salutary to examine the fortunes of political rivals. In British general elections, for example, the chief combatants are the Prime Minister and the Leader of the Opposition, who compete against each other both as individuals and as symbols of all that their own political parties have to offer the electorate.

In 1945 the two contestants were Winston Churchill (birth number 7) and Clement Attlee (birth number 6). Both had, as we have already discovered, strong birth numbers for political success, yet Churchill was favoured by his formidable war record and by the single positive period (1942-50) he was then undergoing. Attlee, by contrast, was in a nine-year neutral period (1939-48). But despite Churchill's advantages he suffered a stunning election defeat. Yet this was not so surprising when we consider the date on which the election was held, 26 July 1945. This was a double negative day for Churchill, but only a neutral one for Attlee.

The two contended again in 1950. Churchill was then nearing the end of his single positive period (1942-50) and Attlee was undergoing a three-year single negative period he had started in 1948. The elction took place on 23 February 1950, which was a double positive day for Attlee and a single positive day for Churchill. Attlee won.

The two leaders fought each other for the third and last time on 25 October 1951. Churchill was then living through a neutral period (1950-52), while Attlee had begun an advantageous double positive period (1951-9). But the date was in Churchill's favour, being neutral for him and double negative for Attlee. Churchill won the election and remained Prime Minister until his retirement in 1955.

In the general election of 1955 Clement Attlee fought against the new Tory leader, Anthony Eden (birth number 7). Both men were evenly matched as far as their life periods were concerned as each was running a double positive period (Eden 1953-62; Attlee (1951-9). But again it was the nature of the day that determined the election outcome. The election date – 26 May 1955 – was neutral for Eden and double negative for Attlee. not surprisingly, Eden won.

The general election of 1959 brought two new men into conflict – Conservative Prime Minister Harold Macmillan (birth number 7), who had taken office when Anthony Eden resigned, and Labour leader Hugh Gaitskell (birth number 2). This was an election, judged on day and period strength, that Gaitskell should have won. The date – 8 October 1959 – was double positive for Gaitskell and neutral for Macmillan. Gaitskell was then running a double positive period (1958-62), while Macmillan had just started a double negative period (1959-62). Yet the victor was Harold Macmillan, who romped home by a mile. But how did he do it? The answer lies in his 7 birth number, which is incomparably stronger for gaining political success than Gaitskell's weak 2. Indeed, only one prime minister of this century has had a 2 birth number and he – Andrew Bonar Law – stayed in office for just seven months.

The general election of 1964 pitted Tory prime minister Alec Douglas-Home (birth number 4) against the Labour leader Harold Wilson (birth number 4). Because both men had the same birth number this meant that the election date – 15 October 1964 – was single positive for both of them. Thus the prize had to go to the man with the life period advantage. Harold Wilson was then enjoying a double positive period (1962-8), while Alec Douglas-Home was in the middle of a single negative period (1959-68). The Labour Party and Harold Wilson won the election. But it was close. The new government only had a majority of five.

The contenders in the election of 1970 were Harold Wilson and the new Tory leader Edward Heath (birth number 6). Wilson was the running a double positive life period (1968-72), which gave him and advantage over Heath, who was undergoing a double negative period (1968-72). But the election date – 17 June 1970 – was strongly in Heath's favour, being double positive for him but double negative for Wilson. The winner was Edward Heath.

The date decided the contest four years later when the same pair again competed for office. This time Heath was in a neutral life period (1972-81), which gave him a slight advantage over Wilson, who was running a single negative period (1972-81). But the election date – 2 March 1974 – was double negative for Heath and double positive for Wilson. Wilson won.

The general election of 1979 was made doubly interesting by the fact that for the first time in British history the Conservative leader was a woman – Margaret Thatcher (birth number 4). Her opponent was the Labour prime minister James Callaghan (birth number 7). But despite Callaghan having the stronger birth number, everything else was in Mrs Thatcher's favour. For not only was she undergoing a double positive life period (1977-81), in contrast to the double negative one that Callaghan was running (1977-80), but the date chosen for the election – 4 May 1979 – was also double positive for her, yet single negative for him. Hardly surprisingly, Mrs Thatcher won hands down.

The most recent general election took place on 9 June 1983. It pitted Mrs Thatcher against the new Labour leader Michael Foot (birth number 8). Foot had the advantage in that he was two years into a double positive life period (1981-9), while Mrs Thatcher had begun a long single negative period (1981-90). The date, however, was favourable to Mrs Thatcher, being single positive for her but single negative for Michael Foot. Yet it wasn't really this that won the election for her. Her victory really stemmed from Foot's weak birth number, which meant that had the election taken place on a double positive day for him he would still have lost. He was, judged on his birth number, a non-starter.

These post-war election contests show that victory at the ballot box in Britain goes to the party leader who has a strong birth number (4, 6 or 7), who is living through a positive life period and who is lucky enough to have the election called on a date that is positive, preferably double positive, for him.

But what of the future, especially now that the traditional two-party system has been upset by the emergence of the SDP/Liberal Alliance? Well, none of this makes any difference because the person who is to become the next prime minister will be decided by the factors mentioned above. Let us therefore examine the likely challengers to Mrs Thatcher in the election of 1987 or 1988.

The new leader of the Labour Party is Neil Kinnock, who was born on 28 March 1942. This gives him a 2 birth number:

$$2 + 8 + 3 + 1 + 9 + 4 + 2 = 29$$
$$2 + 9 = 11$$
$$1 + 1 = 2$$

Kinnock is now running a neutral life period which will last until his birthday in 1988 (1983-8). It will then be followed by a double negative period (1988-94).

The leader of the SDP is Dr David Owen, who was born on 2 July 1938, a date that gives him a 3 birth number:

$$2 + 7 + 1 + 9 + 3 + 8 = 30$$
$$3 + 0 = 3$$

On his 46th birthday in 1984 Dr Owen started a neutral life period which will run until his 52nd birthday in 1990.

Lastly, David Steel is the current leader of the Liberal Party. He was born on 31 March 1938 and thus has a 1 birth number:

$$3+1+3+1+9+3+8=28$$
$$2 + 8 = 10$$
$$1 + 0 = 1$$

Steel began a single negative life period on his birthday in 1984. This will run until his birthday in 1990.

Because Mrs Thatcher is also undergoing a single negative life period which will last until 1990, this means that none of the probable contenders in the 1987/88 general election will have a strong life period advantage. However, should the election be held in the summer of 1988 Dr Owen, who will be in a neutral life period, will be slightly ahead of the rest of the field.

The destiny of these people thus lies in their birth numbers, so what hope can they find in them? Well, for the three men not much. David Owen, who has a 3 birth number, can be immediately given the thumbs down. His birth number, as we have already seen, is a complete non-starter. And Kinnock's 2 is little better. It is a decidedly weak number to field against the strong 4 belonging to Mrs Thatcher and it almost certainly spells defeat for the Labour Party.

That leaves David Steel. His 1 birth number is not a weak one like Owen's and Kinnock's, for although only one prime minister this century has had such a birth number – Herbert Asquith – he held office for an astonishing eight years (1908-16). But even so it cannot match the strength of Mrs Thatcher's birth number. And that means that if Margaret Hilda Thatcher is still the Conservative leader at the next election there can be no doubt that she will win.

At least, just as long as she chooses a date that is double positive for her!

6
YOUR NUMBER ACCORD

In our discussion of numbers and destiny we have seen how your birth number determines your life periods and your number rhythms. But while this is useful and practical knowledge, it cannot tell you if your life will be happy and successful. For everyone with the same birth number has the same sequence of life periods and the same number rhythms, yet the quality of their lives can vary greatly.

So can numerology lift the last of Fortuna's veils and show you the future? Can it tell you if your life will be happy or sad, fulfilling or unfulfilling, successful or unsuccessful?

Yes, it can. And it can do more than that. It can also help you to change the direction of your life so that it follows a happier and more satisfying course.

In this respect numerology is unique. No other method of prediction allows the individual to alter his destiny, for they are mere passive announcers of what will be. And this applies as much to astrology as it does to the reading of tea leaves.

This flexibility arises from the two sorts of numbers that are important to us. On the one hand we have our birth number, which is fixed by fate and cannot be changed, while on the other we have our name numbers, which can be changed simply by changing our names.

Of the three name numbers – the vowel number, the consonant number and the name number itself – it is the last which is most important to us in terms of life success. For it is the accord that exists between it and the unchangeable birth number which determines how happy and fulfilled our lives will be.

To understand how this accord is established it is necessary to examine the diagram opposite which shows the positive, negative and neutral areas of the solar cycle.

Let us now suppose that you have a 6 birth number and an 8 name number. To find out the accord that they enjoy, the 'number wheel' must be turned to bring your birth number to the sunrise position.

We then note the placement of the 8 (see page 206).

Because the 8 falls in the positive area, this means that there is a *positive accord* between your birth number and your name number. The same accord would exist if your name number was 6 or 7 because these also lie in the positive area. Such an accord indicates that your life will be happy and satisfying.

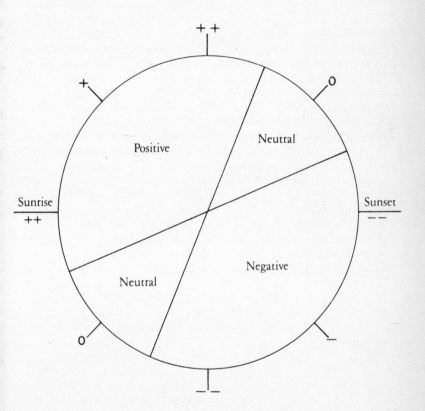

If you had the same birth number – 6 – but a name number that was 1, 5 or 9, then because these all lie in the two neutral areas there would exist a *neutral accord* between your birth number and your name number. This would mean that your life will be moderately happy and satisfying.

However, had you the same birth number but a name number that was 2, 3 or 4, which lie in the negative area, then a *negative accord* would exist between your birth number and your name number. This would show that your life will not be happy and satisfying.

The accord that exists between the birth number and the name number indicates how successful one's life will be in terms of happiness and personal satisfaction, not its success in a material sense. Sometimes, of course, all these go together, so that one becomes rich, famous and happy. But this is an extremely rare state. Riches and fame tend to drive away happiness, not attract it.

For example, let us again consider Elvis Presley, the late King of Rock 'n' Roll, who had a 9 birth number. His name number was 5:

ELVI S   PRES LEY
5 3 4 9 1   7 9 5 1 3 5 7 = 59 = 14 = 5

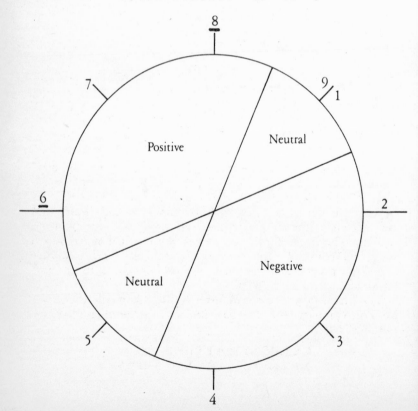

But although Elvis Presley was the most famous popular singer of this century, the accord that existed between his birth number and his name number was *negative* (see page 208).

This reveals that despite his great fame and wealth, Elvis Presley was not a happy or a fulfilled man. And, indeed, a recent biography has described him as psychologically troubled, sexually deviant and physically ill, as well as being a drug addict. He also died prematurely at the age of 42.

If you have calculated your birth number and your name number, the table below will enable you to determine quickly the accord that exists between them, and thus, as a result, the quality of your life.

		Name Numbers		
		Positive	Neutral	Negative
	1	1, 2, 3, 9	4, 8	5, 6, 7
	2	2, 3, 4	1, 5, 9	6, 7, 8
	3	3, 4, 5	2, 6	1, 7, 8, 9
Birth	4	4, 5, 6	3, 7	1, 2, 8, 9
Numbers	5	5, 6, 7	4, 8	1, 2, 3, 9
	6	6, 7, 8	1, 5, 9	2, 3, 4
	7	1, 7, 8, 9	2, 6	3, 4, 5
	8	1, 2, 8, 9	3, 7	4, 5, 6
	9	1, 2, 3, 9	4, 8	5, 6, 7

Let us now examine the accord that exists between the birth number and the name number of some well-known people, to see whether or not it reflects the apparent quality of their lives.

As our first example, we will take the nine men and women who have become prime ministers of post-war Britain. All were successful in their political life and, at least as far as is known, in their family and social life. We would therefore expect, on this basis, for them to have a positive accord between their birth number and their name number.

The first post-war prime minister was Clement Atlee, who was born on 3 January 1883. This gave him a 6 birth number. His name number is 9:

CLEMENT   ATTLEE
3 3 5 4 5 5 2   1 2 2 3 5 5 = 45 = 9

The table shows us that there is a *neutral accord* between a 6 birth number and a 9 name number. However, if we use the name Clem Attlee, which was employed by his family and colleagues, an improved accord emerges:

CLEM   ATTLEE
3 3 5 4   1 2 2 3 5 5 = 33 = 6

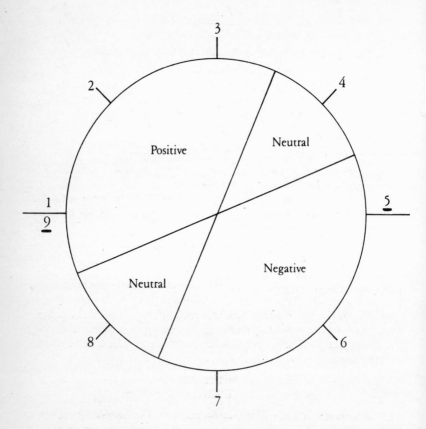

The table shows that a *positive accord* exists between a 6 birth number and a 6 name number.

The man who followed Attlee into Number 10 was Winston Churchill, who was born on 30 November 1874. His birthdate gave him a 7 birth number. His name number is 1:

WINSTON   CHURCHILL
5 9 5 1 2 6 5   3 8 3 9 3 8 9 3 3 = 82 = 10

As the table shows, there is a *positive accord* between a 7 birth number and a 1 name number.

Britain's third post-war prime minister was Anthony Eden, who was born on 12 June 1897 and who thus had a 7 birth number. His name number is 8:

ANTHONY   EDEN
1 5 2 8 6 5 7   5 4 5 5 = 53 = 8

Again, the table shows that there exists a *positive accord* between a birth number of 7 and a name number of 8.

The next prime minister was Harold Macmillan, who was born on 10 February 1894. This gave him a 7 birth number. His name number is 1, like Churchill's:

HAROLD   MACMILLAN
8 1 9 6 3 4   4 1 3 4 9 3 3 1 5 = 64 = 10 = 1

As we have already seen, there exists a *positive accord* between a 7 birth number and a 1 name number.

Alec Douglas-Home became Prime Minister on Macmillan's retirement in 1963. Born on 2 July 1903, he has a 4 birth number. His name number is 6:

ALEC   DOUGLAS–HOME
1 3 5 3   4 6 3 7 3 1 1   8 6 4 5   = 60 = 6

From the table we can see that there exists a *positive accord* between a 4 birth number and a 6 name number.

The next prime minister was Harold Wilson, who held office twice, the first time from 1964 to 1970, the second from 1974 to 1976. Born on 11 March 1916, he has a 4 birth number. His name number is 6:

HAROLD   WILSON
8 1 9 6 3 4   5 9 3 1 6 5 = 60 = 6

With the same birth number and name number as Alec Douglas-Home, Harold Wilson thus enjoys a *positive accord* between them.

Edward Heath was Prime Minister between the two tenures of Harold Wilson. He was born on 9 July 1916 and therefore has a 6 birth number. His name number is 7:

EDWARD   HEATH
5 4 5 1 9 4   8 5 1 2 8 = 52 = 7

And once again, the table shows that there exists a *positive accord* between a 6 birth number and a 7 name number.

After Harold Wilson's retirement in 1976 James Callaghan became Prime Minister. Callaghan was born on 27 March 1912, a date which gives him a 7 birth number. His name number is 8:

JAMES   CALLAGHAN

1 1 4 5 1   3 1 3 3 1 7 8 1 5 = 44 = 8

The table shows that there is a *positive accord* between a 7 birth number and an 8 name number.

Finally, Margaret Thatcher has been Prime Minister of Britain since 1979. Born on 13 October 1925, she has a 4 birth number. Her name number is also 4:

MARGARET   THATCHER

4 1 9 7 1 9 5 2   2 8 1 2 3 8 5 9 = 76 = 13 = 4

Because Mrs Thatcher's birth number and name number are the same, there is a *positive accord* between them.

Thus perhaps not surprisingly, each of these democratically elected British leaders, who were and are successful in both their public and private lives, have a positive accord between their birth number and their name number. Indeed, we find the same accord between the birth and name numbers of most post-war American presidents. Consider, for example, Ronald Reagan, who was a successful film actor before he turned to politics. Born on 6 February 1911, he has a 2 birth number. His name number is also 2:

RONALD   REAGAN

9 6 5 1 3 4   9 5 1 7 1 5 = 56 = 11 = 2

With the same birth number and name number, Ronald Reagan enjoys a *positive accord* between them.

James Earl Carter was the full name of the man who occupied the White House before Ronald Reagan, but he was known to all as Jimmy Carter. Born on 1 October 1924, he has a 9 birth number. His name number is likewise 9:

JIMMY   CARTER

1 9 4 4 7   3 1 9 2 5 9 = 54 = 9

This means that there exists a *positive accord* between his birth number and his name number.

The President before Jimmy Carter was Gerald Ford, who was born on 14 July 1913. This birthday gave him an 8 birth number. His name number is 9:

$$\text{GERALD} \quad \text{FORD}$$
$$7\ 5\ 9\ 1\ 3\ 4 \quad 6\ 6\ 9\ 4 = 54 = 9$$

Again, the table shows that there is a *positive accord* between an 8 birth number and a 9 name number.

But we do not find such a happy accord between the birth number and the name number of the White House's previous occupant, Richard Nixon, who was impeached in 1974. Nixon was born on 9 January 1913, which gave him a 6 birth number. His name number, however, is 2:

$$\text{RICHARD} \quad \text{NIXON}$$
$$9\ 9\ 3\ 8\ 1\ 9\ 4 \quad 5\ 9\ 6\ 6\ 5 = 74 = 11 = 2$$

The table shows that there is a *negative accord* between a 6 birth number and a 2 name number. Such an accord clearly represents, not Richard Nixon's political success, which was considerable, but his paranoia, his unhappy personal relationships, and his disgrace.

A negative accord is frequently found between the birth number and the name number of those who are tyrants and dictators, whose regimes are based on fear and oppression. These people invariably have unhappy and chaotic inner lives.

Let us take Adolf Hitler and Benito Mussolini as examples.

Adolf Hitler, who was born on 20 April 1889, had a 5 birth number. His name is 2:

$$\text{ADOLF} \quad \text{HITLER}$$
$$1\ 4\ 6\ 3\ 6 \quad 8\ 9\ 2\ 3\ 5\ 9 = 56 = 11 = 2$$

The table shows that there is a *negative accord* between a 5 birth number and a 2 name number.

Benito Mussolini, the Italian Fascist leader, was born on 4 December 1892, a date which gave him a 2 birth number. His name number is 7:

$$\text{BENITO} \quad \text{MUSSOLINI}$$
$$2\ 5\ 5\ 9\ 2\ 6 \quad 4\ 3\ 1\ 1\ 6\ 3\ 9\ 5\ 9 = 70 = 7$$

Again, the table reveals that there is a *negative accord* between a 2 birth number and a 7 name number.

Tragedy and unhappiness were frequent visitors to the life of Isadora Duncan, the dancer, who lost her two children in a boating accident, her husband through suicide and her own life when her scarf became entangled in a wheel of the car in which she was a passenger. Miss Duncan was born on 27 May 1878 and so had a 2 birth number. Her name number is 7:

ISADORA   DUNCAN
9 1 1 4 6 9 1   4 3 5 3 1 5 = 52 = 7

With the same birth number and name number as Benito Mussolini, Isadora Duncan's life was marred by the *negative accord* that exists between them.

These examples amply demonstrate that there is a close relationship between the birth number/name number accord and the quality of one's life. However, because this relationship exists, it naturally offers a way of improving one's lot by the simple and relatively painless method of changing one's name. If such a change improves the accord between one's birth number and name number, then it will automatically better one's chances of happiness. This, of course, introduces a new factor into the name changes discussed in Chapter 3, which looked at the name from an internal vowel number/consonant number point of view. Inner harmoney between one's ego and id does form the foundation of happiness, yet the delicate and precious edifice that can be built on it can only withstand the gales of life if it is protected by an encircling positive accord between the birth number and the name number. But all too often, people – actors and entertainers for examples – change their names without realizing the hidden numerological damage they are doing to themselves.

For example, singer and film star Judy Garland was born Frances Gumm on 10 June 1922. Her 3 birth number had a *positive accord* with the name number of her proper name, which is also 3:

FRANCES   GUMM
6 9 1 5 3 5 1   7 3 4 4 = 48 = 12 = 3

Such an accord promises a happy life and this promise was made brighter in Miss Gumm's case by the harmony that existed between her 9 vowel number and her 3 consonant number:

FRANCES   GUMM
  1   5   3   = 9

FRANCES   GUMM
6 9   5 3 1   7   4 4 = 39 = 12 = 3

With such a combination Judy Garland, had she remained as Frances Gumm, would have become a lively, energetic woman, one quite capable of facing life on its own terms and with very few doubts about herself as a person. She would have had a rising spirit, a brash sense of fun and the ability to cope with her problems without resorting to drink or drugs, as indeed Judy Garland was able to before her name change. Thus she would have been, as Frances Gumm, a happy and a stable woman.

By becoming Judy Garland Frances Gumm found stardom yet stumbled into an unhappy bramble bush of marital difficulties, weight problems and a dependence on drugs which undermined her health. She once asked, 'If I'm such a legend, then why am I so lonely?' So why did this happen? Simply because she chose the wrong stage name. Judy Garland's name number is 9 which has, as the table shows, a *negative accord* with her 3 birth number:

$$\text{J UDY} \quad \text{GARLAND}$$
$$1\,3\,4\,7 \quad 7\,1\,9\,3\,1\,5\,4 = 45 = 9$$

Such an accord was able to cause the damage it did to Judy Garland because her name had no inner stability. Her 5 vowel number was out of harmony with her 4 consonant number, suggesting that there were disruptive tensions between her ego and id. Thus her new name gave nothing on which she could build happiness.

$$\text{J UDY} \quad \text{GARLAND}$$
$$3 \qquad 1\quad 1 \quad = 5$$

$$\text{J UDY} \quad \text{GARLAND}$$
$$1\quad 4\,7 \quad 7\quad 9\,3 \quad 5\,4 = 40 = 4$$

Bob Dylan made a similar, yet not quite so drastic mistake. He was born Robert Zimmermann on 24 May 1941, which gave him a 7 birth number. His proper name number is 1:

$$\text{R O B E R T} \quad \text{Z I M M E R M A N}$$
$$9\,6\,2\,5\,9\,2 \quad 8\,9\,4\,4\,5\,9\,4\,1\,5 = 82 = 10 = 1$$

As the table shows, a 7 birth number and a 1 name number enjoy a *positive accord*. Equally important, the vowel number (8) and the consonant number (2) of the name Robert Zimmermann are compatible:

$$\text{R O B E R T} \quad \text{Z I M M E R M A N}$$
$$6\quad 5 \qquad 9\quad 5\quad 1 \quad = 26 = 8$$

$$\text{R O B E R T} \quad \text{Z I M M E R M A N}$$
$$9\quad 2\quad 9\,2 \quad 8\quad 4\,4\quad 9\,4\quad 5 = 56 = 11 = 2$$

With these number combinations Robert Zimmerman would have grown into a well-rounded, happy man. He might not, of course, have found the fame and fortune of Bob Dylan, but his personal gains would have been just as great.

By becoming Bob Dylan, Robert Zimmerman cast a shadow over his life, for the name number of Bob Dylan is 3, which has a *negative accord* with his 7 birth number.

$$BOB \quad DYLAN$$
$$2\ 6\ 2 \quad 4\ 7\ 3\ 1\ 5 = 30 = 3$$

Such an accord means that Bob Dylan cannot be as happy as he would have been as Robert Zimmerman. However, he is protected from the worst effects of this accord by the compatible vowel number (7) and consonant number (5) of his new name:

$$BOB \quad DYLAN$$
$$6 \qquad\quad 1 \ = 7$$

$$BOB \quad DYLAN$$
$$2\ \ 2 \quad 4\ 7\ 3\ \ \ 5 = 23 = 5$$

Because a 7 ego and a 5 id are compatible, they give Bob Dylan sufficient inner stability to withstand the difficulties that life throws at him, so that while he will never be really happy he won't go under either. And because 7 and 5 symbolize strong creative talents and an adventurous spirit, they represent the bedrock on which Bob Dylan built his success as a singer and composer.

This naturally brings us again to you and your life. Like everyone else, you want to be happy. You want to wake up in the morning with a song in your heart, secure in the knowledge that others like you because you are nice to know. You might already feel like this. If so, you are blessed indeed, loved by the gods. If not, then it is time you examined your name numbers and made any name change that might be necessary.

But first, find out the accord that exists between your birth number and your name number. If this is positive, next check which life period you are in. You may be living through a single negative period or a double negative period. These always bring problems of one sort or another, even to those whose birth number and name number are in positive accord. If this is the case, then you should see how compatible your vowel number and consonant number are. Should these be incompatible you can improve your inner strength by changing your name to make them compatible. However, you must make sure that your name number maintains a positive accord with your birth number. Of course, if your birth number has a negative or neutral accord with your name number, you should certainly change your name to produce a positive accord. This is particularly important if you happen to be living through a single negative period or a double negative period.

To make this quite clear, let us consider the case of Rosemary Brown and the disruptive effect that marriage had on her name – and the simple remedy she found for it. Since she was a schoolgirl Rosemary Brown had called herself Rose Brown and she was a happy, well-adjusted girl. Born on 11 March 1960, she has a 3 birth number. Her name number is also 3:

$$\begin{array}{ll} \text{R O S E} & \text{B R O W N} \\ 9\ 6\ 1\ 5 & 2\ 9\ 6\ 5\ 5 = 48 = 12 = 3 \end{array}$$

The table shows that between a 3 birth number and a 3 name number there is a *positive accord*. This favourable accord was backed up by a compatible vowel number (8) and consonant number (4):

$$\begin{array}{ll} \text{R O S E} & \text{B R O W N} \\ \ \ 6\ \ \ 5 & \ \ \ 6\ \ \ \ \ = 17 = 8 \end{array}$$

$$\begin{array}{ll} \text{R O S E} & \text{B R O W N} \\ 9\ \ \ 1 & 2\ 9\ \ \ 5\ 5 = 31 = 4 \end{array}$$

When Rose met handsome George Smith and they fell in love, her happiness seemed assured. But when they married shortly after her 22nd birthday things couldn't have gone more wrong. They had trouble in finding somewhere to live and Rose, quite unaccountably, became depressed, irritable and unhappy. And after an argument with her employer she left her job, which made the Smiths short of money. Things steadily worsened. It soon began to look as though the marriage would not last.

The answer lay, as we might expect, in the name change that Rose had undergone when she married. From Rose Brown she had become Rose Smith, and Rose Smith not only gave her a different name number (9) but a different vowel number (2) and consonant number (7) as well:

$$\begin{array}{ll} \text{R O S E} & \text{S M I T H} \\ 9\ 6\ 1\ 5 & 1\ 4\ 9\ 2\ 8 = 45 = 9 \end{array}$$

The table shows that between Rose's 3 birth number and her new name number there is a *negative accord*. This accord was made worse by the fact that she was then living through the last year of a double negative life period, whose damaging potential it unleashed.

The name change also gave her an incompatible ego and id, which explains why she became a different person so quickly. For

Rose Brown wanted so much to be Mrs Rose Smith.

$$\begin{array}{ll} \text{R O S E} & \text{S M I T H} \\ 65 & 9 \quad = 20 = 2 \end{array}$$

$$\begin{array}{ll} \text{R O S E} & \text{S M I T H} \\ 91 & 1\ 4\quad 2\ 8 = 25 = 7 \end{array}$$

But fortunately, Rose Smith found her own salvation. Quite instinctively, she began calling herself Rosemary Smith, perhaps feeling that Rosemary Smith had more natural dignity than Rose Smith. It was a change that brought her out of her depression and saved her marriage. Indeed, she is now the happy, smiling young woman you would wish her to be. And a bird recently whispered that a Smith Junior is on the way!

The change to Rosemary Smith gave her back her original name number:

$$\begin{array}{ll} \text{R O S E M A R Y} & \text{S M I T H} \\ 9\ 6\ 1\ 5\ 4\ 1\ 9\ 7 & 1\ 4\ 9\ 2\ 8 = 66 = 12 = 3 \end{array}$$

It also gave her a compatible vowel number (3) and consonant number (9):

$$\begin{array}{ll} \text{R O S E M A R Y} & \text{S M I T H} \\ 651 & 9 \quad = 21 = 3 \end{array}$$

$$\begin{array}{ll} \text{R O S E M A R Y} & \text{S M I T H} \\ 9149\ 7 & 1\ 4\quad 2\ 8 = 45 = 9 \end{array}$$

If you believe that a name change can improve your life, you might be able to make the changes as easily as Rosemary Smith or Peter Jones did. But it is quite probable that you might have to adopt a completely new Christian name to bring about the number changes that you desire. In this respect it is pertinent to note that there is no law against you changing your name, so long as this is not done with intent to defraud. However, a radical name change is inconvenient, especially where official documents are concerned.

But while inconvenient in a public and private sense, such a change will bring you positive personal benefits. Within a short time you will find your mood and your confidence changing for the better, and in the wake of these changes will come improvements in your relationships and circumstances that will upgrade the whole quality of your life. For no matter what sort of life period you are now in you can make things better for yourself with a careful name change.

So don't delay. Get the right numbers working for you with a new name. They will change your life more significantly and more positively than a big win on the pools or in a lottery.

For they will give you the greatest blessing of all: happiness.

PART THREE

FORTUNE-TELLING BY PLAYING CARDS

NERYS DEE

INTRODUCTION

The goddess Fortune, it is said, frustrates single-handed the plans of a thousand learned men. To outwit her has been a human pursuit since the dawn of time and, although oracles have come and oracles have gone, divination through the cards has survived, virtually unaltered, to this very day.

The origin of the 52 playing cards is now lost in the mists of time, but it seems probable that it stems from the same mysterious source as that of the tarot and chess. It is often suggested that the playing cards are descendants of the tarot pack itself, but their amazing numerical significance in relation to the solar system, the universe and time seems to give them an importance entirely in their own right.

There is, of course, a close relationship between the 52 playing cards and the 56 cards that go to make up the Minor Arcana of the tarot pack. Both sets have four suits. Each suit contains ten numbered cards plus court cards; there are twelve in the 52-card pack and sixteen in the 56 tarot pack. It is the four extra court cards in the Minor Arcana that completely destroy the obvious yet unique significance associated with the number 52.

In the fourteenth century the 52-card pack was given four additional court cards and annexed to the 22 cards known as the Major Arcana. This made up the 78-card tarot pack we know today. Before this time, the tarot, representing the Qabalistic Tree of Life, consisted of the 22 major trumps only.

Ancient civilizations once had their own versions of the cards. The Chinese engraved copper and silver plates with designs and numbers based on the four suits, which they then reproduced on paper, making them into what is believed to be the very first pack of cards. Later, by introducing the Tao principle of Yin and Yang, black and white, they devised the game we now know as chess. This requires considerable mental skill, patience and foresight for, like the cards, it symbolizes the game of life itself with its surprise encounters and counter-moves.

It is said that the Indians knew of the cards at this time too, with theirs depicting Hindu deities holding swords, sceptres, cups and rings. If this is so, then Ireland may also be considered as the originator of the four suits because this is the homeland of the four prehistoric grails – the sword, the sceptre, the cup and the ring.

Japan, Korea, North and South America and the Pacific Islands have also been credited with introducing the cards to mankind, but it is from Egypt that we find most evidence concerning them in their earliest form. Even so, this still does not give sufficient proof to show that Egypt was the land of their origin. And from here, our trail leads us back to Atlantis, but that is another story.

Court de Gebelin in the eighteenth century wrote: 'If it were known that there existed today a work of the ancient Egyptians which escaped the flames that devoured their superb libraries and which contains their purest doctrines on the most profound and interesting subjects, everyone would doubtless be anxious to acquire the secrets from so valuable a work.'

He was, in fact, referring to *The Book of Thoth*, from which our present day cards are derived. This book is said to contain all the answers to mankind's problems and is made up of a series of plates engraved with hieroglyphics, based on an alphabet depicting gods as letters, letters as ideas, ideas as numbers and numbers as perfect signs. The priests are thought to have assembled this work after consultation with their god of magic, Thoth. They decided to hide within its ancient pages timeless secrets which would always be accessible to future generations, provided they had the desire to seek out such knowledge and wisdom. These same prists also decided that the best way to hide these eternal secrets, yet at the same time keep them within reach of everyone, was to appeal to the vice in man as well as to his nobler qualities. This, then, is why the cards today still carry the profoundest of messages on the one hand, yet are found spread over the seamiest gambling tables of the world on the other.

From Egypt comes the story of yet another book supposedly written by Hermes whose life and times pre-date the pyramids by many centuries. This is said to have contained gold leaves, each of which was impressed with numbers and letters similar to those in *The Book of Thoth*. Together these constituted the Arcanum or secret wisdom of the world. It is to Simeon ben Jochai, a Jewish initiate, that we owe all knowledge of this book, now known as *The Hermetic Book of Destiny*. It was, incidentally, at the command of Pope Clement XIV that Simeon ben Jochai translated it into Latin.

It is said that Moses, who was well versed in Egyptian lore and magic, took *The Book of Thoth* with him when he and the children of Israel left Egypt in search of the Promised land. This he guarded carefully, but after many years it appeared in the Middle East as a text known as the 'taro'. There is seen in this a close connection between the 'taro' and the 'tora', which is, of course, the Hebrew law code in the Old Testament. There is also a close connection between the 'taro' and 'rota', (the wheel of time and fortune). By rearranging the letters alone – tora, taro and rota – we see a glimpse of the magic of the cards and, although the absolute interpretations of both the books of Thoth and Hermes are now lost, we still have the keys to unlock many of their mysteries in our present day 52 playing cards and the 22 cards of the Major Arcana.

The History of the Cards

The cards made their first appearance in Europe around the eleventh century. Exactly how they arrived and who brought them has given rise to almost as many legends as their origin itself, but at least we are certain of one thing and that is that they were not invented by a member of the French court to amuse a bored king.

From A.D. 1200 onwards, Europe has played host to an ever increasing number of travellers from all over the world. Routes between Mediterranean countries, Asia Minor and the Far East were opened up, enabling merchants to bring to the West their exotic goods from lands as far away as India and China. Trade links were formed with Islamic countries too, so it is virtually impossible to discover which of these newcomers actually brought the famous cards with them.

Some sources say it was the Saracens or 'gypsies' – a corruption of 'Egyptians' – whilst other authorities insist it was the Chinese. Although this may have been the case, it is more likely that the Knights Templars were responsible, having learned about them from the Saracens during their crusades to the Holy Land. On their return to England they certainly made no secret of their knowledge of the cards for, in 1230, the Synod of Worcester forbad the Knights to play a card game they called 'King and Queen'.

Until the fifteenth century the cards were alternately banned and approved by heads of State and the Church, both in England and throughout Europe. In France, Italy and England they were as popular within monastic walls as they were with royalty at court and only later did members of the public become familiar with them. So far as England is concerned, if the Knights Templars did not bring the cards, then they reached these shores from France, where they certainly were all the rage. It was, in fact, their national popularity that led to the belief that they originated from the French court, but the following romantic story tells how they most probably found their way into royal circles.

Apparently, in 1390, Charles VI was mentally disturbed, so to divert his attention from terrible bouts of depression, not to mention obsession, Odette, his lovely and attentive mistress, would sing, play the harp and read to him. Always searching for new pastimes, she heard that in Paris there was talk of an exciting new game, brought to the city by gypsies. This game consisted of strange cards, some of which were numbered and others covered with pictures of eastern kings and queens which, when arranged in various combinations created amusement that amazed the players. Wishing above all else to maintain the King's favour, Odette sent for a set of these cards, but before she let him see them she had a court artist decorate a special pack, cleverly designed by herself.

Kings, queens and knaves were easily recognized in this unique pack as none other than members of the royal court. Odette and Charles were prominent among the picture cards and it is said that at the sight of them the King recovered his mental faculty immediately, albeit temporarily, and ordered that the whole world should know about the powers and magic of the cards! From this time on, picture cards in the pack became known as court cards.

The financial accounts for the French court in 1392 show a large treasury payment for 'three packs of handmade cards'. With the King's money and influence plus Odette's talent the cards were soon launched on the royal road to success. Soon every family in Paris possessed a pack and a card-producing business prospered well, but this is not the end of the story. A gypsy heard of the King's interest in the ancient cards and made herself known to Odette, telling her that although she, Odette, knew how to amuse the King with them, she knew nothing of their powers of prophecy.

Taking the pack of royal cards in her hand, the gypsy selected twelve of them and spread these on a table before her. She then proceeded to reel off personal secrets known only to Odette and the King himself, just as if she were reading from an open book. This information related not only to the past and present but foretold future events too, which later proved to be correct.

Odette now saw the cards as an oracle and, although she was told by the gypsy to keep this aspect of them to herself, she could not resist telling an indiscreet friend about her new-found source of wisdom. In no time at all the entire court was using the cards to uncover political plots, hatch new ones and discover secret love-affairs until, in the end, the King himself was obliged to ban all cards, in and out of court, by royal edict.

Their sudden removal was not welcomed within royal circles generally and, in particular, by a famous soldier of the day named La Hire. Through the magic of the cards he had learned of a certain lady's love for him so he had every reason to be grateful to them. He was, therefore, determined to have this royal ban removed at any price. Therefore, he hatched the following devious yet clever plan to do just this.

Calling again on the court artist, he had an entirely new and different pack made. This time it depicted mythological gods and goddesses, biblical characters, historical and national heroes and three members of the present court – the King, Odette and himself. Caesar, Charlemagne, Alexander and Charles VI were the four kings whilst the four braves knaves were Hogier, Lancelot, Hector and La Hire. For the four queeens he chose Pallas, the goddess of arms, Judith the great Jewess, Rachel the symbol of Ysebeau and Argine the gentle fairy, who looked remarkably like Odette.

La Hire extended this patriotic and military theme to the four suits too. Clubs he said represented the sword-guards; hearts the shape of the drawn cross-bow; diamonds he heads of the war arrows and spades the tools of the same name, necessary for digging in in times of siege. When the King saw how the new cards reflected a glorious national image of France, not to mention a touch of personal flattery, he could not refuse La Hire's earnest request that the ban should be removed. In no time at all the cards were back in favour and were spread throughout the court, Paris and France once again.

From now on the 52 cards were consulted before every military campaign as seriously as they were for *affaires de coeur*. In this respect, history tells us how, four hundred years later, Napoleon planned and won many of his batles, including the winning of the famous Josephine, through the cards' revelations. It is said that this lady was delighted when, as a comparatively minor figure at court, the cards foretold that one day she would ascend the great throne of France. Unfortunately, she did not heed the warning they also gave which said that unless she moderated her temper and controlled her moodiness once in favour with the great dictator, she would surely fall from glory. And this is exactly what happened.

Meanwhile, across the channel in England the cards were

enjoying similar popularity and as early as 1463 Edward IV passed a law forbidding the importation of all foreign cards into the country. This was done not to forbid them, but solely to protect and promote the home-produced card market. Although the English king at that time was greatly in favour of the cards, the Church was all for banning them completley; but since it was within monastic walls and royal circles that they were consulted most, it stood little chance of doing this.

By the time of Elizabeth I (1558-1603) the cards were firmly established as aids to political strategy as well as a way to gain personal victory over an opponent. John Dee, Elizabeth's trusted adviser, spelled out messages from the cards which, it is said, laid the foundations for the future British Empire.

In Scotland at this time, David Rizzio, Mary Queen of Scots' adviser, was revealing her future through the cards. This could hardly be called her fortune for, as a famous tapestry still in existence shows, several nasty looking spades and one small heart card revealed the worst. It is a gloomy scene with the Queen and Rizzio staring in horror at the ominous message. Soon after this historical card-reading, the dreadful warning it gave came true. Mary and Rizzio were both executed by order of her half-sister, Elizabeth of England.

After the reign of Elizabeth I the oracular powers of the cards were not called upon again by royalty. They were, however, still to be found in court, but their role was for amusement only. The Prince Regent in the nineteenth century held many exciting parties in London and Brighton, where playing card games for money resulted in the loss of huge country estates and entire family fortunes overnight.

The Victorian era put a stop to all this and saw the cards as distinctly evil. By then their mystical significance and oracular power for the good of the individual and mankind generally had, to all intents and purposes, vanished. The Church condemned them openly from the pulpit, describing them as the devil's invention, intended to encourage what they considered to be one of man's worst traits – gambling.

This attitude towards the cards persisted well into the twentieth century. They were still banned in many homes and most families who did have a pack never played so much as an innocent game of patience with them on Sundays. Since the 1939-45 war, attitudes have changed considerably, with a result that the original mystical purpose of the cards has once again been recognized. In this new-found enlighenment they are now consulted freely in search of guidance and warnings which will help us to steer a more harmonious and rewarding course through life.

The Tradition of the Cards
A pack consists of 52 cards – 40 numbered and twelve court cards. These are divided into four suits – diamonds, clubs, hearts and spades. Each suit has 13 cards – an ace, two, three, four, five, six, seven, eight, nine, ten, Knave, Queen and King. There are 26 black cards and 26 red.

To distinguish these cards from the Tarot pack they are often referred to as 'ordinary playing cards', but this is precisely what they are not. 'Extraordinary' would be a far more accurate description for not only do they reflect the mysterious relationship with our surroundings, they actually symbolize, numerically, the universe on a vast time scale as well. It is this link with time, as we know it, that gives a clue as to how the cards reveal past, present and future events.

Days, Weeks, Seasons and Years
Traditionally, the 52 cards symbolize the 52 weeks in a year and the four suits represent the four seasons. There is, therefore, one card for each week of the year and one suit for each season. Just as a year is divided into four parts or seasons, so too is a day and a lifetime. Each of these quarters is ruled over by one of the four suits.

The Four Elements
Additionally, the suits symbolize the four elements of nature – air, fire, water and earth. In turn, these natural forces correspond with the basic four-fold nature within man himself. Ancient philosophers classified these characteristics as choleric, sanguine, phlegmatic and melancholic, collectively called the four humours. Today, they are better known as intuition, intelligence, compassion and depression.

The Four Suits
Each of the four suits has a unique characteristic of its own. They relate to the four seasons – spring, summer, autumn and winter; the four elements – air, fire, water and earth; the four weeks in a lunar month; the four parts of a day; the four stages in a lifetime – infancy, adolescence, adulthood and old age; and the four basic psychological characteristics – intuition, intelligence, compassion and depression.

The ace of each suit rules the first week of its corresponding season. Kings rule the second week, Queens rule the third week,

Knaves rule the fourth week, tens rules the fifth week and so on, with the twos ruling the last week in each season.

The first week of a cartomancy year is 1 March to 7 March and is ruled by the first card in the pack, the ace of diamonds. The last week in this year is 22 February to 28 February and is ruled by the 2 of spades, the last and lowest card in the pack. The extra day in a leap-year is, appropriately, under the rulership of the Joker.

Duality – Red and Black Cards

Duality plays a vital role in our lives as indeed it does throughout the entire universe. Since this principle is reflected in everything we do and think it is not surprising to discover that it is the underlying principle of the cards too. This is symbolized by the colours red and black. Red cards are generally feminine with all the attributes associated with this characteristic and black cards are masculine and have correspondingly opposite attributes.

Duality is really a question of balance. Night and day, north and south, positive and negative, winter and summer, hot and cold and Yin and Yang are a few examples we take for granted. The nature kingdom also conforms to this duality, with female and male counterparts in plants, animals and man, in an effort to keep the balance. Individually, we are introduced to this principle through our relationship with our mother and father, who symbolize the feminine and masculine characteristics. As we grow older we develop positive and negative moods on a psychological level. These vary from passive, inner seeking to active, outer searching, which are the opposite ends of the scale.

When the cards are consulted specifically for a character reading, this duality is revealed through combinations of the black and red cards. Synchronistically and symbolically they are then interpreted as degrees and types of extrovert and introvert tendencies.

The 365 Days in a Year

The 365 days in a year are not forgotten either for they are found in the cards in at least two numerically disguised ways.

The first is that when any three cards are chosen they give a possible combination of seven separate meanings. For example, if the three cards in question were the ace of diamonds, 2 of diamonds and 3 of diamonds, they are assessed first individually, then in twos and finally all three together, giving a total of seven different combinations. Seven, of course, is the number of days in a week and when this number is multiplied by 52, the number of weeks in a year, the figure reached is 364. Add to this one further unit representing the pack as a whole and the significant total is 365.

Another instance in which the magic number of 365 is produced is by adding the total number of pips on all the numbered cards to the number of court cards, plus their total value, on the basis of ten for each such card, and then finally adding thirteen, the number of cards in each suit. As the following calculations show, the result is 365.

The number of pips on the 40 numbered cards	= 220
The number of court cards	= 12
The 12 court cards counted as ten each	= 120
The 13 cards in each suit	= 13

365

The Numbers Twelve and Thirteen

The thirteen cards in each suit symbolize the thirteen lunar months in a year, the thirteen weeks in each quarter and the twelve calendar months plus the year as a whole. They also represent Jesus and His twelve Apostles, Jacob and the twelve tribes of Israel, King Arthur and his twelve knights, Robin Hood and his twelve merry men, twelve signs of the zodiac revolving around the heavens, twelve gods on Mount Olympus and last but not least, the solar system. According to ancient tradition, this originally had twelve planets, one of which was the moon, orbiting the sun.

The twelve court cards in a pack represent the twelve followers or supporters found in all religious and mythological hierarchies throughout the ages. 'The twelve days of Christmas' referred to in the carol and the significance of the twelfth-night brings this principle down to a more personal level. A recent example of this same theme is found in the popular record a few years ago called 'Deck of Cards', which describes the virtues and lessons to be learned from each card, in religious and philosophical words set to music.

The number thirteen, twelve plus one, plays an important role in astrology and astronomy, as well as in religion and mythology and, whilst there are some who regard this number as unlucky, there are others who see it as a distinctly happy and positive sign. Its negative association arose from the New Testament text concerning the twelve Apostles who sat with Jesus around the table for the Last Supper. Its positive association, on the other hand, also arose from the Bible. In the Jewish faith the thirteenth year is seen as one of fulfilment, so when a boy reaches his thirteenth birthday he is said to have come of age and reached a stage of maturity to be celebrated in a memorable way.

As a number, thirteen is therefore neither fortunate nor unfortunate; it is neverthless of great importance, signifying a completion of one cycle and the beginning of the next. It is the death of the old yet, at the same time, the birth of the new. In the cards this special number is represented by the ace in each suit, ranking high when it follows the King. It is the first and the last card, the Alpha and Omega.

The Trinity
Sacred trinities existed in religious cults long before orthodox Christianity recognized the Holy Trinity. Known as the 'three faces of God', the Egyptians worshipped Isis, Osiris and Horus and in Celtic mythology these same three aspects were Belinis, Taranis and Hesus. In the cards this trinity pattern is represented by King, Queen and Knave in each suit.

The Number Forty
The forty numbered cards in a pack remind us of events in the Old and New Testaments. We read that the Israelites wandered for forty years in the wilderness before entering the Promised Land. Moses remained forty days on Mount Sinai and Elijah was forty days in solitude. Jesus Christ fasted for forty days in the desert. He preached for forty months and was forty hours in the tomb. Jerusalem was destroyed forty years after the Ascension.

It takes forty weeks to have a baby and it is said that forty winks is as good as a full night's sleep! St Swithin, in the ninth century, forecast rain for forty days and forty nights, if it rains on the 15 July, a day now remembered each year as St Swithin's day.

Numerically and symbolically the 52 cards form a collective backcloth in front of which we, as individuals, stand. The relationship between ourselves and our environment is on many levels; some associations we can seel clearly, but others we cannot. With the cards it becomes apparent immediately we recognize their symbolic link with the universe, reflecting, as they do, the principle of 'as above, so below'. The many traditional aspects of all this are equally divided between the four suits.

Conversation and the Cards

There are many sources which enrich a language and the cards have certainly played their part so far as English speech is concerned. When we call someone a 'card' we are paying them a sort of compliment for it shows they have a hidden mystique which is both amusing and intriguing.

If a specific card, like an ace, is chosen to describe a person, then their ability and expertise is established immediately because there is only one definition of an 'ace' pilot or 'ace' driver. For that matter, there is only one meaning for a 'Joker' because everyone knows what to expect when he is around!

The 'Jack' of all trades may be a master of none, but at least he is more suitable than a 'knave'! And what better advice can be given than to encourage someone to 'play their cards right'? If we feel they have a few 'aces up their sleeve' or even 'hold all the aces', so much the better for this will certainly help them 'to follow suit' when the time is right and, who knows, they may even 'win hands down'.

To say 'it's on the cards' sums it all up but often in life, as with the cards, it is not always advisable to 'show your hand' or 'lay all your cards on the table' at once. Try to keep a 'pokeer-face' then, especially if you want to 'come up trumps'!

Games Played with the Cards

It is said that the ancient sages gave the cards a two-fold attraction. One aspect was to appeal to man's nobler quality, his search for knowledge and wisdom, whilst the other was to pander to his lesser virtue, a pursuit of greed and amusement. If this is so, then they certainly succeeded in the last respect because card games, especially those played for money, are as popular today as they were in the days of the French court.

The majority of card games played in Britain today came originally from the Continent, although over the years these have been modified and given new names. Soldiers returning home from wars in Europe brought back most of these, notably 'Napoleon', better known as 'Nap'. And during the First World War the troops played a French game called *'vingt-et-un'* which, after slightly altering the rules, was renamed 'pontoon'.

Emigrants to the U.S.A. took the cards with them, and from the smoky saloons dotted along the highways to the West emerged that well known gambling game, 'poker'. This again was an adaptation of a French bluffing game called *'poque'*, hence the importance of the 'poker-face'. The States later gave birth to 'gin rummy' and 'slippery sam' and with the samba in the 1960s came the latest edition of all, 'canasta'. This belongs to the rummy family.

A typical English card game is 'cribbage', played with cards, a board and pegs. This is said to have been invented by Sir John Suckling a famous gambler of the seventeenth century. More recently, 'Newmarket', named after the racing town in East Anglia, has become very popular in family circles, where only small bets of a few pence or even buttons are at stake.

On a more sober note we have 'bridge' and 'whist'. Bridge parties and whist drives are held regularly in homes and church halls up and down the country. Here, they rarely play for money, but prizes are nevertheless given and although the players would be loath to call it gambling, they still compete pretty fiercely in order to win!

This is by no means a complete list of card games but last and not least we have the solo game of 'patience'. This is said to have been played in French bistros by artists whiling away their time over a glass of wine, testing both the patience of *le patron* and themselves.

The Name of the Game
When remembering that the other purpose of the cards was to reveal our mysterious relationship with our surroundings, it is not surprising that even a game of cards symbolizes the game of life itself. This aspect is the opposite side of the coin from that of gambling and amusement, but is always present.

Take any game of cards you like, gambling or otherwise. After a hand is dealt the players look at the cards to see what they have. Some of these will be good, others will be bad and the rest mediocre. Compare this hand with personal attributes and handicaps, assets and liabilities, credits and deficits and joys and sorrows dealt to us by the hand of Fate. When a good hand is dealt to a player in a card game, it appears that he has an advantage from the start; so too it would seem that the person born with every luxury, good looks and good health, is on to a winning streak. Should both players make the most of what they have, then the chances are they will both succeed. But if they fail to make the right moves at the right time and generally play their cards badly, then they will undoubtedly end up the losers.

On the other hand, players who receive appalling cards, like people born into deprived circumstances, may play what cards they have extremely well and, purely through their own efforts and determination, turn out to win hands down! The lesson to be learned from this is that by making the best of what we have been dealt, whether they are cards in a pretend game or opportunities in the real game of life, we can still win in the end.

1
DIVINATION AND THE CARDS

At one time the observation of virtually everything provided grounds for divination. The clouds – nephelmancy; the winds – austromancy; smoke – capnomancy; a flight of birds – ornithomancy; the flame from a lamp – lampadomancy and the water from a fountain – pegomancy; these were all sources for potential forecasting. The throwing of rice onto a flat surface, tea-leaves left in a cup and pictures in the fire also created signs to be interpreted as omens but, in each case, it was the abstract shapes formed by these that served to awaken the intuitive powers of the interpreters.

The cards are also omens but they are something more than symbolic patterns which depend on the psychic ability of the interpreter for interpretation. Down the ages the four suits have inherited definite characteristics and meanings which are basically constant and each card represents a different aspect of the suit to which it belongs. Intuition, so far as the cards are concerned, comes into play mainly in the interpretation of the symbolic, over-all message which links up with personal circumstances.

Synchronicity – Coincidence and Chance

There is undoubtedly a connection between the human psyche and external events, the inner and outer worlds. All religions teach the existence of an underlying link between ourselves and others and with the universe as a whole. Explanations concerning this vary considerably and none are really convincing, nor are they complete within themselves.

Synchronicity, defined by C. G. Jung as 'a meaningful coincidence', is one way in which this connection manifests itself in our daily lives. More often than not such moments usually pass by unnoticed and nearly always unrecognized for what they are. The concept of synchronicity gives us an insight into just how the cards serve as a bridge or link between the inner and outer worlds. It shows that what may appear to be a coincidence or chance is, in fact, a directly related event. But this event is not by way of the usual chain of cause and effect, action and reaction, so it cannot be traced back and explained in logical terms or in chronological order. This is because the synchronistic event does not arise from linear time but from that 'out-of-time moment', the 'eternal now'.

The English language has only one word for time but the ancients, in particular the Greeks, had two – *kronos* and *kairos*. These describe the difference between the experience of time and the quality of time. *Kronos*, also spelt *chronos*, is measured time as we know it, giving us experiences in chronological order. *Kairos*, sometimes spelt *cairos*, giving us the link with Egypt, is participation within time itself and gives us timelessness. It is during moments of *kairos* that synchronistic events occur, showing we are 'at one with' and not 'separate from' our surroundings.

Oracles and Jung

Having found that humanity was motivated by inner creative instincts as well as outer material drives, Jung began to investigate the unseen synchronistic link between us and our surroundings. This led him to the *I Ching*, otherwise known as *The Book of Changes*. The *I Ching* is considered to be an oracle in book form and is consulted in exactly the same way as the cards. Messages in this book, like those written into the cards, are symbolic, so before they can be understood they have to be interpreted.

Jung found that when we consult an oracle such as the cards, the *I Ching* or any other form of divination for that matter, we are deliberately attempting to produce a reading through synchronicity. We are, by virtue of unconsciously selecting certain cards, putting ourselves into a position whereby we actually cause that coinciding or synchronistic moment of *kairos* – timelessness. The result of this is that we contact the past, present and future.

2

HOW TO CONSULT THE CARDS

A successful reading depends on a truly representative selection of cards chosen by the questioner and the ability of the interpreter to understand them. The questioner and the interpreter may be one and the same person because we most certainly can read our own cards, but an assistant will always give a much more objective assessment of the situation.

The first qualification necessary to become a good cartomancer is a genuine desire to do so! This, backed up with plenty of enthusiasm and lots of practice is all that is needed to succeed. If there is a 'feeling' for the cards then so much the better. Although meanings of individual cards are readily available, it is the intuitive association and linking together of these that gives depth to the over-all message. A psychic and sensitive nature is an advantage, but this is something that actually develops through working with the cards in their oracular capacity.

When first learning to read the cards use nothing more than their basic meanings. This will give an over-all message and assessment of a situation although it may appear somewhat stilted. Remembering that 'practice makes perfect', confidence is soon gained and the intuitive links between one card and another quickly develop.

The most difficult part of an interpretation is telling the questioner that obstacles are ahead, especially when that person is already in trouble. It helps to know that by doing this you are helping them to avoid a problem or, at the very least, saving them from being taken by complete surprise. It is essential that you offer hope where there is despair and give comfort in place of sorrow. Look for a solution, which can always be seen in the cards alongside the problem, rather like the healing dock being found next to the spiteful nettle. Again, practice is necessary to recognize these symbolic antidotes among the hurdles.

Traditional Rituals

There are traditional rituals involved in selecting and reading the cards which should be observed wherever possible. This helps to bring into play those synchronistic moments which allow the questioner, unconsciously, to select the right cards. It also increases the awareness of the interpreter and generally produces harmony between them and the cards.

Ideally, a new pack of cards should be purchased and kept solely for the purpose of divination. These should be handled only by yourself and questioners who select spreads from them for you to interpret. No games of any nature should ever be played with them.

Cards for divination should really be kept in a set place, preferably higher than table-top level. It is said this keeps them above mundane matters and the best place is the top shelf of a dark cupboard. True initiates of the cards advocate that a hand-sewn silk bag is made for them to which they are returned immediately after a reading. This is done to preserve their oracular power which increases with proper use. Mis-handling and using them for card games releases this energy with a result that their harmonies are disturbed, affecting both questioner and interpreter.

The Questioner and Interpreter

Before a spread can be chosen, questioners must decide whether they want a general reading or one that highlights a particular aspect of their life. If, for example, their concern is their love life then a spread suitable for this would be very different from one designed to give an over-all picture of their situation. Again, if a character analysis is required yet another spread would be preferred. The number of questions asked from a spread does not matter, although three is usual, so long as they relate to the subject in question.

It will also be necessary to choose a representative court card for some of the spreads. The secret of discovering the most appropriate one lies in assessing a personal standpoint in relation to a problem or situation, as described later in 'How to Choose a Court Card'.

Preparation for a Reading

Handling the cards is most important for it imprints them with personal vibrations. Before using new cards for a reading, shuffle and cut them as many times as possible and, whilst doing so, look closely at their intricate designs and numbers. The more you familiarize yourself with these the better they respond to your questions.

A relaxed atmosphere is essential when reading the cards. The burning of a joss-stick helps achieve this and so does a warm room rather than a cold one. From a purely practical point of view make sure that the table is large enough to accommodate the spread because if it is bunched up, continuity and expansion of thought are correspondingly hampered. If possible use a round table and then sit with your back to the North and have the questioner facing you with their back to the South.

Procedure

Before placing the pack of cards on the table the interpreter must shuffle them to rid them of any previous influence. If a court card is necessary to represent the questioner it is chosen at this stage, after the initial shuffling by the interpreter. Having decided on this it is then carefully placed to one side, ready to be included in the final selection.

The remaining 51 cards, or 52 cards if a court card is not necessary, are now handed to the questioner who, with the nature of their problem or situation clearly and uppermost in their mind, proceeds to shuffle them thoroughly. The cards are then ceremoniously placed in the centre of the table and are cut by the questioner three times with the left hand. (This hand is nearer the heart, both anatomically and emotionally).

Next, the interpreter picks them up and spreads them face downwards across the table, in a slightly overlapping line. They are now ready for the questioner to make a selection, the number of which will depend on the spread chosen for the reading. This selection is done completely spontaneously when it will be found that the eye leads the hand, the left hand, automatically to certain cards. As they are chosen they are removed and placed face downwards in a small pack, strictly in order of choice. When the required number has been extracted the remaining cards should be removed from the table.

Placing the Court Card

If the spread required a personal court card it is added by the questioner now. Keeping the selected cards face downwards so that their values are not revealed, the personal card is placed among them. This may be a random placing or a calculated, conscious decision as to where it is inserted; it may be exactly in the middle, the third, the ninth, the fifth position etc. This choice is entirely up to the questioner.

The interpreter now takes the selected cards, with or without the personal court card, in readiness to arrange them into a particular spread. At this point it may be necessary to turn the cards over so that the bottom card, the first one chosen, is at the top. This is most important if the cards are to be placed in order of selection.

When a satisfactory reading has been completed the cards are reunited into a full pack and thoroughly shuffled by the interpreter in order to disconnect them from present association. They are then returned to their secluded place of safety in readiness for the next reading.

3
HOW TO CHOOSE A COURT CARD

It is generally supposed that a fair person is represented by a red King, Queen or Jack and a dark person by one of the black court cards. For readings of an over-all nature, covering every aspect of life this basic representation is sufficient, but for a specialized reading, focussing on a particular aspect or problem, a much more characteristic court card is needed. After all, appearance, like beauty, is only skin-deep.

We have, within each of us, the four characteristics symbolized by the four suits. These are proportionately different in every individual and although it may appear that some people are typical diamonds and have no heart, they nevertheless possess this aspect along with the other two, hidden away somewhere. Even the most rigid types have to show their hand sometimes and it is the ability to do this at the right time that makes for a more balanced existence.

Life demands that we play different roles to suit different occasions, so automatically most of us are able to adapt and act the part. An excellent example of this change of role is the hard-headed King of diamonds who falls madly in love and becomes the compassionate King of hearts overnight! But should our work or career be at stake, then our King, Queen or Jack of hearts image is not the one to wear at such times; it is the King, Queen or Jack of diamonds-self who best represents this standpoint; and when money matters are pressing, the King, Queen or Jack of clubs must be 'top dog' then.

In the past, divorced people have always been portrayed by the King or Queen of spades. Unless these are particularly bitter and twisted about their position, these cards are a total misrepresentation and in no way represent them. It is usual for a Queen court card to represent a woman, a King court card to represent a mature man and a Jack court card to represent a younger man. In these days of equality of the sexes, with equal pay for equal work, it may be more appropriate in some cases for a woman to choose a King or a Jack court card and a man to choose a Queen. As time changes, society alters its standpoint; and so, too, do the cards; therefore, from the following descriptions choose the one which best represents you in relation to your looks, problem situation or question.

A Court Card for General Readings

Decide on your outer appearance for these readings and then choose the court card which describes you best.

Diamond Court Cards represent very fair people with flaxen, light red or white hair, light blue or green eyes and a very pale complexion. Slim Nordic types are true diamonds.

Heart Court Cards represent fair people too, but those with slightly richer coloured hair and complexions than diamond types. They have blue, grey or hazel eyes and light brown or auburn hair. Plump, family people are often typical hearts.

Club Court Cards represent those with rich brown hair, brown eyes and colourful complexions. Energetic Latin races are generally club types.

Spade Court Cards represent very dark-skinned people with raven black hair and dark eyes. They always have plenty of energy in reserve and are physically strong.

A Court Card for Specialized Readings

Choosing the right court card for these readings depends entirely on the personal standpoint in relation to a problem, situation or question and has nothing whatsoever to do with outer appearance. Select the most appropriate from the suits below.

Diamond Court Cards represent those concerned with practical matters relating to work, career, promotion, redundancy, ambitions, aims, property, moves, travel and all forms of communication including acting, writing and artistic painting. Efficient, practical people and those who think mainly with their heads, such as professional and business people and manual workers are these diamond types.

Heart Court Cards represent those who are facing emotional problems, romantic entanglements, marriage and heartfelt relationships. All who think with their hearts and the love-lorn are heart types, so too are family-minded people.

Club Court Cards represent those with financial interests and problems involving investments, deals, gifts, monetary surprises, debts and bankruptcy. Bank managers, budding tycoons, misers and paupers are club types.

Spade Court Cards represent those who feel hope is fading fast. They may be in a terrible state facing court cases, worried about a health problem and generally surrounded by negative circumstances. The unfortunate person, albeit temporarily, is the spade type. So, too, are judges, lawyers and all who wield authority.

A Court Card for Psychic Readings

Your standpoint is very important and in this respect it depends mainly on whether you have a positive or negative psychic nature and how long you have been involved with psychism, occultism and philosophy.

Diamond Court Cards represent positive psychics including clairvoyants, astrologers, cartomancers, occultists and healers. If a newcomer to these arts, then choose a diamond court card.

Heart Court Cards represent negative-receptive psychics including mediums, inspirational speakers, intuitive workers and healers.

Club Court Cards represent experienced psychics and those who have returned to the scene after a break for some reason. They may be either positive or negative psychics or a mixture of both.

Spade Court Cards represent those who work entirely alone and not with a group. They are lone workers and seekers but are not necessarily advanced in their understanding. Often they cannot tell the difference between the right and wrong occult path.

A Court Card for a Character Reading

This card should reflect what you consider to be your more permanent personality and not a transient mood of the moment. Find yourself in the suits below and choose accordingly.

Diamond Court Cards represent hopeful positive people with plenty of good ideas and untapped mental resources. They are generally outward-looking and extrovert by nature.

Heart Court Cards represent emotional people capable of great depths of feeling. They are sometimes over-sensitive and compassionate, inward-looking and introvert by nature.

Club Court Cards represent determined people who seek external riches and support from others to gain confidence. They think with both their head and their heart.

Spade Court Cards represent those who see life as a dark, hopeless battle. Most of the time they are depressed and look too closely at themselves and the underlying meaning of life.

4
HOW TO CHOOSE A SPREAD

There are many spreads from which to choose and these are based either on the British system, which uses 52 cards or on the Continental system, which uses only 32 cards. Since the Continental system means discarding all cards below number seven, except the four aces, a reading is bound to give an incomplete assessment of a situation. Simply because a card is numerically low it does not follow that its symbolic significance is correspondingly low. In addition to this, the removal of these so-called lower cards completely destroys the cosmic significance, numerically reflecting the principle of 'as above, so below'.

All numbers are equally important and the number two, missing from Continental spreads, is just one example. This number introduces into the suits questions of duality, opposition, partnership, harmony, disharmony, balance and counterbalance, the basis, in fact, of life itself. When choosing a traditionally Continental method I therefore suggest that cards are selected from a full 52-card pack and not from a watered down version containing only 32 cards.

Continental spreads also distinguish between upright and reversed meanings of a card. This can introduce unnecessary complications into a reading, mainly because foreign authorities vary in their interpretation. Nevertheless, most sources agree that a reversal gives a definitely gloomy meaning even to the most positive and encouraging cards!

Upright and reversed cards belong strictly to the tarot pack where different meanings are clear and important. If this added aspect is desired and your cards are not designed to show which way up they are, then mark them yourself with a 'U' and an 'R' to give them a top and a bottom. British cards do not usually indicate this, except in the cases of the ace of hearts, the ace of clubs and the ace of spades. This is not through design but because their shapes are not symmetrical. The meanings of reversed cards, according to one French source, are given along with the other definitions of individual cards.

A spread represents a situation, problem or question which the suits reflect symbolically on a practical, psychological and psychic level. Each of the 52 cards indicates an event, a quality, a characteristic and an influence and, depending on the spread used, these will be brought to life through the meaning of each card and those surrounding it. For example, the 7 of diamonds on the practical level symbolizes personal ambitions, aims and materialistic plans for the future, but only neighbouring cards will tell us the likelihood of success or failure. Alone, the meaning of this card remains a bare statement of fact.

From the following seven spreads choose the one most likely to reflect your problem, situation or questions. Remember, they symbolize conditions and give symbolic answers which then have to be interpreted on the appropriate level as we are back again to the importance of the personal, fundamental standpoint. Establish this and the rest is easy.

5

THE MYSTICAL CROSS

This is a British spread originating from the Knights Templars. It gives us an excellent over-all assessment of a personal situation on all levels, indicating relationships between lovers, family, friends and acquaintances, career and business prospects, ambitions, money matters and the inevitable obstacles and hurdles in life too. It also shows individual characteristics and psychic potential so may also be used for a character study or psychic reading.

Method

A personal court card is necessary to represent the questioner, plus twelve more, making thirteen cards in all. Having carried out the ritualistic preparation and chosen the most appropriate court card, remove this from the pack. The remaining 51 cards are then spread face downwards across the table in a slightly overlapping line, by the interpreter. Twelve cards are selected from these by the questioner, who keeps them strictly in the order of selection. The court card is then placed significantly among them in the way previously described.

The interpreter now takes the thirteen cards and turns them face upwards, thus revealing the first card selected, and arranges them to form the equilateral cross as shown in Diagram 1 (on page 246).

The line down represents the present situation and the line across reflects influences which will affect this situation. The position of the court card is noted first. If this is in the line down, it shows the questioner's circumstances are likely to control them more than they are able to control their circumstances. If it is in the line across, then it means it is well within their power to control and influence matters. Should this court card be in the middle of the cross then the questioner is assured that the situation will shortly be resolved in a most satisfactory way.

The card in the centre of the cross is interpreted next. This indicates the major aspect around which everything revolves at present. It is both a cause and an effect, with its significance depending on the suit and individual meaning of the card.

Cards in the line down are interpreted individually and linked together to symbolize aspects of the present situation. Finally, the cards in the line across are interpreted individually as influences which will alter the present situation in the future.

THE MYSTICAL CROSS

7 of spades

Queen of hearts

4 of clubs

2 of diamonds/7 of diamonds/9 of spades/4 of diamonds/3 of diamonds/5 of hearts/King of hearts

2 of spades

6 of hearts

8 of spades

Question: What does the future hold for me?

Court Card: Queen of hearts

Combinations and Relationships of the Cards:

Two Twos: Separate ways

Two Fours: Uncertainty at present

Two Sevens: Mutual Love

Position of the Court Card: This is in the line down showing that circumstances control the questioner more than she is able to control them.

The line down represents the present situation.

7 of Spades: The fact that this card heads this line indicates that personal fears and worries dominate the situation. Most of these will come to nothing but, even so, a shadow is cast over everything, producing apprehension and negativity.

Queen of Hearts: This court card represents the questioner. Her family, home and emotional happiness are her life. There seem to be worries on the one hand, 7 of spades, and money troubles on the other, 4 of clubs. 'Thinking' mainly with her heart, not her head, neither of these problems will be easily resolved.

4 of Clubs: This card warns of the loss of an asset. It might be a purse, key or other valuable personal possession but, at the same time, it also indicates difficulties to make ends meet financially.

4 of Diamonds: Much revolves around this card because it is in the centre of the cross. Practical problems are difficult to solve and communications with others seem to break down. Decision making is virtually impossible so this prolongs the issue.

2 of Spades: Two sides of the question are seen but both look equally

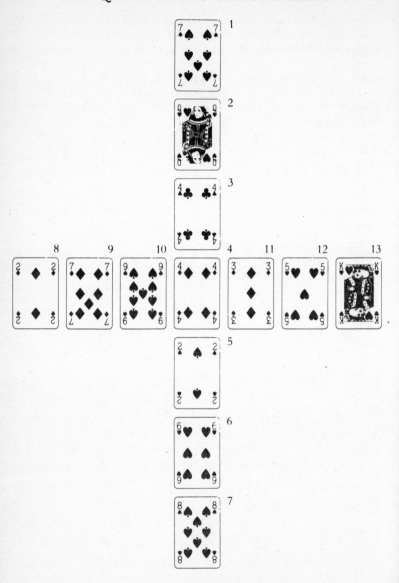

The Mystical Cross

bad. The practical decision reflected in the previous card comes to a head and steps will have to be taken soon.

6 of Hearts: Again, two sets of circumstances are at loggerheads. A compromise is going to be the only way out and this will entail considerable self-sacrifice, emotionally.

8 of Spades: A drain on resources brings depression and lack of energy. It is advisable that the questioner trusts no one but herself. Health must be watched carefully.

The line across reflects influences which will affect the present situation.

2 of Diamonds: This dual influence will help solve the situation in a very practical way, but its value is not recognized at the time.

7 of Diamonds: This influence represents the questioner's practical plans and initiative which, until now, seems to have been sadly lacking. Once this begins to develop, she can expect action. Self-confidence will grow from this point.

9 of Spades: Depressing though this influence is, at least it brings action. By seeing it as a necessary evil the questioner should know that the present is a stage which must be passed through before better times are reached.

4 of Diamonds: As an influence, this card emphasizes loyalties which conflict with what should be done. The head must rule over the heart in this instance.

3 of Diamonds: Practical drive and enthusiasm will develop with this influence. Determination, so necessary to get out of the present rut, will also emerge.

5 of Hearts: A decision to escape from the real issue is felt with this influence. Personal feelings will be overruled by the practical scene, but this is the only way out of a negative situation.

King of Hearts: It can only be assumed that this King represents the questioner's husband. If this is so, then he too is a 'heart-thinker' so is little help in producing a practical solution to his wife's problem. It is, however, a compassionate influence which no doubt gives plenty of comfort and love to her.

Conclusions: The present situation, symbolized by the cards, shows life is getting this person down. Much of her trouble is looking too closely and intently at herself in relation to circumstances. An unknowing selfishness exists which would vanish if she took a different view point of the whole scene.

Future influences help solve all this but the cards also point out that she needs to adopt a more practical approach to life in order to balance the emotional outlook she has at present.

6

THE HORSESHOE OF FATE

The 'horseshoe of fate' originated from the gypsies who took it to France from the Middle East many centuries ago. It is both a simple and effective method, appropriate for a specialized reading relating to all heartfelt problems, changes in work, moving house, travel and money matters.

Method
Seven cards are selected by the questioner, in the ritualistic manner, from the full pack. No court card is needed. These seven cards are then handed to the interpreter who turns them over to reveal the first card selected, and then sets them out in the order shown in Diagram 2 (on page 249).

Card number 1 represents past influences contributing to the present situation. *Card number 2* reveals choices and alternatives. *Card number 3* represents stability or instability. *Card number 4* shows cross-currents, influences and challenges. *Card number 5* shows openings or obstacles. *Card number 6* tells who or what your friends or foes are and *card number 7* indicates the final outcome. This spread is interpreted through the individual meanings of the cards which are then applied to personal circumstances.

THE HORSESHOE OF FATE
King of hearts   8 of hearts
2 of clubs   6 of clubs
  5 of spades   8 of spades
              5 of hearts

Question: Will I win the personal battle arising from business affairs and money complications?
Combinations and Relationships of the Cards:
Two Fives: Personal uncertainty
Two Eights: Inconstency

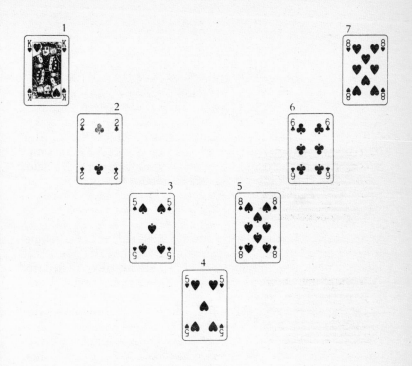

The Horseshoe of Fate

Card Number 1: Past influences contributing to the present situation.
King of Hearts: This card reflects the questioner's own character and influence, revealing he has a pretty easy-going nature. In the past he has let others take an unfair advantage of him. Although usually of persuasive nature, this applies more to emotional situations than to business, so in this respect he would be relatively powerless. Much of the present trouble arises from this and amount almost to neglect of practical matters.
Card Number 2: Choice and alternatives.

2 of Clubs: A change is inevitable but making a choice in conjunction with this is going to be rather difficult because there is not much to choose from. Opposition delays things and money will be the issue. Seeing things from another point of view will help, but beware of an 'out of the frying pan and into the fire' situation developing.

Card Number 3: Stability or instability.

5 of Spades: Troubles are undoubtedly causing insecurity leading to some degree of instability. Complications prolong things but there is one aspect which offers hope for the future; set-backs will be followed by eventual success so despondency is warned against.

Card Number 4: Cross-current challenges and influences.

5 of Hearts: This represents personal reactions to the situation. Inner feelings from the heart are very different from the logic of the head. There is a desire to escape from these emotions but they are part of the battle or challenge. The tendency is to bury the head in the sand so courage is necessary to overcome these personal feelings.

Card Number 5: Opportunities or obstacles.

8 of Spades: A definite obstacle must be faced before moving on to more fulfilling circumstances. False friends are warned against, too. Despondency, with the added problem of depression, become obstacles in themselves so try to keep these in perspective.

Card Number 6: Friends or foes.

6 of Clubs: Help will be forthcoming from a most unexpected source. In this way, friends will prove themselves by giving practical or financial assistance. There are many ways in which they might do this, even as a last minute rescue operation.

Card Number 7: The final outcome.

8 of Hearts: Although the present seems to be in a turmoil, there are hopes for much happier times. A new-found satisfaction is indicated by this card, provided the right cards are played at the right time. In other words, by facing up to obstacles, life will be seen from a fresh standpoint, with new light falling on old, dark situations. In this way, the battle will be won.

Conclusion: In answer to the question, it appears that the outcome depends mainly on a personal, inner battle being won first. Having let things slide in the past, everything has caught up with the questioner so he must take action now to begin to put matters right. A change is coming and when true friends have been sorted out from the false, it will be possible to accept reliable and sincere help. Although an outright win is not seen in these cards, peace of mind will return eventually.

7
THE PYRAMID

Not surprisingly, this spread finds its origin in Egypt. The longer one ponders upon its message, the more it reveals and so in this we see reflections of the great pyramid itself. It is an excellent spread to symbolize a particular aspect of life, but may be used for a concise general reading too.

Method
No court card is needed. Ten cards are selected by the questioner in the true ritualistic manner and handed to the interpreter who turns them over to reveal the first card selected. This card is placed at the top of the pyramid and the others, in sequence, form the lines below, as shown in Diagram 3 (on page 252).

The card on the top line symbolizes the over-all aspect and influence affecting the problem, situation or question. *The second line* shows choice of action. *The third line* reveals underlying forces at work and the degree of stability, and *the base line* tells the questioner how they should play their cards in the future.

THE PYRAMID

9 of hearts

8 of clubs   5 of hearts

3 of spades   Queen of diamonds   Queen of clubs

Ace of diamonds   3 of hearts   4 of spades   6 of hearts

Question: How will my love-life work out?
Combinations and Relationships of the cards:
Two Threes: A choice must be made
Two Queens: Curiosity
9*Top Card:* Over-all aspect and influence.
9 of Hearts: This is the 'wish' or the 'heart's desire' card so it is no secret that this questioner has romance on his mind. It is also the most fortunate card in the pack, offering happiness and fulfilment so long as careful planning is made and put into operation.
Second Line: Choice of action.

The Pyramid

8 of Clubs and 5 of Hearts: The alternatives are to take a chance as suggested by the 8 of clubs, the gambler's card, or not to face up to emotional feelings and responsibilities as shown by the 5 of hearts. Neither are strong decisions nor solutions which would greatly alter the present situation.

Third Line: Underlying forces producing stability or instability.

3 of Spades, Queen of Diamonds and the Queen of Clubs: This seems to reflect a two-to-one chance against a stable situation. The eternal triangle from the 3 of spades, a practical woman in the form of the Queen of diamonds and a determined woman in the Queen of clubs, together put the questioner to the spot.

Base Line: How to play one's cards best.

Ace of Diamonds, 3 of Hearts, 4 of Spades and 6 of Hearts: First of all, practical plans should be made for the future, as stressed by the ace of diamonds. Then, emotional stability, symbolized by the 3 of hearts, should be carefully considered. This is essential before the true heart's desire can be pursued properly. The 4 of spades warns against obstacles, delays and minor upsets and the 6 of hearts makes it quite clear that self-sacrifice is going to be necessary before happiness and peace of mind are found.

Conclusion: There seems to be little doubt that this gentleman is stringing along two ladies at the same time. He must make up his mind and make the choice himself. Although nothing disasterous is going to happen to him, it is hardly fair to keep both ladies in suspense.

8
THE ROMANY WAY

This spread originated from the Balkans and is used extensively by the Romany folk today, in Britain and on the Continent. Most appropriately, it reveals secrets of the heart's desires and all personal problems concerning health and wealth.

Method
No court card is needed. Twenty-one cards are selected in the true ritualistic manner by the questioner. These are handed to the interpreter who turns them over to make sure that the first card selected comes to the top. They are then arranged in sequence, as shown in Diagram 4 (on page 255).

The top line represents the past: *the middle line* represents the present; and *the bottom line* represents the future. The cards are interpreted from left to right beginning with the top line.

THE ROMANY WAY
The Past
2 of diamonds/9 of spades/6 of hearts/Queen of hearts/2 of spades/King of diamonds/7 of hearts
The Present
3 of clubs/2 of hearts/5 of diamonds/Queen of clubs/4 of spades/3 of spades/4 of diamonds
The Future
7 of clubs/10 of diamonds/10 of hearts/Jack of diamonds/6 of spades/9 of clubs/3 of hearts
Question: Will I be healthy, wealthy, happy and wise in the future?
Combinations and Relationships of the Cards:
Three Twos: Change of direction
Three Threes: Stability
Two Sixes: Contradictions
Two Sevens: Mutual love
Two Nines: Eventual contentment
Two Tens: Repayments
Two Queens: Curiosity

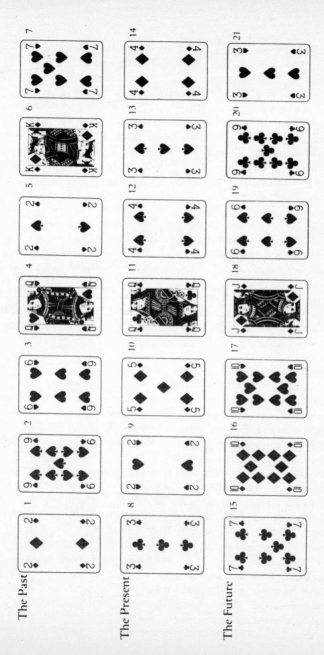

The Romany Way

The Past

2 of Diamonds: A partnership on a practical basis once played an important role in producing the stability enjoyed at present.

9 of Spades: An illness, probably followed by depression, made a considerable impact at the time. Plans had to be altered, especially in relation to a career and this brought great disappointment.

6 of Hearts: Through the set-back seen in the previous card a personal self-sacrifice had to be made. This looked grim at the time, but later proved to have been a blessing in disguise.

Queen of Hearts: A good-hearted person gave help and comfort during those times of stress and was most likely to have been the questioner's mother.

2 of Spades: A difficult decision had to be made and it came at the worst possible time. Opposition and complications must have brought further depression through the delay.

King of Diamonds: This man gave practical help and advice which helped solve many of the difficultis. He was probably the questioner's father.

7 of Hearts: This shows that the questioner found security within himself during, or as a result of, those dark days. His family stood by him and helped in every possible way.

The Present

3 of Clubs: Financial stability gives confidence and security. Progress from now on will be slow but sure and wealth in other ways will begin to accumulate.

2 of Hearts: This shows that an emotional harmonious partnership exists, where successes and heartaches are shared equally. The future will continue to be shared in this balanced way, ensuring family happiness for some time to come.

5 of Diamonds: There are thoughts and discussions concerning property and a possible move, but this is only in the air at present.

Queen of Clubs: Here is a valuable lady who must surely be the questioner's wife. Excellent when it comes to spending money, she has the gift of always making a little go a long way.

4 of Spades: Delays and minor upsets hinder plans for the future. There are difficulties in trying to please everyone, mainly because there are many sides to be considered.

3 of Spades: There seems to be a run of negativity which brings depression and uncertainty. A third person may be interfering and unbalancing everything generally.

4 of Diamonds: It is important that a practical conclusion is reached soon. This should be settled with the head and not too much help from the heart.

The Future

7 of Clubs: Thanks to careful planning in the past there is security in the future. Money will not be a worry and although great financial wealth is not foreseen, there will certainly be sufficient to meet every need.

10 of Diamonds: This indicates the end of one cycle and the beginning of the next. Retirement is on the cards and following this an interesting new life opens up. A move of house is likely at this stage.

10 of Hearts: Having started on a new practical trail, expect this to be accompanied by an equally interesting emotional outlook. Family and friends help to make up this harmony.

Jack of Diamonds: Here is a younger member of the family who gives reliable help when it is most needed. He adds vitality to life and will always be around when most needed.

6 of Spades: A disappointment is to be expected which will overshadow the peace and quiet for a while. This worry could relate to a health problem, but things soon right themselves.

9 of Clubs: Wealth, in every sense of the word, can confidently be expected. Recovery from a set-back seen in the previous card is assured and peace of mind will return.

3 of Hearts: Emotional stability and inner harmony symbolized by this card are the best gifts to bestow on any future.

Conclusion: From disappointments in the past this questioner has learned the lessons of life the hard way. Having fought and won personal battles early on gave him confidence and security. His health has improved over the years and no serious problems are foreseen in this direction. Financially, funds will be just about adequate to provide for necessities, but a wealth of understanding seems to have developed which is worth a lot more than money in the bank. There appears to be a particular problem at the moment, but this will be solved soon and will in no way spoil plans for the future.

9

THE MAGIC SQUARE

This spread was the inspiration of an ancient sage who inherited secrets from the East and the West. As you will see, it is based more on individual potential than on past, present and future events so is ideal for revealing characteristic traits and psychic abilities.

Method

A personal court card is needed to represent the questioner in relation to a character analysis or psychic reading. Having chosen this, it is placed to one side whilst the questioner shuffles the cards. With the pack remaining face downwards, cards are taken from the top by the interpreter, who places then in the order shown in Diagram 5 (on page 259).

The first four cards are taken in order from the pack and placed accordingly. The fifth card is the personal court card, and is placed over square five. The sixth, seventh, eighth and ninth cards are then taken in sequence from the pack to complete the diagram.

Each card relates to the meaning of the square it covers, and is interpreted in relation to this.

THE MAGIC SQUARE

1	2	3
Individuality	*Duality*	*Stability*
Ace of hearts	4 of diamonds	3 of spades
4	5	6
Tenacity	*Potentiality*	*Opportunity*
3 of clubs	Queen of hearts	Ace of spades
7	8	9
Spirituality	*Negativity*	*Positivity*
6 of hearts	8 of clubs	2 of diamonds

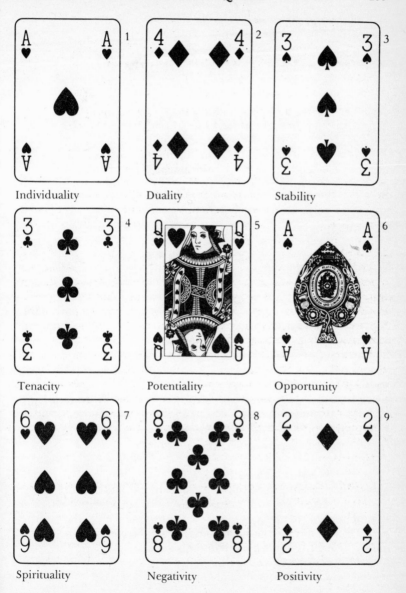

Individuality   Duality   Stability

Tenacity   Potentiality   Opportunity

Spirituality   Negativity   Positivity

The Magic Square

Psychological Reading
Court Card: Queen of hearts

Combinations and Relationships of the Cards:
Two Aces: Reunion
Two Threes: Choice

Square 1 – Individuality: Ace of Hearts
There is no doubt that this lady's heart rules her head. This means her personality is distinctly one-sided and shows she assesses all situations and circumstances from an emotional standpoint. Steps should be taken to develop a more practical approach not only to problems but to life as a whole.

Square 2 – Duality: 4 of Diamonds
This card in relation to this square means there is a strong desire to become an extrovert, but the lady's very nature forbids this. As a duality, these two characteristics attempt to negate each other with a result that a nullity of personality develops.

Square 3 – Stability: 3 of Spades
Mental stability is overshadowed by a form of laziness which prevents true self-expression. Initiative and drive are needed to redress the balance, but first there must be a desire for creativity in a practical way.

Square 4 – Tenacity: 3 of Clubs
A high reserve of mental energy helps to keep up morale and pressure when faced with a battle of wits. Self-confidence will grow from small successes and with the natural characteristic of perseverance these will grow in size and number.

Square 5 – Potentiality: Queen of Hearts
Having selected this queen as her court card it shows the questioner is an introverted lady who needs many more outside interests. She should beware of self-pity and try not to be too sensitive. She should also try to cultivate the characteristics symbolized by the other queens since the Queen of diamonds represents practicality, the Queen of clubs represents confidence and the Queen of spades represents aggression. Just a little of the last queen's characteristic is all that is needed!

Square 6 – Opportunity: Ace of Spades
Unfortunately, this lady is unable to make the most of her opportunities because of a mental hang-up. Whilst she is battling with inner personal turmoil the chance of extrovert self-expression is lost.

Square 7 – Spirituality: 6 of Hearts
Inner peace has not yet been found. Self-realization is desired but at the same time it is feared. Before this state can be reached a degree of self-sacrifice is necessary, involving a change of outlook.

Square 8 – Negativity: 8 of Clubs
Too much self-assessment has produced a negative personality. This is not only a waste of time but more often than not it comes to the wrong conclusion anyway. This situation could, however, be reversed by taking an objective view instead of a subjective one.

Square 9 – Positivity: 2 of Diamonds
Although there is a deep desire to become positive and active outwardly, attention is too divided at present to do so. In order to overcome this, a definite aim or goal must be made first and then every thought and effort directed towards it.

Conclusion: This lady is clearly living too much within herself and is not experiencing fully in the real world ouside. As harsh as she may find this, it is essential that she becomes much more of an extrovert and takes an interest in something beyond herself and her limited domestic scene. Fortunately, she has plenty of mental energy in reserve which is not surprising with such a placid nature as hers.

THE MAGIC SQUARE

1	2	3
Individuality	*Duality*	*Stability*
5 of clubs	8 of clubs	6 of diamonds
4	5	6
Tenacity	*Potentiality*	*Opportunity*
Ace of hearts	King of spades	5 of hearts
7	8	9
Spirituality	*Negativity*	*Positivity*
Ace of diamonds	2 of spades	2 of clubs

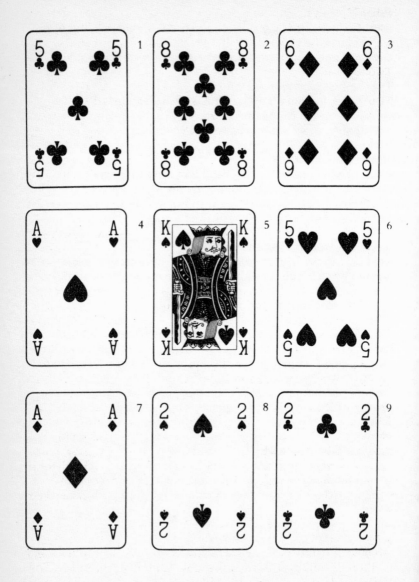

Psychic Reading

Psychic Reading
Court Card: King of spades

Combinations and Relationships of the Cards:
Two Aces: Reunion
Two Fives: Uncertainty
Two Twos: Separate ways

Square 1 – Individuality: 5 of Clubs
It is essential for this questioner to know and accept his psychic abilities and his limitation. To over-estimate this is very dangerous yet at the same time to undervalue it inhibits progress. An intuitive middle course should be sought.

Square 2 – Duality: 8 of Clubs
Over-enthusiasm and confidence in personal psychic ability should not be allowed to overshadow the danger from suspect influences which must always be challenged. False prophets who appear as great masters to the unwary could easily divert energy into wrong channels.

Square 3 – Stability: 6 of Diamonds
The questioner should make sure that harmony exists within himself before committing himself into the hands of unseen forces. At all times he must try to keep the balance because this is the only way to ensure psychic stability.

Square 4 – Tenacity: Ace of Hearts
The combination of this card with this square is most fortunate, showing that the questioner has a natural talent for healing and mediumship. This gives him plenty of patience to persevere in situations which so often seem hopeless. It is this quality that has brought him so far along the occult trail and it will continue to do so, so long as he does not over-extract power from this benevolent source.

Square 5 – Potentiality: King of Spades
Here we discover the lone psychic operator. Obviously he is very enthusiastic and has had considerable experience in most of the basic occult arts. His aim is to increase his power by harnessing forces he believes he can control. His potential, however, is not as great as he himself believes it to be and in this lies the danger.

Square 6 – Opportunity: 5 of Hearts
When completely honest with himself the questioner must admit he is lacking in psychic self-confidence sometimes. Although he may not realize it, this prevents him from making the most of his opportunities and eventually will limit him from further expansion of awareness.

Square 7 – Spirituality: Ace of Diamonds
Considerable spiritual awareness has developed from practical psychic experiences and a stage of initiation has now been reached where the questioner is poised ready to move forward into the next phase. Whether or not he will continue with this expansion depends on him and him alone.

Square 8 – Negativity: 2 of Spades
There is a danger of overstepping the mark psychically. By not realizing the power involved in certain rituals, a negative chain reaction could easily start, dragging down not only the questioner but others who are not even associated with his practices.

Square 9 – Positivity: 2 of Clubs
The ability to work both positively and negatively gives considerable power and advantage. This produces very positive psychic results but only the questioner can say whether these are entirely for the good of others or simply for personal increase of power and glory. At this point there is a choice of two paths: one is positively selfless, the other is positively selfish.

Conclusion: This man is very ambitious, psychically. Undoubtedly he is experienced and has made considerable progress since he started on this trail but now a critical stage has been reached where he must choose the left- or right-hand path. Occultism attracts him far more than mediumship although he has a greater affinity with this, as revealed by the Ace of Hearts. It is on the occult path, however, that he may be tempted to take the wrong steps; and these can never be retraced.

10
THE CELESTIAL CIRCLE

This is a traditional Continental spread, originally using an incomplete pack of 32 cards. When selecting cards from the full pack it gives an excellent indication of events for the coming year, with each card symbolizing one calendar month. The card in the centre reflects the over-all influence for the year as a whole.

Method
Thirteen cards are chosen by the questioner in the true ritualistic way and then handed to the interpreter who turns them over to reveal the first card selected. These are then arranged in the order shown in Diagram 6 (on page 266).

The first card represents the month of the reading so even if it is the last day of the month it must be counted as such. The meanings of each card, on all levels, will reveal the major trends influencing its corresponding month.

If the thirteenth card in the centre is a heart, then a happy year is forecast and if it is a diamond, a successful practical year lies ahead, although probably accompanied by hard work. Should a club occupy this position, money matters and wealth generally will be the centre of attention, but should it be a spade, be ready for a battle.

THE CELESTIAL CIRCLE

9 of diamonds

8 of spades   9 of hearts
3 of diamonds   Ace of spades
2 of clubs   6 of clubs   7 of spades
Ace of diamonds   8 of hearts
Jack of hearts   2 of hearts

8 of clubs

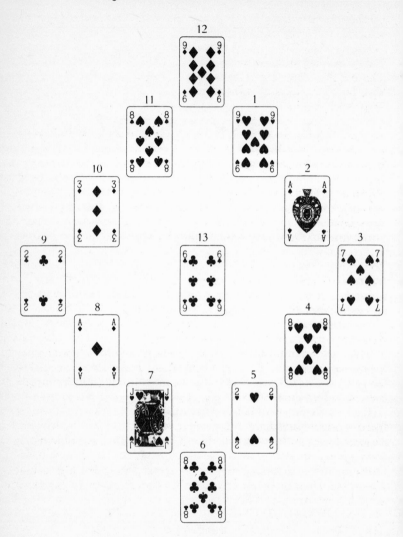

The Celestial Circle

Question: How will my business fare over the coming year? (Cards selected on 30 September 1980)
Combinations and Relationships of the Cards:
Two Twos: Separate paths
Three Eights: Burdens lessen
Two Nines: Successful enterprise
Two Aces: Reunion

Overall Influence for the Year September 1980 to August 1981
6 of Clubs: Attention will be focussed mainly on money in relation to business matters. Pressure and tension produce considerable worry but if this succeeds in stimulating initiative then it will have been worth the trouble. Experiences will prove invaluable and when they are put to work, will pay off handsomely. By enforcing strict economy measures at the beginning of the year a balance of payment should be reached by the end.

First Month – September: 9 of Hearts
This month has been a happy one closely associated with the family. A holiday atmosphere brought relaxation and a general recharging in readiness for hard work in the year ahead.

Second Month – October: Ace of Spades
A pretty formidable obstacle seems to materialize which obliterates all thoughts of the holiday. Strength and courage will be needed to keep things in perspective but whatever this problem is, it must be overcome eventually. The nature of this set-back is not revealed.

Third Month – November: 7 of Spades
Personal fears and worries will do nothing to solve the problem that developed last month. This breeds negativity so be warned. Relationships suffer and stand the risk of deteriorating through lack of emotional control and any display of bad feelings will be regretted later in the year.

Fourth Month – December: 8 of Hearts
Hopes are high once again but there is an underlying fear of insecurity. All that glistens is not gold, unfortunately, so be prepared. On the more positive side, seeing the situation in its true lights dispels all illusion.

Fifth Month – January: 2 of Hearts
An emotional relationship brings a dash of excitement to an otherwise dreary scene. This could be associated with a new romance or it could be that new life revives an old friendship. Socializing plays a bigger part than usual this month.

Sixth Month – February: 8 of Clubs
Financial instability through lack of funds brings worry. Since this card is the gambler's card too, it is worth taking a chance for there is nothing to lose and everything to win.

Seventh Month – March: Jack of Hearts
This could be a most fortuitous month as relaxation and fun bring renewed vigour and hopes for the future. A youthful person livens up the scene and the whole atmosphere is charged with spring.

Eighth Month – April: Ace of Diamonds
The ambition of the year really comes into its own this month. Every effort should be made to attain this goal now or, at the very least, ensure that the road leading towards it is properly laid.

Ninth Month – May: 2 of Clubs
A clash of opinions over money brings progress to a halt. Discussions solve nothing despite joint efforts to reach mutual agreement. Inevitably, a delay is caused but this will be all to the good in the end.

Tenth Month – June: 3 of Diamonds
Having been through a frustrating time, personal determination takes over, ready and keen to achieve that aim. With renewed drive and initiative much will be accomplished this month and although the end object is not quite in the bag, the winning post is now within sight.

Eleventh Month – July: 8 of Spades
Unfortunately, it looks as if an unexpected, last minute set-back turns up this month. Suspicion is in the air so no one should be trusted with confidential information nor should they hear personal secrets either. Sit tight and wait for fate to take a hand.

Twelfth Month – August: 9 of Diamonds
Enthusiasm for business is once again on the cards. New ideas, probably resulting from the previous bad experiences during the year will revolutionize the original plans. Expansion all round can be expected and with it will come adventure and travel.

11
THE HEART'S DESIRE

This is not so much a spread as a way to discover, through the cards, wehther that special wish will come true. Its origin is said to have been with an amorous member of the eighteenth century French court, so it is strictly for lovers.

Method
A court card is necessary to represent the lover, so this will be one of the heart court cards. It is then shuffled into the pack by the questioner who next cuts this into three separate packs with the left hand, and places them side by side as shown in Diagram 7 (below). The search is now on for the personal court card and the 9 of hearts, the card symbolizing the wish or the heart's desire.

If these two cards are in the same pack, then the heart's desire will indeed be fulfilled. Should they be in the first pack on the left of the questioner then their dream will soon come true. If these two cards are together in the middle pack, then a short delay is to be expected before fulfilment. Should they be in the third pack on the right of the questioner, a considerable delay is seen but all will be well in the end.

When the 9 of hearts is alone in the first pack on the left of the questioner, there is still hope for the heart's desire. If it is alone in the middle pack, the chance is less and if this card is alone in the third pack on the right, then do not bank on things too much.

Pack One   Pack Two   Pack Three

The Heart's Desire

12
THE FOUR SUITS

As well as the traditional associations the four suits have with the greater cosmic plan, whereby they represent the four seasons, the four elements and the four weeks in a lunar month, they also have a strong link with us as individuals. Just as they reflect the principles of above, so too do they reflect the principles of below and it is this aspect of the cards that particularly appeals to our nature. This is because they give us a personal glimpse of what fate and fortune have in store for us.

Generally, we are happy with our heart, diamond and club lot in life but we often wish we did not have to put up with the spades and what they stand for. Unfortunately, these are not only unavoidable but necessary if we are going to learn from our experiences and our mistakes. Even so, a warning given by one of these apparently gloomy cards should never be accepted as a predestined omen of fate. It must be seen as a sign urging us to do something about it. After all, if we do not possess free will, what point is there in us trying to solve even the simplest of our problems! Remember then, that ot be forwarned is to be forearmed, so tackle all obstacles positively and determinedly for they must always be far more under our control than we are under theirs!

By looking at life from the standpoint of the four suits, solutions can be seen that are otherwise often missed. Opportunities and successes, true loves and future fortunes shown by the cards help to overcome difficult patches so, in this respect, they are not only prophetic but act as messengers of hope and comfort as well.

Life has four definite aspects, recognized by ancient philosophers and modern psychiatrists and these are symbolized by the four suits. Diamonds represent practical pursuits and material things in life; clubs represent financial matters, riches and wealth; hearts represent emotional feelings and inner responses and spades represent the inevitable problems and obstacles in life.

Everything we think and do arises from one or more of these four standpoints and even a play or film conforms to this four-fold pattern, especially noticed in the characteristic 'surprise ending'. Will it be a diamond-club solution, where the heroine goes for the materialistic jackpot or will she let hearts rule, in spite of an obvious shadow cast by a threatening spade? Real life is just like this.

Diamonds – An Air of Spring
Traditional Aspects
This is the first suit in the pack and symbolizes the spring season and the element of air. It also corresponds with the early part of the day and the morning-time of life. The first breath of spring, with its air of renewal, reminds us of all this for this is the time of birth and rebirth. Buds burst into life and everything in Nature's kingdom starts to grow outwardly. Babies, children and the family tree are associated with this suit.

Practical Aspects
Diamonds are practical, outward-going cards representing material and physical things in life. These include ambitions, aims, work, careers, travel, correspondence and all forms of communication. Logical deductions and clear thinking are expressed, as well as enthusiasm, energy-drives, initiative and high hopes for the future.

Psychological Aspects
From this standpoint, diamonds symbolize the intellect and those who think with their heads. The archetypal intellectual egg-head who often sees no further than the end of his nose when it comes to the real world, extroverts, explorers, high-powered business men and all who follow paths of external pursuit in life are found here. The ancients saw these characters as possessing a choleric nature, one of the four humours recognized by a certain impatience and quick temper.

Psychic Aspects
Psychically, this suit corresponds with positive occultism and all the qualities possessed by those who work in this way. Ability to undertake psychic journeys and astral projection is revealed, along with external forces exerting strong influences. Inspirations materialize as practical ideas.

Clubs – The Heat of Summer
Traditional Aspects

This is the second suit in the pack and symbolizes the summer season and the element of fire. It also represents midday and the peak of life. This is the flowering time and the happy-go-lucky summer of existence, reflecting the heat of the sun, energy and burning desires. Adolescence, with its fires of youth, is associated with this suit.

Practical Aspects

Clubs denote financial situations. Riches and poverty, surprise monetary gifts and sudden expenditures are all within these cards. Personal affinity with money or spendthrift tendencies are shown, as well as indications pointing to the making of potential tycoons, bank managers and accountants, not to mention their opposites, down-and-outs.

Psychological Aspects

From this standpoint, clubs represent determination. Desires to possess money, jewels, property and even other people are indicated. Swinging between moods of hopefulness to states of bloody-mindedness, this type never gives up. Sanguine, the name given to this character by ancient philosophers, sums up their extreme hopefulness.

Psychic Aspect

Psychically, wealth of understanding or poverty of spirit are shown by the cards in this respect. Occult strengths and weaknesses are revealed along with questions of psychic protection. There is a continual quest for enlightenment and psychic fireworks.

Hearts – Refreshing Autumn
Traditional Aspect

This is the third suit in the pack and symbolizes the autumn season and the element of water. It also represents the evening and maturity of life. This is the harvest time when fruitful rewards are reaped and a mellow, more peaceful stage is reached. Adulthood is associated with hearts and, with its experience, can afford to show compassion for others.

Practical Aspect

Hearts are all about emotions and feelings in relation to the family, friends and lovers. Happiness, fun, relaxation and all social events are symbolized by this suit. Comfort and help given to others increases personal inner strength as surely as does reaping what has been sown. Homely ways and motherly love are predominant.

Psychological Aspect
In this respect hearts represent inner feelings and all who think with their heart. The introvert, the do-gooder, whose excellent intentions sometimes lead others and themselves into trouble and the martyr who makes self-sacrifices are shown. Deep feelings of compassion for all forms of life are expressed too. The ancient philosophers called this character phlegmatic because the person appeared adaptable yet apathetic in relation to external, practical matters.

Psychic Aspect
Psychically, spiritual satisfaction, harmony with the elements and the ability to work well and closely with others is shown. Healing and mediumistic attributes and sensititivy to atmospheres are also revealed. External influences are attracted to strong heart-psychics so warnings concerning protection are revealed.

Spades – Bleak Midwinter
Traditional Aspect
This is the last suit in the pack and symbolizes the winter and the element of earth. It also represents darkness and the night-time of life, a time to go to earth, rest and sleep. Benefits gathered from past experiences are mulled over, but cold comfort can lead to depression and sadness. Old age and the human pastime of reflection and regret are associated with this suit.

Practical Aspect
All the hurdles and obstacles in life are represented by this suit. To a certain extent, although these are unpleasant circumstances and events, they serve to straighten out situations in the end. Fair judgment and cold assessment are sometimes very necessary. Health problems and warnings are included among the hurdles and obstacles.

Psychological Aspect
This aspect of the suit indicates ruthless traits, hang-ups and unwarranted aggression. But hard-headedness often acts as a guise for a much softer inner self who is afraid to emerge, making such

people their own worst enemy; they are not as formidable as they seem. Depression and self-pity are revealed. Ancient philosophers saw this character as melancholic, expressing sadness brought on by doubt, lack of self-confidence and bad luck.

Psychic Aspect
From the psychic standpoint this suit represents the dark night of the soul – fears and warnings from the 'great unknown'. Lack of psychic protection and foolhardiness in relation to occult forces invite trouble. Weaknesses and wrong paths are symbolized, as well as downright bad intentions.

13
THE PACK OF CARDS

Each card represents a different aspect, on different levels, of the over-all meaning of the suit to which it belongs. These are its numerical, practical, psychological, psychic, influential and reversed significances which depend on the spread and standpoint from which the cards were selected.

The twelve court cards represent people, as well as certain qualities, whereas the forty numbered cards symbolize situations and circumstances.

The Joker
This card finds its way into a spread in most surprising ways even though it is thought to have been previously removed. The fact that there is a Joker in the pack at all is significant in itself, so he cannot possibly be ignored. So if he does turn up unexpectedly, do not replace him with another card because his presence and message was intended.

Combinations and Relationships
Significant combinations and relationships of certain cards in a spread have collective meanings which give added insight into problems and situations. These are given in the following lists:

Quartets, Triplicities and Pairs
Four Aces	– Triumph
Three Aces	– Harmony
Two Aces	– Reunion
Four Kings	– Honour and success
Three Kings	– Good support
Two Kings	– Good advisers
Four Queens	– Scandal
Three Queens	– Gossip
Two Queens	– Curiosity

Four Jacks	– Battles
Three Jacks	– Quarrels
Two Jacks	– Discussions
Four Tens	– Change for the better
Three Tens	– Repayments
Two Tens	– Change of fortune
Four Nines	– Unexpected good fortune
Three Nines	– Successful enterprise
Two Nines	– Eventual contentment
Four Eights	– Worries
Three Eights	– Burdens lessen
Two Eights	– Inconstancy
Four Sevens	– Equality
Three Sevens	– Fulfilment
Two Sevens	– Mutual love
Four Sixes	– Unexpected obstacles
Three Sixes	– Hard work
Two Sixes	– Contradictions
Four Fives	– Personal happiness
Three Fives	– Personal satisfaction
Two Fives	– Personal uncertainty
Four Fours	– Equal chance
Three Fours	– A fair chance
Two Fours	– Little chance
Four Threes	– Hope
Three Threes	– Stability
Two Threes	– Choice
Four Twos	– Cross-roads
Three Twos	– Change in direction
Two Twos	– Separate ways
The Joker	– Be not deceived, this is an unknown quantity.

Significant Relationships

The ace of diamonds among several hearts	– Business and pleasure do not mix
The ace of diamonds among several clubs	– Matters of business depending on money will come to a head
The ace of spades among several hearts	– Emotional problems
The ace of spades among several diamonds	– Obstacles at work or with a career and ambition

The ace of hearts among several clubs	–	Generosity
The ace of hearts among several diamonds	–	Love and romance connected with a journey or work
The ace of clubs among several diamonds	–	Wealth and an increase of social status
The ace of clubs among several spades	–	Financial problems
A number of mixed court cards	–	Festivity, hospitality and social gatherings
A court card between two cards of the same number or value	–	Soemone is supported or hemmed in by their circumstances
A Jack next to a King or Queen	–	Protection
The Queen of spades between a King and another Queen	–	A break-up of a relationship
The eight and nine of spades together	–	A health problem
A Jack among several diamonds	–	A messenger will bring important information or news
The nine and ten of diamonds together	–	A journey on or over the sea
The nine of hearts and the three of diamonds together	–	A stable love-affair

14
DIAMONDS

ACE OF DIAMONDS

Numerical Significance

This is the first and last card in this suit and represents both numbers one and thirteen – unity and rebirth. It signifies a beginning and an end in itself, thus representing a complete project. In this lies an individual's potential and creativity, as expressed through the intellect. Intellectual striving, which should be directed towards one goal at a time, is necessary, even though the seed of success has been sown. This card also contains the power to transform one situation into another.

Practical Significance

In its purest sense this card symbolizes a clear-cut aim for the future. It is a veritable storehouse of energy, sufficient for putting into action all plans relating to practical and material goals. Like the diamond itself, ambitions should be crystallized, then a single-minded approach utilized to achieve these aims as soon as possible.

This card also signifies new business, a new house or new possession, such as a car, furniture or jewellery. An important document or letter which has the power to alter the future is also represented by this card. Such a communication may be sent or received; and those who have taken exams can expect favourable results. It also symbolizes the renewal of hope through intellectual concentration and a more positive attitude, thus encouraging those who have failed in the past to try again. Originality plus drive will bring practical success and material gain.

Psychological Significance
Tremendous drive and positivity produce a forceful character who means to reach his or her goal by hook or by crook. Crystal-clear thinking allows the individual to cut corners and take risks with safety. Unflagging energy and good health aid the attainment of the highest ambitions which others would see as remote castles in the air. A lack of feeling for others may be displayed as this would contribute little to furthering personal ambitions.

Psychic Significance
An occult achievement of some importance is on the cards. This is an initiation which marks a stage of positive psychic development. Inspirational qualities and telepathic gifts crystallize into rewarding experiences which, in turn, produce the confidence necessary for going on to the next phase. One cycle has been successfully completed and the scene is now set for the future.

Influential Significance
This card has a strong, positive influence enabling the individual to direct his or her forces towards the fulfilment of an aim. Businesses, careers and ambitions receive a boost of energy which revives enthusiasm and helps to bring things to a successful conclusion. This influence will override opposition, especially when the aim is for the good of others.

Reversed Signifcance
Generally this card indicates muddled plans for the future. Good intent remains, but does not receive the stimulation necessary to spark it off. Everything becomes a stumbling-block which overshadows personal potential. A set-back is to be expected.

KING OF DIAMONDS

The King's Significance
This King represents the mature, masculine aspect of this suit. A

combination of experience and action will produce a break-through into new interests. Coming to terms with life has paid off, so the future holds out great promise. On the practical level, stability gives the questions the confidence to help others as well as to further personal aims. Crowned with success materially, a good basis exists on which to develop other characteristics symbolized by the other three suits.

Practical Significance
Traditionally, this King is the fair-haired, blue-eyed man, muscularly strong and essentially practical. He is a clear thinker who uses his head and prides himself on his successes in business and with women. It may signify lack of heart and little consideration for others. He is ambitious, reliable, generally honest and his life appears to be an open book. Really, there is more to him than this although it usually goes unnoticed.

This outward-going personality is naturally disciplined, so a military career would be most fulfilling. As a protector he can be authoritarian yet respected nevertheless. As a business partner he will prove loyal and hard-working, but as a marriage partner he needs to be top dog. Romance usually lasts just long enough to convince a woman that he has a heart – then his work takes first place in his life. Whatever else this King may be, he is an excellent business man.

Psychological Significance
Here is an extrovert who thinks almost exclusively with his head. Strength of character gives him figure-head qualities although this does not necessarily mean that his nature is entirely balanced. As his emotions tend to be inhibited he runs the risk of developing into a dogmatic leader. This characteristic becomes morre pronounced as the years go by.

Psychic Significance
As a potential magician this King could command and direct the positive forces of Nature for the good of others. Both as a healer and an occultist, his powers will depend on his personal level of understanding and, as he progresses in life and evolves, so will he increase his links with the universe.

Influential Significance
The personal influence from this card is strong and positive. It will persuade others to fall in with your ideas and help things to go to plan although over-enthusiasm and drive may be mistaken for ruthlessness. This influence will help all who are willing to accept hard, unsentimental advice.

Reversed Significance
Strong ambitions develop into devious schemes which eventually undermine stability and confidence. Others lose faith in this King and his plans, which the result that aggression creeps in. Disputes create further problems until the only solution lies in travel or moving to a new home.

QUEEN OF DIAMONDS

The Queen's Significance
This card represents the feminine aspect of the suit. She has a practical and fertile imagination which enables her to compete successfully in a man's world. Independence has been won and she is capable of making important decisions speedily and accurately, often to the annoyance of her contemporaries. A loyal supporter of authority, she is seen as a protective female rather than as a motherly soul. Her ambition is to maintain her well-earned position in life

rather than to extend her horizons into unknown territory.

Practical Significance

Traditionally, this Queen has fair hair, blue eyes and a generally pale look. Be not deceived, however, because she is strong, both physically and mentally and knows her own mind. She often thinks she knows other people's too, and this gives her a reputation for being over-authoritative and bossy.

Thinking with her head more than her heart has won her a place in society and brought rewards. As a business woman she succeeds with ease. A career will tend to take precedence over her home and family in the end, although this Queen usually has both these aspects well under control. She is an efficient mother, firm but well-loved. Energy abounds and life always holds out the promise of adventure and change. Organization is second nature to her and demand for her services is therefore great. She is an efficient, positive woman.

Psychological Significance

An unusually positive streak gives this woman an extrovert personality similar to that of a man. Seeing the world as a practical playground, she uses her intelligence to work and play in the best places. Others are jealous of her, but she secretly envies them for their domesticity. As she is so business-like, she is often misjudged as a hard-hearted person.

Psychic Significance

Occult and healing abilities soon develop once this Queen has stepped onto the positive psychic path. Working slowly but surely, she learns to command the positive forces of nature and uses them to help mankind and all other forms of life on this planet.

Influential Significance

Personal influence amounts to self-confidence and self-reliance which, in turn, attracts both friends and hangers-on. These qualities have brought success in the past and will do so again in the future. Others may benefit from this Queen's experience if they take her advice, which is sound and practical, but not always palatable.

Reversed Significance

The hard-headed matriarchal streak is overbearing. When this interferes with other people's liberty, trouble is to be expected. The feamle who knows it all is not liked and is soon shunned by one and all. In family circles this trait causes breaks which can never be breached; and in business it results in enmity and opposition.

JACK OF DIAMONDS

The Jack's Significance
This card usually represents a boy or youth, in which case he is seen to have a practical approach to life and will show an affinity for business at an early age. He is highly intelligent. If this card symbolizes an adult, however, immaturity is revealed. Ambition exists but remains unfulfilled because hopes are rarely put into action, either through laziness or a lack of real know-how. He is, however, a potential King. So this individual needs to re-orientate himself if he wants to achieve this status.

Practical Significance
Like the King and Queen of this suit, the Jack is also traditionally seen as fair in appearance. His nature is outward-going, sometimes to the extent of becoming overpoweringly extrovert. He is usually a know-all, but is popular nevertheless because of his *joie de vivre* which results from an endless supply of energy. He does not grow old quickly and retains his youthful appearance to the end.

His opinions are well-known, but only a fool would take his advice seriously. At work he makes an excellent boss's man but lives in hopes of one day making the grade himself. Sexually and socially, he is more of a success because in these circles no one need take him too seriously. Sport is really his line for it offers him the opportunities he craves. Alertness and swiftness may even earn him the vice-captaincy of the local cricket team. In the home his intentions are always good and he is full of promises which he cannot, rather than will not, keep. This is an ambitious, youthful male who is the Jack of all trades when it comes to work.

Psychological Significance
Although he is ambitious, this individual is too immature and unpredictable to ever reach his goal. A little success goes to his head and he is not wise enough to follow it through to the next logical stage. His arrogance is a form of protection, and brooding over the past for too long prevents him from positive forward-planning.

Psychic Significance
As a positive psychic he is often charged with inspiration. However, he should specialize in one of the more mundane occult arts before setting his sights on the higher ranks. He must also be prepared to take orders and obey them, not only for his own safety but for the sake of others, too.

Influential Significance
The personal influence is essentially energetic and youthful even though sound common sense is missing. It is this energy that has helped to keep him going in the absence of real substance. Others may benefit through contact with him by themselves becoming rejuvenated and even inspired. In this sense, this card has a catalystic influence.

Reversed Significance
Stubbornness is his downfall. Unable to believe that he could ever be wrong, his attitude eventually leads to conflict. Untrustworthy and misleading, others may come unstuck through his actions and, in the end, even his charm will let both him and his friends down.

TEN OF DIAMONDS

Numerical Significance
The tenth card of this suit is a sign of completion, indicating that one particular phase in life has ended and another is about to begin. This relates to intellectual and practical aspects: a stage has been reached which is marked by either a change of some sort or an award. It represents a landmark in a career because one goal has been achieved and a step taken on the path to fulfilment. The foundations for future success have been laid.

Practical Significance
A journey which combines business with pleasure will bring a reward. Effort, both physical and mental, is necessary to spark into action a new plan. Past success is not enough, so do not sit and wait too long because a new opportunity is at hand. It is a time for 'off with the old and on with the new' although any loose ends must be firmly tied. Leave no unfinished business before starting on this next new project.

A letter or document will reveal something very important although great care should be exercised in regard to what is committed to paper. A lot of thought is needed to ensure that things start off on the right foot. New buildings or the refurbishing of old ones bring expansion and success, thus laying the foundations for the future.

Life is satisfying on the one hand, but a certain restlessness is felt on the other. This shows it is time to begin something new, or at least to start again on a firmer footing. Plenty of action is symbolized.

Psychological Significance
Extrovert tendencies help increase personal confidence. An active mind needs controlling in order to avoid head-on clashes. Intelligence alone will lead to frustration and a waste of energy.

Psychic Significance
Powerful external forces will be encountered, therefore occult laws must be observed in order to prevent any adverse rebounds. A point of initiation is reached and all who pass this test will gain confidence.

Influential Significance
The influence from this card will produce action although the outcome is not clear at this time. At least it will start things moving. On the practical level, matters will be resolved after an initial period of movement and a certain amount of upheaval. It is time to

progress, so new plans should be ready for implementation.

Reversed Significance
A threat of failure will bring hopes and plans crashing to the ground. A lack of direction brings matters to a standstill. Enthusiasm and drive are replaced by anxiety and fear, thus making the future appear decidedly dark.

NINE OF DIAMONDS

Numerical Significance
The ninth card in this suit is a sign of courage resulting from previous stability. It indicates leadership qualities but warns that such a position should not be allowed to go to one's head and produce a tyrannical boss or over-enthusiastic superior, whose ambitions are achieved at the expense of others. The warning is that the higher one climbs, the further one has to fall. Numerically, this warning is borne out because number nine is the last of the single figures which then return to nought in the unit column.

Practical Significance
New interests are to be expected. These are associated with work, ambitions or practical pastimes and may be connected with a journey or travel. A holiday could prove both educational and relaxing, with long-term practical benefits.

Promotion is offered and new business ventures are assured of success. It is time to start building for the future, so lay the foundations as soon as it is practically possible. Opportunities must be taken when they arise because second chances are not on offer. Energy will be forthcoming as a result of hard work, whether mental or physical, so the necessary drive will not be lacking. Individuality must be preserved although a compromise with co-workers is also required. Too much thinking could overshadow the human aspect of a project, thus preventing the final goal from achieving its blue print perfection.

Ideas begin to expand, even to the extent of building castles in the air because, with the courage of true conviction, these too will one day become realities. Extended horizons are indicated.

Psychological Significance
Single-mindedness brings success although this way of thinking needs tempering before it develops into self-righteousness. Stubborn ways prevent full expression.

Psychic Significance
A practical approach to occult matters will bring greater rewards than tackling them from a psychic angle. Positive results can be expected as long as feet are placed firmly on the ground.

Influential Significance
This influence brings confidence and encouragement to the scene. If bold steps have to be taken, these will prove to be easier than anticipated or feared. Practical matters will be resolved best by tackling them in a straightforward way. So be brave and honest in the knowledge that unseen forces are working in your favour.

Reversed Significance
Delays and disagreements hinder the completion of projects and any chance of final success. Lack of courage and self-doubt bring matters pretty well to a standstill. Yet obstinacy prevents a new standpoint from being adopted. Energy is soon dissipated and replaced by a general feeling of disinterest.

EIGHT OF DIAMONDS

Numerical Significance
The eighth card in this suit is a contradiction because it signifies either complete success or utter failure. This is a difficult number: it tends to bring too much of everything and therefore usually amounts to nothing in the end. The ancients saw this as equality and negation, numerically symbolized by the dual proportions two and four. Unfortunately, this make for indecision all round.

The Practical Significance

Short journeys connected with business and the furthering of aims will be undertaken. Minor aspects associated with other practical pursuits, including sport, will be to the fore. A visit away from town brings new ideas as well as providing an opportunity to catch up on things.

If things do not go as well as expected, a trip into the country is advised. Getting away, even briefly, gives one the opportunity to see the situation from a fresh point of view.

This card also indicates that too much thought and effort may have been put into a scheme, so take a temporary break. See this stage as a stepping-stone on the way; but ensure that the next move is forwards and not backwards. Much will depend on personal reactions to circumstances, so stand firm. If in doubt, do not make final decisions, but allow time to be the judge. Much will be revealed with patience. There is still plenty of hope and time for a successful outcome, so regard any delays as a necessary evil. Balance and counterbalance are strongly symbolized.

Psychological Significance

Inner conflict produces muddled thinking. Such confusion may appear to be unending because the mind will continually seek outwards for answers. There is little connection between the conscious and unconscious mind at this time.

Psychic Significance

Positive occult forces will accentuate messages from dogmatic religions. These must be recognized and challenged in order to prevent them from influencing the work in hand.

Influential Significance
This influence is likely to bring stalemate and frustration to a situation. It will be difficult to make a move one way or the other: the answer is to wait rather than to be too hasty. Efforts will not meet with immediate results, no matter how much is put into a scheme. However, in retrospect, nothing will have been wasted.

Reversed Significance
Indecision will lead to complications and lost opportunities. Exhaustion results from allowing energy to be wasted in the wrong directions. Loss of drive brings self-recrimination and others, too, are likely to suffer from a wrong move made in haste. It is, however, never too late to start again.

SEVEN OF DIAMONDS

Numerical Significance
The seventh card in this suit signifies completeness in a practical way. It compares with the collectiveness of the seven colours of the rainbow and the seven notes in the musical scale. Representing that aspect which relates to practical hopes for the future, it includes all materialistic possibilities associated with the external world. It is a positive number offering success, provided that the laws of action and reaction are constantly observed.

Practical Significance
This card represents the individual in relation to the outer world. If practical plans for the future have not already been made, then this should be done immediately. It also urges that such plans should be made as simple and concise as possible, then kept firmly in mind as the goal to be achieved.

Representing the personal driving force, this card is closely linked with ideals and ambitions. Artistic talents and everything connected with stage, screen and television are also included. Communicating with others will be easier from now on so, if you have a special message you wish to communicate, get this across as soon as possible. Public speakers and politicians will find this a good time to go into action and the more effort that is put into a project, the greater the benefit is likely to be.

Life will be seen from a fresh angle and renewed hopes stand a good chance of being fulfilled. Energy levels are high, allowing plenty of physical and mental effort to be applied to schemes and activities. A sporting achievement is on the cards too, because the spirit of ambition means to triumph.

Psychological Significance
'Know thyself' through self-discipline is the message here. Yet it is necessary to balance extrovert tendencies with introvert feelings before a true understanding of the self can be accomplished.

Psychic Significance
The spirit will express itself in a very positive way. It may astrally project to far away places and return with gems of wisdom. Dreams will prove most helpful.

Influential Significance
A strong personal influence emanates from this card. Drive, enthusiasm and strength of purpose are ready and waiting to go into action. This will result in the completion of any unfinished business, as well as the initiation of new projects. Material and practical self-reliance is assured, thus generating further self-confidence.

Reversed Significance
Failing to take opportunities will frustrate and annoy unless the general attitude towards life is altered. Wasted talents and an absence of drive and ambition may be due to lack of vitality. A personal stock-taking is necessary: reassess all practical aspects and plans for the future.

SIX OF DIAMONDS

Numerical Significance
The sixth card in this suit symbolizes possibilities and ambitions

which are often difficult to achieve. Practical plans and material possessions tend to lack real substance even though a lot of hard work has been put into them. This number carries a warning message that one can fall to the ground if caught between two stools, so complete one project before starting on the next one.

Practical Significance
Documents in relation to property, business, work, careers and aims are symbolized by this card. A dispute is likely unless extra care is taken when signing important papers or agreements, so read the small print carefully. On a personal level, refrain from committing to paper anything that could not be repeated in public. Information leaks could cause trouble, as could indiscreet statements made in personal letters.

Much is going on behind the scenes although this may not be apparent at this time. A situation could, therefore, appear to be a paradox. Plans to travel may be upset at the last minute although they will right themselves at the eleventh hour. At work, disagreements due to unforeseen circumstances result in delays although no permanent damage is caused; in the home, differences of opinions arise over practical issues. Relying on the intellect too much produces a one-sided view of a situation. If logic is abandoned, a sudden flash of inspiration should occur to throw light on everything.

Psychological Significance
Material worries weigh heavily and cause tension. Difficulties in accepting the true situation aggravate negative tendencies. So beware of disagreements and bad tempers all round.

Psychic Significance
Beware of instability within a group of positive occultists. This could

be due to the absence of negative-receptive psychics who would redress the balance.

Influential Significance
This influence is conveyed mainly through the written word. The pen is mightier than the sword, especially in business matters, so watch out for misconstructions, misleading statements and verbal barbs. Action is necessary to restore stability, therefore this influence should be utilized for this purpose.

Reversed Significance
If allowed to continue, undercover actions will disrupt plans. A lost document or letter will delay the completion of a project and hopes for an early settlement will begin to fade. Be prepared for last minute set-backs owing to the unreliability of others.

FIVE OF DIAMONDS

Numerical Significance
The fifth card in this suit symbolizes mankind, full of practical hopes and potential for the future. From the germ of an idea, it is possible for a far-reaching plan, which has the power to alter one life or many, to develop. This card offers fulfilment, but it is up to the individual to accept or reject the challenge.

Practical Significance
This card holds great promise for the future, providing that opportunities are taken when they arise. There is plenty of originality, but this requires drive to accomplish anything lasting and worth-while. Difficulties may be encountered initially but, once started, the road to success lies ahead.

A move from present property to new or different accommodation is indicated. A journey is in the offing too, providing a change of scenery; this could be a holiday or a business trip. Education and matters associated with the increase of knowledge will come under review, and changes will need to be made in order to get the best results.

Promotions and improvements are there for the asking but, again, it is up to the individual to take the opportunities offered. This is a testing time, but those who are ready and willing to face the challenges will reap the benefits of their hard labours for a long time to come. Personal opportunities which should not be missed are symbolized.

Psychological Significance
Stability of the outward-going aspect of the personality will help achieve extrovert ambitions and goals. This aspect has developed independently from the opposite, introvertive side, so attention should be paid to the heart as well as the head from now on.

Psychic Significance
The urge to work alone should not be encouraged. Positive psychism within the group will bring safer and surer individual progress as well as results.

Influential Significance
This influence highlights practical failings as well as abilities. It gives an opportunity for one to discover weaknesses and strengths and it is therefore worth-while taking the time to learn in which direction your real talents lie. New plans should be laid on the foundations of past experiences. This will make the most of the positive aspects because these hold out the promise of eventual success.

Reversed Significance
Frustration, due to lack of success, does little to put matters right. If ever perseverance was needed, it is now; so try, try, try again. A journey could cause extra inconvenience, but any action is better than none, so make the best of things and go with the stream, not against it.

FOUR OF DIAMONDS

Numerical Significance

The fourth card in this suit is not an easy card to accept. As it represents the square of two, it adds complications to any situation which already offers two alternatives. If determination and logic are applied, the result will be a firm victory and progress; but if dithering and indecision are allowed to take over, then all semblance of a set plan will disintegrate.

Practical Significance

Whichever way you look at this card, difficult decisions arise. Opposition to even the most carefully prepared plans are inevitable; even last minute alternatives are likely to appear as if from nowhere. These difficult choices are likely to arise in matters relating to jobs, business, new houses, material possessions and holidays: everything, in fact, concerned with the practical side of life. Even letter-writing is likely to pose problems.

Too much consideration of a problem or situation is just as bad as too little, however, because both add up to a null and void. In intellectual circles, contradictions produce anger, mainly because there is more than a grain of truth in the opposing points of view. This disrupts stable beliefs, with the result that insecurity creeps into the situation. This is not the right time to make decisions. It may even be a question of the time of the year because the four seasons have a very powerful effect on all mundane matters. What might be easily accomplished in the heat of the summer is an impossiblity in deep midwinter.

Psychological Significance

Instability is expressed in extrovertive ways and other people notice

this. Hang-ups associated with work produce exaggerated characteristics which scare away others, even friends.

Psychic Significance
Occult forces do battle to unbalance the situation. Consant protection
and challenging is necessary. When contacting and manipulating
these powerful forces, they must not only be guarded against but
recognized for what they are and what they can do. To reverse the
balance of power, use their mirror image.

Influential Significance
This influence pulls in many directions t once. Loyalties to colleagues,
on the one hand, are at loggerheads with what is practically best, on
the other. Deals tend to cool off as a result. Communications with
others are difficult because of crossed lines. So, when in doubt
during this period, do not commit your comments to paper or air
them verbally.

Reversed Significance
Fragmented plans and impossible ideas waste time and energy so it
would be better to scrap everything and start again. Only by
concentrating on one aspect at a time will any real progress be made.
There is a lack of co-ordination between hopes and the implementation of them: a stalemate situation exists.

THREE OF DIAMONDS

Numerical Significance
The third card in this suit has a built-in stability which can provide
help for practical aims and ambitions. It is a good sign, indicating
that now is the time to take a step forward because your plans are

based on firm foundation. Creativity should blossom from this point and as this card signifies a source of knowledge, further original ideas can be expected. Confidence in practical ability encourages the expansion and development on all fronts relating to business, hobbies, pleasure and leisure.

Practical Significance
Plans for the future are on a firm footing, but determination to see these through to a successful conclusion will be necessary. If this is lacking, even the best laid schemes can founder, so focus your attention on the final objective and keep this in view all the time.

Energy is available for physical and mental work, so utilize this without delay. Original ideas are waiting to be recognized and, when they are, they should be applied to any old projects which require new stimulus. Academic theses, symbolized by the Cambridge tripos exams, are represented by this card. Thus, intellectual work will suddenly become easier as the barrier to knowledge is pushed back. This is a good time to think about exams and tests because any results from these should be excellent.

Ingenuity, originality and determination make ideal partners in the practical and intellectual fields of life, so it is not surprising that this card symbolizes a blend of past, present and future hopes.

Psychological Significance
Positivity produces a very determined and outwardly stable person. Too much determination could develop into selfishness, however. So, if you do not wish to appear to be on an ego trip, match this determination with thought for others.

Psychic Significance
Harmonious relationships with psychic co-workers and positive occult forces will bring great spiritual rewards. Help and healing directed now will give good results.

Influential Significance
Should lack of enthusiasm slow down practical, material or intellectual progress, then this influence will introduce determination onto the scene. As a result, positivity and drive return, bringing the end object within grasp. Hard work is still necessary, but with this incentive it will seem much easier to achieve positive results. A form of isolation could be experienced as the result of utilizing this determination, but a 'go-it-alone' course is likely to prove far more

rewarding than one which is dependent on the whim of others: the prize does not have to be shared, for one thing!

Reversed Significance
Owing to laziness or lack of drive, a distinct difficulty will be encountered in the achievement of a hope, ambition or project. A plan is desperately needed to escape from the present circumstances which are static and frustrating. Physical efforts are liable to be wasted as things now stand, so try to take stock of the situation.

TWO OF DIAMONDS

Numerical Significance
The second card in this suit is a paradox. Two practical aspects have to be considered and united into a whole, if at all possible. Two heads are better than one – except when they disagree with each other. All or nothing situations develop and the introduction of an alternative is bound to throw something out of balance temporarily.

Practical Significance
This card offers partnerships and delicately balanced relationships between two people linked through business, practical working arrangements or the domestic side of marriage. Both should contribute to the whole by using their individual experiences to bring about a productive joint situation. When the aim is the same, harmony exists; but if one party loses sight of this objective, disharmony will result.

It is difficult to keep a balance all the time because duality tends to make final decisions very difficult; and knowing there is a choice only make things worse. Communication between partners could lead to trouble too, because meanings are not conveyed properly, so extra care must be taken when expressing a point.

If progress with plans slows down, take one step at a time. Good ideas are lacking because parallel lines can never meet – seek out the balanced way. Great tact will be necessary in order to prevent a permanent rift, yet if the right cards are played, agreement and unification will eventually result.

Psychological Significance
Split intentions divide attention on the practical front. Thoughts tend to run in parallel lines which never converge. Energy is wasted, so tiredness is to be expected.

Psychic Significance
Difficulties with two positive aspects confuse occultists. It is easy to go down the wrong psychic track so be careful to challenge all forces in use.

Influential Significance
This influence brings duality which will not always help a current situation. Since this has the effect of introducing a choice or alternative solution it is only later that its true value will be seen and appreciated. Indecision is the worst aspect but, on the other hand, it is important to ensure that the other side of the coin is not forgotten either. The reward from this lies in the future, not the present.

Reversed Significance
Ambitions will be overshadowed by obstacles and practical difficulties. Opposition to a plan makes matters seem impossible and any amount of hard work will have little or no effect. An all or nothing situation has developed, with the result that there is the possibility of falling between two stools.

15
CLUBS

ACE OF CLUBS

Numerical Significance
This is the first and last card in the suit. It combines the numbers one and thirteen which, together, form a pool of wealth. This gives stability and security to individuals as well as firing them with the enthusiasm necessary to search for that proverbial pot of gold at the end of the rainbow. This card is a power in itself and needs careful handling but, if used with discretion and understanding, it attracts all the good things in life. On one level it brings materialistic prizes and, on another, the wealthy reward of wisdom.

Practical Significance
Good fortune lies in this card. Wealth is on the horizon and is well within the questioner's grasp. Speculation has paid off handsomely, bringing material comforts and plenty of worldly goods. There is a warning though; remember the saying: 'Easy come, easy go' because this is a possibility. Permanence is not a special feature of this card, so watch interests carefully.

The way in which such financial wealth is used is most important. If rewarded as one of the talents it will bring help and happiness to many people. So, casting bread on the waters of life can result in rich rewards for everyone. Those who have used personal ability to attain high standards in life will be rewarded with national or even international fame. Industrious folk will reach their goal through inventiveness and devotion, whilst others may well inherit money or titled status.

At one end of the scale this card can signify a big pools win, a legacy or a generous gift; whilst at the other, it represents recognition as a star performer, politician or actor.

Psychological Significance
A strong desire to possess objects of material value overshadows the simple things in life. You should allow those underlying characteristics which lie nearer to your heart to express themselves.

Psychic Significance
A special psychic gift will come to light. If this is used according to occult law, a great wealth of understanding will add to an ever-deepening pool of wisdom.

Influential Significance
The influence from this card instantly helps flagging financial resources. It brings respite from money worries and allows the individual time to reorganize his or her affairs. Although this may not solve the problem, it will certainly give an opportunity to recuperate funds. Speculation and a new approach to wealth will develop, so use this influence to attain a particular goal or standard.

Reversed Significance
Dependence on money for security and pleasures in life will soon reveal the lack of substance such a pursuit brings. Dis-satisfaction, linked to an inability to alter course, produces frustration and poverty of pocket and outlook.

KING OF CLUBS

The King's Significance
This King is the experienced man, crowned with financial success. A stockpile of worldly goods allows time in later life to pursue wealth on a higher plane. Self-confidence arises mainly from material assets, but opportunities will arise later which should put this on a more intuitive footing. Imagination is not lacking, but if this is

directed one way only, it will lead to limitations. A collector of most things – from valuable antiques to a load of old rubbish – this King is seen to be a very single-minded person, with an eye for making a quick profit.

Practical Significance
Traditionally, this is one of the dark, rich-complexioned kings, full of life, sexual vitality and good ideas. Many seek his advice, mainly because he appears to have done so well for himself. Although he is completely trustworthy as far as his intentions go, he may lack sufficient experience to be considered an expert.

Tycoons and financiers are represented by this card and, very often, it is their single-mindedness that has brought them to the peak of their success rather than careful, intelligent planning. Ruthlessness possesses such individuals when they are on this road to success because they know that if they weaken or are deflected off course, they stand to lose.

When this king is the big fish in a little pond, everyone knows it. Modesty is not among his attributes and being in demand is one of his greatest pleasures. Acting as the kingpin suits him and he guards his territory jealously; those who take liberties are castigated, but those who come with cap in hand are more than welcome. In this attitude, shades of insecurity can be seen and this trait is found in even the richest of financial wizards.

Psychological Significance
This king possesses the good quality of perseverence. This attribute should be used with discretion, however, or it might be mistaken for over-forcefulness. He has a rich pool of experience from which to draw but, again, care has to be taken or he could appear boastful.

Psychic Significance
Even though he is an experienced psychic, he still seeks proof that other dimensions really exist. Until he can accept these instinctively and intuitively he will remain at his present stage of initiation.

Influential Significance
This gives control over finances and wealth generally, so influential help with any monetary problems can be expected. This may come from an experienced person qualified in banking or from a changed situation. Loans, if needed, arise from reliable sources and, although expensive, will restore that lost security. A fortunate gift of money or a useful present will brighten life temporarily but, for permanence, this card's influence should be utilized to put personal affairs in order.

Reversed Significance
Miserliness produces a narrow mind that shuts out the true meaning of life. Greed, deception and covetous ways eventually lead to loneliness. The individual's inability to accept changes results in personal limitation and, unless care is exercised, leads to a hermit's life. Fear of losing what has been hoarded encourages false suspicions to develop, so that family as well as friends stay away from the door.

QUEEN OF CLUBS

The Queen's Significance
This Queen is the feminine aspect of the suit. She is an efficient, successful woman who is used to plenty of money and knows what it can buy. Material luxuries often become a necessity so that when times are hard and these are lacking, she becomes unsociable and bad tempered. As a business woman she has her own interests at

heart, rather than those of clients or customers and can, therefore, be regarded as somewhat self-centred. A rich husband is often her source of wealth but, when needs be, she had a good head for making money.

Practical Significance

Traditionally, this queen represents a dark-haired, richly complexioned woman. Active and generous, she enjoys charitable work and organizing others into action. She often acts the lady bountiful, expecting compliments and admiration for her efforts. Wealth, her prop and support, will occasionally be used to promote others, but they are expected to show her endless gratitude in return.

These characteristics show up more and more with increasing years yet, should she find herself alone, she is well able to look after herself and become the bread-winner. Her place, she feels, is in the home but not around the kitchen sink; so any opportunity to go out is seized upon immediately. Lavish in most respects, she is always well and fashionably dressed. Most men admire her cool, sophisticated appearance, but few realize just how expensive she can be until it is too late!

Vitality gives this queen an attraction which makes her the envy of other women, who tend to be jealous of her. This is probably why deep friendships are virtually non-existent. In sports she finds the perfect setting to prove and show herself off; usually, she excels in these and wins many prizes.

Psychological Significance

This woman is an independent thinker, a characteristic which has its benefits although loneliness may develop later through lack of proper communication with others. Her need to possess material objects shows that she looks outwards for security instead of inwards, where personal reserves wait to be recognized and tapped.

Psychic Significance

Occult work is carried out positively and negatively. This brings a wealth of experience but also highlights personal psychic strengths and weakness.

Influential Significance

Personal self-confidence will receive a powerful boost from this positive influence. A temporary self-centredness may develop, but this is just what is required at this time. The effects are generally uplifting, so you can expect an increase in wealth which acts as a safeguard against impending trouble as well as allowing you the time to think and replan for the future.

Reversed Significance
This represents a mean, bad tempered and suspicious woman who cannot keep a friend for long. Always greedy for more and wanting to keep up with the Jones's, she becomes inquisitive and prying, with a result that more doors close than will ever be opened. She is her own worst enemy.

JACK OF CLUBS

The Jack's Significance
When representing a boy or youth this card shows that there is a strong desire to reach the heights and become head boy, captain of the cricket team or the organizer of interests other than the three Rs. Although not an academic, he is a budding tycoon because he has the ability to accumulate wealth and fortune.

If representing an adult, this card represents one who is stuck on the treadmill of life. The result is that this individual never hits the jackpot which was once well within his range.

Practical Significance
Full of vitality, he enjoys taking on responsibility at an early age. Able to save money, he soon learns the advantages that a nest-egg provides; therefore his talents turn automatically towards hoarding more and more. He will always make a determined effort to keep a bargain, although his personal aim or ambition will always be first and foremost in his mind. It is often said that he has an old head on young shoulders yet to put implicit trust in him would be most unwise.

Experience is what is needed and this, combined with the exuberance of youth, holds out great possibilities. To achieve kingly status he must beware of the trap which would keep him at his present knavely level for the rest of his life. How successful he is in this aim will depend on how adventurous he is when opportunities arise.

A degree of risk is involved in making the grade, so chances must be taken if true aims and ambitions are ever to be achieved. This Jack is the only one who can afford to take such chances and get away with it.

Psychological Significance
This character finds difficulty in keeping to one thing at a time. Hopefulness makes up for this defect and carries him through to a limited success. He has the ability to see ahead but does not always rely on his own judgment. Other people let him down yet he does not seem to learn his lesson.

Psychic Significance
Seeking answers to profound occult problems will prevent steady psychic progress. Don't expect too much too soon or a sharp encounter with a restraining occult force will bring a quick realization of your folly.

Influential Significance
This influence will help boost resources and thus restore faith in oneself. It may manifest as a loyal supporter or as a financial improvement. A racy atmosphere will help to relax any previous tension, so be bold and take a chance on a project, idea or hope. Back hunches to the full because this opportunity may not be repeated for some time.

Reversed Significance
Over-enthusiastic drive produces a dicey character who is regarded as potentially dangerous. The higher he climbs, the further he has to fall and, unfortunately, a fall is on the cards through his own stupidity.

TEN OF CLUBS

Numerical Significance
The tenth card in this suit indicates the completion of one phase and

the beginning of the next. The perfection of this number, the first of the multiple numbers, can be compared to the wheel of fate and fortune. Wealth – on all levels – has been accumulated in the last cycle and the future already rests on a secure footing. The phase ahead offers opportunities which, if taken, will provide further increases.

Practical Significance
A welcome sum of money is on the horizon, possibly from an unexpected source. This may materialize in the form of an inheritance, gift or a big gambling win. Security results, thus generating feelings of confidence and anticipation. But be prepared for surprise complications which could temporarily delay the actual arrival of this money.

Much revolves around investments and assets – from the largest fortunes down to post-office savings – so do not let these lie idle for too long. Like the talents in the parable, these will repay you best by being made to work.

This is a good time to spend money on investments for the future, so now is the time to give serious consideration to ways of doing this. Do not sit back and take it easy at this stage or rely too much on past glories. Drive and action is essential to keep the wheel of fate and fortune turning.

Psychological Significance
Hopes will be recharged with energy through personal effort. Fears and doubts are left behind as a new cycle in life begins. Forget the past and look ahead to better times.

Psychic Significance
A gift from the gods helps psychic progress. Philosophically, this

represents the harvesting of a previous sowing: good actions have been followed by good reactions. A new level of awareness is achieved.

Influential Significance
This is a strong, positive, monetary influence which will bring security and confidence to a particular situation. Expect financial matters to stabilize and then steadily improve. Much strength and comfort is given by this material asset and although it is meant to be used, do so only after very careful consideration. Try to insure against future expenditure by acting now. An opportunity to do this will arise shortly.

Reversed Significance
It is virtually impossible to alter present spendthrift habits and, as a result, the last of personal savings ebb and unpaid bills mount up. Without money to act as a form of security, incentive is missing and this keeps the doors of opportunity closed.

NINE OF CLUBS

Numerical Significance
The ninth card in this suit is very fortuitous because it attracts further stability in the form of wealth, in every sense of the word. A peak in financial affairs will be reached shortly and this will bring respite from worries. Also, a milestone has been reached, which puts things on a much firmer footing all round. However, this does not mean that it is a foregone conclusion that the future is going to be rich, without any effort being made. In order to maintain this stability, efforts will be needed and now is the time to make plans for this.

Practical Significance

Wealth is definately on the cards. Bank balances will soon look much healthier, possibly due to inheritances, gifts or money from property. Any money owing will also be repaid. One-man businesses will benefit financially, offering the opportunity for further expansion. Material comforts and a lessening of pressure will follow.

Money connected with marriage and close friendships is closely associated with this card. Over-all richness is indicated, but partnerships will need constant attention in order to continue to function as profitable propositions. Marriage settlements following divorce or separation are to the fore and any uncertainty concerning money will end soon. This is the right time to complete outstanding financial arrangements, even if the sum involved is small. Once this is done, freedom from worry follows – and this is a gift in itself.

A prosperous marriage is also indicated although this does not necessarily signify pounds in the bank. A wealth of happiness and mutual understanding accumulates, too. Count your blessings now and they will become a good investment for the future.

Psychological Significance

Confidence reaches a peak. Negativity vanishes, albeit temporarily, so make the most of this opportunity. Good relationships in the home and at work produce a relaxed and happy atmosphere, resulting in peace of mind.

Psuchic Significance

Positive and negative psychism blend and harmonize, thus opening up even more doors on the occult scene. A wealth of new experiences are offered and confidence in one's own ability increases.

Influential Significance

Decisions will be influenced by money. As a deciding factor, finances rather than emotions should be used as the yardstick. Joint savings will produce unexpectedly good results. This influence has a stabilizing effect too, and although things may appear to slow down it is only temporary. This will give you a valuable opportunity to catch up before moving on to the next phase.

Reversed Significance

Present financial stability cannot last much longer. Expenses will increase enormously and quickly outweight income, so expect high personal inflation. Steps should be taken now to prevent a landslide into poverty.

CLUBS   309

EIGHT OF CLUBS

Numerical Significance
The eighth card in this suit strongly suggests a balance of payments.
Riches, on all levels, are difficult to assess at this stage and can be
compared with a half full or half empty glass of water: it all depends
on the individual standpoint. A rest may be safely taken at this time
before starting on the next phase. There is a danger of covering the
same ground again by repeating the past, but there should be no
turning or looking back, only forward.

Practical Significance
This is the gambler's lucky card. The desire for money and wealth is
strong although, at this point, there does not appear to be a
watertight plan to bring this about. The solution offered is to take a
risk because this is the chance card. Bypass the usual channels and
jump in at the deep end, knowing that you stand a very good chance
of winning.

On the basic level, play your hunches because inspired guesses
about which dog or horse will come in first can be relied upon.
Gambling with property and investments, where financial rewards
are high, are good bets too. Those not given to risking their shirts
should at least be adventurous when investing, buying or selling.

This is a 'nothing ventured nothing gained' situation and unless a
positive move is made now, progress will be circular, so beware of
arriving back where you started. A bottle-neck has been reached,
indicating that the past must be completely settled before turning to
the future.

Psychological Significance
Difficulties in understanding personal motives cause worry. Too

much self-analysis will only lead to confusion and further complications however, so accept yourself and others for what they are.

Psychic Significance
Powerful influences could easily divert good intentions into the wrong channel. Beware of false values and false prophets who unbalance normally stable psychic atmospheres.

Influential Significance
This influence brings out latent gambling instincts and the desire or necessity for more money will develop. This trend will force some form of action to be taken. Opportunities will arise and these should not be ignored or missed because they can save a lot of time and effort by allowing you to take a short cut to the jackpot.

Reversed Significance
By repeating past mistakes more financial losses will be incurred. A negative vicious circle traps the unwary, with the result that it will become impossible to escape even further losses.

SEVEN OF CLUBS

Numerical Significance
The seventh card in this suit signifies personal success in life and offers security and insurance against the future. Carefully planned efforts have paid off and produced a nest-egg of considerable size. On other levels, too, wealth has accumulated and this may be used profitably in many different ways.

Practical Significance
This card represents the natural ability to make money and attain

materialistic goals. Involvement with financial matters at this time is likely and if the right cards are played, success is ensured. Ambitions and plans concerned with making money, or even a modest living, need to be constantly watched. Past experience shows that this will pay off, so don't let go of the reins now or the initiative will be lost as a result.

Since wealth is comparative, individual situations must be seen in relation to personal circumstances and standpoints: £1 seems a lot to some people but nothing to others. Special care must be taken when dealing with other people's money in order to safeguard personal reputations. Honest intentions are not enough: indicate on paper exactly where the money was spent.

Financial success is definitely on the cards, but due more to personal effort than to good luck. However, ensure that your values do not alter and do not make money into a god.

Psychological Significance
Freedom of self-expression should be encouraged now, using the wealth of past experiences to do so. A mature outlook has developed and should be of great help in solving life's problems.

Psychic Significance
Individual psychic development takes a big step forward. After an exciting phase, doors will open on new dimensions. The value of controlled astral travel will result in an important initiation.

Influential Significance
Personal financial matters will improve considerably with the help of this influence. Businesses benefit too and the domestic front will remain in funds despite heavy outlays. New ideas on how to budget and increase income will develop and this will, in turn, bring the security which has often been lacking in the past.

Reversed Significance
Total disregard for simple accounting brings personal financial troubles. Heavy debts will eventually lead to serious circumstances that could involve others who are in no way to blame. The days of borrowing are past.

SIX OF CLUBS

Numerical Significance

The Sixth card in this sit offers a choice of ways in which to make money and obtain wealth but is not a solution in itself. Much hard work and plodding effort are necessary to bring things together, which will be essential before a move forward can be made with any degree of confidence. Pressure and tension are inevitable, yet these will produce the driving force necessary to start to pull things into shape.

Practical Significance

Help will come from a most unexpected source. This could signify a fortunate turn of events or may indicate that a reliable friend will offer profitable advice. Another possibility is that a loan of hard cash could materialize. So, one way or another, some form of enrichment can be confidently expected.

Income and expenditure will just about remain on an even keel. There is nothing to spare, however, and since there is nothing to cover an emergency either, strict economy measures must be implemented at once. This is not a permanent situation but any action taken now will have good repercussions in the future. Careful planning is all-important, so don't be tempted into rash spending or investing in dicey holdings.

Reliable advice is worth seeking before parting with cash, and such help will be found easily although it may not come from a conventional source. Use instinct along with intellect to forge ahead: using both together will allow a more balanced assessment to be made. Everything must ultimately be paid for in one way or another, so do not forget to make provisions for this.

Psychological Significance
Doubts and fears should be seen in perspective or they will upset balanced judgment. Keep negativity under control by replacing dependence on others by self-reliance.

Psychic Significance
Expect occult influences to manifest in strange ways. Personal coincidences will initiate a new train of thought which will lead to new psychic pastures. Psychic development progresses slowly but surely.

Influential Significance
A helpful influence from out of the blue saves the day. Projects and plans relating to business and family matters which depend on money will benefit greatly. Last minute rescue measures will turn up trumps with the result that disappointment will be avoided and good friends will prove themselves to be as good as their word. Faith is restored all round.

Reversed Significance
There is a tendency to underestimate and overspend. An 'easy come, easy go' attitude may work for a while but, once the scales have been allowed to tip too far in the wrong direction, poverty is on the cards. Such conditions are self-imposed although this does nothing to stop the negative, downhill slide.

FIVE OF CLUBS

Numerical Significance
The fifth card in this suit denotes hopes for a better future. With drive and initative, plus plenty of inspired guesses, it is possible to

work up from nothing to a richly endowed position in life. This could result through an accumulation of material assets or, alternatively, through a wealth of experience. The end objective is quite clear although the road to this success has yet to be fully laid. Taking a new track altogether could provide a solution.

Practical Significance

Money associated with marriage and partnerships is indicated. This may take the form of sharing gifts and inheritances or the taking of rewards from joint business efforts. If equality is absent, a financial arrangement may leave one partner hard up, however, so changes might be necessary. Even though this might mean starting from virtually nothing, it will be worth all the hard work in the end.

Seen as a challenge, an opportunity will present itself which will bring better returns than a previous investment. There is nothing to stop progress once a firm plan is made and, should money troubles develop, they will soon vanish because, once started on that positive road leading towards the end objective, cash will begin to materialize.

Long-term monetary plans, including pension schemes and insurance policies, should be considered now. With an eye on the future – looking especially in the direction of old age – it pays to ensure that the nest will always remain well feathered.

Psychological Significance

Difficulties in dealing with others could become a worry. Weakness of character can lead to mental oppression, so it is important to recognize this tendency before it is too late. To keep the peace is one thing, but to be overpowered is another.

Psychic Significance

Positive psychic protection is necessary when controlling occult forces which are stronger than is realized. Harmony within the group will help to develop this, but if harmony is lacking, unwanted influences will creep into the situation and cause havoc.

Influential Significance

This influence will have long-term effects on wealth generally. At least this will settle things one way or the other and reveal the true financial state, down to the last penny. This can be regarded as a definite starting point, so loook ahead and make those much needed plans for the future. This card holds out great promise that things will go well, provided that personal dedication is applied positively.

Reversed Significance
Lack of initiative in the past continues into the future and there is little hope of any opportunity, however good, being taken now. Financially broke, friends are thin on the ground. Devious means of recouping losses will not provide a solution, however, so such thoughts should be squashed.

FOUR OF CLUBS

Numerical Significance
The fourth card in this suit indicates a struggle to keep things on an even keel. Resources could be drained in several directions at once, leaving little in reserve. However, if a halt is called now, a firm basis is left, upon which a secure, four square future could be built. If arrangements involve partners, special care must be taken to maintain the necessary harmony and balance or all could be lost completely.

Practical Significance
There is a strong warning in this card concerning the loss of a valuable article. Extra precautions should be taken to ensure that material possessions such as keys, jewellery, purses or gloves as well as cash, cars or furniture are not stolen or lost. The call on financial reserves could be a lot heavier than anticipated and limitations imposed as a result. The solution lies in keeping well within the bounds of solvency.

A loss of faith in oneself leads to lack of self-confidence and to lack of trust in others who have, in the past, been most reliable. This can cause insecurity, so keep the question of balance in mind when trying to regain equilibrium. Equal but opposing forces will either negate or destroy each other or harmonize into a positive force which can help to stabilize the situation.

Psychological Significance
Inhibitions seek outlets and, in so doing, may appear as extreme behaviour. Mental highs and lows produce mood swings, but this is only a temporary stage and will pass. Try to steer a middle course, especially when in the presence of others.

Psychic Significance
There is a risk that too much psychic work will drain off too much energy. This will not help anyone, so take a rest from occult encounters in order to keep at least one foot on the ground.

Influential Significance
Demands from several directions at once produce an influence that draws heavily upon resources. So, expect savings to dwindle and, on a physical level, be prepared for energy to drain away. Since it is difficult to do much about things at present, it is best to sit tight, relax and wait for a change of atmosphere.

Reversed Significance
Extreme difficulties will be encountered regarding money matters. Distrust of everyone and everything brings negotiations to a halt and produces an infuriating stalemate. Snap decisions will invariably be wrong, so do nothing rather than make more mistakes.

THREE OF CLUBS

Numerical Significance
The third card in this suit offers stability in respect of resources. Acting as a reservoir from which to draw, businesses will recover and

thrive, and the launching of new projects will prove remarkably easy. Enthusiasm fires ambitions into action and things will grow from this point into profitable reality. Those who have experienced failure in the past should try again, for the time is now right to make another attempt.

Practical Significance
Financial stability gives the materialistic self-assurance which has been lacking until now. Progress in all directions is on the cards, although opportunities still need to be recognized and grasped before they will pay off. There will be good co-operation between partners and this, plus firm financial backing, signifies that plans, schemes and proposals stand every chance of success.

A stage has been reached where new and profitable ideas will emerge on many levels. In a mundane respect, financial benefits from an expanding business can be expected. From a personal standpoint, valuable past experiences will be put into action to form a source of wealth from which to draw when in trouble and in need of strength of purpose.

Individual potential invested in business, artistic pursuits or on the domestic front now will express itself in very rewarding ways. Excellent foundations exist on which to build for the future, and now is the time to do this with every confidence. There is more than a grain of truth in the saying 'third time lucky', so prove this right by acting on intuition backed up by experience.

Psychological Significance
Reserves are high, bringing mental stability and confidence in oneself. Unification of ideas will blend into a new creative stream of thought, leading to future fulfilment.

Psychic Significance
The occult 'law of three requests' is encountered. When challenging entities and forces, use this law in order to be absolutely certain of their true identity.

Influential Significance
This is a stabilizing influence which gives confidence and introduces security into schemes and projects. Money matters will begin to look a lot healthier soon and will continue to improve for some time. A prosperous atmosphere shines on the domestic front, so extravagances are excusable just now.

Reversed Significance

Self-reproach for wasted opportunities leads to aggression and anger. As hopes fade, they are replaced with despair but, since no effort is made to really alter, this must be expected.

TWO OF CLUBS

Numerical Significance

The second card in this suit indicates a duality which is likely to produce head-on clashes and opposition associated with wealth and its distribution. Discussions with partners or financial advisers appear to offer no solution, yet, at the same time, efforts must be made because nothing ventured means nothing gained. Eventually, the balance will be restored, but keep an eye on both sides of the fence until this happens.

Practical Significance

A change of circumstances brings uncertainty but this is inevitable. In practical terms, money matters prove worrying although real fears for the future are quite unfounded. The joining of forces is one answer to the problem but, since this is not yet possible, it is better to go it alone.

Although joint efforts may appear to halve responsibilities and liabilities, they could, at the same time, double mental strain through such an arrangement. One aspect has, therefore, to be weighed against the other. On the whole, any pressure to pool resources should be resisted in the knowledge that a lone effort will more than double rewards.

The reckless spending of money or energy will not be recouped easily, so this is not the time for action generally. Projects launched now have only a fifty-fifty chance of success; therefore, it is better to wait for a sign that leaves no doubt whatsoever that the time is right and the door wide open.

Psychological Significance
The conscious and unconscious minds form a link which increases awareness and understanding of oneself and others. Care must be exercised, however, in order to maintain a good balance between the emotions and the intellect. Further development of the character will grow naturally from this duality as long as a careful balance is maintained.

Psychic Significance
Working as both a positive and negative psychic will increase the individual's powers tremendously and result in a greater degree of responsibility. A good, balanced philosophy of selflessness and compassion is very necessary therefore because the welfare and safety of others is at stake.

Influential Significance
Although this is an opposing influence it often does a lot more good than harm in the end because it lessens the urge to spend unwisely on non-essentials. The twin nature of this card inhibits positive decisions, yet, again, this acts as a brake just at the right time and thus protects resources. Do not throw caution to the winds however, but stand with both feet firmly on the ground in readiness for the next phase.

Reversed Significance
Opposition destroys every vestige of hope and kills enthusiasm. Vindictive partners inhibit self-expression and make life thoroughly miserable. Double the price has to be paid for innocent mistakes.

16
HEARTS

ACE OF HEARTS

Numerical Significance
This is the first and last card in the suit: a combination which produces fulfilment and wisdom. Nourishment to feel and sustain all heartfelt desires stems from this and happiness is initiated too, which affects all emotional situations. New friendships and reunions are activated, offering lasting friendship and love in the future. As a source of energy, this manifests on many levels, beginning with sexual and physical attractions and going on to compassionate feelings for humanity and all living creatures as a whole.

Practical Significance
Everything the heart desires is in this card. A happy family, true friends, passionate lovers and continued peace of mind are all definite possibilities. Heartfelt hopes and wishes stand a very good chance of being realized because fate and fortune shine benignly on the happiness scene at this time.

A surge of benevolent energy from this source of plenty rejuvenates and heals tired bodies and minds. Having received this, kindly feelings and thoughts for others are generated which, in turn, reward the individual with a satisfying, inner harmony.

Socially, opportunities arise which offer the chance of meeting many new friends and those in search of a lover will find themselves in the right place at the right time. Romantic settings materialize in the most unexpected places and relationships blossom speedily in this atmosphere. Sex and excitement soon enter the scene and these are followed, more often than not, by long-standing arrangements. Fertility is also symbolized by this card, so the beginnings of a new family circle could follow suit and the whole cycle of life begin once again.

Psychological Significance
Strong emotions need to be controlled because the heart definitely rules the head at this time. Judgment could well be very unbalanced from this singular standpoint although a good balance should develop eventually, once it is realized that a one-sided outlook exists.

Psychic Significance
A pool of compassion and understanding is ready and waiting to be tapped by those who wish to do so. Healing energy arises from this source and may be utilized for self-healing or directed towards others who need it. This force pours oil on troubled waters and protects the innocent.

Influential Significance
This is a strong, compassionate influence which can be used in any situation that lacks love and understanding. It will calm down the irate, bring balance to an over-materialistic situation and, by introducing humour into a worrying monetary problem, remove fears completely. Purely in its own right, this card has the power to introduce emotional happiness and inner satisfaction.

Reversed Significance
A barren situation is to be expected. Lack of understanding, absence of feeling for others and a general bleakness dispels all hope of emotional happiness. A big disappointment results in loneliness – with a broken heart hiding beneath a shattered exterior.

KING OF HEARTS

The King's Significance
This King is the great lover of the pack. He expresses himself with deep feelings coloured by the dictates from his heart. His ambition is to collect plenty of admirers and notch up sexual conquests but, with the increasing years, he turns more towards philosophical concepts. In many ways, he is a self-centred person and cannot see himself as he really is. He sincerely believes his heart is in the right place and that this is enough.

Practical Significance
Traditionally, this King is a fair-haired, blue-eyed man who is very emotional and thinks mainly with his heart. Above all, he is a great lover. This makes him a warn-hearted person who is friendly, kind, generous, well liked and popular. He is the home-loving type and therefore puts this side of life before his career and materialistic ambitions. As a father he plays for hours with the children.

Since he is an incurable romantic, he attracts the opposite sex and takes them in completely. Flattery and compliments pour from him and he has the gift of bestowing himself on one woman at a time, creating the impression that she is the only person in the world so far as he is concerned. Inwardly though, he is really a loner who exists in a secret place surrounded by his own thoughts. Others rarely know him although they often think they do.

His artistic nature can be channelled into various directions and, in the home, often manifests as a pretty garden and, at work, as a tidy desk. This neatness makes up for his apparent lack of originality although this trait is not lacking when it comes to pursuits nearer to his loving heart.

Psychological Significance
Heartfelt emotions nearly always hold sway over reason and logic. He has a great need to love and be loved, compassionately as well as sexually. There is a danger, however, that this individual will become withdrawn as he grows older.

Psychic Significance
Strong receptive qualities show good mediumistic ability which, when partnered by positive psychic communications, will extend well into the 'great unknown'. This King may also represent masculine discarnate beings such as departed fathers, uncles or grandfathers.

Influential Significance
This is the loving influence, whether from a lover, parent or good friend. It has the power to persuade and charm the birds off the trees, if necessary. Sometimes glib words accompany it and are accepted as pearls of wisdom, but only time will tell if these are true or false. Advice flows freely from the heart although, since this is based on emotions not on sound, practical experience, it cannot really be taken too seriously.

Reversed Significance
A tendency towards selfish sexual gratification does nothing to fulfil the desires in the long run. This attitude may attract a wide circle of off-beat acquaintances, yet such company will only end up by being despised thoroughly.

QUEEN OF HEARTS

The Queen's Significance

When young, this character represents the lover, and the blushing bride. As she grows older, she becomes the comfortable little woman in the home whose limited outlook extends little further than the end of the garden. She tends to develop interests which focus solely around the kitchen sink, and a bit of gossip. Ambitions are at a minimum beyond this point, yet contentment seems to grow rather than diminish with time.

Practical Significance

This Queen is generally regarded as a fair-haired person, yet this exterior, like the superficial image of all the court cards, is unreliable. When a girl, her hopes dwell on an early marriage, a home of her own and a family.

Potentially a ready-made mother, a good friend to the neighbours and a thoroughly domesticated person, she asks for no more than peace and quiet in the home. Romantic notions make her the queen of the kitchen where she takes pride in cooking, cleaning and everything within the scope of the domestic scene. Once married, however, her standpoint changes. She drops the glamour – which once lured every male in sight – for a stouter, almost dowdy image of the mistress of the house.

Artistic talents grow with middle-aged spread and what emerges usually surprises everyone: pretty paintings and romantic story-writing were invented for the typical Queen of Hearts.

Emotions are slowly conquered over the years and self-assurance grows from inner self-satisfaction rather than from intellectual confidence.

Psychological Significance

Seeing life from an emotional point of view gives a very one-sided picture. This leads to over-sensitivity and, eventually, to self-pity. Introversion should be counteracted by more outside interests in order to restore the balance as soon as possible.

Psychic Significance

This Queen is a natural medium. It is important that she learns to control this gift properly, however, before uninvited influences intrude and take over. Good protection is essential, therefore. This card may also represent feminine discarnate beings, such as departed mothers, aunts or grandmothers.

Influential Significance
This influence offers good motherly advice. Compassion and a
reliable shoulder to cry on help to release tension, particularly as
confidences will be respected. A friendly atmosphere restores
harmony both inside and outside the home and, generally, happiness
reigns.

Reversed Significance
A self-centred outlook limits a fertile imagination and this eventually
frustrates and demoralizes a normally placid nature. Friends become
few and far between and interests diminish. Day dreams replace
practical plans and further obstacles prevent emotional happiness.
Dreariness overshadows the domestic scene.

JACK OF HEARTS

The Jack's Significance
As a boy or young man this knave is full of fun. If he matures
emotionally he will become the King of Hearts, yet he will always
retain that boyish look throughout his life. Potentially a kind person,
he seems to miss out when it comes to hand outs and experiences
difficulties in being taken seriously. This causes frustration. A
general aura of immaturity – a characteristic which, once recognized,
is never forgotten – makes him the symbolic Peter Pan.

Practical Significance
He is, like the King and Queen of this suit, traditionally fair. Easy-
going all his life, he enjoys sport more for the sociability it offers than
for the exercise. Although a competitive spirit is lacking, a sporting
attitude to life is not – so he is very popular, especially with the ladies.
At work, promotion seems to pass him by, but since happiness and

an easy-going life are his chief aims, this does not bother him unduly.

When in love he can be hurt easily and shows it, too. His habit of wearing his heart on his sleeve does not help in this respect and he is prone to make unfortunate relationships anyway. When married, he is often thought to be his wife's son because he is virtually ageless.

Even when he draws his retirement pension this individual still has a boy's face. But this youthful exterior does nothing to alter the funny old character who has developed over the years, inside. Kindness must be acknowledged, however, for this is basic to his naive nature.

Psychological Significance
This Jack does not take himself seriously and should, therefore, not expect others to do so either. He is amiable, poetic and a day-dreamer, yet becomes bored very quickly. Practical interests should be developed or depression will creep in all too soon.

Psychic Significance
Intuitive and meditative, he has the makings of a good initiate. However, this enthusiasm quickly fades when it is discovered he has to start at the bottom in order to reach the top. Be warned: psychic dabbling could develop if persistence is lacking.

Influential Significance
Without a doubt this influence brings a dash of renewed vigour, especially to a flagging sex life. Such physical rejuvenation surprises everyone and a much more relaxed atmosphere replaces tension, so life will be happier and more fulfilling than of late. Friends rally round and social gatherings provide opportunities for meeting new faces and visiting exciting places.

Reversed Significance
As the unhappy lover of the pack, he makes himself more miserable than is necessary by wallowing in self-pity. This – and pride – prevent him from snapping out of it and, eventually, he takes on the role of the dejected lover, permanently.

TEN OF HEARTS

Numerical Significance
The tenth card in this suit shows that another round of the emotional

side of life has been completed. The culmination of this cycle manifests as inner peace and confidence. A new phase begins soon, built upon the foundations of the past, and plans for the future concerning family, love-affairs and all happy events should be made without delay. Changes are inevitable, but these will be welcomed.

Practical Significance
A very special and pleasant surprise brings happiness and joy. Rewards from past efforts bring unexpected gifts and a happy event. This could be news of a baby, an invitation to a wedding, a family gathering, a party or a reunion with a long-lost friend or lover.

There is a feeling of anticipation in the air, This acts as a protection against negative acts by producing a buffer effect. Progress for the family as a whole is to be expected and inner satisfaction brings long hopes for happiness to the individual. Romantic encounters are on the cards, so lovers can look forward to an especially exciting time when they will be able to devote more time to each other than they thought possible.

Although business and pleasure do not usually mix this is one of the few occasions when one will help the other. Social contacts and entertaining lead to expansion of material benefits, so do not hesitate to invite the boss to dinner. If you are the boss, then give employees a treat and you will be repaid by loyalty in return. This is a time when compassion, friendship and generosity can well be afforded.

Psychological Significance
The prospect of destiny suddenly becomes very important. Inner motives can be examined by deep thinking, yet there is no time for this now because action is needed, not more inaction.

Psychic Significance

A successful cycle, concerned mainly with negative receptivity, mediumship and clairvoyance, has been completed. A change in psychic direction will follow, and this will introduce the more positive side of occultism onto the scene.

Influential Significance

This is a strong protective influence which guards against emotional agony and trauma. Personality clashes will bring no lasting damage and quarrels and misunderstandings will soon be patched up. There is an element of surprise in the air and the introduction of unexpected events will result in much happiness, making life lighter and more relaxing.

Reversed Significance

Romantic opportunities are missed, with a result that self-recrimination follows. Negative emotions create tension which builds up to bursting point. This will clear the air, but also warns that the same unrewarding cycle will begin all over again unless the situation is recognized for what it is and changes made.

NINE OF HEARTS

Numerical Significance

The ninth card in this suit is considered to be the most fortunate in the pack and is known as the 'wish' or 'heart's desire' card. Therefore, all who are concerned with serious love-affairs and matters close to the heart can expect complete fulfilment. As the square of three, this number has stability as its main characteristic. Courage to make romantic approaches and confidence to see things through to the end will suddenly develop as a result of this.

Practical Significance
A high romantic note is reached where the world seems a beautiful place. Since everyone loves a lover, everything in the proverbial garden is lovely too. Those who harbour a secret wish can expect this to come true ... with just a little effort. Positive steps must be taken to ensure that the desired result is achieved because it takes two to make a bargain.

Apart from these good romantic indications, family affairs will prosper too. An abundance of goodwill flows from within and this affects all who come into contact with it. Life seens really rosy and troubles are at a minimum.

An opportunity will soon be offered to fulfil the heart's desire yet this could be missed unless personal effort is added to it. To a great degree, future happiness depends on the outcome of this opportunity, so be prepared to grasp it with both hands.

Psychological Significance
Solitude becomes a most satisfying experience. Experiencing a complete inner life strengthens purpose and causes illumination to shine into the lesser known, dark corners of the mind. Complete peace of mind brings great happiness.

Psychic Significance
Harmonious relationships between psychics produce excellent results for the good of all living creatures. Healing acts are particularly effective at this time and hopes in this direction will be more than realized.

Influential Significance
This influence is truly romantic. Hidden desires will be ignited and an imminent meeting with a lover is on the cards. Life in general is going to become happier and more exciting as a result of this prevailing atmosphere. Now is the time to make a wish, knowing that it stands a good chance of coming true.

Reversed Significance
The over-romantic atmosphere encourages lovers to make fools of themselves, so beware. Over-enthusiastic behaviour will result in your intentions being misunderstood and the object of the heart's desire will be thoroughly put off. Too much sentimentality, on the other hand, could ruin a plan just as easily as could an overtly sexy approach.

EIGHT OF HEARTS

Numerical Significance
The eighth card in this suit is a paradox because it signifies possibilities which result either in perfect harmony or in bitter disappointment. There are no half measures, so expect all or nothing situations to develop. The difficulty arises when final decisions have to be made; yet, if this can be accomplished, immediate peace of mind is achieved. If friendships are not as satisfying as they should be, now is the time to make a break and start again.

Practical Significance
Happiness is offered, at a price. Superficially, everything appears to be going well but, inwardly, a feeling of emotional uncertainty exists. Apply positivity to the situation and ignore negative signs as much as possible because these are less important than they seem. Forget the past, if possible.

If proffered gifts are accepted as tokens of true affections and not as appeasement presents, any temporary disagreements with family, friends or lovers will soon be forgotten. Social events, romantic moments and sentimental journeys will bring joy to the heart, but again, try to ignore all aspects which threaten to undermine present happiness.

Sensitivity is now at an all-time high, so be careful not to jump to the wrong conclusions, especially where affections are concerned. Feelings of guilt are likely and this could lead to inner conflict. Hasty action will be regretted later, so turn a blind eye to certain things.

Psychological Significance
A split mind exists which takes time to put together again. Deep

feelings are at loggerheads and the only way to unite these is to turn your attention to outer, practical aspects where a real solution may be found.

Psychic Significance
A choice between two psychic paths has to be made. This must be decided by the individual, who should in no way be influenced by the group. Forces of equal intensity will make this a difficult decision, however.

Influential Significance
The influence from this card throws new light onto old situations associated with the heart. There are two sides to every question and these will be shown up very clearly. Even so, do not expect to reach conclusions easily because patience will be needed in order to maintain harmony.

Reversed Significance
Prejudice will prevent an alternative course of action from being seen, let alone taken. One-sided views, if allowed to persist, will bring eventual destruction of emotional relationships and leave a void which will be very difficult to fill. Obstacles in the path of love and opposition to sentimental journeys will be virtually impossible to avoid.

SEVEN OF HEARTS

Numerical Significance
The seventh card in this suit is complete within itself and signifies great personal potential for happiness in the future. Everything the heart desires is contained within this card and, provided the game of

life is played according to the rules, wishes and hopes will surely be granted. Self-satisfaction is justifiable for this has been earned as a result of philosophical reactions to life's problems.

Practical Significance
This card represents individual desires for personal happiness and reflects the emotional aspect of the self: that which is known only to the individual concerned. Secrets of the heart suddenly become very important because now is the time to do something about them. Stability has developed from past experience, bring a quiet confidence with its own attractiveness and mystique. So, if this is combined with positive drive, all those romantic dreams can come true. However, if indecision is allowed to creep in, they will, unfortunately, fade all too quickly.

An opportunity will occur shortly which will offer the chance to express artistic talents. This could have far-reaching effects and lead to considerable success or even fame. So now is the time to take stock of dreams and hopes and begin working towards achieving them. New avenues should be explored, too, especially those which bring a diversion from everyday problems.

Psychological Significance
An excess of emotional energy must be allowed to express itself freely or there is a danger of it rebounding as nervous tension. This represents the libido, the basic driving force which, according to Freud, needs a regular sexual outlet.

Psychic Significance
A mystical experience will bring enlightenment and understanding. The symbolism of this signifies a key to the store of unconscious wisdom and, depending on the school of occultism followed, will appear in relation to the Holy Grail, The Tree of Life or the Tao.

Influential Significance
This is a strong personal influence, capable of steering emotional and heartfelt circumstances towards desired conclusions. Compassion and understanding has a calming effect on disturbed individuals and on difficult situations. Lovers may confidently expect a good response from those they desire most and should ensure, therefore, Cupid's dart aims for the right heart.

Reversed Significance
Failure to make the most of a romantic situation will be bitterly regretted. Hopes for a special meeting with someone will be frustrated through lack of initiative and courage. A disappointment in love is on the cards, entirely due to personal neglect and not through lack of opportunity.

SIX OF HEARTS

Numerical Significance
The sixth card in this suit brings the heart's desire nearer, but at a price. Two sets of circumstances are at loggerheads, yet, for peace of mind, they must eventually merge somehow because a compromise is inevitable. One may hope for the best of both worlds but, since this card does not symbolize actual fulfilment but only a step on the way, no immediate conclusion should be expected.

Practical Significance
This card symbolizes some form of self-sacrifice, either self-imposed or the result of unfortunate circumstances. Acceptance is the only answer at this stage, although this does not mean that everything has to remain unchanged. One may be willing to pay a high price for something the heart desires above all else, yet it is foolhardy to take this to the extreme of enforced martyrdom.

To be at the beck and call of the family or having to take a back seat in someone's affections amounts, in principle, to the same thing. A one-sided love-affair or an eternal triangle situation is a notorious breeding ground for willing self-sacrifice.

This card warns that the heart should not be allowed to dictate unconditionally because self-destruction moves in all too quickly, replacing happiness with pain. If this is regarded as a necessary experience then much can be learned but, when looking back on things, nothing should ever be regretted.

Psychological Significance
There is no inner peace at present. Independence is desire but fears of standing alone prevent progress towards this. At least this is an aim in the right direction, so it should become the goal for the future.

Psychic Significance
Psychic abilities should be used in the service of others. This is a testing-time, so expect clairvoyance and all the occult arts to be thoroughly scrutinized and challenged by superiors.

Influential Significance
This is a personal influence which could eventually make a rod for your own back. It allows others to take advantage and exploit your loyalty, yet, at the same time, it encourages the pure sacrificial act which is a gift to those who are genuinely in need of help.

Reversed Significance
Masochistic tendencies attract other people's burdens as well as your own, which will all weigh heavily upon your back. Emotional energy drains away and physical hard work is on the cards too. If this situation is allowed to continue, inner rebellion will cause untold trouble and mental turmoil. Self-help is the first line of defence, therefore.

FIVE OF HEARTS

Numerical Significance
The fifth card in this suit symbolizes the need to communicate with

someone and fulfil that friendship. Sexual relationships, especially
on the romantic level, need careful handling because emotions
could destroy practical stability and ruin everything. Happiness is
encouraged although this could be missed through the implementation of a short-sighted policy. So, play for time: think of tomorrow as
well as of today.

Practical Significance

'Still waters run deep' is the message of this card. It signifies a strong
urge to escape from true feelings, due to divided loyalties or a guilt
complex. The heart and soul have been put into an amorous pursuit
at the expense of reason, so caution is needed before all bridges are
burnt.

This is a severely testing time when heart-searching questions
need honest answers. Actions taken now will have far-reaching
effects, and, since these arise from the emotions, considerable
restraint is needed. Sexual desires must be strictly controlled or they
could be misunderstood. Equally, other strong emotions which also
need curbing are those likly to erupt as passionately religious beliefs
or nationalistic outbursts.

At this time the truth is difficult to recognize and face. Sometimes
it lies beneath excuses which lead to negativity and inaction; at others
it manifests in positivity and over-reaction, bordering on extreme
fanaticism.

Psychological Significance

Guilt emerges as self-pity one moment and as aggression against
others the next. Frustration due to lack of emotional outlets causes a
build-up of mental energy which should be released physically, in
the form of sex or sport, or expressed mentally through philosophical concepts.

Psychic Significance

A lack of confidence in one's psychic ability brings development to a
halt. Communication between the conscious and unconscious mind
has been neglected, but the way will open up again once this fact has
been recognized.

Influential Significance

This influence encourages one to escape from real issues. It is the
'bury-the-head-in-the-sand' card but, unfortunately, such behaviour
will not send troubles packing. A brave heart is needed above all else.

Strength seems to gather from nowhere once the world has been faced because others will then make moves which will help to improve the situation tremendously. The first move must, however, come from within the individual.

Reversed Significance
Turning a blind eye to personal affairs presents others with the opportunity to take unfair advantage. Laziness plus cowardice heaps more troubles on the old ones, so there is an urgent need for a change in direction. Heaven-sent opportunities still arise but are consistently ignored.

FOUR OF HEARTS

Numerical Significance
The fourth card in this suit tugs at the emotional heart-strings. There is a fear of toppling too far one way so that life appears to be rather like walking a tightrope just now. Beware of jumping out of the frying pan into the fire, yet, at the same time, do not simply sit there: something must be done but the question is, what and when?

Practical Significance
Emotional independence is represented by this card. This has developed not so much from happiness but more through painful experiences which tore at the strings themselves. Having reached this singular stage, fear of showing one's true feelings exist and emotions now act as a barrier which keep romantic encounters at bay as a result. Members of the opposite sex are viewed with distinct mistrust and lack of confidence in them and oneself has formed a negative alliance.

In family circles disharmony rules. Arguments and disagreements may well give cause for concern yet, if this situation is faced fairly and squarely, much of the heat can be removed and things will then be able to simmer down generally.

Swinging from the heights to the depths emotionally makes for unstable situations and relationships, so this is not the time to make bold decisions which could very well be regretted later. It would be better to do nothing than to spoil the future but, if action is unavoidable, try to take steps which are not guided solely by the heart's wishes. Remember, the head should have its say too.

Psychological Significance
Swinging emotions produce manic-depressive moods. If external circumstances are to blame, concentrate on keeping a middle of the road course. If it is inner feelings which colour and trigger matters off, learn to recognize the two extremes of temperament and blend them mentally.

Psychic Significance
The importance of the four-fold nature of matter is indicated with this card. This suit represents water which, in turn, symbolizes compassion, understanding and feeling for others. The further development of these qualities is needed before a four-square psychic footing can be achieved, however.

Influential Significance
This has an unsettling influence on the emotions. Its origin is found in past bitter experience which is best forgotten if future happiness is ever to be won. Sometimes is provides protection against complicated love affairs; at others it opens the door onto one-sided relationships which drag on to become forlorn romantic hopes. Sit tight and wait for the winds of change to blow.

Reversed Significance
Unfair deals in love bring inner misery. Nothing will ever happen to change things, therefore it is advisable to try to forget the past, accept the present and plan for a better future. Familiarity breeds contempt, so do not make this mistake on top of all others.

THREE OF HEARTS

Numerical Significance
The third card in this suit shows emotional stability with considerable

control over personal feelings. A quiet confidence attracts others of like natures and a new-found emotional stability increases attractiveness, so lovers should find life particularly fulfilling. Friends and family appear more amenable than usual and everything goes smoothly and swimmingly.

Those who are madly in love can expect a reward for their devotions and one way in which this expresses itself is in an increase from two to three. A new baby could be the one to make up this number . . . so be prepared.

Fertility of imagination is also ready to produce its brain child which, like its physical symbolic counterpart, is full of potential and hope for the future. It is as if a long period of training is over and, having completed the course of sowing, the reaping is about to begin. What follows is the harvest: a prize of which to be truly proud. Abundance of emotional happiness should be stored and treasured for a rainy day.

Psychological Significance
Emotional stability has been won through personal effort. This is a superior mental state which bestows strength of purpose to aims and ambitions of a practical nature. Expect progress with underlying plans.

Psychic Significance
The still, inner voice of intuition should always be heeded and respected. Original psychic techniques and unique remedies for healing arise from this source.

Influential Significance
This influence restores any lack of self-confidence. If there is a yearning for a particular partner then this new-found inner stability

will attract him or her in the right direction. A surplus of mental energy creates a much more stable atmosphere, so life should grow happier and easier all round.

Reversed Significance
Emotional effort is wasted in the wrong direction. Relationships prove most unsatisfactory owing to poor judgment of character. Lovers and friends seem unreliable, but the truth is that the fault lies much nearer home. Do not take sides in three-cornered arguments where no one can win.

TWO OF HEARTS

Numerical Significance
The second card in this suit holds the key to harmonious relationships where two hearts beat as one. Whether two can live as cheaply as one is another matter however, so the diamonds and clubs must be consulted in this respect. Individually, a good relationship has developed between the inner and outer selves, resulting in a much more expansive outlook on life.

Practical Significance
Marriage and all romantic partnership are represented by this card. Chance meetings and renewed acquaintances will blossom into deep and happy friendships, some ending in marriage, others not. All sexual relationships – from the first kiss to the finality of making love – are also symbolized by the two hearts on this one card. Plenty of give and take, partners in themselves, are needed to maintain this delicate balance, but this can be done quite successfully when there is a joint aim.

Apart from lovers, relationships between friends, neighbours, workmates and family flourish, so there should be plenty of fairness and equality all round. This is a good time to iron out any difference and long-standing disagreements. Such troubles may well come to a head, so be ready to deal with them with a compassionate heart.

The merging of ideas will more than double the rewards and you should not let pride keep progress from the door any longer than needs be. This is the time to unite in theory, if not in practice.

Psychological Significance
A natural sense of justice and fair play paves the way for a greater understanding of action and reaction, sowing and reaping, Yin and Yang. These are the basic principles of psychology as well as those of the universe as a whole and produce inner peace as well as an out atmosphere of harmony.

Psychic Significance
Telepathy between well balanced psychic partners leads to further occult initiations. Working in pairs will increase awareness safely and surely as long as a unified aim exists.

Influential Significance
This is a dual influence affecting hearts and emotions. The opportunity for shared romance and joint happiness is offered, probably arising from social activities or holidays. A generally peaceful atmosphere reigns, allowing time to rest and catch up on the more neglected aspects of family life. Shared experiences bring joy and laughter.

Reversed Significance
Disharmony between lovers, friends and family is on the cards. Emotional relationships are very unstable and disagreement all round makes life intolerable. Revealing personal feelings to others will lead to further misunderstandings and only make matters worse.

17
SPADES

ACE OF SPADES

Numerical Significance
This is the first and last card in this suit and combines numbers one and thirteen into a source of trouble. This is seen as a necessary evil because it brings into the open that which festers beneath the surface. The force behind this has the power to leave no stone unturned and in so doing reveals some pretty unpleasant surprises.

Practical Significance
An enormous hurdle or challenge in life lies in this card. It brings to a close one phase and starts off the next so this is why it is often seen as the death card. Life is staged throughout in phases and many of these end on climactic notes; the symbolic death of a love-affair is one such example. Death, therefore, is by no means the only finality we have to face, as this card signifies.

Underlying problems relating to health, business, money matters, love-affairs, ambitions, careers and hopes for the future will be affected and are bound to come to a head soon. Action will be forced upon those who ignore the warning signs so be prepared. A sense of justice rules too, which often appears ruthless for the natural law of action and reaction does not take feelings into account. On a practical level, law suits are possible concerning tussles over rights and possessions, but a philosophical approach, where everything is fair in love and war, helps soften such blows. So face up to the challenge and, where necessary, accept these events as inevitable stumbling blocks along life's highway.

Psychological Significance
A mental hang-up prevents real enjoyment, satisfaction and happiness from life. This is the iceberg of the mind where only the tip shows and the rest lies dangerously submerged beneath the surface of the unconscious. The first step towards thawing out this condition is to accept its existence and know its extent.

Psychic Significance
Beware of unseen dangers. Occult attacks through foolhardiness could bring fear and trepidation to even the most experienced psychic workers. Keep up protection and challenge every entity and force thoroughly. The effects from this cause disharmony within the group and loss of confidence in the individual.

Influential Significance
This influence adds fuel to the fire that needs just a spark to set off an inferno. Once this happens it must be fought with might and main. It has the power to disrupt situations and turn placid people into aggressive lunatics who collectively start riots and even wars.

Reversed Significance
If things could get worse then they will. Forsaken by friends and life generally, injustices appear on all fronts producing a trap from which escape seems impossible. Enormous personal effort is needed to alter the present downward trend where problems are forming into immovable obstacles.

KING OF SPADES

The King's Significance
This King is the archetypal judge attracted to authoritarian positions in life. He is often found in local government, politics and the professions, especially law. Dogmatic and severely critical, he is quick to see faults in others but fails to notice his own. With a ruthless logic devoid of all compassion his intellect rules stubbornly over his

instinct and intuition. It is better to have him as a friend than a foe.

Practical Significance
Energy surrounds this dominant and positive character. He uses this ruthlessly and unstintingly to further his own ends and once he is on the ladder of success he means to stay there until he reaches the top. He is most professional in everything he does and nothing short of perfection, often at the expense of others, will do. This leaves no room for the slightest criticism from others but, to be fair, he does his job very well indeed.

When at work he crosses swords with everyone who stands in his way. Since popularity does not go with either his job or his character he remains a loner. There are two types of women who are attracted to him; the masochist who enjoys being the underdog and the more than equal female who means to be top dog. She controls him from the start, much to everyone's delight and surprise.

Beneath the armour of over-confidence and self-opinionated superiority there actually lies a streak of insecurity. To cover this up he over-reacts and, in so doing, reveals his weakness.

Psychological Significance
There is a danger of a dynamic personality being ruined in later years through greed. In pursuit of power, patriarchal tendencies could become tyrannical but if these are tempered with wisdom, true leadership qualities emerge. Cruel traits exist which must be curbed.

Psychic Significance
Striving to invoke the four elements, this potential wizard or warlock seeks power and not wisdom. By contacting forces which he later finds to be beyond his control, he eventually falls under their spell although would never admit this.

Influential Significance
This influence produces single-mindedness and a ruthless approach to life. It gives power to enforce decisions and law and order which, in certain circumstances, is essential. There is always the danger of overstepping the mark and becoming too dicatatorial, so the utmost discretion is needed.

Reversed Significance
A lonely destiny lies ahead for this cold, calculating character. Pursuits of power have led him along a path strewn with obstacles and trouble which eventually build up into insurmountable barriers. Chaos and disorder rule completely.

QUEEN OF SPADES

The Queen's Significance
This Queen is ambitious and ruthless in pursuit of power. She rules the roost wherever and whenever she can and makes others well aware of their subordinate pecking order. A stickler for discipline she rarely takes other people's feelings into account when she lays down the law. Thinking exclusively with her head enables her to achieve feats more sensitive women would never desire, let alone strive for.

Practical Significance
There is no need for an enemy with a friend like this woman. Friends to her are there to do her bidding and nothing else, but she loses most of these after their first encounter with her selfish temperament. Committee work attracts her and it is not long before she takes command, including the chair. Since she is far from stupid she plays her cards right from the start, so it is not really surprising that she is

applauded for her organizing abilities and devotion to the cause.

This Queen is sure to be found in every office and place of work. Age does not matter, for both young and old alike play the same overbearing role, with the result that they are known as witches and worse. Regarded as a diffficult, bossy and thoroughly dangerous woman she sees herself as a dutiful, honest and forthright person who is greatly wronged by everyone, including her family.

Psychological Significance
Hard-hearted and headstrong this character lacks every trace of feminine warmth. Inhibited emotions cause frustration which adds to the outer veneer of ruthlessness. A close relationship with the opposite sex is desperately needed, but there are few men who feel inclined to take her on. When they do the partnership does not last long.

Psychic Significance
In the past this Queen would have been recognized as a witch whose practices were suspect to say the least. Considerable occult knowledge gives her power over those who become her initiates and, once in her clutches, it is virtually impossible to escape.

Influential Significance
This is a ruthless influence lacking all compassion and wisdom. It is reminiscent of the iron hand in the velvet glove which delivers blows swiftly and passes on silently leaving behind confusion and disruption. Good may result from this havoc eventually, but this will depend on other factors as well. Beware of the person who helps others into trouble.

Reversed Significance
Selfishness develops into a rigid characteristic that blots out every trace of feeling for others. As a female recluse, everyone keeps well away for fear of being attacked verbally, if not physically. Loneliness is inevitable, but this woman is her own worst enemy.

JACK OF SPADES

The Jack's Significance
This card rarely represents a boy but if it does it depicts a delinquent. As a man it symbolizes an emotionally immature, inadequate and totally impractical person. He is misinformed and is misinforming

so his word and advice should never be relied upon. Even so, he is full of self-importance, self-confidence and big ideas. As he grows older he lives more and more in a world of his own.

Practical Significance
Although this man lacks authority, he takes it upon himself to boss others. This does not make for popularity but he has only himself to blame. Insincerity in the past has given him a bad reputation, so when it comes to promotion at work he is passed over. Friends are few and far between but, since 'birds of a feather flock together', those he has are unreliable and devious. They are the proverbial dogs who have been given a bad name so it is difficult to shake off this bad image. This Jack is usually the leader of the gang.

As a husband he is hard going for any woman who is foolish enough to have him. A Queen of spades is the only one who has any degree of control over him, but this is never a happy arrangement. Should a romantic Queen of hearts misguidedly take him on, she will rue the day and every succeeding day she stays with him. His mother and older women are the only ones who have any time for him. Maybe this is because his mentality remains that of a spoilt child all his life.

Psychological Significance
Gross emotional immaturity is the cause of this mixed-up character. Inner turmoil manifests outwardly as aggression and wanton behaviour. Leadership qualities are only temporary and disappear altogether with increasing years.

Psychic Significance
Entering the psychic scene like a flash of lightning, all attention focusses on this startling newcomer. But thunder will surely follow

and these rumblings should arouse suspicions, so beware of him. He will certainly have a few tricks up his sleeve, but only the naive and gullible will be taken in.

Influential Significance
This disturbing influence brings out the worst in individuals and agnifies the negative aspects in every situation. Everything will be revealed through this, so expect secrets to be thrown to the wind and confidences to be broken. Courage is needed to face up to all this, but to compensate there is a feeling of distinct relief.

Reversed Significance
A thoroughly despicable character like this should not expect much from anyone. Untrustworthy and unreliable he is shunned and lonely. At work he is avoided and in the home he receives little love since he gives little in return. When confronted with his own mistakes and faults he flies into a childish rage.

TEN OF SPADES

Numerical Significance
The tenth card in this suit completes a round in life which has been difficult to say the least. From this point things can only get better. Looking back on events shows how things went in circles with nothing accomplished in the end. Even a downward spiral may be discovered, from which it will take time to recover, but as an obstacle course this phase has ended.

Practical Significance
Personal frustration is to be expected as a result of past and present circumstances, so tears and jealousy are excusable although they do nothing to solve things. Enthusiasm and hopes are likely to be

dashed to the ground so do not expect too much yet. Difficulties with practical plans, emotional hopes and money matters bring delays and minor upsets. Communication proves to be a major problem which causes misunderstandings all round.

Loss of jobs and failure to find new ones take their toll on emotions and domestic scenes suffer from intolerance and frayed nerves as a result. Relationships naturally become tense so watch out for trouble spots which trigger off fiery reactions. This is generally a negative card; therefore every possible precaution should be taken, on every level, to keep things on an even keel. This will be a lone task and it will be difficult to recognize true friends but, if it is of any comfort, many are in the same boat with you. An end to the present trouble is in sight, so keep going.

Psychological Significance
Depths of depression are reached through external circumstances. This is understandable but it must not develop into a regular response pattern where every obstacle, however small, triggers off this extremely negative reaction.

Psychic Significance
Occult work in a group faces a severe challenge. The weakest link in the chain places everyone in danger, so whoever this person is must be discovered, psychically cleared and re-aligned. Strengthen protection against external, interfering forces which seek to break up a circle trying to work harmoniously.

Influential Significance
Enthusiasm will be drastically dampened down by this negative influence. Any lack of drive must be fought and overcome if survival on practical, emotional and financial fronts is to be maintained. Stick to original plans until something better turns up, which it will shortly. Beware of misunderstanding which could trigger off a long chain of events which blight the future.

Reversed Significance
Just when things look to be at their worst they deteriorate even more. A rough ride, going over the same old ground frustrates to breaking point. It is difficult to see where all this will lead as the wheel of fate continues to turn much as it did before.

NINE OF SPADES

Numerical Significance

The ninth card in this suit is consistant in that it keeps up its promise of further negativity. An all-time low is reached which affects any one of the three other suits representing practical, emotional and financial matters. Even so, everything happening now helps to clear the air but this will be realized only after the event and when the edge has worn off a painful memory. Numerically, it is still a fortunate number if only because it prevents an even worse fate.

Practical Significance

Worries over health and, to a lesser extent, wealth drain energy, allowing depression to take over. A stage is reached where action must be taken so whatever happens, expect something of a change. Illnesses will be brought to light and revealed for what they are; these range from minor complaints to conditions needing urgent medical attention. Suspense comes to an end with this comparative peace of mind, as long-feared enemies are recognized for what they are.

Scandals and idle gossip bring unhappiness to many innocent people. Although this could result a long time after the event which started off the negative trail, it still causes suffering. It is important to try to rise above these difficult circumstances, as impossible as it seems and above all, conserve personal energy. This is the key to solving all trouble, physical and mental, so rest and relax whenever possible. Beware of wasting valuable energy on trivialities that do not really matter and ignore pettiness in others for this is a trap which distracts from the main issue.

Psychological Significance

Lack of energy lowers resistance to everything. Apart from feeling under the weather physically, the emotional threshold to stress is so weakened that a break-down is on the cards. It is far better to do nothing rather than do the wrong thing, because this simply piles on the agony.

Psychic Significance
Occult battles with negative forces test defences. Rituals involving astral projection should not be attempted at this stage for fear of a serious attack. Watch out for danger signals inside as well as outside the group or circle, which seek to cause a rift.

Influential Significance
As a negative influence of a parasitic nature this will deplete even the strongest characters. Beware of wasting energy on self-pity and self-recrimination as a result of this; instead, reverse the process into positive thinking and planning. Tiredness and lack of drive unite into a destructive partnership and, if allowed to continue, they demolish every hope for the future.

Reversed Significance
Serious troubles associated with poor health and lack of wealth bring increasing bouts of depression. Help is no longer offered because it has been rejected in the past. Underhand schemes to make money fail and, even worse, past devious plans designed to extract profits by undesirable means will be exposed. Further misery results.

EIGHT OF SPADES

Numerical Significance
The eighth card in this suit is negative and most unfortunate, causing

disputes which are extremely difficult to understand, let alone resolve. This is because only half the picture can be seen at any one time and somewhere between the two lies a no man's land where there is nothing to win and nothing to lose either. This is a thoroughly frustrating situation which cannot be ignored.

Practical Significance

Obstacles and indecisions rule over every aspect of life. Business schemes, travel arrangements, including holidays and ambitions for the future suffer particularly so expect delays before matters are sorted out satisfactorily. In arguments, both points of view are evenly matched, making it virtually impossible to make progress but, sooner or later, the scales will tip one way and end the present deadlock. Time must not be wasted during this temporary lull, so use this to prepare for the final fray and the action which is bound to follow. No good will come from forcing the issue at this stage so sit tight.

On the domestic front there will be clashes within the family probably between younger and older members. Love-affairs will face a testing time too and only the really well adjusted relationships will survive. A strong warning is also given with this card concerning trust. Do not reveal personal secrets nor give away confidential information relating to other people to anyone.

There is a possibility of enforced isolation such as a stay in hospital or, in extreme cases, it could be a prison sentence. Whichever it is, this should be taken as an opportunity to recover from personal difficulties. It will also act as a future safeguard and protection.

Psychological Significance

Definite strength of will exists, but without a specific aim this is like a journey without a destination. Make sure that an end object is in view and that mental energy is properly controlled and directed towards this. Intellectual powers will be wasted too, unless a strict discipline and routine is laid down and kept to.

Psychic Significance

Beware of working in the dark both literally and metaphorically. Lone workers are in particular danger of an occult attack since they lack protection from a psychic partner or from a group. These attacks will take unexpected and unusual forms and will by no means be confined to psychic levels only.

Influential Significance
This influence frustrates the individual by placing obstacles in the way and brings wheels within wheels grinding to a halt. Attempts to communicate with others fail, so take advantage of this uneasy quiet to make watertight plans and better policies in readiness. Strained emotional relationships run the risk of reaching breaking point, especially if enemies have a chance to have their say.

Reversed Significance
No good will come from a scheme, in spite of all the effort and hard work put into it. This leads to despondency, depression and dejection which does not lift easily. Lack of self-confidence does little to help an already bad situation.

SEVEN OF SPADES

Numerical Significance
The seventh card in this suit has strong personal associations of a distinctly negative nature. Secret fears and worries cast despondent shadows over the brightest scenes and bad characteristics are allowed to express themselves. These override compassion from the heart and logic from the head. Individual selfishness rules and will continue to do so until a realistic and honest approach to life is adopted.

Practical Significance
Although personal worries exist, they are no excuse for bad manners and hasty tempers. By allowing fears of what might happen to control and colour every aspect of life, a dark cloud hangs over the present. Eventually this will bring a depletion of energy, and invite

more trouble in the form of physical illness and depression.

There is a risk that attitudes to life become increasingly selfish and, although rarely recognized as this, other people see it all too clearly. Negative situations are attracted to negative people, so much of the present trouble could have been avoided. Practical and emotional problems may well exist but these can become complicated through wrong thinking and consequent wrong handling. Disputes with friends and workmates are unavoidable and these strike deep at the roots of individual standpoint. Obstacles and misfortunes, however, are necessary experiences meant to teach lessons in living, but the present chain of negative events is being fostered by a poor philosophy and understanding of what life is all about.

Psychological Significance
Difficulty in altering fixed patterns of thought form a barrier around the mind which blinkers the sight. Expansion and expression of the personality is inhibited and an altogether bigoted character develops. If freed from this self-imposed bond, a new positive life-style develops and one way to begin to do this is to seek out a good basic philosophy.

Psychic Significance
Insufficient belief in powers beyond this world must be reconciled with the continued pursuit of psychic phenomena. It is extremely dangerous to venture further along the occult path without complete acceptance of these, plus recognition of symbols and archetypes. Rebound reactions are to be expected until a definite conclusion is reached.

Influential Significance
Personal problems reach a crisis point as a result of this influence. Worries concerning health, the family or matters at work cast gloom over everything else. Fears will be exaggerated and although most of these will never happen, they still have the power to produce a negative atmosphere and interfere with peace of mind. Control has never been more necessary than now, because things could deteriorate even more if left to their own devices.

Reversed Significance
Spite and malice are fostered like vipers in the bosom. Seeing life as an errand of vengeance can only reap more disasterous reactions, so

until it is realized that one negative action produces another negative reaction, things will continue on the downward path until rock-bottom is reached.

SIX OF SPADES

Numerical Significance

The sixth card in this suit represent hard work which shows little reward for all the effort. Attempts to preserve that which has already been achieved will meet with opposition, but the fight must continue. There are always two aspects to be considered and these have to be manoeuvred into a position which produces some degree of equilibrium.

Practical Significance

Disappointments are inevitable, but this does not mean all is lost. Although a 'wet blanket' atmosphere dampens down enthusiasm, in no way does it extinguish the spark of ingenuity so there is still hope. Set-backs such as this, when viewed in retrospect, will be seen to have been for the best.

Minor health problems will prevent complete fulfilment of plans, but again, all will be for the best so do not waste time and energy worrying about what might have been. Depression is likely but this should not be allowed to overshadow the hatching of plans for the future. From a practical point of view, just when contracts concerning property are about to be signed, along come doubts and everything stops short. Diplomacy and time will work wonders in this situation whereas attempts to force the issue will only make things worse. Have faith and wait for a change in circumstances which will be for the better.

Psychological Significance

Difficulties in reconciling the inner realm of dreams with the outer world of harsh realities causes mental conflict. One without the other is incomplete and therefore unfulfilling, so the answer lies in a blend of the two. These two aspects represent the conscious and unconscious minds, between which there should exist strong links.

Psychic Significance

Forces beyond control impose self-sacrifice that greatly disturb psychic workers. Those who operate alone are in particular danger. Difficulties with astral projection will be the first warning sign, followed by garbled messages from outer space.

Influential Significance

This influence brings disappointment, tears and set-backs. Even when things seem to be going really well, a negative feeling manages to creep in and spoil everything. Undercover actions are suspected although there is no proof that they exist. Matters will improve shortly but meanwhile, be prepared for delays, unexpected obstacles and being let down by others.

Reversed Significance

News which should have arrived some time ago arrives too late to prevent a catastrophe. Obstacles now seem like permanent fixtures and trying to escape them is impossible, certainly at the moment. A long chain of disasters, fortunately none of which are devastating, look like continuing for some time.

FIVE OF SPADES

Numerical Significance

The fifth card in this suit has the power to demolish every hope that once stood a good chance of succeeding. Misunderstandings and misinterpretations have laid a false trail leading to the downward path. Aims and ambitions for the future must not be lost, in spite of the present obstacles because this is a testing-time. Those who emerge will greatly increase their strength and understanding of life. Personal involvement with certain unpleasant situations cannot be avoided and it will mean carrying other people's burdens.

Practical Significance

This card warns against discouragement. Although trouble seems to heap upon trouble, there is still a bright spot on the horizon. Success is still within the grasp, so long as it is sought with courage and determination. Whatever the odds, try hard to see it through to the end and do not give up now.

Plans for a career, business projects, holidays and moving house are all at risk due to temporary set-backs, but last minute reprieves suddenly put everything right again.

Money matters take a knocking but again final calculations will show them to be far better than was feared. On the emotional level, relationships will suffer from misunderstandings which complicate things so much that there is a risk of a complete break. By accepting the inevitable and flowing with the stream there will be an improvement of circumstances, but do not expect to solve difficulties easily for this is impossible. Original plans and hopes should not be allowed to become submerged beneath the present trouble. Confidence and strength is needed to carry on, so concentrate on the future and not on past regrets. Accept that everything is going to take that much longer than was first thought and reorganize the calendar to fit in with the new schedule. Once this is done there will be a feeling of relief at having tried to do something about the situation.

Psychological Significance

Beware of speaking your mind in the so-called name of honesty. Brutal truths should be delivered with discretion and more often than not they should be replaced with white lies anyway. It is not a sign of a strong character to be able to tell others their fortunes in this way.

Psychic Significance

Entities from the lower astral plane masquerade as innocent spirits.

These test the power of challenge and call for accurate recognition of signs, symbols, archetypes and all unseen forces. Use the pentacle, the five-pointed star, for protection.

Influential Significance
This influence has the power to complicate and disrupt even the simplest of plans. On the positive side it will single out unseen obstacles which are better brought to light now than later so in this sense it is not bad. Eventual success is on the cards, but only after difficulties have been ironed out. Doubt and lack of faith in ones own ability is also introduced with this influence so see it as a real personal challenge.

Reversed Significance
Beware of the stab in the back which could have far-reaching disastrous effects. This may result from the past, so try to put an end to a negative chain of events before it reaps more havoc. Legal battles will prove costly and in the end nothing will have been proved. Try to avoid such action.

FOUR OF SPADES

Numerical Significance
The fourth card in this suit combines an unstable number with the negativity of the suit as a whole. The effect from this is to halt previous progress in different ways and create trouble all round. Battles are foreseen and these range from court cases down to battles of wits.

Practical Significance
Legal battles, arguments and disputes are to be expected. Watertight

cases suddenly spring a leak and everything looks like collapsing. The weakest link in the chain should be found and examined carefully for signs of trouble and, small though these may be, they have the power to wreck everything. Practical, emotional and financial plans will all be affected. Love-affairs will develop into frustrating experiences especially if clandestine meetings are involved. As a warning, divorce or separation is on the cards. Unfortunately, there is little one can do about the present situation except wait and see.

A rest from worry and strife should be considered, which is not the same as trying to escape personal responsibilities. Health problems could be an added burden so this must be preserved above all else. Loss of sleep from a worry could start a vicious circle, ending in either physical or mental illness, so make sure a good night's rest is a regular occurrence. Relax during the day-time whenever possible.

Psychological Significance
Primitive instincts should be recognized as such and therefore controlled. These go with mundane pursuits and whilst they continue to rule, intellect and wisdom, let alone compassion, do not have a look-in. Brute force and ignorance lead to self-imposed imprisonment.

Psychic Significance
Be prepared for a battle with occult forces. Difficulties in knowing the enemy, who will be heavily disguised, confuse and disrupt the harmony within the group. Long-term after-effects will further disturb and bring trouble but at least it will sort the sheep from the goats.

Influential Signficance
This influence introduces a heartless atmosphere. Disputes arising from business and matrimonial affairs could end in court and in lengthy legal battles. On a less formidable level, troubles will be brought into the open where they can be dealt with fairly and squarely. Although unpleasant at the time, the air will be cleared as a result.

Reversed Significance
Lack of courage does nothing to help the present wave of trouble. Ignoring the true facts only postpones the final outcome and this

gets worse the longer it is left. Delaying tactics should not be tried and although this may seem one way out it is, in fact, only putting off the evil moment.

THREE OF SPADES

Numerical Significance
The third card in this suit represents a three-sided problem which undermines stability and equality. Emotional relationships and business partnerships are particularly susceptible as a third person or principle tries to interfere with the present harmony. Destructive forces seek to destroy long-established arrangements and will often try to do this in the name of progress.

Practical Significance
This card symbolizes the eternal triangle, a situation that can never be a happy arrangement. When relating to marriage and business partnerships no stability or progress will ever be made whilst this unsatisfasctory structure exists. A blind eye may be turned to an ever increasing threat but this cannot be swept under the carpet forever. Evntually, the truth will out.

  As a warning, every precaution should be taken when considering a third partner for he or she may sooner or later throw a spanner in the works. On emotional levels a third person enters the scene who has the power to disrupt an old-established relationship. This is usually presumed to be a secret lover but the culprit might be a child or relative who proves the theory that two are company but three is a crowd. Even an obsession which one of the partners has for a hobby or sport could be the third interloper but whoever or whatever it is, it will take three times as much effort to keep the status quo.

Psychological Significance
Creative thoughts are self-inhibited so the result is third-rate work and lack of originality. A complete change in attitude, not only to work but to life as a whole is needed, but this must be voluntary and not something imposed by a third party.

Psychic Significance
Beware of matriarchal tyranny ruling through emotional blackmail, mental enslavement and jealousy. This will be cleverly done so do not expect the obvious. Feminine vibrations of a destructive nature must be anticipated and, as destructive as these are, they will not be easily recognized.

Influential Significance
This influence introduces a third aspect which thoroughly upsets plans and relationships. Arguments develop and there is the likelihood of great enmity stemming from a once harmonious situation. The breaking of agreements is likely and applies to emotional commitments as well as to business pledges. As an early warning sign look for an atmosphere of aggression.

Reversed Significance
The breaking of an agreement can lead to personal strife and collectively to group or even national hostility. Action of a most despicable nature is taken and this is not done in the name of humanity. Disorder rules in place of harmony, so the future looks bleak and without a lot of hope for some time to come.

TWO OF SPADES

Numerical Significance

The second card in this suit brings duality and opposition. Complications arise and the disharmony produced by this has the power to sever long-standing relationships and agreements. Indecision delays everything with stalemate situations on emotional, practical and financial fronts. Neither side of the fence offers a balanced solution so wait for further developments before taking the next step.

Practical Significance

This card warns of a dividing of the ways but there is little to choose from either path. Split into two, neither half is complete within itself so difficulties will undoubtedly develop. These will grow unless the situation is faced, understood and accepted. Then, and only then should further moves be considered. A change in direction will bring the present stalemate to an end but determination and patience are needed to do this. Expect the depths of depression on the one hand, but hope on the other because from this point the only way out is up.

Emotional relationships will be charged with disharmony through clashes of temperament and business partnerships will suffer from opposing views. Separate ways are on the cards but there is no reason why these paths should not unite in the future when both parties are on the same track again.

Since this card represents an all-time low everything associated with it can only be described as negative too. Seen symbolically as the last week of winter, spring cannot be far behind.

Psychological Significance

Obsessions reach a peak or trough, as the case may be. The truth is distorted out of all proportion as complete fantasy takes over. There is a danger of entering a dream world from which there is no escape and no return.

Psychic Significance

The dangers of evoking names of power are realized too late. Dual forces clash causing psychic fireworks and a chain reaction is started which encircles and enslaves those who first sought to raise them.

Influential Significance

This influence negates and opposes all hopes and plans for the future. Indecisions and uncertainty shatter personal confidence, so balanced outlooks suddenly suffer a split down the middle causing confusion and depression. In all relationships, both sides will find that this influence highlights their partners defects which leads to more trouble. Since plans become impossible to fulfil and finances are greatly reduced, hibernate mentally and wait for the first breath of spring.

Reversed Significance

This card represents the depths of depression and despair. Deliberate and downright bad intentions have produced negativity, so gloom and darkness overshadows everything. As the dark night of the soul, all hope seems to have gone but a final chance to redress the balance will be offered soon.

18
THE JOKER

The Joker's Significance
This card is not numbered but traditionally it is represented as zero, a sign embracing all and nothing, sense and nonsense, happiness and sadness and wisdom and folly. Looking at this lively figure it is difficult to decide exactly what his message is until, that is, it is realized that he is in disguise. His costume is that of a court jester, a buffoon who was supposed to make a King laugh. A jester, however, was far from a fool and in this lies the Joker's secret.

Practical Significance
This card symbolizes individual potential latent within each of us which may or may not express itself fully during one lifetime. On the surface, this appears as the innocence of a child, the wisdom of Job, the stupidity of an idiot or as pure tomfoolery but whichever it is, it has the power to deceive and take others by surprise.

Progress in practical and financial affairs can confidently be expected as unlimited energy drives on towards a most satisfactory conclusion. Powers to transform are at work so anything is possible as new life is given to flagging projects. Emotionally, an unexpected experience has a profound effect on relationships and, whether happy or disillusioning, it certainly throws a new light onto the whole affair. Intellectually, a flash of brilliance and originality brings success to those striving for academic awards and again, this comes out of the blue.

Untapped energy and individual possibilities express themselves when least expected with a result that lives and situations could be transformed overnight. A carefree attitude replaces an old cautious approach, making life much easier to face, if nothing else.

Psychological Significance

Here is the eccentric who harbours the seeds of a genius but these will grow only if sown in a conventional way. In doing this lies the difficulty. Unable to accept society as it is, he or she attempts to alter it but, since this cannot be done without first becoming part of that establishment, the task seems impossible. The Joker, however, is a clever juggler too and takes everyone, including himself, by surprise!

Psychic Significance

A psychic awakening opens the door on a new dimension and the journey into another world has begun. Seeking enlightenment in this way reveals the path of the mystic and this is one strewn with pitfalls and rewards but, above all, surprises.

Influential Significance

Expect the unexpected with this influence. Surprises will alter situations in a flash, bringing last minute help, changes in fortune, recovery from illnesses and instant friendship, both platonic as well as romantic. Be prepared for sudden illogical events involving people and circumstances that are most unusual and perhaps comical.

Reversed Significance

Living up to the ordinary reputation of the Joker, expect status to be downgraded to the level of a fool, a vagbond and a mindless seeker of pleasure. There is indeed nothing much of a character beneath a superficial top dressing.

PART FOUR

FORTUNE-TELLING BY RUNES

DAVID & JULIA LINE

INTRODUCTION

'Just a few pieces of stone with symbols on them' – that's how many people regard runes, associating them, perhaps, with ancient northern European cultures and some obscure branch of occultism, but crediting them with little else.

Opinions vary as to the original purpose of runic symbols. Were they a form of alphabet for pre-Christian tribes in northern Europe and the British Isles or were they developed only for use in ancient magical rites?

In later years the word 'rune' came to mean a spell or poem, yet many experts believe that runes were simply a convenient alphabet for secular documents, legal records and contracts. There is no sure evidence of a wide literary use of runes in very early times. A few runic manuscripts have survived, but most of these come from a later period.

Curiously, the word 'rune' is derived from two roots: the Germanic 'ru' and the Gothic 'runa' – two related forms which mean mystery, secret and secrecy. Does this endorse their original usage, reinforcing the secrecy and mystery of both secular and legal matters?

One only has to look at the legal jargon of today to see that it is carefully contrived to make understanding by lay people no easy task. Or did this association with mystery and secrecy refer to something much deeper and much older?

Certainly runic characters have not taken on their shapes – combinations of straight and angular lines – for any particular symbolic reason. There is no cause to doubt that they developed in this way because it was easiest and most practical for letters to be carved in wood, always in such a way that the single lines did not follow the grain and thus weaken the timber 'tablet'. Straight line characters were also eminently suitable for carving on stone and bone – even metal.

But even such a simple concept as an alphabet composed of a series of straight and angled lines cannot remain simple for long. As with the development of different languages and, in turn, regional dialects, so runic characters evolved into numerous patterns. Like today's world languages, runes can be categorized into major groups and, for convenience, fall into three main categories.

The basic Germanic series of runic symbols can be found on about a hundred inscriptions believed to date from the third to the eighth centuries AD. This alphabet was called a Futhork, and just as the word 'alphabet' took the first two letters from the Greek, so runes took 'futhork' from the first six letters: F, U, TH, O, R, and K. This runic alphabet was divided into three groups each comprising eight characters, giving a total of twenty-four characters in all. Known as 'aettir', these basic divisions were sometimes named after Norse deities: Freya's eight, Hagal's eight and Tiu's eight.

Each runic character had a dual meaning – outwardly material, and inwardly spiritual. It is these runic symbols on which the divinations in this book are based.

Freya's Eight

ᚡ	*feoh*, cattle or fee
ᚢ	*ur*, yore or ox
ᚦ	*thorn, thurs,* thorn or giant
ᚨ	*oss, Asa,* god
ᚱ	*rit,* sunwheel, sun-wain
ᚲ	*kaon,* torch, life-strength
ᚷ	*gifu,* blessing, gift
ᚹ	*wunna,* bliss, Woden

Hagal's Eight

ᚻ	*hagal,* hail, health
ᚾ	*naut,* need
ᛁ	*is,* ice
ᛃ	*yer,* year, harvest
ᛇ	*yr,* yewtree
ᛈ	*peorth,* paddock, berg
ᛉ	*aquizi,* stone axe
ᛋ	*sig,* sun, winning

Tiu's Eight

ᛏ	*tiu,* the god Tiu
ᛒ	*birca,* birch tree, berg
ᛗ	*eh, eoh,* horse, steed
ᛘ	*man,* mankind, world

ᛚ	*lagu,* lake, water of life
ᛜ	*ing,* kin, offspring
ᛟ	*odal,* homeland, holding
ᛞ	*dag,* day

The Runes

It is safe to assume that each rune corresponded to what is now accepted as the guttural sound of German. There was not the scope, however, to convey the more resonant vowel sounds of our pre-Norman Anglo-Saxon language and, in order to cope, the number of characters in the futhork increased first to twenty-eight and then later to thirty-one. This Anglo-Saxon variety of runes is believed to have appeared around the fifth century AD in the British Isles.

As with all languages and scripts, changes continued, especially in phonetic values. Two of the old Anglo-Saxon characters – 'thorn' and 'wynn' – were adopted by the old English alphabet while the third rune, 'th', was used in early English script to supplement our own familiar alphabet. Through careless calligraphy it came to resemble the letter 'y' and yet retained the sound 'th'. Today we can see the remnants of this in such antique signs as 'Ye Olde Englyshe Teashoppe'.

The third major subdivision of runes belongs to Scandinavia. Here the reverse happened and the parallel linguistic development of Scandinavian languages resulted in the number of runes being reduced to a mere sixteen characters.

So we have a very straightforward account of runic development – nothing very mysterious or secret, just a simple alphabet. But there's usually two sides to any story: let's look at the other.

According to ancient Norse legend and described in the Icelandic poem 'The Elder Edda', the god Odin (or Woden) was the original master of the runes. The story goes that in order to rediscover the already existing secret of the runes, Odin was submitted to the barbaric and painful ordeal of being hung upside-down on a gallows for nine nights as a sacrifice. The gallows in this context are synonymous with the sacred Ash Tree of Nordic mythology, Yggdrasil. The meaning of the world 'Yggdrasil' can be interpreted in three ways and, as Bill Butler says in *The Definitive Tarot*, the gallows, rood and tree are all Yggdrasil – The World Tree.

Whether or not Odin was a god or just a warrior king, the rediscovery of the runes is, in legend, attributed to him. Legend also tells us that Odin's eight-legged horse, Sleipnir, had runic symbols carved on his teeth. It is equally worth noting that all Anglo-Saxon kings claimed descendency from Odin and in pre-Norman times it was a necessary 'qualification' for kingship to be of his blood.

Curiously, there is a link – perhaps coincidental – with Tarot cards and the twelfth card of the major Arcana, the Hanged Man, which symbolizes the dying god. Regardless of the difference between

The twelfth card in the major arcana of the Tarot pack illustrates, perhaps by coincidence, the sacrifice to which Odin subjected himself in order to regain the knowledge of the runes. The symbolic components of this card point towards the theory of spiritual enlightenment through suffering – a principle adopted by many religions.

packs, this particular card contains the same pictorial components. We see a man hanged by one foot, the free leg crossed at right angles to the other and the arms positioned behind his back to form the hint of a triangle. The symbolism of a triangle surmounted by a cross represents the descent of light into darkness in order to achieve redemption. (This has parallels in many Christian teachings.) In short, it represents redemption or spiritual awakening through suffering – just as Odin discovered the runes through personal sacrifice. This link between Odin and the Hanged Man id illustrated in the following extracts from the translation by Paul B. Taylor and W. H. Auden of 'The Words of the High One from The Elder Edda' (*The Elder Edda: A Selection,* Faber & Faber, 1973).

Wounded I hung on a wind-swept gallows
For nine long nights,
Pierced by a spear, pledged to Odin,
Offered, myself to myself;
The wisest know not from whence spring
The roots of that ancient rood.

They gave me no bread, they gave me no mead;
I looked down; with a loud cry

I took up runes; from that tree I fell.
and:

I know a twelfth: if a tree bear
A man hanged in a halter,
I can carve and stain strong runes
That will cause the corpse to speak
Reply to whatever I ask.

The runes as a means of divination are not well documented, although some academic works have been published on the historic origins. We know that the spread of Christianity, via the Roman Church, to the outermost parts of Europe, brought with it the essence of the alphabet we use today. The pagan use of runes for purposes of divination was outlawed by the Church and categorized as 'a tool of the devil'. Although the Church actively tried to stamp out runic divination, it continued to be practised in secret and became inevitably linked with witches, warlocks and their arts.

Runes, both esoteric and practical, continued to be studied throughout history until this century and nowhere else were they held in such high esteem as Germany. Runes became a vital component of the Third Reich's belief in Aryan superiority. From the theory of the Urrunen – an ancient north German script and the forerunner of the runes as we know them – the Nazis tried to prove that this alphabet was the root from which all others developed – Phoenician, Greek and so on. With this theory, another coal was added to the fire of the Nazi's belief in Aryan racial superiority. But, as with the way that the Third Reich tried to prove a racial link between themselves and their allies, the Japanese, this idea should not be considered seriously.

Nevertheless, runic associations with Nazi Germany only served once again to bring runes into some vague disrepute as they had once been when linked with witchcraft.

Another illustration of how runes were adopted by Hitler's Germany was in the way that the SS used the runic form of ⚡ as symbols for their collar badges. The letter, ⚡ 'Sig, also stands for victory – which is something they achieved, albeit briefly. But we must not forget that runes, like the swastika, are very ancient symbols which were in use long before Hitler appropriated them.

Two artifacts – a ring and a mount – which are adorned with runic inscriptions. They were found beside the Thames and can now be seen in the British Museum, along with numerous other examples of the runic art.

Runes had another outlet still: they were used on perpetual calendars known in Norway as Primstaves and in Denmark as Rimstocks. These precursors of the Staffordshire clog almanacs were timber or bone tablets or rings bearing characters representing the days of the year, the prime or golden numbers and seasonal symbols.

Clog almanacs were still in use in this country at the end of the seventeenth century and have been well documented by Dr Plot in his book *A Natural History of Staffordshire* (E. J. Morton, 1973). These clog almanacs were similar to the earlier runic primstaves and were constructed from oblong lengths of wood, brass, bone or horn, marked with notches representing the days of the months of the year on each of the four edges. Flanking left and right were symbols indicating the lunar cycle, saint's days and so on. They could be hung on a wall, stood on the mantlepiece and even carried in a pocket.

Another unusual runic link is with our old currency: pounds, shillings and pence. The solidus was a Roman silver coin which bore a runic inscription and was still in use in this country until the seventh century. Our £sd originates from the Roman coins of libra (£), solidus (s) and denarius (d), so even today runes still have some connection with day-to-day life.

There are still many fine examples of runic inscriptions to be seen both in this country and abroad, in museums and in their original settings. One such example is the Franks' Casket dated about AD 650-700. The right side is in the Museo Nazionale del Bargello in Florence and the rest can be seen in the British Museum. The Hunterston brooch, now in Edinburgh, was marked with runes in the tenth century, perhaps by Norse settlers in Man, which has yielded twenty-four inscribed crosses. There are runes on the Collingham stone in Yorkshire (seventh century) and the Bewcastle Cross in Cumberland; the Ruthwell Cross in Dumfriesshire is somewhat later. Other runic inscriptions can be seen in Ireland, Wales, Devon, Cornwall, Silchester and Scotland. In Denmark and Schleswig there are over fifty inscriptions dating from the third to the sixth century and in Norway over sixty such inscriptions dating from the fifth to the eighth century. Manuscripts are rare and relatively late but examples may be seen in the British Museum.

1
WHAT YOU NEED
FOR CASTING RUNES

The basic tools you will need for runic divination are a set of 25 rune stones and a casting cloth. there are 24 stones inscribed with runic symbols and one blank stone. While this might appear complex and expensive to set up, this is in fact not so. In its basic form your set of rune stones could simply be twenty-five dominoes with runic symbols drawn or painted on the reverse sides. The runic cloth needs to be no more than a sheet of ordinary paper big enough to carry a 10″ (230mm) diameter circle.

Serious practitioners of runic divination are likely to go to greater lengths in their production or purchase of runes and runic cloths. Examples of runes produced in timber, terracotta and porcelain are shown on these pages along with more flamboyant designs for the cloths which can, of course, be adapted to suit individual needs but, in principle, must contain common essential components. Sources for purchasing craftsman-made rune stones and cloths are given at the end of this book.

The basic runic cloth, or casting cloth, consists of a sheet of paper or material onto which are drawn or sewn three concentric circles. Working on the basis that the runes themselves will measure about 1″x1″ (25mm x 25mm), the ideal diameters for the three circles are 3″, 7″, and 10″ (75mm, 178mm and 254mm). In no way should these measurements be treated as absolutes – they are only general guides.

From the three circles you can see that four areas are created: the inner circle, middle circle, outer circle and the space beyond. Each of these areas is significant in determining the meaning of runes as they fall across the cloth.

The centre circle is called 'skjebne' – the Norwegian word for destiny. In other philosophies the term 'karma' could possibly apply but this implies that, while fate is not haphazard and subject to chance, it is determined by an individual's actions in previous lives or spiritual conditions. While one might subscribe to the principle of

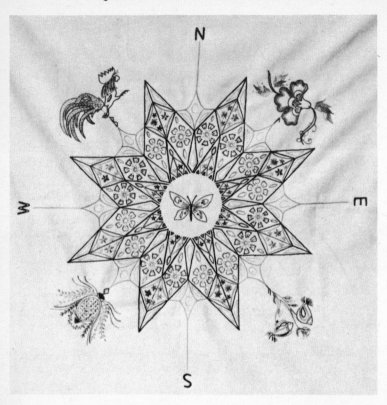

Many practitioners of runic divination will adapt the basic pattern for the runic cloth to suit their own purposes. This flamboyant design still retains the essential 'areas' of the simple concentric circle design. But more elaborate symbolism is used here and the reader will need a keener eye to identify the exact location of cast stones. This is not recommended for the novice.

'destiny', it associations with 'past lives' isn't necessarily acceptable.

The middle ring is known as 'outside skjebne', while the outer ring is divided into four segments, each with its own attributions. In broad terms, working outwards from the centre of the runic cloth, the circles take the querent from purely spiritual matters to those of a more immediate emotional or physical nature.

Various labels can be applied to the outer four segments. Some students of runic divination nominate the segments under the headings of health, home, wealth and success, but in practice such bald and obvious labels can often only serve to confuse the results of a cast. Other alternatives in use are the equally obvious division of earth, air, fire and water, conjuring the symbolism of alchemy which again is capable of causing some confusion when interpreting results. Another fallacious system – this time incorporating the runes themselves – is to apply astrological symbols and significance to both cloth and stones. As the use of alchemic elements remains popular, we have retained them in the explanatory chapters but added them to the more appropriate symbols.

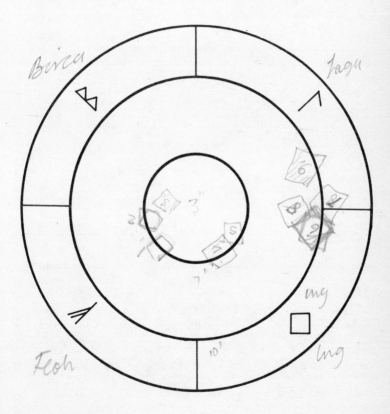

The basic casting cloth comprises three concentric circles. The outer area is segmented and a rune stone can land on any one of seven possible locations – each determining a specific meaning for the rune in question.

In fact, the labels for the outer circle segments should simply be a means to identify the spaces relative to one another and the angle from which the runes were cast. The significance of the segments is primarily dependent upon the nature of the stones which land on them.

To this end, the simple runic system of labelling is least likely to cause confusion. These are 'Feoh' (ᚠ), 'Birca' (ᛒ), 'Ing' (◇) and 'Lagu' (ᛚ).

By dividing the outer circle into four segments, the cloth offers the option of seven possible 'landing sites': skjebne, outside skjebne, Feoh, Birca, Ing, Lagu and outside the runic circle. It is interesting to note

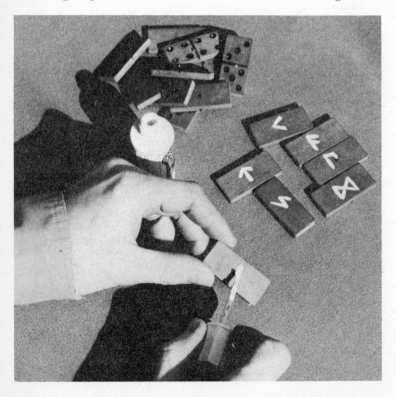

The quickest and easiest way to produce a set of rune stones is to paint or draw runic symbols on the back of a set of dominoes. Here correcting fluid is being used but chinagraph, ink, felt tip or even enamel paint can be used.

that the number seven has long been thought to hold substantial occult significance. Hippocrates said that because of its occult virtues number seven has a tendency to bring all things into being. There is also an association between seven and the image of Odin suggested in the twelfth card of the Tarot major arcana which was described in a previous chapter. Here the symbol for seven is the same as the symbolic components of 'The Hanged Man' (Odin) – a triangle above a square. All the sides add up to seven.

Also, perhaps coincidentally, the rune stones themselves have an association with the number seven. By applying the rules of numerology and adding together the digits of 25 – the number of stones used – you arrive at seven: $2 + 5 = 7$.

It is likely that, originally, the runic casting cloth had such positive occult components designed into it. But beware of trying to extract

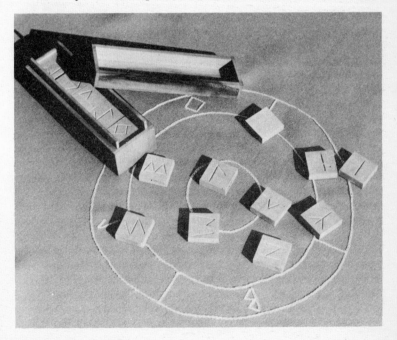

This set of boxed runes has been professionally made using 'pear'. The stones are ideally sized at 1″ x 1″ x ¼″ and the symbols have been lightly carved into the surface of the wood. Other appropriate timbers are oak, elm, ash, yew, rosewood and birch. This set was produced by Michael Westgate.

too much symbolic meaning from the relationships of the three basic circles and the four segments.

The casting cloth in its simplest form can be a sheet of paper, and the runes can be as easily manufactured. As already suggested, dominoes with the runic letters painted on the reverse side will serve the purpose. Even if the prospect of carving symbols into wood is a deterrent, there is no great problem in drawing runic letters onto 'stones' cut from a length of inexpensive batten.

As the runic querent has to select and then hold nine runes from the total of twenty-five, prior to casting, the size of rune stones is critical. Runes measuring 1"x1"x¼" (25mm x 25mm x 6mm) are recommended as the optimum size. While material thinner than ¼" (6mm) can be used, it reduces the possibility of runes landing on edge – which in itself is significant to an interpretation.

Rune stones can be produced in a variety of materials. Those on the left are made from terracotta and are roughly moulded. They certainly give a 'stonelike' feel, are heavy and very durable. The stones on the right are made from porcelain and are shown before final glazing and firing. Here the symbols will be picked out in a second colour. These stones are very smooth to the touch.

Although runes made from pine or ramin are adequate, they do not have the same intrinsic quality and 'weight' as those cut from elm, walnut, oak and other more appropriate timbers. The wooden set illustrated in this book has been made from pear – even more esoteric!

All the Northern European trees known to the followers of Odin had their own magical qualities. It would therefore be inappropriate for the serious runic diviner to use such timbers as African or South American mahogany, teak, afrormosia and iroko, all of which, in realistic terms, are perfectly suitable for the job, but would probably not have been known then.

Since neither Letraset nor Meccanorma produce instant rub-down runic lettering, the job must be done by free-hand. As runes consist only of straight lines the work does not require any great calligraphic skills and pleasing results can be achieved with Indian Ink, felt tip pen or even black paint.

For the more adventurous who intend to carve the letters into the wooden stones, two sharp chisels measuring ½″ (12mm) and ¼″ (6mm) will be all that is needed. Here it's a good idea to first draw the letters onto the stones, making sure that they are centred and not too close to the edges. With straight grain softwoods there is a risk of splitting the timber. Simply cut into the wood at an angle of about 45° from each side of the drawn lines to achieve a 'V' shaped cut. If you wish, the carved letters can then be painted in and the stones finished in clear varnish. Remember that one stone – skjebne – is left blank.

2

CASTING AND READING RUNES

Amongst the many advantages runes are claimed to have over Tarot, I Ching and other methods of divination, is the fact that casting and reading is an uncomplicated and relatively speedy process.

With the casting cloth laid out on a suitable surface – a table top, tray or board – the diviner spreads out the stones and shuffles them face down in much the same way as you would for dominoes. From the twenty-five stones the querent selects nine and shuffles these around in cupped hands. When the querent is ready, he or she simply casts the nine stones over the cloth. At this stage it is a good idea to point out that runes are not cast with the vim and vigour of a spin bowler. The action is almost akin to pouring them from an upturned hand with just enough impetus to scatter the runes over the cloth.

Why select only nine stones – why indeed? Some diviners stick to the traditional eleven while others determine the number of stones the querent selects by applying rules of numerology. There are no hard and fast rules here but practice has shown that nine stones can be held in even the smallest hand and provide sufficient numbers to produce a detailed and worthwhile reading.

Another reason for using nine stones with, perhaps, a more appealing justification takes us again to the legend of Odin hanging on Yggdrasill, the World Ash. Here it took nine nights for Odin to gather the knowledge of the runes so, in turn, in order for the querent to gain his knowledge, nine stones should be thrown: one for each night.

Any application of numerology should be treated with some caution. Numerology is, after all, a method of divination far removed from the geographic and cultural origins of runes. It could be argued that applying any aspect of numerology to runes is like trying to mix oil and water. Nevertheless some exponents claim success in this direction, so it is worth giving some mention to this system of stone selection. The number/letter associations used are as follows:

1	2	3	4	5	6	7	8
A	B	C	D	E	U	O	F
I	K	G	M	H	V	Z	P
Q	R	L	T	N	W		
J		S		X			
Y							

The above system, generally favoured by numerologists, is based on the Hebrew alphabet with some assistance from the Greek. The number nine is omitted as it was believed to be the numeral equivalent to the nine lettered name of God and the letters are not listed in the normal order.

Here the diviner locates those numbers corresponding to each letter in the querent's name and, along with the birthdate, adds them together from left to right. All the compound numbers are added together until a single total is reached.

The following example illustrates how a diviner would allocate the number of stones to be selected by John Smith born on the 2nd November 1958.

J O H N   S M I T H   2. 11.   1958
1+7+5+5 +3+4+1+4+5 +2+1+1+1+9+5+8 = 62 = 8 stones

Once the runes have been cast, the diviner must look for a number of key patterns made by the falling stones along with those stones which fall face down or on edge. Although this might outwardly appear difficult it is really just a matter of detailed observation.

More often than not a large proportion of stones will fall together in a clump, some overlapping, some just touching and others very close together. These stones are of prime importance and refer to the most immediate concerns or problems of the querent. The diviner must also gauge the 'order' in which they fell to arrive at the appropriate sequence for reading. Apart from paying close attention to the stones at the moment they are cast, sequences within a group can generally be numbered from the point nearest to the querent outwards.

In some cases an obvious 'progression' of stones will be observed by the diviner – not close enough to each other to warrant labelling as a group but, nonetheless, forming a discernible pattern. A progression can also be generated by a series of stones which have closely linked meanings. Sometimes it will be the sequence of meanings rather than a physical pattern which will indicate a progression.

Secondary groups – perhaps consisting of only two or three stones – can fall in the same cast. These are exactly as the name implies; secondary in importance to the main group. Other stones will scatter singly across the cloth. Again, their initial value is as would appear – one-offs or isolated events but still relevant to the querent.

Stones which fall face down indicate that the meanings are hidden to the querent's conscious mind. They refer to unseen events in the past, present or future which could have a direct bearing on the querent's situation – for good or bad depending on the meaning of the stone and its position on the cloth. They often serve to provide the missing link to something about which the querent is only half aware.

Occasionally runes will land on edge. The simple interpretation for this is that whatever the stone represents, the result could go either way. If a rune lands on edge within an obvious bunch or group, then its position relative to the others and its place on the casting cloth must be noted with special care.

With the position of each rune observed, its attitude and relationship to other groups and single stones noted, the diviner can begin to assemble overall meanings.

If you imagine that each rune is like an isolated word in a sentence, you can see that, in order to complete the sentence, each rune must be fully identified and its meaning interpreted in the light of all the other stones. It's rather like constructing a correct sentence when you know all of the nouns and none of the verbs. For this a small degree of intuition helps but, like mastering any art, it is practice which counts in the end.

Things are made easier by the fact that runes are each allocated a label giving a generic meaning, one which stays with the stone no matter where it falls. This is the key meaning which identifies the nature of the rune and the area in which it operates. The generic meaning is backed up with seven specific meanings, each determined by where the stone falls on the cloth. The only exception here is the rune Hagal – not a good stone to throw!

Combining generic and specific meanings to achieve a particular image or meaning for one stone is straightforward. But remember that with a group of stones, this result must be aligned and related to the others. You must therefore grasp the broad picture painted by all the runes based on 'isolated' compounds.

All the meanings are given in later chapters of this book and, because there are so many ambiguities in the English language, various possible, and still appropriate, alternatives are given to help you tie the meanings of individual stones together.

One final and important point is that not all stones will fall neatly into one of the seven allocated 'slots'. Some will be half in one area and half in another, perhaps with only just a corner of a stone across a border. In cases like these the meaning of a rune in a dual position must be considered carefully and the reading adjusted according to how much of the rune falls into another section. This is best illustrated by example.

If the rune Ing (◇) which affect direct family, falls half in Skjebne (change leading to improvement) and half into outside Skjebne (move of house) this would indicate that by moving home the querent and his family will benefit, perhaps by gaining more space, or in terms of health in a better environment, or they would just get on better generally in a different place.

If the rune Naut (⸕), which is a warning, falls mainly in the Lagu section (⌐) (refusals) with just a corner in outside Skjebne (patience) the probable interpretation would be that plans which the querent is making will be turned down. However, there is just a little hint of encouragement not to give up, to keep at it; that all is not completely lost as it would have been if the rune was entirely in the Lagu section.

3

SAMPLE CASTS

Probably the most practical way to illustrate how to read runes is by example and, for this reason, we have detailed six genuine casts showing where the runic stones landed and how they were interpreted.

While the names of the querents have been changed – for obvious reasons – other details remain true.

On each of the drawings shown note the arrow which indicates the direction from which the stones were cast and the grey shading of stones indicates those which landed face down. The stones are numbered in casting order.

FIGURE 1

Name: Nicola
Age: 32
Occupation: Craftswoman
Background: Currently involved in setting up a new pottery but supported by only a small private income. A new emotional attachment is very much in mind at the moment.

Major progression: Stones 1-5
1. Yer in Lagu and outside Skjebne: This points to a period of setting up when little in the way of results are forthcoming.

2. Odal in and outside Skjebne: It will be some time before her work is recognized but she must still work hard. There could also be problems over property or legacies.

3. Peorth in and outside Skjebne: Her new found sexuality and emotional involvement could do more harm than good as far as work is concerned. Probably only a pleasant distraction but the querent is reading too much into it. She would be advised to turn it to her own good.

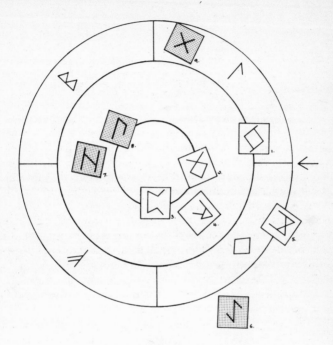

FIGURE 1

4. Rit outside Skjebne: This reinforces the idea that success can only come through her own efforts and that work must be treated very seriously. It could result in travel.

5. Man in Ing and outside the circle: Not everyone is on her side. She must keep her ears and eyes open for any signs of deceit.

Progression summary: Work must come first and foremost and should be taken very seriously in order to succeed. She should avoid distractions and be prepared for unexpected obstacles.

6. Single stone – Yr face down outside the circle: This indicates that she could create health problems in the search for her ambition. It could equally apply to her emotional attachment or work or the conflict between the two.

Secondary progression: Stones 7 and 8

7. Hagal outside Skjebne: Disruptions are indicated over which she has no control or indeed knowledge.

8. Ur mostly outside but also slightly into Skjebne: Distant influences could be beneficial but she must be prepared to respond quickly to new opportunities.

Progression summary: Things are happening behind the scenes which could bring improvement – even though, on the face of it, this might not seem the case. She should be prepared to act quickly.

9. Single stone – Gifu in Lagu: This points towards a joint venture as being one way to achieve success.

Cast summary

Nicola will not achieve success overnight. Whatever happens it will involve considerable singlemindedness, determination and hard work. There will be a variety of obstacles and distractions in the way and these will need to be put into perspective and treated accordingly. Many of the immediate problems could be solved by thinking about joint activities or a partnership.

Result

Nicola has allowed emotional distractions to interfere with her work. At the time of writing her business venture is not coming up to expectation.

FIGURE 2

Name: Geoffrey
Age: 35
Occupation: Engineer
Background: Lives on a houseboat with wife and four children. Recently sold up business with intention of moving abroad. Has spent considerable amount of time and money to refurbish boat in order to take it abroad.

Major progression: Stones 1-5

1. Thorn hidden outside the circle: There is a danger that something vital to his immediate plans has been misunderstood and he must check this out.

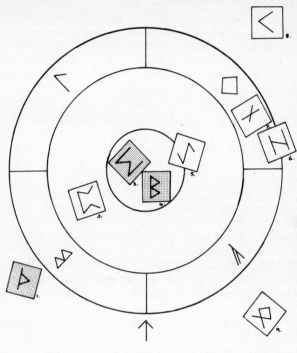

FIGURE 2

2. Peorth outside Skjebne: It looks as if there are problems over assets or possessions he is trying to sell or dispose of. Once out of the way, things will go smoothly.

3. Eh in Skjebne: While there are problems to overcome the conclusion to his plans is in sight. All loose ends should be tied up.

4. Birca in Skjebne: Because his home is closely linked to his plans and, with it, his family, the scheme or future plan will further unify his family.

5. Yr in and outside Skjebne: This clearly says that the querent should avoid short cuts – rushing things in order to speed events. He should not make false economies and not overdo it.

Progression summary: This part of the cast clearly ties in with the querent's aims and ambitions. It warns the querent to make sure that every avenue has been explored in order to avoid delays, to do all necessary work properly as, in effect, he and his family will depend upon it.

Secondary progression: Stones 6 and 7

6. Hagal in Ing and outside circle: This clearly indicates events beyond the querent's control which will cause disruption.

7. Naut in Ing: This offers a warning to the querent to be prepared for problems and obstacles but to cope with them patiently and logically.

Progression summary: Outwardly not good news for the querent – the combination of these two stones reinforces the fact that difficulties will continue.

8. Single stone – Kaon outside the circle: The moves the querent intends will result in the loss of friends, and saying goodbye to people he knows. He must give this serious thought.

9. Single stone – Odal outside the circle: The querent must ensure that he is careful with any deals he undertakes. It could also point to machinery which is either unsafe or just unsound or unsuitable.

Cast summary
The cast clearly reveals that Geoffrey's intended venture will be a success although many frustrations before departure will cast doubts on the whole idea. He must also realize that he will be leaving many friends behind with, perhaps, the only benefit being a further unification of his family. He must prepare for his venture as best he can and not take short cuts. It indicates probable mechanical problems and other difficulties prior to departure.

Result
At the time of writing Geoffrey has had considerable expenditure on his craft. He discovered that it would not clear bridges on the French canals and so the craft had to be ballasted to lower it in the water. He has experienced numerous difficulties with items such as generators and pumps. While the sale of remaining stock from his business has been agreed, it has not been concluded.

FIGURE 3

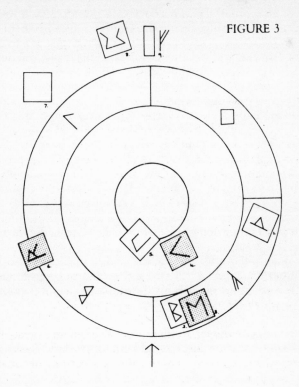

FIGURE 3

Name: Michael
Age: 36
Occupation: Reporter
Background: Recently divorced and now living with another worman. His working situation is very insecure with a real chance of impending redundancy.

1. Single stone – Thorn in Feoh: He can have what he most wants but it will be a question of biding his time and taking no undue risks. This stone points towards a major ambition or desire.

2 & 3. Group stones overlapping. Eh hidden on top of Birca both in

Feoh: Here the combination of stones point towards a doomed marriage or partnership, but because this is closely linked to the existing family circle it might not necessarily involve the querent.

4. Single stone – Kaon hidden outside Skjebne: Regardless of the truth in the previous two stones, this single rune points towards the probability of the querent getting involved in an enjoyable yet unimportant affair.

5. Single stone – Ur in and out of Skjebne: In career terms, the querent must be ready to grasp a new opportunity from abroad. It will result in betterment, not possible in the present working situation. Delay in taking advantage of this opportunity could mean the loss of this chance – one which will not be repeated.

Stones 6 and 7 (not strictly a group but make better sense when read together):
6. Rit in Birca and outside the circle: The risks the querent has taken in his career or marriage will be his downfall and he will have to massively rethink his plans. This downturn will result in financial outlay for which he will have to make provision.

7. Skjebne outside the circle: The reversal of plans forecast in the previous rune were not just bad luck but a necessary lesson to be learned. The message here is clear: he must learn by his mistakes.

Group stones 8 and 9:
8. Peorth outside the circle: The querent must be prepared to be more content with his emotional lot, and not look for 'that impossible dream'.

9. Feoh on edge outside the circle: This couples closely with rune eight pointing out that the querent has the chance to avoid further emotional upset, quarrels and clashes and possibly even separation, if he makes a positive effort with what he has. It could go either way – the result will be up to him.

Cast summary
This was an interesting cast in that the groups and single stones were not all observably connected. Here interpretations tended to dictate the logical groupings rather than the physical points the stones landed on. Clearly this cast warns the querent that all his ills are very

much of his own making – there is no-one else to blame. Success, in both career and love, can be achieved if the querent gets his head out of the clouds and works hard in both areas. New opportunities will arise.

Result
Michael eventually lost his job but new opportunities arose – none from abroad but from elsewhere in the country. His new career is proving to be successful although his income is lower. His new family environment is a great success.

FIGURE 4

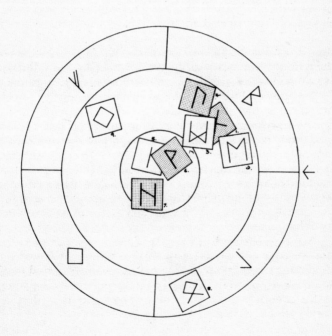

FIGURE 4

Name: Derek
Age: 53
Occupation: Representative
Background: Has been divorced for many years and has a girlfriend of many years standing. Lives alone and works as a freelance salesman.

Major group: Stones 1-4

1. Gifu hidden outside Skjebne: Someone, probably a woman, whom the querent has been close to and very fond of in the past is likely to return. This could result in him rethinking his current emotional status.

2. Eh outside Skjebne (resting on Gifu): This warns the querent that the 'lady from the past' must be viewed with caution. It could result in disruption and he must ask himself if his feelings are sincere or if it could be just a resurrected affair.

3. Man in and outside Skjebne (resting on Gifu): This is a complex situation for this rune with various interconnecting considerations. The stone points towards the querent's business activities but still affecting his overall lifestyle. The woman in stones one and two could also be involved. This stone warns the querent to 'beware of the small print' or any details in a forthcoming contract. Treat any 'experimental' ideas with caution and simply pay attention to detail.

4. Ur hidden outside Skjebne (resting on Gifu): Again, this stone involves life's harmony, keeping things even and stable. An opportunity, unknown to the querent at the moment, will arise and could involve a change of home. This may not be for some time.

Group Summary: Clearly a warning is given to be careful when it comes to detail in business and thinking things through at an emotional level. Both could cause problems if not treated correctly. Further disruption, but beneficial this time, is likely to come in the future.

5 & 6. Wunna hidden on top of Is in Skjebne: The querent is likely to leave the person he is truly fond of in the future and it will result in considerable sadness and the need for him to 'harden his heart'. Through Wunna it can be seen that a reunion will eventually take place under far better circumstances.

7. Single stone – Hagal in and slightly out of Skjebne: This stone indicates disruptions caused by natural events. The most obvious interpretation is that the querent is likely to suffer an illness in the future which could thwart or alter plans.

8. Single stone – Odal in Lagu: Personal goals for the querent will not be achieved the easy way; he must show will power and determination.

9. Single stone – Ing outside Skjebne: A clear pointer for the querent moving home to meet new faces and have new opportunities.

Cast summary
The querent should very much let his head rule his heart over business and emotional matters and pay attention to detail where both are concerned. New moves and a change of home are likely and while not achieved easily, will ultimately be successful.

Result
While the lady from the past has not yet reappeared, the querent has already lost business opportunities by not studying details or clearly communicating his wishes. At the moment plans are underway for the querent to move to a Mediterranean country within the next year and work is being geared to this end.

FIGURE 5

Name: Eileen
Age: 40
Occupation: Shopkeeper
Background: Having brought up her family alone for some years she is now established with a new man – someone who has his own clearly defined business interests, some of which overlap with those of her own. Considerable emotional upset preceded the new established home arrangement. She is an astute businesswoman.

This cast shows six hidden stones and means that many unexpected events are likely to take place.

1. Single stone – Dag in Ing and outside the circle: Plans the querent is making and actively working towards will be more of a labour of love and will not be fully appreciated.

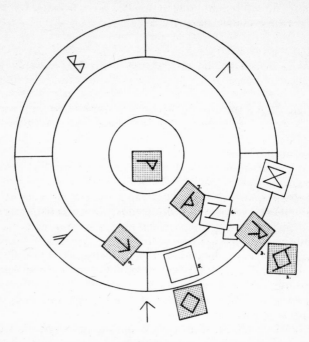

FIGURE 5

Group stones: 2 and 3 read together
2 & 3. Yer hidden outside the circle and Rit hidden in Ing: This warns the querent to try to keep her plans to herself for the time being. Also a subject which the querent is studying will prove to be a waste of time.

Group stones: 4 and 5 read together
4 & 5. Ing hidden outside the circle and Skjebne in Ing: Unknown to the querent someone is likely to give a false account of something which affects her family and could result in a delicate situation which will have to be dealt with.

Group stones: 6 and 7 read together
6 & 7. Hagal outside Skjebne and in Ing resting on Thorn hidden

outside Skjebne: Here again the querent will find herself in a situation not of her choosing and not to her advantage. In order to counter the stones' forecast, the querent must avoid hasty decisions.

8. Single stone – Wunna hidden in Skjebne: Someone close to the querent will return home unexpectedly – probably another woman. It will be an occasion for celebration.

9. Single stone – Tiu hidden in both Feoh and outside Skjebne: Something the querent has been secretly hoping for will soon happen. It could mean an extension of something which already exists – but on another 'wave-length'.

Cast summary
Part of the querent's time is spent on productive work but these activities will not be fully appreciated by someone else – maybe her new husband? It will, however, stand her in good stead for the future and have a bearing on new prospects both at home and work. Much of what happens will, apparently, be by 'accident' or out of her control. Stone eight is self-explanatory. Despite minor hiccups, the future looks assured.

Result
New business ventures are finally under way although this will mean a move of house. Her existing business has suffered following a reduction in passing trade caused by the opening of a new bypass nearby. She has taken up craft studies at a local college. Her eldest daughter recently returned home from South Africa. With the move of house comes the opportunity to involve herself in work in which she has always been interested.

FIGURE 6

Name: Marjorie
Age: 51
Occupation: Theatrical Properties Manager
Background: Marjorie had an extremely unhappy childhood resulting from a broken home. She lives with an aged relative and her only leisure activity is boating. She has no emotional involvement – her last affair was with a well-known actor.

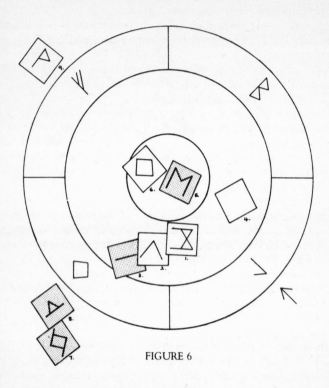

FIGURE 6

Major group: Stones 1-3

1. Man outside Skjebne: This indicates possible problems of a contractual nature and warns that misunderstandings are likely. The solution is to delegate nothing and act as her own messenger.

2. Kaon outside Skjebne: It follows that the misunderstanding will be between her and someone she knows well – either a close friend or relative. Certainly the person in question is someone she much admires.

3. Is hidden in Lagu and outside Skjebne: Here some ambiguity comes in. It covers emotional cooling and it could refer to the querent seeing this friend or relative in a different light. But it could also refer to some asset being 'frozen', or tie in with the contractual problems already outlined.

Group summary
The querent is likely to lose something – possibly an asset or a friend – especially if she fails to attend to details and make herself clear in what she means.

Major progression: Stones 4-6
4. Skjebne outside Skjebne: The querent will soon be involved in a difficult situation which cannot remain unsolved and has been brewing for some time.

5. Eh hidden in Skjebne: Reforms, alterations, changes: these are impending. It will give the querent an opportunity to do what she wants to do for a change.

6. Ing in Skjebne and slightly outside Skjebne: Changes or alterations to circumstances will be beneficial and will result in an entirely new phase in her life. It could indicate a change in home or living conditions.

Progression summary: All the stones so far point to a domestic rearrangement which will probably result in more freedom for the querent.

Group stones: 7 and 8 read together
7 & 8. Yer hidden in the outside circle and Thorn hidden outside the circle: This points again to poor communications and misunderstandings and warns that the querent should always make her intentions crystal clear. Some benefit the querent is waiting for or expecting will not happen and therefore plans must not be geared to this direction.

9. Single stone – Wunna outside the circle: While unattached at the moment the querent has deep affection for someone who she can see is doing everything wrong. She must take it upon herself to point that person in the right direction.

Cast summary
The querent should stop expecting that which will not happen and readjust her life accordingly. She will benefit from domestic changes. Her great weakness is in not making herself clearly understood and this could affect her forthcoming good fortune. She should have the courage to warn a close friend of his/her muddled thinking.

Result

Not a clear and concise cast and this probably reflects the way the querent is currently thinking (or not thinking!). None of the veiled benefits or changes in family circumstances have, at the time of writing, materialized.

Study of these six samples will show areas where ambiguities can crop up and it is in these situations that the diviner must carefully link the main themes, if not the primary meanings, of each stone in a group or progression. It is also an area where some intuitive application is needed.

It is interesting to observe, however, that those querents who treat the matter seriously and concentrate on what is at hand when they cast the stones, generally get the clearest, least ambiguous results. Is this a coincidence? Certainly the last querent in the six samples treated the whole matter with little regard and, as a result, the cast's results were, at best, trivial.

Before going any further, it would be a useful exercise for the budding practitioner to go through the samples shown here again and, without reference to interpretations offered, but using the meanings detailed in the following pages, produce his or her own set of results. Comparison between those published and your own will certainly indicate how satisfactorily you will be able to interpret your own runic casts.

4
FREYA'S EIGHT

FEOH ᚠ

This Rune governs *LOVE*.

Key words include: a feeling, kindness, tenderness, liking, affection, friendship, sentiment, longing, desire, romance, passion, hold dear, value, care for.

The Rune of FEOH (ᚠ) in SKJEBNE (◻)
Primary meaning: love that transcends the norm.
Subsidiary meanings: greater than usual, gigantic, vast, enormous, complete, collosal, breath taking, out of this world;
knows no bounds, soars, overwhelms, is superior to:
the normal, customary, standard pattern, model, the rule, formula, the usual, everyday.

The Rune of FEOH (ᚠ) outside SKJEBNE (▣)
Primary meaning: conserve to gain.
Subsidiary meanings: keep on ice, preserve, keep, protect, keep alive, store up, save up, build up a store, look after, cherish, treasure, maintain, service, feed;
in order to: win, profit, benefit, accumulate, earn, harvest, be rewarded, attain, reach, come into, win the jackpot, succeed.

The Rune of FEOH (ᚠ) in the Air quadrant (ᚠ)
Primary meaning: love hopes realized – contentment.
Subsidiary meanings: desires, longings, expectations, wants, needs, wishes for affection, tenderness, unity, passion;
converted into fact, given reality to, made to happen, come about, be done, exist;
bringing with them: pleasure, well-being, delight, happiness, pleased with one's lot, enjoyment.

The Rune of FEOH (Ⴤ) in the Earth quadrant (ꓭ)
Primary meaning: well-being.
Subsidiary meanings: contentment, comfort, at ease, euphoria, peace, delight, happiness, agreeable, relish, feel pleasure, health and wealth, crest of the wave, success, good run of luck, golden touch, halcyon days, doing well, smile of fortune, bed of roses.

The Rune of FEOH (Ⴤ) in the Water quadrant (◇)
Primary meaning: increase in love both physical and spiritual.
Subsidiary meanings: become greater, grow, enlarge, make bigger, tenderness, friendship, sentiment, longing, desire, romance, passion, hold dear, value, care for;
of the body, sensuous, natural, sexual; of the soul, mind, deep inner feelings, divine, inspired, almost sacred or religious.

The Rune of FEOH (Ⴤ) in the Fire quadrant (Γ)
Primary meaning: marriage.
Subsidiary meanings: matrimony, wedlock, union, life together, conjugal bliss, love-match, nuptials, elope, man and wife, partners, good match, marry off, join, tie the knot, handfasting, pair off, for better for worse, set up house, repent at leisure.

The Rune of FEOH (Ⴤ) outside the Runic circle (⊘)
Primary meaning: discord/divorce.
Subsidiary meanings: disagreement, controversy, argument, rows, bickering, clashes, rupture, breach, at odds, hostile, antagonistic, incompatible, quarrels, fighting, dissidence, loss of harmony;
go separate ways, break it up, cut loose, withdrawal, parting, be free, be alone, isolation, segregation, disconnect, untie the knot.

UR Ⴖ

This Rune governs *DISTANT INFLUENCES*.

Key words include: far away, remote in time or relation, not close or intimate, action invisibly exercised, exert upon affect.

The Rune of UR (Ⴖ) in (☐)
Primary meaning: opportunities from afar – be ready to act.
Subsidiary meanings: possibilities, openings, well-timed, chance to capitalize, twists of fate, scope, freedom, choices;

coming from: a distance, remote, out of range, ahead, back of beyond, far away, not locally, at a distance, out of sight, at the limit of vision.

Be prepared: alert, standing by, poised, forewarned, ready to go, come into play, do, operate, try, move, have a go, perform, participate.

The Rune of UR (⋂) outside SKJEBNE (▣)
Primary meaning: improvement through change.
Subsidiary meanings: betterment, an uplift, good influence, the making of, enrichment, recovery, enhancement, increase, restoration, rallying, turn the corner;
brought about by: alteration, variation, modification, adjustment, contrast, variety, a break from routine, versatility, substitution of one for another, ringing the changes, a shake-up.

The Rune of UR (⋂) in the Air quadrant (⩑)
Primary meaning: chance not to be wasted.
Subsidiary meanings: possibility, the right time, suitable opportunity, opening, heaven sent, stroke of luck, fortuitous, happy accident, a gamble;
use it, exploit it, put to good use, must not be missed, get the best out of it, turn it to account, profit by, avail yourself, capitalize, cash in, take with both hands.

The Rune of UR (⋂) in the Earth quadrant (ᛒ)
Primary meaning: think of tomorrow – do not be headstrong.
Subsidiary meanings: consider the future, study, meditate, worry about, take into account, reflect, weight up:
the day after today, prospects, the outlook, future, coming events, what is to come, lies ahead, later, in due course, eventually, ultimately.
Don't be: rash, reckless, impetuous, over-hasty, stubborn, unyielding, perverse, obstinate, pig-headed, foolish.

The Rune of UR (⋂) in the Water quadrant (◇)
Primary meaning: visitors from afar.
Subsidiary meanings: people who: come, go to see, as an act of friendship or social ceremony, on business, for curiosity, callers, drop in, come back, return, stay temporarily;
from far away, not locally, at a distance, other countries, continents, ways of life.

The Rune of UR (⌐) in the Fire quadrant (Γ)
Primary meaning: have faith in your own judgement.
Subsidiary meanings: have: belief, credence, assurance, trust, accept, admit, swear by, go by, know, understand, rely on, have no doubt, depend on, hold:
your personal, not another's, independent, unaided, private opinion, sagacity, discernment, discretion, views, decisions, findings, rules, feelings, calculations, assessment.

The Rune of UR (⌐) outside the Runic circle (⊘)
Primary meaning: a chance wasted.
Subsidiary meanings: a possibility, the right time, suitable opportunity, opening, stroke of luck, happy accident, gamble:
gone forever, let slip, said goodbye to, irredeemable, misused, mishandled, not taken, spoiled, let go, missed, advantage not used.

THORN ▷

This rune governs *BENEFITS*.

Key words include: something to one's advantage, on one's behalf, in your own interest, for your own good, good turns, blessings.

The Rune of THORN (▷) in SKJEBNE (□)
Primary meaning: beneficial if you stay your hand.
Subsidiary meanings: it will be advantageous to: hold in abeyance, keep, reserve, hold over, delay, gain time, keep waiting, temporize, shelve, keep on ice – something which you are intending to do.
Don't: divulge, be too open, blurt out, spill the beans, come out with it, confide, confess, admit, let into the secret, tell what you are up to.

The Rune of THORN (▷) outside SKJEBNE (▣)
Primary meaning: quick action leads to mistakes.
Subsidiary meanings: doing something at maximum speed, in a hurry, jumping in, at a gallop, in a short time, without reflection, break-neck, high speed, like a flash – will lead to:
errors, wrongness, faults, bad ideas, blunders, miscalculations, slips, being misled, being deceived, inaccuracty, clumsiness, being in the wrong, led up the garden path, playing into someone's hands.

The Rune of THORN (▷) in the Air quadrant (⋎)
Primary meaning: everything comes to he who waits.
Subsidiary meanings: if you: look on, wait and see, do nothing, be cautious, wary, heedful, discreet, take no risks, bide your time, leave nothing to chance – then, to you wil come:
all things, all that matters, chances, rewards, credit, winnings, a rich harvest, you will collect, come in for, get the proceeds, inherit, things will fall to your share, come to you.

The Rune of THORN (▷) in the Earth quadrant (ß)
Primary meaning: aggravating another will cause them to lash out; danger.
Subsidiary meanings: by exasperating, irritating, fanning the flames, complicating matters, making bad worse, you:
run the risk, skate on thin ice, tempt providence, court disaster, it's chancy, perilous; you will cause someone to:
erupt, be rude, violent, bellicose, run riot, rampage, see red, fume, explode, blow up, let fly, become maddened and angry.

The Rune of THORN (▷) in the Water quadrant (◇)
Primary meaning: not a time to gamble.
Subsidiary meanings: now is not the time to: take a risk, take the plunge, start a new venture, speculate, experiment, leap in the dark, play the market, hazard a try, chance it, try your luck.

The Rune of THORN (▷) in the Fire quadrant (⌐)
Primary meaning: do not let another manipulate you.
Subsidiary meanings: do not let someone else: pressure you, turn your head with honeyed words, goad you, crack the whip, motivate you with tempting offers and sales talk, work on you, call the tune, override your own feelings, shame you into something, manage you, set the pace, induce, persuade, win over.

The Rune of THORN (▷) outside the Runic circle (⊘)
Primary meaning: misunderstandings – you did not make yourself clear.
Subsidiary meanings: because you were not: understandable, explicit, lucid, emphatic, did not use plain English and make things known – someone will: get the wrong end of the stick, be at cross purposes, misconstrue your meaning, twist the words, get a false reading.

OSS ᚠ

This Rune governs *INTERACTIONS*.

Key words include: acting reciprocally or on each other, give and take.

The Rune of OSS (ᚠ) in SKJEBNE (▢)
Primary meaning: speedy decisions called for with an elderly person.
Subsidiary meanings: swift, fast, quick, lively, smart, expeditious, judgements, conclusions, decisions, settlements, evaluations, appraisals, summing up, taking stock –
will be necessary concerned with someone – of pensionable age, of declining years, with grey hairs, in their dotage, second childhood, senile, old, wrinkled, doddering, past it.

The Rune of OSS (ᚠ) outside SKJEBNE (▣)
Primary meaning: gain in knowledge that leads to an important action.
Subsidiary meanings: acquiring, getting, increasing, attaining more: comprehension, cognition, understanding, grasp, mastery, wisdom, learning, experience, know how –
this will lead to a: serious, grave, urgent, vital, supreme, weighty, solemn, critical, fateful, no joke, life and death –
gesture, conduct, occurrence, step, tactic, manoeuvre, measure, move, behaviour, deal, transaction, attempt, commitment.

The Rune of OSS (ᚠ) in the Air quadrant (ᛦ)
Primary meaning: love to cross the age barrier.
Subsidiary meanings: affection, friendship, sentiment, fondness, longing, lust, desire, harmony, closeness, appeal, charm, fascination, attraction;
between two people years apart, a young lover, father figure, mother substitute, sugar daddy – people with similar interests but from different age groups.

The Rune of OSS (ᚠ) in the Earth quadrant (ᛒ)
Primary meaning: long life.
Subsidiary meanings: longevity, ripe old age, long duration, long innings, into extra time, outlive others, wear well, endure, last, survive, evergreen, long run.

The Rune of OSS (ᚠ) in the Water quadrant (◇)
Primary meaning: partnership improved by quick action.
Subsidiary meanings: a joint effort: duet, team work, mutual
assistance, give and take, relationship, marriage, unity, think alike,
inseparable, hand in hand, work together, pull together;
will be made better: built up, stronger, developed, increased, gain,
advance, amplified, enhanced;
by: speedy, swift, fast, lively, smart, expeditious, gestures, conduct,
steps, tactics, manoeuvres, measures, behaviour, moves, deals,
transactions, attempts, commitments.

The Rune of OSS (ᚠ) in the Fire quadrant (ᚱ)
Primary meaning: an older person's advice benefits partnership.
Subsidiary meanings: an opinion given as to future action – counsel,
information, knowledge, hints, suggestions, warnings:
Received from: someone advanced in age, not young, with experience, older and wiser, long established, mature, of another age;
will: do good, help, make better, enhance a relationship, marriage,
joint effort, team work, unity.

The Rune of OSS (ᚠ) outside the Runic circle (⊘)
Primary meaning: do not delegate. Be careful – small accident.
Subsidiary meanings: do not: deputize, act for, on behalf of, appear
for, negotiate or stand in for, replace, do duty of, substitute, hold the
baby, pass the buck.
Be warned: take heed, caution, pay attention, on guard, forewarned,
painstaking, watchful.
Not large, little, paltry, trifling, silly, slight error, unexpected event,
chance mishap, unintentional act, fluke, unpredictable event.

RIT ᚱ

This rune governs *CAREER*.

Key words include: trade, profession, calling, life-work, bread and
butter, craft, job, employment, occupation, calling, chosen work.

The Rune of RIT (ᚱ) in SKJEBNE (▢)
Primary meaning: success where most deserved.
Subsidiary meanings: happy ending, accomplishment, achieve-
ment, victory, win, attainment of object, reach goal, triumph, make

out, come off well, conquer, breakthrough;
whger most: merited, earned, due, owing, credited, expected,
warranted, valid, worked hard for.

The Rune of RIT (ᛉ) outside SKJEBNE (▢)
Primary meaning: through own effort there is success. You go far –
travel.
Subsidiary meanings: because of, by, by way of: personal, private,
individual, not aided by anyone else –
steps taken, doing, performance, labour, stress, trouble, hard work,
will power, exertion –
there will be: happy ending, accomplishment, achievement, victory,
winning, attainment of object, reach goal, triumph, break through.
You will also: journey, visit other countries, see the world, move
from place to place.

The Rune of RIT (ᛉ) in the Air quadrant (ᛉ)
Primary meaning: a love adventure.
Subsidiary meanings: office romance, love affair, flirtation, amour,
entanglement, intrigue, lover, admirer, infatuation, passing ships,
something that takes your fancy, light relief, escapade.

The Rune of RIT (ᛉ) in the Earth quadrant (ᛒ)
Primary meaning: risk, be prepared, unexpected expenses.
Subsidiary meanings: element of uncertainty, not one hundred per
cent sure, gamble, chance, peril, dangers, hazards;
be warned, ready, take care, precautions, tread carefully, be alert,
keep your eyes open;
unforseen, unknown, not bargained for, taken aback, surprise, out
of the blue, jolt, a start;
expenditure, outlay, costs, outgoings, not budgeted for, out of
pocket.

The Rune of RIT (ᛉ) in the Water quadrant (◇)
Primary meaning: hold back knowledge, do not reveal your hand.
Subsidiary meanings: keep back what you know, have learned, are
aware of, informed about;
don't disclose, communicate, leak, give away, confess, let on,
indicate, admit, expose, show, confide, betray, come out with – what
you are up to, keep your plans secret, keep things to yourself, don't
be too open, play it close to your chest.

The Rune of RIT (R) in the Fire quadrant (⌐)
Primary meaning: much patience needed.
Subsidiary meanings: what is required – good temper, calmness, imperturbability, steadiness, composure, coolness, forebearance, endurance, long-suffering, longanimity, tolerance, toleration, sufferance, resignation, acquiescence, submission, keep calm, master your feelings, put up with it, grin and bear it.

The Rune of RIT (R) outside the Runic circle (⊘)
Primary meaning: an upset of plans.
Subsidiary meanings: inversion, turning back to front, inside out, overturning, change, turnabout, shuffle, otherway round, reversal, spoiling, messed up:
intentions, calculations, purpose, decisions, designs, schemes, plots, pursuits, aims, course of action, desired object, resolves, aspirations, targets, dreams, desires.

KAON ‹

This Rune governs *RELATIONSHIPS.*

Key words include: involvements, concerns, rapport, bonds, links, relativity, comparisons, friendships, ties with, bearings upon.

The Rune of KAON (‹) in SKJEBNE (☐)
Primary meaning: someone from your past to return.
Subsidiary meanings: a person you once knew, an old school friend, colleague, lover, friend, acquaintance, known to you before;
come back, re-enter, make an appearance, crop up, recur, reappear, afresh, now, echo of the past.

The Rune of KAON (‹) outside SKJEBNE (▣)
Primary meaning: a light relationship.
Subsidiary meanings: love affair, flirtation, entanglement, intrigue, lover, admirer, amorous adventure, infatuation, passing ships, light relief.

The Rune of KAON (‹) in the Air quadrant (Ⱶ)
Primary meaning: for a lady, a gift; for a man, the joy of giving.
Subsidiary meanings: a present, treat, surprise, unexpected present, little thank you, chocolates, an expression of love or thanks;

Pleasure in giving, thing that causes delight, emotion of pleasure, better to give than to receive.

The Rune of KAON (⟨) in the Earth quadrant (ꞵ)
Primary meaning: improvement leading to revitalization.
Subsidiary meanings: betterment, uplift, amelioration, change for the better, transfiguration, conversion, enrichment, enhancement, upswing;
leading to new strength, fresh energies, resuscitate, regenerate, recurrent, freshen, rekindle, rejuvenate, revive, pick up, come to life again.

The Rune of KAON (⟨) in the Water quadrant (◇)
Primary meaning: an opportunity or a relationship which must be acted upon.
Subsidiary meanings: a chance, access, well-timed possibility, opening, scope, choice;
or an involvement, friendship, link, bond, concern, which must be: followed up, not ignored, put into operation, worked on, brought into play, handled, manipulated, taken advantage of, seized.

The Rune of KAON (⟨) in the Fire quadrant (ᚱ)
Primary meaning: much to be gained by encouraging.
Subsidiary meanings: a great deal, a large amount, something vast: to be acquired, learned, got, won, earned, obtained, piled up, got hold of, increase, expansion, profit by, get rich, gain by inspiring, approval, egg on, allow or promote continuance or progress of, inspire with courage, embolden, stimulate by assistance.

The Rune of KAON (⟨) outside the Runic circle (∅)
Primary meaning: loss of a friendship through a silly mistake.
Subsidiary meanings: be deprived of, forfeit, waste, sacrifice, privation, missing, said goodbye to:
a friend, relationship, closeness, amity, concord, fellowship, compatibility, warmth, kindness;
because of, by way of, caused by: an absurd, foolish, stupid, ridiculous, trifling error, slip, bad idea, fault, misunderstanding.

GIFU

This Rune governs BALANCE.

Key words include: equilibrium, even sided, correspondence, equality, parallel, harmony, rhythm, even, both sides equal.

The Rune of GIFU (✕) in SKJEBNE (◻)
Primary meaning: a coming together brings rich rewards.
Subsidiary meanings: an assemblage, gathering, rally, meeting, celebration, social group, reunion, crowd, put together, join, attract, unite;
causes, results in, brings about, conveys, great compensation, gratitude, high fees, great honours, much acclaim, generosity, tributes, presents, hearty thanks.

The Rune of GIFU (✕) outside SKJEBNE (▣)
Primary meaning: reunion in the near future.
Subsidiary meanings: harmony, unison, agreement, see eye to eye, come together again, not be parted, reunite, join together, be one again, reconciliation, another try.

The Rune of GIFU (✕) in the Air quadrant (Ⲫ)
Primary meaning: not a time to stand alone.
Subsidiary meanings: circumstances warn against, not apt, not right, not now, don't, take note, be warned, omens are not right, the wrong moment –
to: go it alone, stick your neck out, attempt by yourself, seek help, advice, counsel, someone or other people to assist you, get some backing, someone behind you, don't take it all on your own shoulders.

The Rune of GIFU (✕) in the Earth quadrant (ß)
Primary meaning: more give than take needed.
Subsidiary meanings: a greater degree of, an increase in, additional devotion, dedication, concessions, allowances, impart more, relax, yield to pressure, elasticity, presents;
not so much: seizing, obtaining, exacting, using, capturing – is required, called for, necessary, demanded, wanted, what must be done.

The Rune of GIFU (✕) in the Water quadrant (◇)
Primary meaning: seek advice.
Subsidiary meanings: look for, search, find, ask for, hunt, quest for: counsel, words of wisdom, criticism, tips, hints, reference, consult, suggestions, recommendations, refer, confide in, listen to, be

advised, submit one's judgement to another's, put heads together, compare notes, sit in conclave, ask for opinions.

The Rune of GIFU (✕) in the Fire quadrant (⌐)
Primary meaning: success linked to another.
Subsidiary meanings: attainment of object, favourable issue, happy ending, time well spent, take the prize, triumph, gain, glory, victory; connected with, joined, caused, in conjunction with:
someone else, additional, different, similar, some other person, a second party.

The Rune of GIFU (✕) outside the Runic circle (∅)
Primary meaning: a quarrel.
Subsidiary meanings: bickering, friction, fall out, severance of friendly relations, at odds, aggression, feud, tiff, squabble, occasion for complaint, have differences, at loggerheads, nag, spoiling for a fight, bellicose, dispute with, cat and dog, row.

WUNNA ᚹ

This Rune governs EARTHLY LOVE.

Key words include: terrestrial, of or on the earth, not a spiritual or higher affection, friendship, fondness, closeness, passion, desire, physical attraction, bodily.

The Rune of WUNNA (ᚹ) in SKJEBNE (☐)
Primary meaning: a loved one returns – celebrations.
Subsidiary meanings: a close friend, member of the family, old flame, someone who is loved and has been parted from you – comes back, comes home, arrives, drops in, turns up, puts in an appearance, returns to the nest.
This causes cheerfulness, happiness, mirth, jollity, occasions for rejoicing, merry-making, parties, family get-togethers.

The Rune of WUNNA (ᚹ) outside SKJEBNE (☐)
Primary meaning: good news connected with a loved one.
Subsidiary meanings: pleasing, beneficial, first rate, most desirable, excellent, couldn't be better – information, communication, letter, phone call, results;
concerned with: a friend, member of the family, husband, wife.

The Rune of WUNNA (ᚹ) in the Air quadrant (ᚤ)
Primary meaning: prospects are golden.
Subsidiary meanings: the future outlook, coming events, what is to
come, in the fullness of time, in due course, show very good signs,
have the makings of, show promise, good omens, of turning out:
balmy, halcyon, favourable, auspicious, doing well, smile of fortune,
Midas touch, blessed, couldn't be better.

The Rune of WUNNA (ᚹ) in the Earth quadrant (ᛒ)
Primary meaning: take what the future offers.
Subsidiary meanings: convert to use, enjoy what's at your disposal,
exploit, use, avail yourself, employ, make use of, use to the full, take
up;
what is to come, in the offing, in view, about to be, on the point of,
imminent; turns up, provided, furnished, given, supplied, produced,
yielded.

The Rune of WUNNA (ᚹ) in the Water quadrant (◇)
Primary meaning: gain from giving to a loved one.
Subsidiary meanings: a chance to: increase, get, win, acquire, reap,
profit, earn a dividend, succeed,
by: bestowing generosity, gifts, presents, something extra, token,
labour of love, offering, sacrifice, contribute, hand over;
to someone close: a friend, relative, husband, wife, sweetheart.

The Rune of WUNNA (ᚹ) in the Fire quadrant (ᚱ)
Primary meaning: open your heart to a loved one.
Subsidiary meanings: uncover, lay bare, expose, unveil, show, keep
nothing back or hidden –
affections, feelings, passions, emotions, mental and spiritual make-
up, soul, inner self, sentiments, responses, eagerness, deeply felt,
sincere, be deomstrative, don't hide your feelings – to someone
close: a friend, relative, husband, wife, sweetheart.

The Rune of WUNNA (ᚹ) outside the Runic circle (⊘)
Primary meaning: risks around a loved one.
Subsidiary meanings: chance of bad consequences, perils, dangers,
pitfalls, traps, threats, warnings, danger signals, evil omens, chancy
dangerous courses;
on every side, all about, surrounding, encompassing, enclosing,
ringing round, closing in;
around: a close friend, relative, husband, wife, sweetheart.

5
HAGAL'S EIGHT

HAGAL ᚺ

This Rune governs DISRUPTIONS.

Key words include: upheavals, splits, separations, shambles, scenes of chaos, violent dissolutions.

The Rune of HAGAL (ᚺ *) in SKJEBNE (* □ *)*
Primary meaning: disruptions caused by nature.
Subsidiary meanings: scenes of chaos, upheavals, splits, separations, havoc, plans wrecked, hopes suffocated,
all brought about by natural forces: floods, fire, earthquake, lightning, death, illness, acts of God.

The Rune of HAGAL (ᚺ *) in any other position on the Runic Chart*
Primary meaning: events beyond your control.
Subsidiary meanings: it is: out of your power, influence, cannot be manipulated, there are no strings to pull, you have no sway, no say in or authority over:
happenings, occurrences, opportunities, mishaps, emergencies, the state of affairs, current happenings and concerns, what is on the agenda, arises, in the wind, falls to one's lot.

NAUT ᚾ

This Rune governs WARNINGS.

Key words include: danger signals, omens, writing on the wall, predictions, forecasts, prophecies.

The Rune of NAUT (ᚾ *) in SKJEBNE (* □ *)*
Primary meaning: warning: care and constraint.
Subsidiary meanings: this is a danger signal: be cautious, look out, keep watch, take notice, be on your guard.
You must be prepared to: take pains, give attention to detail, take heed, be thorough, exact, feel your way.
Also required are: temperance, restriction, self-control, keep things on a lead, under control, within bounds, confined, with strings attached.

The Rune of NAUT (ᚾ *) outside SKJEBNE (* ▢ *)*
Primary meaning: patience.
Subsidiary meanings: the following qualities may be called for: be resolute, single-minded, have staying power, be steady, unflagging, undaunted, never despair, you must have what it takes to continue, stick to it, keep at it, be good-tempered, calm, tolerant, enduring, forebearing, resigned and prepared to put up with matters.

The Rune of NAUT (ᚾ *) in the Air quadrant (* ᚹ *)*
Primary meaning: perseverance.
Subsidiary meanings: the following qualities may be called for: persistence, tenacity, stubbornness, single-mindedness, concentration, plodding on, staying power, grit, be a willing horse, unfailing, never discouraged, keep at it, never say die, stick to your guns.

The Rune of NAUT (ᚾ *) in the Earth quadrant (* ᛒ *)*
Primary meaning: rash acts hold back plans.
Subsidiary meanings: by being incautious, heedless, inconsiderate, flippant, over-confident, dare-devil, irresponsible, frivolous, playing with fire, having a couldn't-care-less attitude; this sort of conduct, behaviour, exploits will only serve to:
retard future intentions and ambitions, delay the reaching of goals and targets as well as aims, hopes and calculations.

The Rune of NAUT (ᚾ *) in the Water quadrant (* ◇ *)*
Primary meaning: stumbling blocks.
Subsidiary meanings: the following all have a certain nuisance value and can get in the way or hinder progress: impediments, obstructions, frustrations, checks, snags, a spot of trouble, interference, hurdles, blind alleys, brick walls, handicaps, meddling, sabotage, teething troubles, problems.

The Rune of NAUT (ᚾ) in the Fire quadrant (ᚱ)
Primary meaning: refusals.
Subsidiary meanings: non-acceptance, a shake of the head, saying no, a slap in the face, unwillingness, something withheld, being turned down, declining an offer, turning a deaf ear to suggestions, frowned upon, refusal of consent, not wanted.

The Rune of NAUT (ᚾ) outside the Runic Circle (∅)
Primary meaning: gossip.
Subsidiary meanings: something to tell, tit-bits, causing a sensation, unconfirmed reports, hearsay, talk of the town, tittle-tattle, scandal-mongers, the inside story, common knowledge, indiscretions, nudges and winks, interference, side glances, whispering, talking behind someone's back.

IS |

This Rune governs EMOTIONAL COOLING.

Key words include: indifference, loss of interest, lukewarm feelings, half-hearted, unresponsive, no enthusiasm, no passions, no longer eager, no longer deeply felt.

The Rune of IS (|) in SKJEBNE (◻)
Primary meaning: spiritual pain caused by partings.
Subsidiary meanings: in the soul, heart, mind, breast, bottom of one's heart, deep-felt, sincere feelings of:
distress, strain, hurt, ache, torment, prolonged agony, wretchedness, bruised, miserable, sadness, having a thin tine, brought about by: separation, a break-up, someone gone away, divorce, being kept apart, disunion, a wedge between you.

The Rune of IS (|) outside SKJEBNE (▣)
Primary meaning: cooling of emotions.
Subsidiary meanings: feelings of indifference, disinterest, half-hearted, lukewarm, unresponsive, no enthusiasm, no passion, no longer eager, no deep feelings, go off someone, see the person for what they are.

The Rune of IS (|) in the Air quadrant (ᛉ)
Primary meaning: one-sided love.

Subsidiary meanings: uneven, by one party only, friendship, affection, tenderness and fondness which is not shared, love-hate, infatuation, a crush, calf-love, an idol, heart-throb, only out for what they can get, being used.

The Rune of IS (|) in the Earth quadrant (ᛒ)
Primary meaning: broken hearts.
Subsidiary meanings: melancholy, heart-broken, sorrowful, woe-begone, unhappy, tormented, wretched, misery, tears, anguish, regretful, feeling ill-used, taking things badly.

The Rune of IS (|) in the Water quadrant (◇)
Primary meaning: frozen assets.
Subsidiary meanings: matters are being kept on ice, suspended, preserved, kept alive but cooled, reserves and resources are frozen until needed.

The Rune of IS (|) in the Fire quadrant (ᚱ)
Primary meaning: static.
Subsidiary meanings: immobile, at rest, still, asleep, stagnating, at a standstill, unmoving, stuck, riding at anchor, staying put, lying low, keeping quiet.

The Rune of IS (|) outside the Runic Circle (⊘)
Primary meaning: divorce – spearation.
Subsidiary meanings: disconnect, withdrawal, parting of the ways, isolation, segregation, break-up, cut loose, break away, unclasp, detach, go separate ways, be alone, avoid each other, be free.

YER ᛉ

This Rune governs LESSONS.

Key words include: examples, cautions, warnings, profit by example, what must be learned, take heed, learning, self improvement, study, gain knowledge.

The Rune of YER (ᛉ) in SKJEBNE (☐)
Primary meaning: a waiting period.
Subsidiary meanings: passivity, dormancy, nothing-doing, stagnation, doldrums, inactivity, in abeyance, lying fallow, inert, wait and see,

look on, procrastinate, unemployed, unprogressive, idle, slack water.

The Rune of YER (⟡) outside SKJEBNE (▣)
Primary meaning: static.
Subsidiary meanings: stagnation, asleep, immobile, rest, stillness, at a standstill, unmoving, stuck, stay put, ride at anchor, keep quiet, unruffled, poker-faced.

The Rune of YER (⟡) in the Air quadrant (Ⱶ)
Primary meaning: legal documents – you gain after waiting.
Subsidiary meanings: official, required or appointed by law, based on or within the province of the law;
written papers, manuscripts, contracts, deeds, treaties, writs, warrants;
you will: acquire, profit, succeed, come by, increase, later, subsequently, following;
bide time, be patient, hold on, abstain from action, pause, tarry, keep watch.

The Rune of YER (⟡) in the Earth quadrant (ß)
Primary meaning: slow up – regain energy.
Subsidiary meanings: decelerate, don't overdo things, don't take on too much, ease up, put on the brakes, shorten sail, reduce speed, rein in, check, curb, back pedal;
give yourself a chance to: revive, pick up, recharge your batteries, rally, come round, recover, get well, recuperate, return to normal, become yourself again.

The Rune of YER (⟡) in the Water quadrant (◇)
Primary meaning: look to the long-term – safeguard yourself legally.
Subsidiary meanings: watch out for, be aware of, have regard for, attend to, take notice of, keep an eye on, remember;
long duration, future, permanence, long standing, security, not now but in years to come, future generations, the remainder;
make provision, stipulations, precautions, protect, officially, binding, based on or within the province of the law.

The Rune of YER (⟡) in the Fire quadrant (Γ)
Primary meaning: look closely to detail.
Subsidiary meanings: pay attention, take notice, have regard, attend to, take heed, keep an eye on, take pains, concentrate, have a care, watch out;

seemingly insignificant matters, be exact, precise, be thorough, right to the last detail, careful, diligent, meticulous, check and re-check, an eye to detail, exact, minute.

The Rune of YER (◇) outside the Runic circle (∅)
Primary meaning: you wait in vain.
Subsidiary meanings: you are patient, hold on, defer action with a view to something expected, bide time, keep watch, do nothing, don't make a decision –
to no purpose, without success, empty, doomed to failure, without regard, achieve nothing, to no avail.

YR ∫

This Rune governs OUTWARD JOURNEYS.

Key words include: directed towards the external, material, visible, apparent, travels, expeditions, quests, searches.

The Rune of YR (∫) in SKJEBNE (□)
Primary meaning: trouble averted by going the long way round.
Subsidiary meanings: bother, inconvenience, exertion, vexation, grief, pains, the thing which causes this, anxiety;
turned away, warded off, missed,
by taking not the shortest, far-reaching, no short-cuts, method, procedure, course, manner, form, means, channel, road, technique, course of action.

The Rune of YR (∫) outside SKJEBNE (▣)
Primary meaning: success if you don't overdo things.
Subsidiary meanings: attainment of object, favourable issue, happy ending, time well spent, triumph, glory, victory,
if you don't: go to extremes, overtire yourself, take on too much, strain yourself, bite off more than you can chew, exaggerate, over-act, aggravate, over-emphasize, make too important, enlarge, magnify, make mountains out of molehills.

The Rune of YR (∫) in the Air quadrant (ⴸ)
Primary meaning: don't over-react.
Subsidiary meanings: don't exaggerate your emotions or feelings, don't go into hysterics at the slightest little thing, keep cool, don't get

flustered or heated by events, don't make too much out of a situation.

The Rune of YR (ʃ) in the Earth quadrant (ᛒ)
Primary meaning: pause.
Subsidiary meanings: calm down, cool off, unwind a little, don't go dashing about wildly, sit back and take stock, ease up, take some time off, cool your vibes, don't get so angry, worried, involved, upset, take a deep breath before starting again.

The Rune of YR (ʃ) in the Water quadrant (◇)
Primary meaning: look calm when flustered.
Subsidiary meanings: look still, serene, unruffled, unabashed, undisturbed, not in the least bit bothered or worried –
when inside you are: confused, in a flurry, nervous, at sixes and sevens, agitated, in a bustle, panicking, don't quite know what to do but must do something.

The Rune of YR (ʃ) in the Fire quadrant (ᚨ)
Primary meaning: irksome problems.
Subsidiary meanings: tedious, tiresome, boring, wearisome, same, repetitious, no fun, uninteresting, unamusing, try your patience, monotonous, unvarying;
difficulties, perplexities, enigmas, burdens, troubles, tasks, jobs, predicaments, tough assignments, things to be sorted out, coped with.

The Rune of YR (ʃ) outside the Runic circle (∅)
Primary meaning: overtired, strain, the rope snaps.
Subsidiary meanings: made excessive demands on person's strength, damaged by exertion, weary through toil, labour, over-taxed, exhausted, on your knees;
tension, distorted from body stress, stretched beyond normal degree, sudden breakdown, fracture, collapse, sudden giving way, failure, stop of mental energy, sudden loss of courage and spirits.

PEORTH ᛈ

This Rune governs SEXUALITY.

Key words include: of sex, occurring between the two sexes, desires, passions, animal instincts, urges.

The Rune of PEORTH (⋈) in SKJEBNE (◻)
Primary meaning: keep the secret.
Subsidiary meanings: secrecy, silence, mystery, keep it dark, keep close, under your hat, mum, reserve, withhold, let it go no further, be taciturn, to yourself, tell no-one, don't breathe a word, lock up, bottle up, conceal, protect, guard, hide, lock in, never tell.

The Rune of PEORTH (⋈) outside SKJEBNE (▣)
Primary meaning: material gain.
Subsidiary meanings: concerned with bodily comforts, things, assets, possessions, worldly not spiritual, money, belongings, goods and chattels;
acquisition, getting, winning, earning, obtaining, build up a store, get hold of, come by, increase, expand, profit, grow rich.

The Rune of PEORTH (⋈) in the Air quadrant (Ⱡ)
Primary meaning: a gift.
Subsidiary meanings: a natural flair, inborn ability, aptitude, knack, genius for, present, token, reward, consideration, prize, something extra, free of cost, given away, had for the asking, windfall, acquistion, come by.

The Rune of PEORTH (⋈) in the Earth quadrant (ᛒ)
Primary meaning: be on your guard – sexual health hazard.
Subsidiary meanings: be warned, take care, precautions, be alert, watch out, careful;
something damaging or injurious to health, well-being, constitution, brought about sexually: unwanted pregnancy, V.D. – who knows? you are warned.

The Rune of PEORTH (⋈) in the Water quadrant (◇)
Primary meaning: take no chances – all it not what it seems.
Subsidiary meanings: take no risks, make certain, calculate the odds, do nothing casually, unintentionally, on the spur of the moment, whatever happens make sure, avoid doing anything hasty;
appearances are misleading, deceptive, it is not as good as it may appear, misguiding, unreal, a delusion, contradiction, sham, make-believe, imitation, farce, concealed.

The Rune of PEORTH (⋉) in the Fire quadrant (Γ)
Primary meaning: reveal nothing.
Subsidiary meanings: disclose, communicate, leak, give away, confess, let on, indicate, admit, expose, show, unveil, blurt out, spill, come clean, confide, come out with, betray, report; tell nobody, not a soul, don't say a word, blank, nought, zero, hold back, don't reveal anything.

The Rune of PEORTH (⋉) outside the Runic circle (⌀)
Primary meaning: be more realistic or you will be disappointed.
Subsidiary meanings: get matters in their proper perspective, sorted out, don't expect or hope for too much, what is not possible, get your feet on the ground, face up to things, see it as it actually is, what is genuine, not artificial –
or you will: feel let down, disenchanted, disillusioned, made unhappy, desires and expectations not fulfilled.

AQUIZI ᛉ

This Rune governs THE HIGHER LAW, THE SOUL.

Key words include: spirit, heart, mind, the inner you.

The Rune of AQUIZI (ᛉ) in SKJEBNE (◻)
Primary meaning: circle out more.
Subsidiary meanings: find new company, ideas, pastimes, try something new, make new friends, broaden your horizons, widen your knowledge, stretch yourself, branch out, let yourself go, seek new interests and circles to move in.

The Rune of AQUIZI (ᛉ) outside SKJEBNE (▢)
Primary meaning: new career, changes in work and home.
Subsidiary meanings: a change of job, activity, occupation, employment, duties, what one has to do, their field, department, line of country;
alterations, a shift of scene, pastures new, a turning point both at home and work.

The Rune of AQUIZI (ᛉ) in the Air quadrant (⼷)
Primary meaning: decision about long-term future – do not hold back.

Subsidiary meanings: a time to judge facts, recapitulate, inspect, assess, consider, form an opinion, do a survey, find solutions which will affect:
what is to come, your destiny, what's on the agenda for a long time to come, something permanent, deep-rooted, lasting.
Don't be tempted to keep quiet about something which bothers you, bottle things up, curb your feelings; if you want to express an opinion or an idea, now is the time to do so.

The Rune of AQUIZI (Y) in the Earth quadrant (B)
Primary meaning: don't be used; spiritual vampires drain.
Subsidiary meanings: don't be: exploited, taken in, duped, manipulated, utilized;
don't allow others to: prey on, become parasites, wring out, dry up, soak up, absorb, dehydrate, reduce your:
unconscious, personality, ego, mind, heart, soul.

The Rune of AQUIZI (Y) in the Water quadrant (◇)
Primary meaning: study (hidden factors); expansion, strength from outside.
Subsidiary meanings: be careful, surveillant, attentive, take notice, be aware, look out, pay attention, be alert;
opportunities for increase, enlargement, amplification, reflation, growth, flowering out, deepening, heightening, building up, development, making more mighty and potent, will be found externally, lie beyond.

The Rune of AQUIZI (Y) in the Fire quadrant (⌐)
Primary meaning: give more of yourself, the all-embracing nature.
Subsidiary meanings: make your identity known, don't hold back, come out of your shell, show your personality, be outgoing, put in more effort, be wholehearted, body and soul, one hundred per cent, every inch, no omissions, totally, entirely, undivided attention.

The Rune of AQUIZI (Y) outside the Runic circle (⊘)
Primary meaning: serendipity – happy accident.
Subsidiary meanings: accidental discovery, finding, treasure trove, hit upon, no assignable cause, fortuitous, turn of fate, fall to one's lot, chance upon, unaccountable, lucky shot;
brings pleasure, enjoyment, a pleasant time, good luck, will delight, be appreciated.

SIG $

This Rune governs *DECISIONS*.

Key words include: chose, calculate, conclude, deduce, appraise, consider, pass judgement, sum up, make up mind, course of action.

The Rune of SIG ($) in SKJEBNE (□)
Primary meaning: wait – answers found through time.
Subsidiary meanings: wait and see, mark time, while away, do nothing for the time being, tread water, hang fire, delay, be inactive, don't decide yet, suspend operations –
because: explanations, reasons, light, clarification, solutions, keys, clues, illustrations, courses –
will be found: in due course, in the future, in a while, later, to come, lie ahead, yet to come, not now, another day.

The Rune of SIG ($) outside SKJEBNE (◎)
Primary meaning: you try what is beyond you.
Subsidiary meanings: you attempt, strive after, tackle, endeavour, search, struggle for, venture, undertake, take on, devote yourself, gamble, quest, take on obligations –
which are: outside your range, scope, capabilities, not possible, too much, hopeless, no chance, impracticable, out of the question, unfeasible, unworkable, unachievable.

The Rune of SIG ($) in the Air quadrant (Ⴤ)
Primary meaning: stop now and regain energy.
Subsidiary meanings: now is the time to halt, desist, refrain, down tools, switch off, relax, rest, finish, break off, withdraw;
give yourself a chance to revive, pick up, rally, come round, recover, recharge your batteries, get well, recuperate, return to normal, sleep it off, become yourself again.

The Rune of SIG ($) in the Earth quadrant (ß)
Primary meaning: worry – negative feelings, concentrate, mind over matter.
Subsidiary meanings: there are feelings of uneasiness, disquiet, cares, problems, headaches, anxiety, woe, bad feelings generally, undercurrents, pulses, tremors;
you must think, collect your thoughts, be attentive, consider,

contemplate, reflect, get it together,
and also: use your brain, intelligence, perception to sort things out,
not physical strength.

The Rune of SIG (⚡) in the Water quadrant (◇)
Primary meaning: necessary expenditure will lead to gain.
Subsidiary meanings: force of circumstances will dictate, impose,
require, give no choice, be unforgoable, bring about unavoidable,
outgoings: costs, expenses, outlay, investment, disbursements,
spending, out of pocket expenditure;
but this will lead to: profit, gain, winnings, acquisition, success,
earning a dividend, making money, reap rewards, a rich harvest.

The Rune of SIG (⚡) in the Fire quadrant (Γ)
Primary meaning: stay calm and stay put.
Subsidiary meanings: it is necessary to remain imperturbable,
steady, composed, cool, serene, tranquil, content, unexcitable,
unworried, good-tempered, relaxed.
It is also necessary to be inert, stand firm, mark time, quiesce, sit tight,
ride at anchor, don't move, be immovable.

The Rune of SIG (⚡) outside the Runic circle (⊘)
Primary meaning: you must continue to wait.
Subsidiary meanings: it is necessary to carry on, remain, still –
passing time, being dormant, inactive, inert, looking on, wait and
see, procrastinating, not progressing, at slack water.

6
TIU'S EIGHT

TIU ↑

This Rune governs *INTRIGUES.*

Key words include: underhand plotting, secret amour, employ secret influence, rouse the interest or curiosity of.

The Rune of TIU (↑) in SKJEBNE (□)
Primary meaning: completion of project.
Subsidiary meanings: conclusion, end of the matter, maturity, readiness, culmination, climax, summit, achievement, *fait accompli*, finished product, executed, discharged, realized.
Plan, scheme, design, programme of work, policy, strategy, undertaking, engagement, obligation, matter in hand, business venture, promise, enterprise, goal, ambition.

The Rune of TIU (↑) outside SKJEBNE (⧈)
Primary meaning: new beginnings.
Subsidiary meanings: not existing before, brought into existence, invented, introduced, discovered, unfamiliar, further, additional, lately arrived, modern, recent, newfangled, not worn or exhausted, fresh, original, not yet accustomed.
Start, set about, time when something starts, openings, channels, opportunities, chances, pastures new, fresh avenues, new fields of experience/work, fresh starts, another chance.

The Rune of TIU (↑) in the Air quadrant (ᚠ)
Primary meaning: hopes now need action.
Subsidiary meanings: at the present time, this moment, immediately, expectations, presumptions, aspirations, beliefs, ambitions, goals, visions, dreams, wishes, secret desires.
Require, what is called for, necessary, wanted, lacking, missing,

demanded, claimed, stipulated, ordered.
Performance, doing, transaction, dispatch, execution, force, energy, handling, act upon, operation, take steps, attempt, try, implement.

The Rune of TIU (↑) in the Earth quadrant (ᛒ)
Primary meaning: show feelings more.
Subsidiary meanings: reveal, divulge, disclose, express, present, be unreserved, open, candid, exhibit, expose to view – emotions, sensations, sympathy, understanding, sentiment, impressions, passions, desires, needs; don't hide things, keep back, bottle up, show feelings to a greater degree, extent.

The Rune of TIU (↑) in the Water quadrant (◇)
Primary meaning: when you have what you want – move on.
Subsidiary meanings: when you – possess, have at your disposal, obtain, get, achieve, succeed, experience, reach – what you – require, desire, need, are without, lacking, wish for, strive after, work for, seek after, search for, aspire to, covet, it is the time to – change, go on, advance, try something else, progress, aim higher, set things into motion again, be ready to roll, start again, travel, transpose.

The Rune of TIU (↑) in the Fire quadrant (ᚱ)
Primary meaning: new ways to be tried.
Subsidiary meanings: not existing before, brought into existence, invented, introduced, discovered, unfamiliar, further additional, lately arrived, modern, recent, newfangled, fresh, original, not yet accustomed to.
Potentials, methods, styles, fashions, avenues, doors, openings, procedures, techniques, routes.
To be tested, examined, sampled, experienced, experimented with, explored, sounded out, practised, verified, researched, analysed, inquired into.

The Rune of TIU (↑) outside the Runic circle (⌀)
Primary meaning: danger of excess and losing control of the situation.
Subsidiary meanings: tendency to, liable, likelihood, probability, good chance, to be expected, forseeable, show signs, in the making, by all odds;
of overdoing things, going over the top, exaggerating, overacting, magnifying, straining, taking on too much, running riot, going to extremes;

by so doing becoming inert, disorganized, impotent, have no say, no grip, no drive, chaos, powerless, incapable of controlling what's going on, circumstances, environment, factors, appearance.

BIRCA ᛒ

This Rune governs *HOME*.

Key words include: where you live with your family, personal life, where you abide, inhabit, carry out your life from, refuge, where you feel comfortable and at ease.

The Rune of BIRCA (ᛒ *) in SKJEBNE (* ◻ *)*
Primary meaning: unity.
Subsidiary meanings: get togethers, meetings, counsel of war, gathering of the clan, relatives, brothers, sisters, parents, aunts, uncles, cousins, in-laws, husbands, wives, the whole tribe, anniversaries, weddings, funerals, christenings, birthday parties, Christmas reunions.

The Rune of BIRCA (ᛒ *) in the Air quadrant (* ▢ *)*
Primary meaning: news of a marriage or a birth.
Subsidiary meanings: information, hear about, be told of;
mention of: a wedding, church ceremony, registry office, engagement with a wedding in the offing, handfasting;
beginning of a new life, baby being born, offspring, new beginning, arrival of the stork.

The Rune of BIRCA (ᛒ *) in the Earth quadrant (* ᛒ *)*
Primary meaning: regain energy.
Subsidiary meanings: decelerate, don't overdo things, take on too much, ease up, put on the brakes, recharge batteries, shorten sail, reduce speed, rein in, check, curb, back-pedal;
give yourself a chance to revive, pick up, rally, come round, recover, get well, recuperate, return to normal, make a comeback, sleep it off, become yourself again.

The Rune of BIRCA (ᛒ *) in the Water quadrant (* ◇ *)*
Primary meaning: look to the long-term and safeguard legally.
Subsidiary meanings: watch out for, be aware of, regard to, attend to, take notice of, keep an eye on, remember;

long duration, future, permanence, long standing, security, not now
but in years to come, future generations, remainder;
make provision, stipulations, protect, precautions –
which are: official, binding, based on or within the province of the
law.

The Rune of BIRCA (Β) in the Fire quadrant (Γ)
Primary meaning: attend to small detail.
Subsidiary meanings: pay attention, notice, regard, take heed, keep
an eye on, application, take pains, concentrate, take care of, find time
for, watch;
seemingly insignificant matters, be exact, precise, thorough, right to
the last detail, careful, diligent, meticulous, check and recheck, take
pains, an eye to detail, minutely, take heed, care, be fastidious.

The Rune of BIRCA (Β) outside the Runic circle (∅)
Primary meaning: unwanted pregnancy/miscarriage.
Subsidiary meanings: not needed, too many, last straw, burden,
parenthood, conception, produced in shame, outside marriage, at
an inopportune time, in the family way, carrying, call into being;
stillborn, abort, premature, lose the baby, induced abortion.

EH Μ

This Rune governs *CHANGES.*

Key words include: changes of opinion, tastes, reforms, character,
turn upside-down, alterations, substitution, differences, new situations, the familiar becomes different.

The Rune of EH (Μ) in SKJEBNE (□)
Primary meaning: completion of plans.
Subsidiary meanings: conclusion, end of the matter, result, issue,
maturity, consummation, executed, discharged, achieved, accomplished, seen through, all ends tied up, clinched, finished off,
disposed of.
Schemes, designs, schedules, programmes, arrangements, policies,
what you wanted to do, achieve, attain, goals, work towards, strive
for.

The Rune of EH (M) outside SKJEBNE (▣)
Primary meaning: love one-sided.
Subsidiary meanings: uneven, by one party only, friendship, affection, tenderness and fondness which is not shared, love-hate, infatuation, a crush, calf-love, an idol, heart-throb, only out for what they can get, being used.

The Rune of EH (M) in the Air quadrant (ⴼ)
Primary meaning: transitory love.
Subsidiary meanings: not permanent, fading, passing, for the time being only, short and sweet, short-lived, cursory, fleeting, doomed, momentary, not enduring, easy come – easy go, temporary, here today and gone tomorrow, an affair, flirtation, intrigue, light relief.

The Rune of EH (M) in the Earth quadrant (ᛒ)
Primary meaning: new friendship.
Subsidiary meanings: recent, novel, the latest, budding, not existing before, fresh starting, coming into existence, embarking upon, entering into, cropping up;
amity, compatibility, intimacy, relationship, warmth, companion, on good terms, inseparable, close, thick as thieves, loyal, fast, firm.

The Rune of EH (M) in the Water quadrant (◇)
Primary meaning: caution – but appear bold.
Subsidiary meanings: watchfulness, keep watch, hold back a little, don't be too forthcoming, care, heed, vigilance, don't show your hand, don't rush in, watch –
but seem to be by your behaviour; look to be aggressive, red-blooded, daring, adventurous, hardy, audacious, venturesome, ready for anything, unflinching, fearless, intrepid, unshakeable, brave, full of fight, spirited.

The Rune of EH (M) in the Fire quadrant (ᚱ)
Primary meaning: reveal nothing.
Subsidiary meanings: do not disclose, communicate, leak, give away, confess, let on, indicate, admit, expose, show, unveil, blurt out, spill the beans, come clean, confide, betray, report, tell anybody, not a soul, don't let on, keep quiet, mum, to yourself, secret, hold back, don't reveal anything.

The Rune of EH (M) outside the Runic circle (⊘)
Primary meaning: foolish mistakes.

Subsidiary meanings: unthinking, brainless, moronic, stupid, care-less, wanting, crass, idiotic, not clever, trifling, fatuous, pointless, puerile, conceited, vain;
errors, blunders, misjudgements, miscalculations, inexact, bad ideas, loose thinking, sloppy, off-target, do the wrong thing, slip-ups, clumsy.

MAN ᛗ

This Rune governs *COMMUNICATIONS*.

Key words include: information, transmission of knowledge, news.

The Rune of MAN (ᛗ) in SKJEBNE (□)
Primary meaning: experiment with caution.
Subsidiary meanings: test, try, put to the proof, by guess and God, analyse, get the feel of, branch out, venture, practice upon, research – with care; mindfully, with heed, be on guard, beware, sharp-eyed, pay attention to detail, do your homework, be thorough, meticulous, prepare your groundwork carefully.

The Rune of MAN (ᛗ) outside SKJEBNE (▣)
Primary meaning: contract problems due to lack of communication – do not delegate.
Subsidiary meanings: doubts or difficulties, things hard to under-stand, sort out; in connection with mutual agreements between two parties, business agreements, legal documents, marriages. Because of the absence of or a deficiency in speech, transmission of ideas, expression of feelings.
You must not deputize, send a representative or agent, pass on authority; but do things for yourself, don't let someone else do them for you.

The Rune of MAN (ᛗ) in the Air quadrant (ᛟ)
Primary meaning: reasonableness is called for.
Subsidiary meanings: practice moderation, control, keep in check, keep within bounds, be calm, don't get agitated, expect too much, be fair minded, hold the scales evenly. This is what is required, wanted, needed, essential, a must, a requisite.

The Rune of MAN (ᛗ *) in the Earth quadrant (* ᛒ *)*
Primary meaning: health hazard caused by strain.
Subsidiary meanings: if you wish to remain fighting fit, have a good constitution, have health and strength, vitality, fitness, good condition, bloom, well-being, be sound as a bell, robust –
do not take chances which cause danger, take risks, overdo things, get tired and fatigued, push yourself to the limit of endurance, or these will bring about the opposite effect.

The Rune of MAN (ᛗ *) in the Water quadrant (* ◇ *)*
Primary meaning: circumstances are against you – whispers.
Subsidiary meanings: you are propelled without resistance, other influences contrast with your own wishes, opposition, collision course.
Insinuations, rumours, secret hints, gossip, slander, scandal, undercurrents, soft rustlings.

The Rune of MAN (ᛗ *) in the Fire quadrant (* ᚠ *)*
Primary meaning: in-depth relationship now develops after the real intent is hidden.
Subsidiary meanings: with a deeper meaning, not just physical, intellectual understanding, far reaching, rapport, regard, affinity, alliance, liaison, twin souls.
Increases, becomes clear, enlarges, expands, matures, blossoms, builds up, widens.
After the real intention, purpose, pursuit, object, goal, design, meaning, aim, context, idea has been concealed, disguised, veiled, kept secret, not confessed, unnamed, glossed over, bottled up.

The Rune of MAN (ᛗ *) outside the Runic circle (* ∅ *)*
Primary meaning: untrustworthy.
Subsidiary meanings: doubtful, dubious, uncertain, vague, anybody's guess, treacherous, unpredictable, unreliable, unsure, chancy, risky, unstable, shady, slippery customer, untried, untested, have a suspicion, crooked, scoundrel, rascal, criminal, dishonest, underhand, unfaithful, corrupt.

LAGU ᛚ

This Rune governs *THE EMOTIONS.*

Key words include: feelings, sensations, senses, perception, experience, passions, hopes and fears, affecting your inner self.

The Rune of LAGU (⌐) in SKJEBNE (☐)
Primary meaning: psychic powers lead, but know your limits.
Subsidiary meanings: your subconscious, perception, reasoning
power, ideas, conceptions, thoughts, from your soul, heart; these
serve to direct, point the way, command, spur you on, set the pace.
Take care not to overreach yourself, take on too much, bite off more
than you can chew, do only what you know you can safely cope with,
know when to draw the line.

The Rune of LAGU (⌐) outside SKJEBNE (▣)
Primary meaning: answers found within yourself: outside influences
mislead.
Subsidiary meanings: solutions, the key to the matter, the right
course of action will be found in your own mind, is for you to bring
out, search for, conceive, formulate.
Situations, monetary problems, responsibilities, commitments,
other people's opinions will cloud the issue, give the wrong slant,
colour your decision, deceive.

The Rune of LAGU (⌐) in the Air quadrant (Ƴ)
Primary meaning: physical attraction will cloud the issue: seek
deeper understanding.
Subsidiary meanings: attractions – of the body not of the mind, on
the surface, externally, bodily, sensual will:
colour your decision, give the wrong slant, deceive, give a false
picture, pull the wool over your eyes.
It will be necessary to dig deeper, fathom out on a different level,
look below the surface, probe, enquire, plumb, seek within in order
to see through, find the real meaning, gain knowledge.

The Rune of LAGU (⌐) in the Earth quadrant (Ɓ)
Primary meaning: rise above personalities to see.
Subsidiary meanings: look for other meanings and depths that may
be hidden by outward appearances, don't be blinded by traits,
features, idiosyncracies, qualities, peculiarities, identities, mannerisms.
These will not help you to see matters in depth, to understand,
comprehend, recognize, know, discern, make out, grasp: following
these will only deceive and take you in.

The Rune of LAGU (↑) in the Water quadrant (◇)
Primary meaning: darkness; do not stop, feel your way.
Subsidiary meanings: ignorance, unawareness, lack of knowledge, unknown quantities, you are unenlightened, in the dark, uncertain, have nothing to do, but you must:
continue, keep going, persist, carry on, follow through, don't waver or hesitate. Sound things out, be tentative, grope, fumble, get the feel of things, probe, venture, explore, prospect, keep trying.

The Rune of LAGU (↑) in the Fire quadrant (↑)
Primary meaning: a more positive approach is called for. Look to the past.
Subsidiary meanings: a new method of attack, way of doing things, style, manner, *modus operandi* is needed, which must be sure, self-confident, unquestionable, know all the answers.
Base this on knowledge and experience already gained, learn from past mistakes, remember what has gone before, earlier happenings, look to your roots.

The Rune of LAGU (↑) outside the Runic circle (∅)
Primary meaning: don't be sidetracked by opposition.
Subsidiary meanings: don't be disorientated, misdirected, take the wrong course, go off at a tangent, be led astray, put off the scent, held back by –
antagonism, hindrance, interference, opposing causes, non-co-operation, rivalry, resistance, protests, obstacles, obstructions; you must make a stand and stick to your guns.

ING ◇

This Rune governs *DIRECT FAMILY*.

Key words include: close relations, wife/husband, parents, children, brothers, sisters, aunts, uncles, etc.

The Rune of ING (◇) in SKJEBNE (◻)
Primary meaning: change leading to improvement.
Subsidiary meanings: difference, variation, alteration, fresh phase, substitution, something new, not routine;
causing, bringing about, directly responsible for, inspiring, originating from, resulting in, bringing to pass, sparking off, provoking:

progress, forward motion, betterment, advance, showing promise, make strides, headway, development, furtherance, gain, achievement.

The Rune of ING (◇) outside SKJEBNE (⊡)
Primary meaning: move of home.
Subsidiary meanings: change of residence, new environment, new surroundings, fresh place to live, new roots, pastures new, beginnings, adventure, new faces, different house.

The Rune of ING (◇) in the Air quadrant (ᚠ)
Primary meaning: change your plans – be versatile and giving.
Subsidiary meanings: differ, vary, alter, substitute, something new, project, schemes, designs, undertakings, ventures, engagements, programme of work, strategy.
What is needed is: elasticity, be prepared to hand over, variety, readiness, ease, become many-sided, faceted.

The Rune of ING (◇) in the Earth quadrant (ᛒ)
Primary meaning: personal attitude must show change.
Subsidiary meanings: your own, private, no one else's, individual, way of thinking, behaviour, point of view, way of judgement, reasoning, reactions, thoughts;
have to be seen to alter, vary, become different, a new angle, a new slant.

The Rune of ING (◇) in the Water quadrant (◇)
Primary meaning: outside influences lead to change.
Subsidiary meanings: events beyond your control, out of your power, another person's actions, something in which you have no sway, authority over, force of circumstances, general state of affairs, fate, destiny;
cause, bring about, are responsible for, result in, spark off, provoke, bring to pass, underlie, found –
a difference, variation, alteration, something new, substitution, not routine, new angle, new slant.

The Rune of ING (◇) in the Fire quadrant (ᚲ)
Primary meaning: your actions to benefit another.
Subsidiary meanings: your own, personal private, individual, no one else's – movements, doings, energy, influence, steps taken, deeds, functions, chosen course;
will be to the advantage of, do good to, bring privilege to, help, assist,

profit, aid – someone else, not you, some other person.

The Rune of ING (◇ *) outside the Runic circle (* ∅ *)*
Primary meaning: misrepresentations.
Subsidiary meanings: represent wrongly, give false account of, false light, travesty, parody, caricature, distorted image, mis-information, over-dramatized, exaggerated account, be false, detract, toned down, bumped up.

ODAL ᛟ

This Rune governs *MOUNTAINS TO CLIMB.*

Key words include: obstacles to be overcome, scaled, risen above, work one's way up, struggle up, ascend from bottom of the ladder.

The Rune of ODAL (ᛟ *) in SKJEBNE (* ☐ *)*
Primary meaning: gain from own effort.
Subsidiary meanings: getting, winning, acquiring, thrift, savings, profit, earn a dividend, succeed, make money, come by, reap, increase;
brought about: personally, not by another, independently, unaided, in private, on your own;
and by your own: exertion, struggles, drive, force, energy, muscle, work, labour, perseverance.

The Rune of ODAL (ᛟ *) outside SKJEBNE (* ▢ *)*
Primary meaning: legacy/property buying or selling difficulties.
Subsidiary meanings: inheritance, possessions, chattels, belongings, estate, birthright, heritage, bequest, moveables, effects, assets. Obstacles requiring effort to be removed, embarrassment, objections, awkward situations, problems, worries, hurdles, stumbling blocks; concerned with exchanging for money, purchasing, procuring or disposing of, finding a purchaser, trading in, making over.

The Rune of ODAL (ᛟ *) in the Air quadrant (* ᛉ *)*
Primary meaning: the need is a willing sacrifice.
Subsidiary meanings: what is called for, requirement, necessary, missing, demanded, claimed, stipulated, ordered –
is a: voluntary, spontaneous, consenting, ready acquiescence, of free will, with a good grace, nothing loth, gladly, with pleasure, happy;

surrender, offering, victim, devotion, resign oneself, giving up something for the sake of another.

The Rune of ODAL (ᛟ) in the Earth quadrant (ᛒ)
Primary meaning: strength given for the climb up.
Subsidiary meanings: capacity to bear, reinforcement, power, energy, courage, will power, guts, potency, might, tolerance, support, perseverance, fight, what it takes;
is bestowed, presented, donated, granted, conferred, invested, vouchsafed, provided –
for the ascent, struggle up, rise, take off, climbing the ladder, try for the top, upward motion, upsurge.

The Rune of ODAL (ᛟ) in the Water quadrant (◇)
Primary meaning: now you must dare – expand.
Subsidiary meanings: at the present time, this moment, immediately, you are obliged, commanded, have no choice, the only course open, it is imperative, a necessary move;
attempt, exert yourself, take a chance, venture, speculate, gamble, have a go, do;
broaden, widen, stretch out, stretch yourself, extend, unfold, throw off reserve, increase, extend trade, territory, new horizons, new avenues, greater scope and understanding.

The Rune of ODAL (ᛟ) in the Fire quadrant (ᚴ)
Primary meaning: determination wins.
Subsidiary meanings: resolution, a sticking point, earnestness, seriousness, resolve, decision, being intent upon, endurance, carry through, stand no nonsense, will power, resolve, tenacity, concentration, single mindedness, constancy, grit, courage;
will mean: a happy ending, success story, time well spent, triumph, accomplishment, pays dividends, victory, fruitless, unbeaten, make the grade, pull it off, arrive, achieve mastery.

The Rune of ODAL (ᛟ) outside the Runic circle (∅)
Primary meaning: beware of moving wheels.
Subsidiary meanings: caution, be warned, take care, pay heed, mind out for, danger signal, hint, forewarned, be on your guard, be prepared;
wheels in motion, wheels within wheels, a puzzle, clockwork, machinery, wheel of fate turning; might be an accident concerned with wheels, a car, train, bicycle, machine.

DAG ⋈

This Rune governs *AMBITION*.

Key words include: hopes, expectations, aspirations, visions, dreams, desires, goals, what one strives for/towards, intentions, pursuits, targets, have in mind.

The Rune of DAG (⋈) in SKJEBNE (☐)
Primary meaning: effort rewarded.
Subsidiary meanings: measures, steps taken, something done, performed, executed, implemented, administered, laboured at, exertion, stress, strain, trouble, employment, hard work, do one's utmost, keep at it; pays off, brings prestige, remuneration, compensation, thanks, profit, just desserts, compliments, honours, has not gone unnoticed, brings repute, acknowledgement.

The Rune of DAG (⋈) outside SKJEBNE (▣)
Primary meaning: be positive in a negative situation.
Subsidiary meanings: be certain, sure, confident, convinced, reliable, steadfast, unquestionable, undeniable, guaranteed – in circumstances, environment, predicaments which seem to express or imply denial, prohibitive, unsuccessful, frustrating, losing battle, profitless, abortive; don't let them grind you down.

The Rune of DAG (⋈) in the Air quadrant (Ⅴ)
Primary meaning: stay your hand.
Subsidiary meanings: delay, wait and see, play for time, postpone, adjourn, procrastinate, hold back, put off, shelve, temporize, stall, hold in abeyance, keep your plans secret, don't be too open, forthcoming.

The Rune of DAG (⋈) in the Earth quadrant (Ᏸ)
Primary meaning: make advances where you can.
Subsidiary meanings: make progress, take steps forward, gain headway, steal a march, gain, develop, achieve, make ground, forge ahead, move up, surge forward;
when able, at every opportunity, opening, every chance, whenever possible, use what comes to hand, within your grasp.

The Rune of DAG (◻ *) in the Water quadrant (* ◇ *)*
Primary meaning: action seen to be in progress.
Subsidiary meanings: movements, doings, energy, influence, steps taken, deeds, functions, chosen course;
apparently, visibly, noticeably, by the look of it, observable, manifesting, happening, appearing, actually, perceptibly, recognizable, happening, being done, making headway, evolving, coming about, going on, occurring, becoming, taking place, the order of the day.

The Rune of DAG (◻ *) in the Fire quadrant (* ⌐ *)*
Primary meaning: a new and better lifestyle.
Subsidiary meanings: not existing before, brought into existence, invented, introduced, unfamiliar, fresh, improved, of a more excellent kind, surpassing what has gone before, change for the better;
existence, way of living, nature, improved standard of living, manner of existence.

The Rune of DAG (◻ *) outside the Runic circle (* ⌀ *)*
Primary meaning: effort unrecognized.
Subsidiary meanings: measures, steps taken, something done, performance, executed, implemented, labour, exertion, stress, strain, trouble, employment, hard work, stuggles, do one's utmost, keep at it;
no word of praise, not rewarded, labour of love, unsung, ignored, forgotten, unnoticed, glossed over, no word of thanks, without payment.

7
SKJEBNE

This Rune governs *DESTINY*.

Key words include: kismet, one's lot, predestination, fortune, destiny, in the stars, god's will, prescribed course.

The Rune of SKJEBNE (☐) in SKJEBNE (☐)
Primary meaning: that which must be accepted.
Subsidiary meanings: that which must be tolerated, put up with, the inevitable, fate, destiny, fortune, gone along with, no choice in the matter, out of your hands, conform to, in the stars, one's lot, foreordained.

The Rune of SKJEBNE (☐) outside SKJEBNE (▣)
Primary meaning: a problem that must now be faced.
Subsidiary meanings: difficulty, predicament, quandary, cornered, complication, trouble, worry, difficult situation, headache, enigma, concern, something hard to handle, a burden, fly in the ointment; must now be dealt with, recognized, handled, sorted out, not left unsolved any longer, tackled, owned up to.

The Rune of SKJEBNE (☐) in the Air quadrant (Ͱ)
Primary meaning: you meet your match.
Subsidiary meanings: you come up against someone just like you, your twin soul, doppelganger, your double, someone just as crafty, same personality, cannot be bettered, one jump ahead, equal, corresponding exactly, up to all your own tricks.

The Rune of SKJEBNE (☐) in the Earth quadrant (ᛒ)
Primary meaning: a price to pay.
Subsidiary meanings: not something for nothing, a penalty, account to settle, levy, face the music, forfeit, pay the costs, damages, compensation, return favour, as you sow so shall you reap, come-

uppance, settle up, reckoning, make an example, lesson to learn.

The Rune of SKJEBNE (☐) in the Water quadrant (◇)
Primary meaning: the situation is not in your hands.
Subsidiary meanings: circumstances, what is going on, environment, lay of the land, predicament, position, prevailing conditions – not in your control, unmanageable, intractable, not your decision, down to someone else, brought about by outside influences, in the lap of the gods, in the air.

The Rune of SKJEBNE (☐) in the Fire quadrant (⌐)
Primary meaning: you succeed.
Subsidiary meanings: happy ending, success story, triumph, fruitful, undefeated, make the grade, accomplish, achieve, reach your goal, show results, hit the jackpot, arrive, graduate, qualify, make out, pull it off, make a breakthrough, do marvels, bear fruit.

The Rune of SKJEBNE (☐) outside the Runic circle (⊘)
Primary meaning: a necessary failure.
Subsidiary meanings: no alternative, had to happen, no choice, force of circumstances, required, unforgoable, indispensable, unavoidable, fated, imposed;
faux pas, blunder, error, non-event, mistake, miscalculation, slip-up, wrong idea, clanger, oversight, mistiming.

GLOSSARY

Aeromancy
Divination by atmospheric conditions. For example, thunder and lightning before a wedding is bad luck.

Ailuromancy
Fortune telling by cats. A grey cat is good luck, but a white cat crossing your path is an omen of illness.

Alectryomancy
A form of fortune telling by roulette. A circle of letters is scattered with grain, and chickens spell out a message by picking grain from selected letters.

Aleuromancy
Predictions are written on slips of paper and baked inside cakes. A well-known example is the Chinese fortune cookie.

Alphitomancy
A method of trying a suspected criminal. The accused has to swallow a piece of specially baked barley loaf – if he chokes he is guilty.

Arachnomancy
Fortune telling by spiders. Killing a spider is bad luck, seeing a spider spinning in the morning brings good luck.

Arithomancy
Fortune telling by numbers. Letters in a name can be given numerical equivalents, or the numbers in a birth date used, to produce a personal number, giving an indication of personality.

Astragalomancy
Divination using dice. For example, one means yes, five good luck.

Austromancy
Fortune telling by the study of winds. The effects of wind on, for example, bells hanging on a tree, or ripples on a pond, are noted and interpreted.

Belomancy
A form of casting of lots. Specially marked arrows are either thrown on the ground, or picked from a container at random.

Bibliomancy
When seeking advice, choose a book, open it at any page at random and the first words read will give an answer to the problem.

Botanomancy
Fortune telling from the burning of leaves and branches. One of many forms of pyromancy. The appearance of smoke, clearness of the flame etc. are interpreted, as well as pictures seen in the fire.

Capnomancy
Another form of pyromancy, this involves interpreting the smoke from incense and burnt offerings. The smell and direction of the smoke is noted.

Cartomancy
Fortune telling with playing cards. Hearts are lucky, spades spell danger.

Catoptromancy
Mirror gazing. For example, to see your future partner, look into a mirror at midnight on Halloween while holding a candle. Your future partner will be seen looking over your left shoulder.

Causimomancy
Another type of pyromancy. Divination is made from the burning of objects cast into a fire.

Cephalomancy
Fortune telling using the skulls of donkeys or goats. The heads are boiled and the shape and condition of the skulls used for divination.

Ceraunoscopy
Predictions made using the appearance of thunder and lightning as omens.

Ceromancy
Divination from patterns of melted wax dropped into a dish of cold water.

Chaomancy
Fortune telling from atmospheric conditions generally.

Cheiromancy
Well known as palm-reading. As well as the lines of the palm, the shape of the fingers and hand is noted. For example, short fingers indicate impatience, square hands practicality.

Cleidomancy
A form of dowsing. A key is suspended by a thread and the direction in which it swings, whether backwards and forwards, clockwise or anti-clockwise, indicates a positive or negative reply to an inquiry.

Cleromancy
The drawing of lots, using beans, stones or siips of paper to gain answers to questions.

Coscinomancy
The earliest form of dowsing. A sieve is held between the blades of a pair of tongs held by two people who each push the blades in opposite directions. The direction in which the sieve begins to turn gives the oracle's reply.

Crithomancy
Divination using corn or grain. There are many methods, including observing the patterns on the crust of freshly baked bread and forming patterns with flour or kernels of grain.

Cromniomancy
Fortune telling using onions. To predict an election winner or future marriage partner, write the initials of the contenders on several onions, leave them to sprout, and the first onion to sprout will bear the initials of the winner.

Crystallomancy
The practice of crystal gazing. The questioner gazes into a crystal ball and interprets the images which are revealed in it. For example, a frog indicates fertility, a lighthouse means danger ahead.

Dactylomancy
Another form of dowsing, using a suspended ring. Often used to predict the sex of unborn children. The mother suspends her wedding ring on a hair from her head. If it swings backwards and forwards the child is a boy, if in a circular motion it is a girl.

Daphnomancy
Another form of pyromancy, using the burning of laurel leaves. The louder the sound the leaves make while burning the better the omen.

Entomomancy
Fortune telling using the behaviour and appearance of insects.

Geomancy
Divination of marks made in dust, sand, soil, or more recently, paper. For example, a small circle indicates a forthcoming marriage, a triangle means a successful career.

Halomancy
Divination by casting salt into a fire, another form of pyromancy.

Hippomancy
Fortune telling by horses. One white horse means bad luck, while two white horses seen together is a good omen.

Hydromancy
Divination by water. The many methods involved include gazing into still water such as a pool, and drinking from sacred springs to induce visions.

Ichthyomancy
Divination by the examination either of the entrails of dead fish, or the behaviour of live ones.

Lampadomancy

Fortune telling using the flames of lighted lamps. For example, a flame with a single point means good luck, but the unexpected extinguishing of a flame indicates coming disaster.

Lithomancy

Fortune telling with precious stones. A red stone predicts romance, a purple one foretells a quarrel.

Lychnomancy

Divination using the flames of three identical candles. If one flame burns brighter than the others this is a very good omen. Candles burning unevenly spell danger.

Meteormancy

Omens taken from the appearance of meteors and shooting stars.

Molybdomancy

Divination using molten lead dropped either onto a flat surface or into water. Predictions are based on the patterns created, and when water is used, from the hissing sounds made when the lead hits the water.

Myomancy

Fortune telling by mice and rats. Omens are taken from the sudden appearance of vermin, their behaviour, and the sounds they make.

Necromancy

The calling up of the spiritis of the dead for divination. One of the most well known methods is the use of the ouija board.

Numeromancy

Fortune telling by number. See Arithomancy.

Oenomancy

Divination from patterns made by wine poured out as a sacrifice to the gods.

Oneiromancy
Fortune telling from dreams. A complex subject, there are many methods of interpretation.

Ophiomancy
Divination from the behaviour and colour of snakes.

Ornithomancy
Prediction from the appearance, flight, song and feeding habits of birds. The most commonly used method of taking omens in Roman times.

Pegomancy
Similar to mirror gazing but using water, such as springs, pools or dishes of water.

Pessomancy
Divination using pebbles, either of different colours or with special markings. Blue stones, or those marked with flowers, for example, indicate success or prosperity.

Phyllorhodomancy
Fortune telling using rose petals or leaves. Either the pattern of falling petals is interpreted, or the sounds of rose leaves clapped in between the hands.

Psephomancy
Another word for Pessomancy – pebble divination.

Pyromancy
Divination by fire. There are many variations, including interpretation of smoke patterns, behaviour of burning substances in the fire etc. See botanomancy, caponomancy, causinomancy, daphnomancy, halomancy and sideromancy.

Rhapsodomancy
Similar to bibliomancy, this method of divination involves opening a book of poetry at random and taking an omen from the first words read.

Scapulomancy
Divination using the pattern of cracks on the burned shoulder bone of an animal, particularly a sheep.

Sideromancy
Another form of pyromancy. An odd number of straws is cast onto a red-hot iron, interpretations are made of the movements, smells and patterns of the burning straw.

Stichomancy
Another term for bibliomancy – a stitch is a line of verse or short section of prose.

Tasseography
Fortune telling with tea leaves. For example, leaves left in the pattern of a beehive promise prosperity, while that of an arrow predicts bad news.

Tephromancy
Taking omens from the patterns in the ashes after a sacrificial fire has been burnt.

Tyromancy
An ancient method of divination using cheese. The coagulation of the cheese during manufacture is observed, and omens drawn.

Zoomancy
Fortune telling by animals. Either the appearance and behaviour of real animals, or visions of imaginary animals, are used as portents.